ALMA MAHLER-WERFEL
Diaries 1898–1902

ALMA MAHLER-WERFEL

Diaries 1898–1902

SELECTED AND TRANSLATED BY
Antony Beaumont

From the German edition
transcribed and edited by
Antony Beaumont and
Susanne Rode-Breymann

Cornell University Press
Ithaca, New York

First published in 1999
by Cornell University Press
512 East State Street, Ithaca, NY 14850

Photoset by RefineCatch Ltd, Bungay
Printed in England by Clays Ltd, St Ives plc

This translation © Antony Beaumont, 1998

A CIP record for this book is
available from the Library of Congress

ISBN 0-8014-3654-0

2 4 6 8 10 9 7 5 3 1

Contents

List of Illustrations

Acknowledgements
1, 2, 18: by courtesy of the Österreichische Staatsbibliothek, Bildarchiv; 4, 7, 8, 14, 15, 16: collection Susanne Rode-Breymann; all others: collection Antony Beaumont

Introduction

from the editors' correspondence files

AB 1 December 1993
Dear Dr Rode-Breymann,
In search of material for a forthcoming monograph on Alexander Zemlinsky, I recently visited the US, where I found an unpublished manuscript of extraordinary interest: Alma Mahler's diaries (actually Alma Schindler's, for they end shortly before her marriage to Mahler). Altogether there are 22 volumes (Alma calls them 'Suites'), covering a period of four years.
Surprising as it may seem, none of Alma's biographers (Monson, Giroud, Wessling et al.) have made much use of this material, restricting their quotations from it largely to passages published as long ago as 1974 in La Grange's *Mahler*. Surprising, because the diaries, housed in the Van Pelt Library at the University of Pennsylvania, have been accessible to the public since the early seventies. When I saw the manuscript, the reason immediately became clear: Alma's handwriting. I myself spent two totally frustrating days in Philadelphia trying to decipher it; on many pages I could make out Zemlinsky's name, but I failed to reconstruct a single complete sentence. Growing familiar with the handwriting will clearly take time and patience. I have therefore ordered photocopies of the entire manuscript to be sent to me at home in Germany.
Knowing that intractable handwriting is a speciality of yours, and aware that you share my passion for *fin-de-siècle* Vienna, I thought you might perhaps be interested in collaborating on a transcription. Am I right?

SR-B 4 December 1993
Dear Mr Beaumont,
What a splendid idea – a fascinating task and not only of value to Zemlinsky research! As far as I know, many of the riddles surrounding Alma Schindler-Mahler-Gropius-Werfel have never been solved: the wilful termination of her career as a composer, for instance, customarily described as 'typical of the fate of the creative woman' (cf. Herta Blaukopf's introduction to Alma Maria Schindler-Mahler's *Complete Songs*, published by Universal Edition) and for which Mahler is always depicted as the guilty

party. Allegedly it was he, as Eva Rieger wrote in *Frau und Musik*, who 'suppressed and hence destroyed' Alma's 'remarkable talent'. The evidence commonly quoted is found in a letter to Alma from Dresden, dated 20 December 1901. For me it was a sobering experience to read these twenty pages (published in Françoise Giroud's *Alma Mahler ou l'art d'être aimée*), but then I began to wonder if Mahler's stipulation that Alma abandon her creative ambition could really be interpreted as unconditional. One passage in particular arouses my doubt:

> And here, unfortunately, I have to turn to you, for I find myself in the curious position of being compelled – in certain respects – to compare my music, with which you are actually unfamiliar and which you certainly do not yet understand, with yours, to defend it against you and to place it in its true perspective. [. . .] Could you really visualize such a marriage of composers? Do you understand how ridiculous such a strange rivalry would be, how detrimental it would later be to both of us? [. . .] One thing is certain: if we are to be happy, you must give me what I need, you must be my spouse and not my colleague!

Inasmuch as Mahler refused to contemplate marriage in a situation of artistic rivalry, there can be no doubt that this passage represents an unconditional demand. But if Alma Schindler set such store by her own artistic activity, why did she bow to Mahler's sexist views and comply with his wish? After all, they had not known each other long, and Alma could easily have gone her own way. Confronted by Mahler with the dilemma of choosing between creativity and partnership, she could, proudly and independently, have made her own career as a composer – even if her marriage would not have lasted. This change of direction in her life, marking the point at which she abandoned her personal artistic ambition, was surely not just occasioned by Mahler, but must also have been the outcome of her free will. Mahler's letter is concerned with an essential element of her personality – freedom of choice. Why then did she forswear it? Surely other considerations – both personal and social – must have influenced her decision as well.

In search of an answer, Giroud proposes an interesting theory, namely that Alma may have become 'intoxicated' with the idea of capitulating to Mahler, as if to spite her mother, who saw his letter as offering sufficient grounds for breaking off relations at once. Was the mother–daughter relationship really as 'highly ambivalent' as Giroud sees it? Compared with Alma's own account in *And the Bridge is Love*, Giroud's is considerably more complex and also, in certain respects, divergent. Time and again she supports her theories with quotations from the diaries. In search of a closer understanding of Alma's personality, it would of course be most interesting to be able to evaluate not merely the brief excerpts quoted by her, but the text in its entirety.

AB 27 March 1994
Dear Dr Rode-Breymann,
The photocopies from Philadelphia arrived earlier this week, and I have started looking at them more closely. One does eventually grow a little more accustomed to the handwriting, and the few passages I have so far succeeded in deciphering appear to offer interesting new insights.
In the new, unexpurgated edition of Mahler's letters, one passage currently arouses my particular sympathy:

> Oh Almschi [...], I wish you would write more clearly! [...] Dear girl, do make the effort: separate the letters clearly from one another and write the consonants more distinctly.

And one of her first letters to Zemlinsky provoked a characteristically sarcastic tirade of quasi-biblical ire:

> And the Lord Sabaoth brought down great misfortune upon my unworthy head. [...] For he conferred upon me a scripture from the hand of the blessed Alma Maria, and I scourged my sinful eyes full sixty minutes to read the message which I, miserable sinner, was destined to receive.

Meanwhile I have spoken to Donald Mitchell, who assured me that it would be of great value to Mahler scholarship to see the diaries in print. At his suggestion I contacted Alma's granddaughter Marina, who was equally enthusiastic about the project and unhesitatingly gave her permission for an original-language edition, to be published by S. Fischer Verlag.
I enclose copies of Suites 4–15, i.e. almost exactly half the material. Good luck!

PS. We should meet soon to discuss the editorial problems involved, and decide how to approach them.

SR-B 1 April 1994
Dear Mr Beaumont,
Working on the diaries is proving utterly fascinating. Many an episode is so intriguing that I often feel loath to interrupt work on even very long sections before reaching the end. But there are problems too, particularly of

legibility. Sometimes this is due to the use of purple ink, which tends to fade – I experienced similar difficulty with Alban Berg – at other times there are problems of a psychological nature. Whether under the influence of Wagner or in other strongly emotional situations (in connection with her step-sister Maria, for instance), Alma's handwriting frequently becomes irregular and uncontrolled. These are her moments of 'wildness', as she herself describes it.

As far as editing is concerned, the main problem is one of scale: the text is incredibly long. Should we publish the entire diary, or abbreviate it? This is something which we, in consultation with the publishers, will have to discuss in greater detail. I would prefer the transcription to be as complete as possible, for otherwise we would run the risk of becoming party to the dissimulation and camouflage of which Alma herself has often been accused. I have just been rereading a conversation between Eleonore Vondenhoff and Andreas Maul, published in the ÖMZ, on the subject of the alterations implemented by her in the first edition of Mahler's letters. As soon as one begins to abbreviate, one enters a similar labyrinth of prejudice and prevarication. And surely: our edition must allow readers to form their own picture.

AB 16 April 1994
Dear Susanne Rode-Breymann,
D'accord. Perhaps we will have to prune the text a little before going to print, but any such decision can be taken at a later stage. For the time being, let us transcribe the diaries in their entirety.

Another thing: I find it difficult to separate mode of address from ambience, figure of speech from orthography, and would therefore consider it desirable, wherever possible, to retain the original spelling (except, of course, for errors and inconsistencies in place names etc.). We shall also need to find a way of organizing the highly unorthodox punctuation . . .

AB 4 October 1994
Dear Susanne,
Hurrah: the transcription is complete! A few pages in our photocopy appear to be missing, however, and a few words obdurately resist positive recognition. Let's hope our forthcoming research trip to Philadelphia will help to tidy up these corners.

Alma describes her three principal love-affairs – with Klimt, Zemlinsky and Mahler – in meticulous detail. Strangely enough, almost every episode of the Klimt saga is recounted weeks after the event. I found the explanation in *And the Bridge is Love*:

> At last, in Genoa, my mother cruelly killed our romance. Day after day she broke her word of honour, studied the stammerings in my diary, and thus kept track of the stations of my love. And in Genoa – oh horrors! – she read that Klimt had kissed me!

Realizing that her mother was prying into her affairs, she took great pains not to write anything down that could have been used in evidence against her. But this one, searing experience proved just too much. The consequences were disastrous . . .

Now that *The Diaries* can at last be properly evaluated, several riddles come closer to being solved. Above all, my hope of discovering the truth about Alma and Zemlinsky has been abundantly fulfilled. By collating the diary entries with Zemlinsky's surviving letters, his tragic tale can be reconstructed from beginning to end.

The charming story of how Mahler courted his bride has been recounted often enough, but new light is thrown on it here, particularly with regard to the dizzying speed at which it all took place.

After the birth of her step-sister Maria, it became a matter of increasing urgency for Alma to find a husband – and one who not only appealed to her but also fulfilled the expectations of her mother. Youthfulness and good looks were essential, but also artistic talent, wealth, fame and – if possible – Gentile parentage. Zemlinsky failed to qualify on most counts; indeed, even Mahler did not entirely fill the bill.

New, critical light is now also shed on Alma's self-promulgated 'portrait of the girl as a young artist' – a budding talent forced into silence by a husband fearful of rivalry. For six years, from the age of fourteen, she had taken composition lessons with the highly esteemed Josef Labor. But Labor was blind, and he was obliged to judge his pupils' work on a purely aural basis, assuming that what he heard corresponded to what was written down. Yet the few scraps of musical notation in Alma's diaries betray a woefully defective ear and an astonishing ignorance of the fundamentals of theory and notation. As a rule she would limit her efforts to piano music and song; but once she started on a piano trio, only to abandon it for lack of knowledge of the stringed instruments. And on another occasion (not recorded in *The Diaries*) she asked Zemlinsky to send her a copy of his A-major String Quartet. With the unflattering remark, 'You wouldn't be able to read it anyway', he refused. He set her the task of writing a piece for mixed chorus, but once again her technique let her down: the tenor part,

Zemlinsky remarked, was 'beyond the range [...] of a man's voice, unless, that is, he were a castrato.' And yet she cultivated an intense friendship with the principal heldentenor of the Hofoper, Erik Schmedes. Altogether I suspect that Mahler's ban was motivated more by fear of professional embarrassment than by any emanation of male chauvinist *angst*, envy or the like.

Is my verdict too harsh? What do you think?

SR-B 10 October 1994

Dear Antony,

Your verdict on Alma's artistic status does strike me as a little harsh. After all, we don't even know the works dating from this period and, surprising as it might seem, even the Five Lieder, published on Mahler's initiative in 1910, don't appear to have been written at this time. Until now it had always been assumed that they were composed *c.* 1900–01, but *The Diaries* mention only 'In meines Vaters Garten' and two of the songs published in the group of 'Five Songs' of 1924. When were the others written?

I have two hypotheses. The first is controversial: that Alma composed them during her years of marriage to Mahler, and the idea that she observed her husband's ban is no more than a myth. My theory is supported by the fact that during her period of courtship, i.e. before the arrival of the fatal letter, she scarcely mentions any creative activity at all. Reading *The Diaries* in sequence, one can observe a regularly recurring phenomenon, indeed she comments on it herself: her vacillation between periods of intense productivity and what she describes as her 'sterile' phases. The most productive periods, it seems to me, were the loveless ones. Was composition for her primarily an ersatz for emotional life?

My second hypothesis concerns the numerous works mentioned in *The Diaries* but which evidently no longer exist. These do not appear to have been lost during the flight to America, for Eleonore Vondenhoff, who visited Alma for a last time shortly before her emigration, writes that she had broken up her household on the Hohe Warte, packed everything of value into metal crates and deposited them in a safe place. Did she intentionally destroy these early compositions, and perhaps also the diaries dating from her years with Mahler? We can but speculate.

SR-B 15 March 1996
Dear Antony,
Having pored over the original manuscript in Philadelphia for twelve days, we have managed to fill almost all the gaps in the text and to decipher all but the most obscure of hieroglyphics. I think we can safely say that the transcription is now complete. Now for the footnotes!

Alma often writes about painting and, in the earlier suites, displays remarkably discriminating taste in artistic questions. Her frequent commentaries on events in the art world contribute substantially to the interest of *The Diaries*. She discusses several of Klimt's most famous pictures (*Schubert at the piano*, for instance, or the controversial mural paintings for Vienna University), enthuses over Segantini, expresses her admiration for Böcklin and many others. Her remarks sometimes also help untangle certain strands of the closely woven fabric of Viennese art history: Klimt's *Portrait of Marie Henneberg*, for instance, appears in an entirely new light, and one discovers that Alma shared Webern's love for Böcklin's *Idealized spring landscape*.

All in all, I feel we should consider incorporating a substantial number of illustrations in the published edition.

AB 23 December 1995
Dear Susanne,
How best to present *The Diaries*? Could one perhaps translate Alma into the new millennium as 'infotainment'? I could well imagine it: a double-click on 'Clémenceau', and up pops the family tree, complete with potted biographies; move the mouse over 'Katzmayr', and you hear the lady singing – in digitally re-mastered stereo. An endless amount of background information could be incorporated: paintings and drawings, books and scores, town plans and hiking maps, biographies, news cuttings, concert and theatre programmes, letters, hyperlinks to archives and art galleries . . . But actually, our task is simply to transform twenty-two illegible exercise books into one easily navigable volume of clear print. We shall have to annotate the text in detail – researching that will be arduous enough – and we should include Alma's own pen-and-ink drawings, none of which have been published before.

To me, reading *The Diaries* is like raising a curtain, behind which stands the Vienna of 1900 in all its majesty, and so close that one can almost reach out and touch it. The vitality of everyday life, eye-witness accounts of significant artistic events, unique insights into the behavioural patterns and linguistic conventions of *homo austriacus* – all these serve to make the book unique.

Having split the diaries, for purely organizational reasons, into two sections (Suites 4–15 and 16–25), it transpires, quite by chance, that this division precisely mirrors the dramatic structure. The story unfolds as in a Wagner opera, deliberate in pace but with a cumulative momentum; and towards the end the tempo increases appreciably. Act I ends (with Suite 15) on a climactic note, with a banquet celebrating the inauguration of the Vienna Secession; at the same time Alma rings down the curtain on her affair with Klimt. Act II introduces a new protagonist, Zemlinsky, who becomes involved in a long, tormented love-duet. Not until the finale does the actual hero take the stage: Mahler. The heroine's closing aria is self-critical and submissive: 'I must strive to become a real person, let everything *happen to me of its own accord.*' The end, as in the *Ring*, is also a new beginning. But, as in the *Ring*, the future is uncertain: will better times follow, or is a new catastrophe in the offing?

One of Alma's most human traits is the rapidity with which she changes her mind. 'Odi et amo' – one day she loves, the next she hates. Only Wagner, her musical god, Schindler, the deceased father, and Nietzsche, her household philosopher, remain sacrosanct. Doubtless the most critical area of her *Weltanschauung* is the problem of Judaism. I find her standpoint baffling and irritating in equal measure. *The Diaries* include remarks on Jews and Jewry which, in my opinion, cannot go to press without comment. Two of Alma's three husbands were Jews, men whose physical presence and intellectual stimulus she loved, cherished and respected. But her comments are often offensive, and can neither be softened by mitigating circumstances nor excused with a shrug of the shoulder as being irremediable attributes of the *Zeitgeist*. Later her anti-Semitic attitude hardened to the point where she no longer numbered amongst those rated as 'harmless'. Yet she remained loyal to Werfel and accompanied him, if at first unwillingly, into exile.

I feel almost as uneasy about the indiscreet account (1 January 1902) of her first experience of sexual intercourse with Mahler. And when she exclaims, 'I *long* for *rape*! – Whoever it might be' (24 July 1901), one's hair stands on end. But censorship is not our concern. As you once wrote, the image of Alma has too often been distorted and obscured.

SR-B Memo 30 December 1996
Dear Antony,
One thing more. We mustn't forget to thank those who helped us:
the many archivists and librarians, particularly Nancy Shawcross and
her staff in the Special Collections department of the Van Pelt Library in
Philadelphia; the many friends who gave us invaluable information and
advice; our German publisher, S. Fischer Verlag, who generously supported
our research in Philadelphia and Vienna.

AB Fax 31 December 1996
Dear Susanne,
Just before going to press, it occurs to me that our list must also include
Jörg Hockemeyer, who made a substantial contribution to the first rough
version of the transcription. And 'rough' was the word! For he it was who
succeeded in deciphering most of the passages that Alma later deleted – I
mean the ones you shouldn't be showing the children. He contributed
much else as well; his name should take first place.

AB 25 January 1998
Dear Susanne,
I finished the translation last night. Two major decisions had to be taken in
advance, one concerning content, the other style:
    how much to include;
    how best to transform Alma's Viennese German into English.
A complete translation of the original Tagebuch-Suiten would have placed
the book in a very high price category. Rather than seeing a few hundred
copies being sold to specialists and university libraries, the publishers and I
agreed on a limit of 150,000 words, i.e. half the length of the German
edition, and on a presentation designed to appeal to the non-specialist
reader.
We have already discussed the dramaturgical structure of the Diaries: in
that spirit, I have selected and rejected in much the same way as I would
have made cuts in an opera. Such a process is inevitably subjective, but
as far as possible I have restricted the omissions to complete 'scenes'
and 'arias', i.e. those days which were dull, repetitive or inactive. The
hierarchy of Alma's dramatis personae is clear enough, and it soon
became clear that extended dialogues with lesser figures (the unfortunate
Krasny, for instance) could well be omitted without harming the narrative
flow; the same goes for the long quasi-Socratic dialogue between Alma

and Buckhard, shortly before the breakdown of their strange, licentious relationship. Passages with putative readings have been reduced to a minimum, for there seemed little point in translating material about people who could not be precisely identified, and descriptions of the art treasures of Florence, Rome, Pisa and Venice (Suites 10–11) can be found in any tourist's guide, where they are probably more reliable than Alma's own. I would gladly have summarized everything that has been omitted, but that would, in the end, have taken up almost as much space as the omissions themselves.

Even before her years with Mahler, Alma's world was immense, and to annotate it exhaustively would have amounted to writing a new cultural and social history of *fin-de-siècle* Vienna. But since it has been my concern to give the reader as much of the original text as possible, the editorial apparatus has been kept to a minimum. Certain aspects of the text strike me as more deserving of comment than others (the self-contradictions and deliberate misrepresentations in Alma's published writings, for instance); some personages appear only briefly but seem nevertheless to warrant more extended commentary; others, such as the architect Felix Muhr, appear frequently, but almost nothing is known about them. Every editor will have his own priorities; objectivity is not always possible.

An abbreviated edition, you may object, lays itself open to renewed suspicions of censorship. In principle I would agree. But I have taken great care to maintain the balance and spirit of the original, and if, by excluding passages of a more run-of-the-mill character, Alma's life appears to move at an even more breakneck pace than it really did, this is surely a fault on the right side. The cuts are exponential, i.e. the earlier Suites are more extensively abbreviated than the later ones; and from November 1901 to the end there are no cuts at all. Scholars still have the option of consulting the more lavishly annotated German edition, and out-and-out purists will anyway wish to consult the autograph. You will be pleased to know that our index, carefully structured to clarify family relationships and to provide as much factual information in as little space as possible, has been taken over with no substantial alteration, and that a few errors, oversights and minor blemishes in the German edition have now been corrected.

As for the translation: after some experiment, I found it best to use a basic vocabulary of 'upper-crust' English, spiced with expressions of the kind I heard in the north-west London of my youth, spoken by Austrian refugees. In places the book acquires a certain Wodehousian flavour (one can almost picture Alma as a Bloomsbury debutante), but, as you know, she also liked to assume more serious roles: the Catholic agnostic, the Nietzschean immoralist, the art critic, the femme fatale. I have done my best to vary the shades of purple accordingly. And on the few occasions where she uses Viennese or Salzkammergut dialect, Cockney and West Country English proved viable equivalents.

It was most kind of you to help me unravel several obscure passages in the German, and thank you, too, for the loan of several photographs. While on the topic of gratitude, I must also thank my nephew, Dr Christopher Reuter, for providing the medically exact translation of *Lungenspitzencatarrh*, Stephen Barber for gently scraping the rust off my English syntax and Christopher Hailey for his valuable comments on the first draft of the manuscript.

What a coincidence: The Diaries open on 25 January 1898 – exactly a hundred years ago today.

Bibliographical references

ix *Monson*: Karen Monson, *Alma Mahler, Muse to Genius*, Boston, 1983.

ix *Giroud*: Françoise Giroud, *Alma Mahler ou l'art d'être aimée*, Paris, 1988.

ix *Wessling*: Bernd W. Wessling, *Alma. Gefährtin von Gustav Mahler, Oskar Kokoschka, Walter Gropius und Franz Werfel*, Dusseldorf, 1983.

ix *La Grange*: Henry-Louis de La Grange, *Mahler*, Vol. I, London, 1974.

ix *Blaukopf*: Herta Blaukopf, 'Alma Mahler as Composer', foreword to Alma Maria Schindler-Mahler, *Sämtliche Lieder*, Vienna (UE 18016), n.D. (1910, 1915).

x *Rieger*: Eva Rieger, *Frau und Musik*, Frankfurt am Main, 1980.

x *Mahler's letters*: Günther Weiss: 'Gustav Mahlers Briefe an Alma', *Musica*, 45. Jg., 1991, p. 230–233. The new edition was published in 1995 with the title *Ein Glück ohne Ruh* (q.v.).

xi *quasi-biblical ire*: unpublished letter from Zemlinsky, dated 26 October 1900; typewritten copy (Special Collections, Van Pelt-Dietrich Library Center, University of Pennsylvania).

xii *similar difficulty with Alban Berg*: Susanne Rode, *Alban Berg und Karl Kraus. Zur geistigen Biographie des Komponisten der 'Lulu'*, Diss., Europäische Hochschulschriften xxxvi/36, Frankfurt am Main, 1988.

xii *ÖMZ*: '"Mich hat auch der Mensch ungemein interessiert, der hinter dieser Musik steht." Eleonore Vondenhoff im Gespräch mit Andreas Maul über die Entstehung des Gustav-Mahler-Archivs "Sammlung Eleonore Vondenhoff"', *Österreichische Musikzeitschrift*, 1990, p. 17.

xiii *Klimt had kissed me*: cf. Suite 10, 29 April 1899.

xiii *unflattering remark*: unpublished letter from Zemlinsky, dated 26 April 1901 (source: as above).

xiii *piece for mixed chorus*: unpublished letter from Zemlinsky, dated 22 August 1901 (source: as above).

Always act as if the maxims of your will-power could be accepted as the principles of a collective legislation.
  Kant

Typographical note

Postal addresses are cited as follows:

district (Roman numeral) – street name – street number

Currency

Principal unit is the Florin (Gulden, abbr. fl), divided into 100 Kreuzers. 1 fl in 1900 was approximately equal in purchasing power to £1.50 or $2.50 today (1998).

Bibliographical references

AtB: Alma Mahler-Werfel, *And the Bridge is Love*, Hutchinson & Co., London, 1959

MaL: Alma Mahler, *Gustav Mahler. Memories and Letters*, trans. Basil Creighton, ed. Donald Mitchell and Knud Martner, Sphere Books Ltd, London, 1990

GoR: *Ein Glück ohne Ruh'. Die Briefe Gustav Mahlers an Alma.*, ed. Henry-Louis de la Grange and Günther Weiss, rev. Knud Martner, Siedler Verlag, Berlin, 1995

Mein Leben: Alma Mahler-Werfel, *Mein Leben*, Fischer Taschenbuch Verlag, Frankfurt am Mein, 1963

Suite 4

Tuesday 25 January 1898
Skipped the Labor[1] lesson. A little hung-over. Took a stroll on the Ring with Carl.[2]
p.m. out with Carl again. Called on *Lilli* and *Marie Lehmann*. Everything Lilli does and says has a certain inner commitment. Her whole being vibrates . . . At present she's campaigning intensively against vivisection.
In the evening: Dr Pollack[3] and Krieghammer. T.[4] picked a bone with Kriegh., accused him of anti-Semitism, although Kriegh. never even mentioned the subject. He said, quite rightly,

    You must be crazy,

and Carl brought the conversation to an end. It was very unpleasant.

Thursday 27 January
This morning: practised.
This evening: Dr Pollack and Narziss Prasch.[5] Yesterday I played 'Die Walküre' until late at night. I like the first act best, particularly the close, 'Blühe, Wälsungen Blut'. And the passage where Siegfried draws Sieglinde passionately towards him is wonderful – such fire, genuine erotic ardour. Is there *anything* to equal it?
My throat is very sore today. –

1 Josef Labor (I., Rosengasse 4), organist and composer, blind from birth, was A.S.'s composition teacher. He also taught Julius Bittner, Paul Wittgenstein and, for a brief period *c.* 1894, Arnold Schoenberg.
2 Carl Moll, a pupil of A.S.'s father, the painter Emil J. Schindler, who died in 1892. In 1895, Moll married Schindler's widow, Anna Sofie *née* Bergen. He was a founder-member of the Vienna Secession. The family had an apartment at IV., Theresianumgasse 6, close to the Belvedere and the Südbahnhof; Carl Moll's mother (A.S. refers to her as 'Mama Moll') lived at XIII., Maxingstrasse 28.
3 Theobald Pollack, a close family friend. Thanks largely to the influence of A.S.'s father, he was appointed to a high-ranking position in the Ministry of Railways (cf. *Mein Leben).*
4 i.e. Theobald (Pollack).
5 Narciss Prasch, an engineer, and his wife Anna Prasch-Passy, singer and voice-teacher (IV., Pressgasse 22).

Wednesday 2 February
I'm completely hoarse. Gretl[6] went to the Lanners[7] on her own, Mama
to the Zierers' with Carl, who later went to Burckhard's[8] banquet
(Hotel Sacher). I stayed home alone. Composed a setting of 'Wanderers
Nachtlied' (Goethe).

Friday 4 February
This morning: a wealthy collector by the name of Schreiber. I sat at the
piano, shivering. 'I hope to God he buys something,' I thought to myself.
But no – the silly ass didn't. He promised to come again. But that was it. If
someone doesn't take the plunge straight away, they'll think twice before
doing so later.

Tuesday 8 February
Labor. I'd learnt *his* pieces in secret, and today I played them to him. He was
absolutely thrilled, made a few comments, then played me his latest organ
work, nine variations on a theme ('The Kaiser hymn'), for the forthcoming
Jubilee. He played me the introduction, which is really magnificent.
In the evening: alone. Carl left for Munich.

Wednesday 9 February
This morning: Frau Radnitzky[9] came to give Gretl a lesson. Mama and
I called on Frau Engelhart. It's really lovely, the stairway of a very old
house, decorated with paintings and reliefs. We were shown into Frau E.'s
boudoir, which is quite enchanting. Full of delightful pictures and lovely
vases, some with synthetic flowers, others full of fresh ones. Frau Engelhart

6 Gretl Moll, Anna Bergen's illegitimate daughter; her father was allegedly syphilitic. She
died in a mental home *c.* 1940, a victim of the Nazis' euthanasia programme. In *AtB* there
is virtually no mention of her.
7 The Lanner family (I., Opernring 19) owned a textile factory in Telč (Southern Moravia).
Ernst Lanner had been a friend of A.S. since her childhood.
8 Max Burckhard was an influential civil-law reformer. In 1890 he abandoned his career in
politics and became director of the Burgtheater. Despite the hostility of a conservative public,
he introduced modern literature into the repertoire, including works by Ibsen, Hauptmann,
Schnitzler, Hofmannsthal and Bahr. He abandoned the post in 1898 after clashes with court
officials, becoming councillor to the High Court and co-editor of the Secessionist journal,
Ver sacrum.
9 Orig. (and *passim*): 'Adele', 'Frau Adele' or '(Frau) Mandlick' (in the English translation,
consistently: 'Frau Radnitzky'). Adele Radnitzky-Mandlick (IV., Margarethenstrasse 25),
A.S.'s piano teacher, was a pupil of Julius Epstein. She also taught several of A.S.'s friends,
including Else and Melitta Lanner.

is preg . . .[10] once again. But I really like her. She showed us her little boy – a child, just like any other. Stares at everything with a silly, vacant expression and stretches his arms out in front of him. –
This evening:

Fidelio

Guest appearance of *Lilli Lehmann*. Marcelline: Forster, sang quite nicely, the same goes for Grengg, Schmedes & Neidl. But the moment *Lilli Lehmann* came on stage she was the centre of attention. What a voice! She sang the first aria ('Abscheulicher, was hast du vor') with such heartrending beauty that she had to come in front of the curtain to acknowledge the applause. It was just wonderful! Such talent, such fire, such genius puts Mark & Renard[11] completely in the shade. – During act II, Gretl and I looked at each other and almost began to cry. I often cry at the slightest provocation, but today I was in such rapture that my heart began to pound, so hard I feared it would burst. It was a performance never to be forgotten . . .
If only I were a somebody – a real person, noted for and capable of great things. But I'm a nobody, an indifferent young lady who, on demand, runs her fingers prettily up and down the piano keys and, on demand, gives arrogant replies to arrogant questions, likes to dance . . . *just* like millions of others. – Nothing pleases me more than to be told that I'm exceptional. Klimt,[12] for instance, said:

> You're a rare, unusual kind of girl, but why do *you* do this, that and the other, just like anyone else?

And Dr Schuster said to me:

> I don't know, I like you because I've never met anyone quite like you.

Yet I'm just one of many, for I relish such shallow compliments!
I want to do something really remarkable. Would like to compose a really *good* opera – something no woman has ever achieved. In a word, I want to be a somebody. But it's impossible – & why? I don't lack talent, but my attitude is too frivolous for my objectives, for artistic achievement. – Please God, give me some great mission, give me something great to do! Make me happy!

10 Orig.: 'schw . . .'. A.S. avoids writing out the word 'pregnant' in full.
11 Paula Mark and Marie Renard, both singers at the Hofoper.
12 Orig. (and *passim* in Suite 4): 'Klimpt'. A.S. later deleted the 'p'. Together with his brother Ernst and the painter Franz Matsch, Klimt opened a studio for mural decoration, collaborating principally with the architects Ferdinand Fellner and Hermann Helmer. After the death of his brother, in 1894, Klimt freed himself from academic traditionalism, became spokesman of the younger generation and, in 1897, co-founder of the Vienna Secession.

Friday 11 February

Siegfried

Frau Hellmann invited us – {myself,} Gretl and Paul – to sit in her box. Oh, it was wonderful! It didn't finish until 11:30. Mahler had opened all the cuts. As far as I'm concerned, it could have lasted until morning. Who could be bored by such an opera? The beginning of act II, the 'Forest Murmurs', is so enthrallingly beautiful that I held my breath and was astonished – *astonished* that I'd seen the opera two years earlier and hadn't been bowled over as I was today. Maybe it's because I know the Trilogy better now and can better understand how the individual motifs merge and blend. The end of act I is wonderful too, not to mention the 2nd part of act III – the 'Magic Fire'. It's so well done, the tongues of flame quietly flickering – I find the phrase 'wabernde Lohe' so felicitous. 'Wabern' is inexplicable, a purely emotive word. This time Siegfried wasn't sung by Winkelmann but by a new tenor named Schmedes. A new tenor in every sense, because he only recently changed from being a baritone. He was pretty good, above all his youthfulness was refreshing, especially as it's really essential for the part. He sang and acted well and with feeling, but he still has to learn to manage his resources. By the end of the opera he was showing signs of considerable strain. But anyway, that's expecting too much of so young an artist. –

The second newcomer of the evening was Friedrichs as Alberich, who sang with truly elemental passion. Sedlmair (Brünnhilde) was good, but not up to her usual standard, her voice sounded worn. Walker (Erda) as good as ever. Michalek (Woodbird) out of tune. Grengg (Wotan) good.

The opera gave me immense pleasure, and now it's my dearest wish to see 'Götterdämmerung' on Sunday.

Sunday 13 February

Spent the morning with the Lichtenheld[13] girls. Mizzi gave me a delightful picture of herself.

This afternoon Gretl Hellmann called and, since today marks the Death of Richard Wagner, I played 'Tristan', 'Walküre' and 'Götterdämmerung' to her all afternoon. The latter was supposed to be performed at the Opera but was cancelled due to the indisposition of Winkelmann. They gave 'Norma' instead. – How mean not to play W. on the anniversary of his death.

13 The Lichtenheld family (I., Hohenstaufengasse 6). Dr Adolf Lichtenheld was a teacher at a state-run Gymnasium in the 4th *Bezirk*.

Monday 14 February
Had my picture taken by Moeller, together with the Hardys.[14] He made a gigantic facial study, something like this, with my hair down. Could be quite attractive.

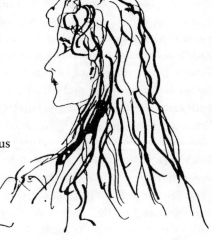

This afternoon: we stayed home, utterly exhausted after all the standing still.
This evening: alone.

Friday 18 February
This morning: thoroughly browned off . . .
p.m. first dressmaking, then to the Loews – they weren't home – then Moritz Meyer. Herr Meyer showed us around, and we were astonished by the *sheer* splendour. The Zierers' apartment is mere wallpaper by comparison. – So many antiques, so many treasures!
Pictures – Makart, Papa, Achenbach,[15] Grützner, Ferraris,[16] old Spanish masters, Troyon and several by Gabriel Max. Also some lovely pictures by Rosenthal – virtually a museum (tapestries and carpets). When he's no longer with us, and these treasures are scattered over the face of the earth, *angels will weep*!

Saturday 19 February
This morning: lesson in Frau Radnitzky's studio in the presence of all her pupils – ughhh. Tomorrow, namely, Savart is playing {the horn} with us, so the grand piano was moved into the studio.[17]
p.m. at the Leglers'.[18] A young composer was there too. His opera,

14 The Hardy family (IX., Ferstelgasse 6). John George Hardy's firm, Paget, Moeller & Hardy, manufactured brake-units for rolling stock.
15 Identity not enirely certain: possibly the landscape painter Andreas Achenbach, or his younger brother Oswald, who specialized in Italian landscapes in a folkloristic style.
16 Artur von Ferraris, favoured painter of royalty. His portraits include those of Kaiser Wilhelm and Kaiser Franz Joseph I.
17 Louis Savart was not only a horn-player, but also appeared as vocal soloist in concerts of the Wiener Männergesangverein.
18 The Legler family (IV., Heugasse 18). Wilhelm Legler was an engineer; his son Wilhelm, a painter, later married Gretl Schindler (cf. Suite 19, 4 September 1900).

'Sündige Liebe', is soon to be performed.[19] Lots of other people were there too. –

This evening: 'Norma'. Lilli Lehmann was *magnificent*. But the opera – 'Norma'? Particularly at the beginning, the meagre orchestration, the hackneyed melodies, m-ta-ta, m-ta-ta etc., the choruses (they always have the most important things). Only comprehensible, of course, if you know the libretto by heart. It made me laugh and annoyed me at the same time. Later I grew more reconciled. 'Casta diva' and the second act were very fine.

Monday 21 February
Had lunch yesterday at Mama Moll's.
This evening: dance at Dr Loew's. At home: *Lilli & Marie Lehmann*, Egner,[20] the Nepallecks, the Molls, Fischel and Klimt. When we saw the Lehmanns, we simply didn't want to leave. We got home at 4:15. The others left at 3:00. The next day, when I heard that *Lilli Lehmann* had sung 'The Erlking' etc., I cried. She was the most boisterous of all. Between the main course and the dessert she carried the plates out and, seeing how much Klimt had eaten, she said:

> You know, Moll, the way your president stuffs himself! Enough for the whole Secession.

Then both sisters began to take the micky out of Willy Nepalleck. Teased him about his medals, asked him how often and how deeply he'd 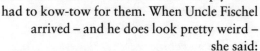 had to kow-tow for them. When Uncle Fischel arrived – and he does look pretty weird – she said:

> I shan't shake hands with you, you frighten me. She called him 'Sammael' and wanted to dress him up as the devil. Altogether she was so witty, sang, joked, *danced*. Yes indeed, they danced, even a quadrille. That meant: every man had

to kiss his partner. Carl, never one to miss a chance, grabbed Lilli and gave her a couple of smacking kisses. She laughed heartily. He said he'd been given them, she said he'd taken them.

This afternoon we went to see her, and she mimicked all yesterday's guests. Then she said:

19 *Sündige Liebe*, opera by Franz Soukup (libretto by Heinrich Glücksmann), was first performed in Brno on 4 March 1899.
20 The painter Marie Egner was a pupil of A.S.'s father.

Alma, with *your* complexion, if you powder your face, you look like a
wax doll.
When we left, she kissed Carl twice, each of us three times.

Tuesday 22 February
This morning at breakfast, Carl said:
> I'm certain you've met of one of the most interesting women alive. Not
> to mention her artistry. She has such a *big*, noble soul. An angel.
Today: Labor. He was really sweet.
p.m. dressmaking. Fräulein Rosa,[21] my teacher, told me some time ago that
she was in love with an Italian, but couldn't marry him because he was a
Christian and her father a devout Jew. Clandestinely she wrote to him and
received *his* letters poste restante. Today we called on her. She'd been crying, and immediately it occurred to me that something was up: they're
bound to have found out about the letters. I sounded her out and told her
what I suspected.
> How did you know? It's unbelievable.
And she told me her father hadn't eaten for three days, and when she asked
him why, today, he said:
> To avert the dishonour you are bringing upon our family.
Suddenly he stood up and said:
> I shall not eat again until you sign this document.
And he gave her a piece of paper, saying he would dictate her a letter, in
which she would tell him (Adelso) that it was all over. She refused,
thank God, and Dr Pollack, whom we told about it, promised to help
her . . .
This evening: Mama & Carl went to see Yvette Guilbert, a Parisian
chansonnière, with Herr and Frau Zierer. Dr Pollack discussed Spinoza
and Goethe with us for a while, then went home.

Wednesday 23 February
Monsieur.[22] Frau Radnitzky.
Yesterday we discussed the superfluousness of religion. Dr Pollack said:
> Look how much havoc it causes. Just consider the martyrs, the
> crusades etc.
I contended that religion was of enormous benefit to the arts. Almost all

---

21 Rosa Kornblüh, A.S.'s sewing teacher and retailer of lingerie (shop address: XV.,
Dingelstedtgasse 1).
22 A.S.'s French teacher, Léon Dubrot (VIII., Josefstädterstrasse 3).

surviving Greek and Roman sculpture portrays the gods. What would have come of the most beautiful poem in the world, the Song of Songs, if the Jews hadn't preserved it? And later, during the Renaissance, at the time of Titian, Michelangelo, Dürer and Holbein, almost all the paintings were of saints. Dr Pollack is certainly right in maintaining that religion, particularly Christianity, ruins public morality. Good deeds are often the result not of conviction or inner compulsion, but are done, almost without exception, in order to shorten the doer's time in Purgatory and assure him a place in Heaven. Hence many people generally considered kind-hearted are in fact nothing of the sort. They are merely concerned that their deeds be seen and acknowledged. –

This evening: alone. Had a real go at 'Walküre' act I and the 'Magic Fire' music.

Siegfried—Faust I—Wilhelm Meister

Brünnhilde—Gretchen—Philine:[23]

23 Text on the picture (bottom left): This is supposed to depict his shield and helmet.

Thursday 24 February
The second number of 'Ver sacrum' has just been published.[24] I'm not much impressed by the title page, a drawing by Koloman Moser. Of *him* I would have expected something better. Klimt's first picture was rather disappointing too.[25] There are some excellent nudes by Engelhart[26] and a 'Leda' by List, on the other hand, and Böhm's 'Lamb-clouds'. A 'Snake dancer' by Moser won me over completely. Bertha Zuckerkandl has contributed an excellent article and there's a slightly weaker satire by Kurzweil.[27] Cobbler, stick to your last, painter to your easel.

We argued with Carl in the evening about certain untruths in other landscapes of Böhm, and he said that was *stylization*. For me that word is like a red rag to a bull. What harm have the wonderful beauties of nature done to them, that they have to be stylized or, in plain language, messed about?

Wednesday 2 March
Mama, Carl and I inspected the Gartenbaugesellschaft for the Secessionist exhibition. It makes a very good impression. The halls are big, but unfortunately they're in *urgent* need of repair . . .
This afternoon: Frau Hardy and Lydia looked in to bring the photographs that Herr Moeller had taken. They've turned out very well, particularly the ones of Gretl, whose face is really photogenic.

24 *Ver sacrum*, the official journal of the Vienna Secession, was inaugurated in 1898. It appeared for six years.
25 *The Witch.*
26 Josef Engelhart, co-founder of the Vienna Secession, was noted for his contacts with leading foreign artists. Having begun his career as a painter (notably with a tempera-mural, *Oberon*, in the Palais Taussig), he later concentrated primarily on sculpture. He created several fountains and statues, including the memorial in the Zentralfriedhof to the baritone Leopold Demuth.
27 Bertha Zuckerkandl, 'Wiener Geschmacklosigkeiten' (pp. 4–6), Maximilian Kurzweil, 'Der Erfolg' (pp. 10–14), in *Ver sacrum*, I, ii, February 1898.

Dinner at the Geiringers'. Apart from us, the Lichtenheld girls (with parents) were there, also Anton Geiringer, Dr Pollack, Ernst and Hanna and a young (boring) Russian. It was great fun, particularly when Anton arrived. He sat next to me at table, Ernst opposite me. The latter talked of nothing but Anton, but he didn't notice. After dinner we all smoked, and Geiringer played the piano quite wonderfully. I was asked to play, but didn't want to. Mizzi sang 'Morgen send' ich dir die Veilchen' (by Meyer Hellmann, a tear-jerker). She has a frightful vibrato. Mama sang too, but rushed dreadfully in the Pasman-Waltz, because she'd forgotten the text. Later Ernst asked me to dance, and it went very well. Finally everyone joined in. This Anton G. is the very essence of ugliness. He says as much himself too.

Wednesday 9 March
Concert: Messchaert and Röntgen.[28] Röntgen played the 'Moonlight' sonata. Apart from the first movement, it was very fine. Mes. sang 'Die Winterreise' – it was lovely. If only he'd sung Schumann, though – I would have liked that even better.

Thursday 10 March
This evening: tarot party with the Zierers, Frau Duschnitz, Spitzer,[29] Lehmann, Hellmer,[30] Epstein & Klimt. After dinner we took black coffee in the studio, danced and sang. Lehmann sang Rubinstein's duet 'Über allen Gipfeln ist Ruh' with Mama. Klimt is such a dear man. – I'm writing this because they went back to playing cards and roped Klimt in too.
At 2:00 the Zierers and Frau Duschnitz went home. Then the fun really began. Mama and Marie Lehmann danced a pas de deux, then we all sang glees and had a whale of a time. After we'd danced our fill, the party ended at 3:30. – Mama said:

> The Zierers are bound to make remarks, because Klimt sat with you (Alma) all evening and spoke to you so much.

But he was delightful, talked about his painting etc., then we talked about

28 The Dutch baritone Johannes Messchaert and the pianist-composer Julius Röntgen frequently gave mixed programmes of lieder and piano music.
29 Dr Friedrich Victor Spitzer, heir to a sugar refinery in Moravia, studied chemistry at Vienna University. In the 1890s he took up photography. Josef Hoffmann designed his villa on the Hohe Warte (XIX., Steinfeldgasse 4).
30 Edmund Hellmer, also referred to by A.S. as 'Uncle Hellmer', was professor of sculpture at the Vienna Academy. His sizeable *oeuvre* included a memorial to A.S.'s father, completed in 1895.

'Faust', a work which he loves as much as I do. – No, he's a really delightful fellow. So natural, so modest – a true artist!

Tuesday 15 March
Labor. I played him two of my lieder and he expressed the opinion that they were too Secessionist.

Thursday 17 March
Today I restyled my hair. It suits me. The same way Clara Taussig does hers.

This evening: alone. Composed a little song. Goethe of course! –
Carl had a committee meeting at Hotel Bristol. Earlier he told us he'd unpacked some wonderful paintings of Kroyer and one by List. Everyone is in the best of spirits.
Mama wasn't at home. This evening I played the most *beautiful* passages from {Schumann's} 'Faust'. The music is unbelievably sweet (not sugary) and charming.

Saturday 19 March
Yesterday afternoon I was at the Hardys'. We embroidered our names on a quilt for Herr Moeller.
Today: Frau Radnitzky. She'd been talking to Epstein junior, who'd taken such a liking to me last spring (due to my piano playing, namely). Recently, when he was here with Klimt and all the others, I didn't want to play but finally consented and played a bit of 'Tristan', but badly. He mentioned it

to Frau Radnitzky and asked her not to let me play Wagner. – He's absolutely right, and I hereby resolve not to play any W. operas for a month. It's a resolution I can't keep, but it's worth trying. Otherwise she was pretty satisfied with me. –

Dr Pollack gave me a magnificent book, Reimann's 'Johannes Brahms', with reproductions of pen-and-ink drawings by *Max Klinger*. I'm overjoyed. I simply adore Klinger. Klinger & Böcklin!

No. 3 of 'Ver sacrum' – special Klimt number. First a short biographical note, then the poster for the exhibition, then the 'Study for a ceiling fresco, "Hygeia"' – wonderful, delightful studies of faces. I wasn't so taken with 'Fish-blood', 'Tragedy' is superb. Also a group picture in a theatre ('Totis'), a nude and some exquisite posters. – My favourites are the spandrel pictures[31] in the Museum of Art History. Also a study for the Dumba picture, which I don't understand. A fabulous blue picture and, as I said, some delightful studies of faces. What versatility – perhaps one should say: genius.

Sunday 20 March

This morning: Felix Fischer with his over-dressed but very pleasant wife, Rat Watz etc.

Lunch at Mama Moll's.

In the afternoon we drove to the Prater. On the way, Gretl and I got out at the Gartenbaugesellschaft to deliver a letter from Kuehl to Carl. Nowak, Olbrich, Hoffmann and Bacher were busy painting. Engelhart came over right away and said:

Look, it's Schindler's daughters.

The painter Eugen Jettel[32] (he left Vienna 25 years ago and lives in Paris, one of Papa's best friends in his early years) greeted us very affectionately and showed us the big cartoon by Puvis de Chavannes.[33] I was immensely taken by it – its freshness and vigour. Nice, straightforward people. How I'd love to paint stylized, grey flowers. Jettel came with us to where Mama

31 Spandrel: the triangular space between one side of the outer curve of an arch and the ceiling or framework. Klimt painted spandrel and intercolumnar pictures for the Kunsthistorisches Museum in 1890–91.

32 The landscape painter Eugen Jettel, whose home in Paris was a meeting-point for Austrian and German artists. He returned to Vienna in 1897. In 1902 the Künstlerhaus presented a major retrospective exhibition of his work.

33 A focal point of the 1st Secessionist Exhibition were the cartoons for a triptych, *St Geneviève feeds the starving of Paris* by Puvis de Chavannes. Puvis died shortly afterwards, on 24 October 1898.

was waiting in the cab, and told her *that Vienna had never seen a comparable exhibition.* – It's said that the French and English contributions are superb, but that Austria also cuts a fine figure.

In the Prater we saw many of our friends. Later we were at the Hellmanns'. This evening: at home with Jettel & Hartwig. Since Jettel is a Wagner enthusiast, I played Wagner all evening (*despite the ban*). He said he was initially staggered how much I resembled Papa in his early years. He was very enthusiastic about Klimt and said:

> One of Austria's leading artists.

Monday 21 March

Wanted to try out the Bösendorfer grand (English mechanism), but it had already been delivered to the Kaufmännischer Verein. Then to the Sewalds'[34] and with them & Mama to Bertha Kunz in her wine-bar.[35] I drank a quantity of champagne and was given canapés with caviar.

This evening: committee meeting at the Kaufmännischer Verein. It was delightful, except for my débâcle. Everyone made some contribution, and I too had to play. – I played 'Elsa's Dream' (Liszt) and 'La Fileuse' (Raff). I played like a pig. Frau Radnitzky, who was there, was furious. Afterwards it was quite fun: one after the other, seven men came and sat close by. I didn't know where to turn, and Rudolf (who was there with Mimi) said I should turn around with my back to the table and hold court.

Tuesday 22 March

Despite yesterday's debauchery, I went to Labor – at 10:00 – and didn't regret it. I played him my most recent song ('Ein Blumenglöckchen'). When I'd finished, he said:

> Quite good really.

But suddenly remembering that praise was against his principles, he pointed out lots of mistakes. I was happy for just the little bit of praise. It helped soothe yesterday's wounds.

This afternoon, at the Hardys', we solemnly presented our quilt to Moeller.

This evening: Prasch concert. It was mediocre. Her voice is small and extremely well-schooled, but leaves you utterly unmoved.

34 Probably the lawyer Dr Bernhard Sewald (office I., Elisabethstrasse 4).
35 Bertha Kunz's wine-bar was at I., Führichgasse 10. She later became the proprietor of Café Schwarzenberg.

Wednesday 23 March

Frau Radnitzky came to give Gretl her lesson. I avoided her, like a dog that's committed some misdemeanour. – She vented her fury on the innocent Gretl. Well, on Saturday I'll probably hear all about it. I'm looking forward to it already. Mama and I went to Taubenrauch[36] to order our spring oufit – frightfully expensive – 90 fl! Mama said:

> You know, Alma, I still have 100 fl in a savings account that nobody knows about, I shall use it to foot the bill.

My eyes filled with tears, and I resolved to withdraw the 20 fl in Gretl's and my post office book and give them to Mama. Gretl agreed.

This evening: Mama was at Dr Herz's. We went to the Zierers'. Something funny happened: Flora[37] wasn't quite certain whether we'd be coming, and had invited Amelie Engel. All of a sudden she came along, kicked up a hell of a fuss and said:

> Do you think I came here to hobnob with the Schindlers?

But she stayed all the same, and we – Lilli, Gretl and I – treated her with utter contempt. Lilli was even rude to her, just for our sake. After dinner I was asked to play. I didn't. Then Amelie came to me and said:

> Fräulein, you must have heard what I said. I'm really sorry, you must surely have misunderstood me.

And she made her apologies as prettily as you could imagine – far better than I ever could. So then I played, and so did she. She played waltzes beautifully, and I played quite well for the first time in days.

Friday 25 March

At 12:00 we went to the Gartenbaugesellschaft to look at the pictures. I won the bet with Klimt. He was delightful, and we – he, I and the critic Vincenti – went up to look for Thoma.

Carl's enthusiasm was exaggerated. I was disappointed. Such an old fogy can surely be no genius, for truly great artists remain eternally young. Is his contemporary Böcklin out of date (since I was told it was the fashion) – I ask you?

A wonderful room of Meuniers, a female nude by Klinger. A magnificent picture by Klimt, then St{uck}, Khnopff, the large Puvis de Chavannes

---

36 There were two firms of ladies' outfitters in Vienna under the name of Taubenrauch: the first at I., Seilerstätte 7, the second, Josef Taubenrauch & Cie, at VII., Mariahilferstrasse 70.
37 Flora Zierer, daughter of a merchant banker, was married on 27 April 1899 to the coal-wholesaler Oskar Berl. From his Viennese office on the Schottenring, Berl controlled several subsidiary firms in Prague. He was also a co-founder of the Deutsches Volkstheater.

cartoon, a sweet dancing female nude by Engelhart etc.[38] I can't mention them all, there are too many. I hope and believe that the exhibition will be well received. It's simply beautiful. There's a wonderful memorial sculpture by Bartholomé, and Alt & Jettel and so many others, I can't name them all.

Lunch at the Sewalds'. Afterwards: played 'Tristan' four hands with her. Then to {Café} Demel.

This evening: Marie Lehmann.

Saturday 26 March

Opening of the Secession[39]

It was delightful! This morning Frau Radnitzky came and scolded me for last Monday. What do I care! This afternoon at the Gartenbaugesellschaft there was art, true art, and real people. I led the Winkelmanns around, then Duschnitz, Hardy, the Jettels and the Lanners. When they'd all gone, Jettel, Kuehl, Mayreder[40] and Klimt came to talk to us. – That was when the fun began. – Then we all went home for high tea, Klimt too, and this evening there was a banquet at the Rote Rössl. Thirty pictures have been sold – one of Carl's for 2,000 fl. Not at all bad.

In the evening: alone.

Sunday 27 March

This morning: at the Zierers'.

Klimt, Jettel, Kuehl, Mayreder and Krieghammer came for lunch. Afterwards we drove to the Prater, Kuehl, Carl, Klimt and I in one cab. Carl was my vis à vis. On the way home Klimt said:

I tell you what, let's change places,

and sat down opposite me. – He's such a dear fellow. I was actually a little annoyed with him, because he said I was spoilt by too much attention, conceited and superficial. – So I didn't speak to him, except for saying that

---

38 In the Meunier room were pastel drawings, landscapes from the Belgian mining district and fourteen statuettes of artisans. The Klimt picture was *Music* (destroyed by fire in 1945), painted for the Palais Dumba. Khnopff exhibited *Silent water*, which today hangs in the Modern Gallery of the Kunsthistorisches Museum.

39 1st Secessionist Exhibition at the Gartenbaugesellschaft on the Parkring (25 March–20 June 1898). One room was reserved for presentation of the journal *Ver sacrum*. The closing date is often wrongly cited as 15 June: due to public demand, the exhibition ran for a further five days.

40 Julius Mayreder, architect, and Dr Rudolf Mayreder, engineer (I., Seilergasse 7).

he should get to know me better before passing judgement. He pulled such faces, I had to laugh. –

I really don't understand why Klimt is considered a poseur etc. – I find him really very dear and significant.

Everyone came to us for high tea.

This evening: alone with Uncle Fischel, as there was a banquet at Hotel Victoria. He discussed Böcklin, Thoma etc. with us.

[Revisions completed early January 1963.]

Suite 5

Wednesday 30 March
This evening: 'Bartel Turaser' by Philipp Langmann. – Mama Moll sat in our box. It was wonderful – terribly moving. A worker, living in abject poverty, is bribed by his rich superior to give false evidence. His wife encourages him and, since his children are sick, he commits perjury. In return he receives 200 fl. All his comrades are furious, but he has his money, and intends to use it to buy food with which to restore his children's health. The third act begins with their coffins being carried out of the house. There he sits, philosophizing about poverty etc. (naturally the Social Democrats greeted the scene with loud calls of 'bravo'). Suddenly his grief gets the better of him, and he sinks onto his dead son's bed. Very softly he hears the word 'Pa-pa', just as the little boy had always spoken it. Naturally one can follow Bartel's line of thought. Overjoyed that the child, for whom he has committed a crime, forgives him, he gives himself up to the police. The whole thing is so sad, so well written and so well performed that it's a real pleasure, even if the play isn't exactly cheering. Tyrolt and Schmittlein were fantastic.

Thursday 31 March
First thing this morning to the Secession with Carl. He went straight to the office to fetch money for Mama. That's why I went, because Carl didn't want to entrust the money to anyone else and wasn't planning to come home all morning. Of the artists, Engelhart, Kurzweil and Klimt were there, but I didn't see them until later. First I went around on my own and looked at the pictures for the umpteenth time. Klimt came to me, and we spoke about everything imaginable. Suddenly he was gone. Evidently he was very busy. After a while Carl returned with the money, and I left. Walked very quickly, as is my wont. Suddenly I heard hasty steps behind me, *guessed* that it was Klimt, but just kept walking, and hid behind my umbrella. – So it went on, but then he took a few strides and ended up beside me:

> You can hide behind your umbrella and walk as fast as you like, but you still can't escape me, he said. Will you get into trouble if I walk beside you?

I said not, although I was inwardly uncertain. So he walked with me and was delightful company. He said he wanted to escort me home, but I declined and got on the bus (the wrong one), had to get out at the next stop and walked home alone. Mama wasn't put out at all. Why didn't I walk home with him? It would have been such fun!

Lunch at Mama Moll's.

This evening: Anzengruber's 'Die Kreuzelschreiber' at the Volkstheater. An excellent play – a splendid evening. Mama Moll came with us. Giampietro was delightful, but I like him anyway. Glöckner and Greissnegger were excellent too. The play is brilliantly conceived. –

Mama and Carl took a box at the Carltheater to see

Die Kindsfrau

with {Marie} Geistinger. The play is said to be weak, and when I asked how Geistinger had acted, Carl replied:

> They should put her in a museum.

Good Friday 8 April

The weather is fine, our little fruit trees are already blossoming – I'm sitting at the window, drumming my fingers against the panes. – Out, out! Freedom – fresh air!

Tuesday 12 April

Labor. He was quite satisfied and really sweet to us. – Unfortunately it got late, and after the lesson we'd planned to go the Secession. Mama, meanwhile, was already there, and looking for us like a needle in a haystack.

This afternoon we wanted to go . . . but it started to rain, with thunder and lightning – the first real *thunder storm*, simply because we wanted to go to the Secession. Why does fate always intervene?

This afternoon I practised for two hours. Earlier, at Labor's, I'd bewailed the fact that I don't take music-making seriously enough, that I lack depth.

> Depth is indeed necessary if you want to get anywhere, he said.

I can *feel* it too, I know it, and yet I'm so superficial. That, unfortunately, is just the way I am.

Wednesday 13 April

This afternoon: to the Secession, for the first time since falling ill. Gretl and I looked round the paintings on the first floor, which I all liked except for those of Thoma, Pauer and . . . Stuck. Yes Stuck, my dear Stuck, seems to be growing kitschy. There's a picture entitled 'Sin' – well! Then three studies of heads – commercial, that's the only word. First we were on our own, then we bumped into Dr Spitzer, later also Jettel. Khnopff the painter, a sensitive Belgian Symbolist, is in Vienna. Later Carl arrived with the Hennebergs,[1] Klimt, Engelhart etc. I wandered around for a while with Olbrich. Hoffmann and Bernatzik were there too. It was very nice. Carl introduced us to Khnopff. During the course of the conversation he said:

Ça ma petite (about Gretl).

When he was leaving, Khnopff said:

Adieu, mademoiselle la grande et mademoiselle la petite, laughing heartily.

I didn't exchange a word with Klimt.

This evening: with Mama to Gerhart Hauptmann's 'Der Biberpelz' at the Volkstheater. A vicious satire on officialdom. Oh, what a wonderful play! Schmittlein acted magnificently.

Thursday 14 April
Carl had general assembly yesterday until 1:00 a.m.

This morning I practised, then tormented myself mercilessly – wanted to write a quick movement. It's not as easy as it looks, especially with Mama running in and out all the time. I got as far as the middle section in B minor, but even to get that far I'd sweated blood. I fear it won't come to much.

Sunday 17 April
In the morning: in town.

Dr Pollack to lunch.

p.m. Jettel and Khnopff. We all drove to the Prater. – Khnopff walked with me and Gretl all the time, and was terribly nice. We understood each other very well. First he called me 'Alma viva', then 'Alma Tadema'. Finally he managed to pronounce the word 'Fräulein' Alma. He's a very refined, aristocratic person and an artist of immense stature. –

This evening: Fischl and Mayreder. Carl was at the Taussigs'. Fischl and Mayreder debated on the Secession, Fischl pro and Mayreder contra – primarily against Olbrich. It's all very well to dismiss him, to criticize – but

1 Hugo Henneberg (IX., Höfergasse 12) read physics, chemistry, astronomy and mathematics. Later he experimented on reprographic techniques, and eventually embarked on a career as graphic artist and photographer in his own right. The fourth issue of *Ver sacrum* was dedicated to the process of rubber-plate printing, perfected by Henneberg and Heinrich Kühn, both members of the Vienna Camera Club. Together with his wife Marie, Henneberg became one of the closest friends of A.S.'s family. In 1902, he exhibited his work in an exhibition promoted by the Vienna Secession.

just try doing it better yourself, dear Mayreder! It was the fourth time that
M. had called on us in the last few days, and we're heartily glad to be rid of
him. Nobody misses him, myself least of all. – I wonder if he's still fond of
me? He's very taken with the Secessionist painters, being particularly
'enamoured' – as he puts it – of Bacher, Engelhart and Klimt. Of the latter
he says he can well understand young ladies falling for him *in a big way*.

Oh yes, that was fun: while Kuehl, Klimt, Mayreder, Jettel etc. were here,
Klimt gave me the idea of shaping my bread into a heart. I did so, then he
formed a toothpick into an arrow and plunged it into the heart. He took
red wine and made it flow from the wound. It looked really good. He gave
it to Mayreder as 'my wounded heart'. On reflection, I can see that it was a
very brutal joke and I regret it, for at the time Mayreder gave me a look
that went straight through me.

Incidentally, Klimt knows that M. is fond of me. He noticed – and said as
much as well. I didn't deny it.

Monday 18 April
Carl had a wonderful time at the Taussigs' yesterday and is just mad about
Emmy's husband, Herr Redlich, who takes a lively interest in art and has
bought himself a Meunier. He asked Carl for a copy of the first number {of
'Ver Sacrum'}. – Keep at it! The circulation has already risen to over 2,000.
The Klimt number alone caused it to rise by over 1,000. –

Thursday 21 April
Practised hard.

p.m. Dressmaking. Very enjoyable. Grete Jockl told me that for days (since
they first met me) their conversation has been about nothing but 'Alma
Schindler', so much so that her Mama said:

> Well, I shall have to take a look at this young lady, she must be some-
> thing quite out of the ordinary.

This evening we met up with Herr Zierer. He was red in the face and said
we should tell Carl that if he didn't come soon, he was through with him.
Carl is absolutely right. Zierer, who always pretended to be a particular
friend of Carl's, really could have done something for his child – the
Secession. After all, in buying the Khnopff picture he knew he wasn't doing
Carl any favours. He knew he'd found a bargain, knew that in a few years'
time he'd be able to sell that magnificent picture for twice or three times
the price. – That doesn't come into it. But slipping several 1,000 fl bills to
underwrite the Künstlerhaus – that was really mean of him.

The catalogue for our exhibition looks roughly like this. It's orange-yellow. The poster is about the same, except that on the left there's a scene of Theseus with the Minotaur: Art conquering Indifference.

Saturday 23 April
Frau Radnitzky – and Chopin. In the Db-major Nocturne I see my whole life reflected. It's almost as if Chopin had written it specially for me, for my emotions . . .
This evening we have a party – what a drag.
p.m. at Bertha's.
The evening was delightful – Klimt was there too. On his place-card I'd written his name incorrectly, as 'Klimpt'. I was furious with myself. He put the card in his pocket. Then I noticed that he still had the card from last time – and was very pleased. I talked to almost no one else. Hermine & Frau Geiringer teased me about that. Herr Müller sang very nicely. Geiringer played magnificently. Mama sang (without spirit) & Spitzer

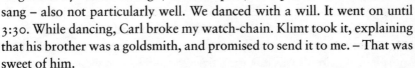

sang – also not particularly well. We danced with a will. It went on until 3:30. While dancing, Carl broke my watch-chain. Klimt took it, explaining that his brother was a goldsmith, and promised to send it to me. – That was sweet of him.
We drank a toast of brotherhood with Geiringer – that was a struggle. They all grabbed hold of me – Klimt to the fore – and Geiringer grasped the opportunity: on the cheek, of course.
Ernst and Flora Zierer were there to speak to Carl as emissaries of their father. One thing was very amusing: Hancke, business manager of the Secession, was there too. He was sitting next to me. For a joke, I took everyone's rings and put them on my fingers. Hancke asked me, teasingly, which one I liked best.
    This one here, I imagine?
And he pointed to Klimt's. Klimt was talking to Uncle Fischel all the while. After dinner, he said:
    Hancke was evidently trying to sound you out. It's unbelievable: without even listening or looking, he never misses a thing. He also knows how to speak so discreetly that nobody hears him except the person he wants to talk to.
I told him as much.

Sunday 24 April
In the morning: to Flora. She's still talking about the affair in the Künstlerhaus. We saw Ernst as well.
Lunch at Mama Moll's. – Mimi's attitude towards me was very kind and
gentle. She said, in the cab she couldn't stop thinking about us, and
couldn't sleep. 'No,' she said to herself, 'Klimt and Alma are getting on
really well together,' and all of a sudden it occurred to her that I too might
one day get married. She couldn't get the idea out of her head – made her
quite depressed.

> That he's fond of you, she said, that's nothing new. But whether
> you . . .

Well, I wonder whether Klimt could answer for everything he told me
yesterday:

> Look before you leap! You can't trust an artist – and a painter least of
> all. It's in the blood. High-spirits – frivolity. Here today, gone
> tomorrow.

Monday 25 April
The week began beautifully. I hope to God it goes on like this. I was busy
letting my hair down, when Mama called:

> Children, a surprise! Come quickly!

I ran, just as I was, into the dining-room. Khnopff had sent us delightful
little pictures. Gretl's was less attractive & smaller – two violets – mine was
of a girl holding a vase. I was absolutely overjoyed. Carl wants to repro-
duce it in 'Ver sacrum' – but *I* don't want to – as owner. Do I really deserve
it? No, not in the world. He wrote an accompanying note:

> Mademoiselle Alma la grande, a souvenir à {la} délicieuse promenade
> au Prater (the time we walked on ahead with him).

What a nice man – I would never have expected anything of the kind.
This evening: Mayreder. I felt sorry for him – I believe he's still very taken
with me. The look in his eye and – well, in a word, I'm really sorry for him.

Tuesday 26 April
Early in the morning to Labor. He was so kind, and when he heard that
we were driving out to the Zentralfriedhof this afternoon he showed such
deep sympathy that I had difficulty suppressing my tears.[2]
At midday we met M. Lichtenheld, the two Jolys etc. Got back home – who

2 On 27 April 1898, A.S.'s father would have celebrated his fifty-sixth birthday.

was in the garden with Carl? Klimt, who'd come to bring me my gold chain. It was so kind of him. Mama invited him to drop in while she's away. Oh, he's so nice. I said something rather impulsive. I said:

When I was given my watch, I liked it so much, I took it to bed with me.

Oh, he said, is that your yardstick for loving something?

Aunt Xandi,[3] Gretl and I had to laugh, although under such circumstances one should pretend to be totally innocent.

p.m. we drove out to the Zentralfriedhof, saw Koloman Moser and Hoffmann. Came home shattered.

Hearing that Carl had a visitor, we didn't go in – but when the visitor had gone, Carl told us it was Max Klinger. He was annoyed that he hadn't known of our return, otherwise he would have fetched us. We were no less annoyed at missing the chance of meeting such a famous man – too stupid. In the evening: Dr Pollack, who teased me about Klimt – I really don't know what's the matter with everybody. If you talk to one person a little longer than you talk to others, everyone immediately thinks you're in love. They should keep out of it, look to their own salvation. 'Twould make more sense.

Wednesday 27 April

Monsieur. *Mama has left* {for Hamburg}! I planned the menu, was given money – am in charge of the household now.

p.m. dressmaking – didn't do very well at all. Towards evening – I was practising a Bach fugue – Emma announced that Klimt was there. I went down to greet him. He didn't know anything about the Loïe Fuller story, at least that's what he said. Then Carl joined us and he {Klimt} stayed to dinner. He really loves his food. But he's a dear, sweet fellow. Nevertheless I think he was offended by my behaviour yesterday. I don't understand exactly why, but I have that feeling, and my feelings never deceive me. Nor do I expect to see him here again in a hurry.

Thursday 28 April

Early this morning: Mama Moll, who told me that Erna Moll said that the talk of the town was – that I was engaged. Nothing could be more idiotic, really – engaged to *Mayreder. He'd be just ideal! Ughhhhh.*[4]

Aunt Xandi just stopped by. We were talking about the abovementioned and she said:

3 Alexandrine Nepalleck (IV., Favoritenstrasse 52).
4 Orig. (and *passim*): 'Brrrrrr'.

Whether you like it or not, they'll soon be talking about you and Klimt.
Yes, I said, there's often been such talk, even with Richard.[5]
(It was she who'd spread that particular story.) I said:
I wonder whether I can raise the number to twenty.
She laughed. I find it revolting, the way people love to wag their tongues.
Before leaving for Mama Moll's, I treated the maids to an extra litre of beer
– from my own money – and revelled at their pleasure.
Later Carl came to Mama Moll's too. I didn't do any dressmaking because
I'm not well, and C. went to the
                Laying of the foundation stone of the Secession.
In the evening: at Flora's. I never laughed so hard in my life.

Sunday 1 May
This morning: to the Künstlerhaus.[6] I most liked the sculptures of Ries and
Klinger (some at least), of the pictures, Hirschl & some of the French
painters. I was disappointed by Böcklin, also by Klinger's picture. 'The
struggle for fortune' of Rochegrosse I found enthralling. We stayed for two
hours – saw about a third of the exhibition. I was dead tired.
Lunch at Mama Moll's.
Spent the afternoon in the garden. I fetched a volume of Byron from
Mama's library and read 'Cain' from beginning to end. I really liked it. So
imaginative – so magnificent. This evening I started on 'Don Juan'.
Later, Krieghammer and Reininghaus[7] came to dinner. It went without a
hitch.
{in the margin:} From Mama Moll's window we could see the workers
marching.

5 The neurologist Richard Nepalleck, a relative of A.S.'s mother.
6 At the Jubilee Art Exhibition, which opened in the Künstlerhaus and the Musikverein
on 19 April 1898, the Künstlerhaus artists – probably in reaction to the 1st Secessionist
Exhibition – exhibited paintings of a more advanced style than hitherto.
7 Carl Reininghaus, heir to a brewery in Graz, was a munificent patron of the Secession. It
was he who, in 1902, took the initiative in saving Klimt's *Beethoven-frieze* from destruction.
He also sponsored Carl Moll and several of his colleagues on their 'grand tour' of Italy in
1899 (cf. Suites 10–11). In the *Neue Freie Presse*, 17 November 1929, Moll published a
perspicacious obituary of him: 'In Graz, his house was built by Julius Mayreder, a Makart
ceiling adorned his living-room, intriguing 18th-century Viennese *objets d'art* bore witness to
his inquisitive nature, to his love of art. The Viennese "holy spring" {*Ver sacrum*} cast its spell
over him: he left his home in Graz and moved to Vienna. When a Secessionist Exhibition was
announced, he could scarcely control his enthusiasm. Even while the pictures were being
hung, he would besiege the house, turn every picture round, disturb the workers. He was
feared and – loved. [. . .] A curious fellow, the warmest, most outgoing of people – but
sometimes his mind would cloud over, he would appear confused, mistrustful, belligerent.'

Tuesday 3 May

Today I was really pleased with myself: Labor was *very* pleased with me.

> You see, he said, today it's been a pleasure teaching you – it wasn't one of those lessons in which I have to drum everything in. I felt I was discussing Beethoven with a fine young lady.

I'd never imagined I'd get that far. Considering my thoughtlessness – and perhaps intellectual shortcomings – that's saying quite a lot.

I'm reading Byron's 'Don Juan'. I don't understand how the man who wrote 'Cain', a magnificent, serious work of great dramatic and imaginative power, could write such a frivolous 'Don Juan'. He revels in mud-slinging – altogether the tone is abominable, irresponsible. I'm not impressed. One further thing annoys me: he attacks contemporaries, such as Wordsworth, Coleridge, Southey, Campbell, Moore and Sotheby.[8] *That* may be appropriate for satire but not for epic poetry. Goethe never did anything of the sort: he did write one satire, 'Wyland and the Gods', but in his other poems you never find the names of contemporaries.

Thursday 5 May

Yesterday p.m. Olbrich and K. Moser looked in and made very amusing conversation. Great fellows.

Yesterday evening: general assembly. Despite massive resistance, Klimt was re-elected as president. The vice-presidency still has to be decided.

This morning: practised until Aunt Xandi and Mama Moll arrived. Went out with the latter. Lunch at Mama M.'s After lunch we drove with her to Habig, where she bought us new hats. Then to Toresti.[9]

In the evening: Dr Pollack.

Mama is having a good time in Hamburg. She's happy to be with her family again. My God, how long will she still have them?

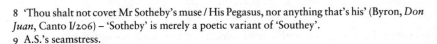

Friday 6 May

Whenever I play the D♭ major Nocturne of Chopin, I grow sad – it's the story of my life. It begins yearningly, uncertainly, becomes ardent and passionate, then (when the theme returns for

---

8 'Thou shalt not covet Mr Sotheby's muse / His Pegasus, nor anything that's his' (Byron, *Don Juan*, Canto I/206) – 'Sotheby' is merely a poetic variant of 'Southey'.
9 A.S.'s seamstress.

the third time) a question is proposed and decisively rejected – it ends in a mood of sad resignation.

Saturday 7 May
Die Walküre
What's all this talk of sad resignation? I, indeed all mankind, should rejoice that such a work was ever written. Such passion, such magical sounds – Wagner, you surpass all your predecessors, not to speak of your successors. Other than after 'Tristan', I never felt so enraptured, so breathless, so crazy. Schmedes was brilliant, a guest ({Paula} Doenges) was exquisite, a Sieglinde of rare poetry. Sedlmair was magnificent as usual. The close of act I and the final scene of act III are unsurpassed. Wonderful, great, impressive!

Wednesday 11 May
Yesterday vol. 5 of 'Ver sacrum' was published (exhibition brochure). I don't much approve of it, neither a) with the choice of pictures (Bernatzik chose them), nor b) with the quality of reproduction. Some are so dark, you can scarcely make anything out, and then for instance there's a portrait sketch by Stuck. Is that really necessary? The face is so bad, so repulsive. This evening I wrote the fair copy of my little song.

Monday 16 May
To lunch: Reininghaus with his little girl. Mama invited him to discuss an idea of his. The last time he was here, he spoke a lot about Italy, warmly urging Carl to go there and study the old masters. Carl said:
    Certainly, if I had the money.
And yesterday Reininghaus wrote Carl a delightful letter, informing him that a sum of money had been deposited at the Austro-Hungarian Bank to be placed at Carl's disposal, and that he, as a friend, had the right to do him this small favour. Carl won't accept, naturally, but it's most thoughtful of R. Mama talked it over with him today, while I took Hanna, who's eight years old, for a walk in the garden. She's an uncommonly bright child and has already developed a certain feeling for art. We heard that R. is getting a divorce. He made a few allusions which left me in no doubt of it.

Wednesday 18 May
I was in the middle of my Dubrot
lesson when there was a ring at the
door: the interpreter of some rich
American had come to ask whether
the gentleman could look at the
pictures in the studio. Mama
assented, and I had to show him
round. In my excitement, all I
could think of was 'Yes, yes, yes'.
He's very friendly, by the way, is
roughly middle-aged and very
good-looking. He said he was
staying at Hotel Bristol. Let's hope
that Carl calls on him there.
Scarcely had the English-speakers
departed, when the door opens and,
naturally, in walks Madame van
der Stappen. 'Come, Alma.' Now
it was time to parle in French,
and Mme. v. St. found that I spoke
it very well. She and her husband are
coming to dinner with us tomorrow.

Götterdämmerung

It was wonderful, *Lilli Lehmann* (Brünnhilde) quite breathtaking, adorable, such a stature, such a voice, such an actress. A great artist and a great
personality! And 'Götterdämmerung' . . . the world doesn't deserve it –
nobody appreciates, nobody understands just what this genius of a painter-
cum-poet-cum-musician has actually created – for us, for humanity, for the
benefit of all. One should take it with the same fervent passion with which
it was given. But there are still those who look askance at it – they should
be *ashamed* of themselves, ungrateful wretches. One thing about the pro-
duction bothered me: the actual twilight of the gods, for my taste, wasn't
sufficiently grandiose or overpowering. There was a rumbling sound like at
8:00 p.m., when the shopkeepers let down the shutters.

Sunday 22 May
A ring at the door and I saw {Crown-Prince} *Luitpold* [of Bavaria], ran
and told Mama, who immediately said that *I* should receive him. I came

downstairs (*didn't* curtsy) [that was too revolutionary] and said that Carl wasn't at home, but that I'd sent for him. – He asked:

With whom do I have the honour?

I said:

Schindler.

[He embraced me twice, each time exclaiming:

My friend Schindler{'s daughter},

his eyes full of tears], and he was terribly kind, spoke a lot about Papa, of Munich and Nimpfenburg, and was really most kind. His two adjutants introduced themselves, and I showed them the pictures and everything (he doesn't have much of a clue). Carl soon arrived and showed him everything all over again. Meanwhile I conversed with the two adjutants, both of them very pleasant individuals. I was able to speak quite uninhibitedly with Luitpold and his two appendages. I even said 'Your Imperial Highness', which was wrong because he's a Royal Highness. But I didn't care, because when you look into those jovial, blue eyes it doesn't make any difference. When he left, he shook hands with me twice and I curtsied beautifully twice over. I can scarcely imagine it. [Looking at the Tilgner fountain, he asked me if it was by Carl (what a feeling for art).][10]

This evening:

Tristan

my favourite opera.

Lilli Lehmann was brilliant. I shan't write anything more about the piece. I can only repeat: incomparable, unearthly – thoughts not of a man but of a god. In my eyes, Wagner is just as *holy* a person as Lilli Lehmann. People who can make so many others happy and blissful,[11] do more to benefit mankind than the saints or martyrs (I have no time for them), who let their bodies be slit open, their eyes be put out, without so much as a murmur. They are the holy ones, they live *for* humanity. –

If I go on like this I think I shall go mad, just like King Ludwig of Bavaria – for sheer rapture over Wagner's operas and enthusiasm, yes, love for Wagner.

10 Victor Oskar Tilgner created several monuments and fountains in Vienna, including the Mozart Memorial in the Burggarten and the Makart Memorial in the Stadtpark. A.M.-W.'s numerous later additions to her diary entry about the visit of Crown-Prince Luitpold indicate that the event was of considerable significance to her.

11 Orig: 'selig' – in this context either blissful or blessed (in the ecclesiastical sense).

Tuesday 24 May
Labor lesson.
This evening: alone. Today we hatched out a really wonderful plan. Reininghaus remitted 15,000 fl to Carl, who replied that he could never accept such a gift, but that he, R. should leave the money in the bank until such time as he so liked a picture of Carl's that he wanted to buy it. At all accounts, C. agreed to use the money for a journey to Italy. So now we have to wait and see. All being well, we'll go to Rome, Naples, Capri, Florence and Milan next March. Carl will be away for eight weeks. I scarcely dare think about it, I'm so overjoyed. Mama's behaviour is classic: Already now, she's exploiting the affair to her own ends. 'You've got to be good,' otherwise we'll call it off – or 'drink more milk, so you're strong and healthy when you're there.' In Mama's opinion, milk is good for everything anyway – pimples, debility, colds etc. Recently I said:

> If ever I have a corn on my toe (so help me God), you'll still say, 'Drink milk and it'll go away.'

Thursday 26 May
(Secession) They must have had a riotous time yesterday. My goodness, Carl came home without his umbrella, Böhm with only half of one. Fortunately they're anything but 'holy' youths.[12]

Monday 30 May
Bowled, cycled, went for a stroll.
The book I'm currently reading is rather out of the ordinary:

Also sprach Zarathustra

by Friedrich Nietzsche, highly interesting. Although (as I can't deny) I don't understand everything, I like it immensely. – Right at the beginning (the foreword) it's so wonderfully done that even the most uninformed of laymen can get a good deal out of it.

Monday 6 June
In the early morning I went to the station with Alois to collect two bicycles, a man's and a woman's. Mama won't accept them for us and I don't agree either. It looks very strange if we accept such gifts from Dr Pollack. It rides less easily than the Hennebergs', but it's perfectly all right all the same.

12 Word play on 'Ver sacrum'.

This evening: alone (Rosa is due on the 17th).
Yesterday and today I wrote five variations on an original theme.

Tuesday 7 June
Today I had a very pleasant experience: I played Labor the five variations –
and he was pleased. He said:
    You always have taste.
Didn't find any mistakes and was really kind and good-humoured. I was
so thrilled! As the theme was rather short, he asked me to write variations
on a longer theme.

[Checked in early January 1963. A.M.-W.]

Suite 6

Monday 13 June

Unveiling of the Makart monument

This morning we went to Mama Moll's, then collected
Carl from the Secession, met Engelhart and Nowak and
walked with them to the Stadtpark. Quite a crowd had
already gathered: Makart's mother, his son (his daughter
didn't arrive until it was over), members of the Künstlerhaus
and the Secession.[1] Klimt was most endearing. He came over
to me immediately and chatted away. The moment when he
and Felix stood side by side and laid the wreaths was very
effective. Afterwards I spoke to Klimt for a while. He
asked when we were going away etc.

Frau Lanner treated us to breakfast in the Stadtpark.

> You have good taste, Alma, she said. You know, when two people
> look alike, they usually marry. –

I must admit it had never occurred to me that Klimt and I looked alike. –
Everyone teased me (I couldn't care less). Later Carl, Jettel, Engelhart &
Klimt came looking for us but couldn't find us, as we were sitting quite
hidden away. [Later he told me he had suggested to Carl that they should
breakfast in the Stadtpark – and was furious at not finding us.]

Tuesday 14 June

Last lesson with Labor. I was so sorry. I asked if he'd take me on again next
year, and he said:

> I'm looking forward to it already and shall receive you with open
> arms.

Wednesday 15 June

The Secessionist Exhibition was supposed to close today, but it's in such

---

1 The memorial address for Makart was given by Nikolaus Dumba; music to accompany the
unveiling of the monument was provided by the Vienna Männergesangverein, conducted by
Richard von Perger.

demand that they've prolonged it for six more days. Spitzer and the Hennebergs wanted to come to Vienna specially – and they came, although it wasn't the closing day. We were very pleased.

The Hennebergs, Spitzer and Klimt came to lunch.

After lunch, Frau Henneberg and her husband drove home, and we had a rendezvous at the Secession at 6:00. Meanwhile Klimt stayed with us and drank schnapps. He spilled a glass, but disguised it by covering the stain with all the utensils on the table. Carl didn't even notice.

Kl. and C. then went off to the funeral of little Ottenfeld, returned a quarter of an hour later and walked over to Jettel's.

Uncle Fischel came and drove us to the Secession. From there, all eight of us drove to the Prater to see the Jubilee exhibition. It isn't up to much. All the same, I had an amusing time with Klimt. He took the menu cards, which he always carries with him, out of his wallet: 'Alma & Klimt – too bad'. Mama hinted darkly that I shouldn't walk with Klimt. But he was so delightful. He'll probably call later this week to collect my fan. After the Prater, at 11:30, everyone came back home with us. |It was rather fun.|

Monday 20 June
This evening: end of the Secession {exhibition}. Klimt gave a speech in honour of {Franz} Alt, who replied with wit and good humour. Together with Redlich and Felix Fischer, I went round all the rooms once again. Not until the end did Kl. see me. – He asked if I'd just arrived. Gretl, who wanted to leave, pestered me so much that I decided to leave. Kl. couldn't believe it:

What, you're leaving before the exhibition is over? Impossible!
We went all the same – [and lived to tell the tale!]
I'm in such a dreadfully bad mood. Went into the garden on my own and . . .

Tuesday 21 June
This morning each of us received a postcard from the Secession, signed by all the artists. The addresses were in Klimt's writing. On mine he'd written: 'Very dreary Alma', and on Gretl's: 'Gretl even more dreary'. Just because we didn't stay until the exhibition was over. – I was sorry too. Of course I took the postcard with me.

Later this morning a gigantic picture [by Henri Martin] arrived from France. It took eight men to carry it into the studio. – Then we packed our bags, and at 11:25 we took the train from the Nord-West-Bahnhof to Budweis and from there to Teltsch.[2]

In the evening we went for a little stroll.

Wednesday 22 June
Slept well, cycled, read & wrote letters. Unpacked.

p.m. a frightful storm, hailstones as big as pigeons' eggs. The two ponds beyond the factory merged into a lake, and we were afraid we'd all be washed away.

In the morning, the girls all run around with their hair loose. I said that they looked like the holy women in the picture of the same name at this year's Künstlerhaus exhibition.

Yesterday we had a hilarious time. Whenever I play at theatre (with other girls), I always take the leading male role. Yesterday we distributed the parts of 'Walküre': Wotan, Brünnhilde, Siegmund and Sieglinde.

Naturally I shall play Siegmund, I said.

We laughed till we cried. Later Melitta said:

Let's write a pastoral play. Gretl, naturally, will play the silly cow, (she always gets the smallest parts anyway)

then comes Else, then Melitta. And Alma, *naturally*, will be top dog. – So now we say 'naturally' to everything. Often it sounds quite daft – all right, but it's good fun.

This evening Melitta and I started on a new play. It's called 'Be faithful'. –

Friday 24 June
Wonderful weather – we rowed across the lake towards the forest, and when we'd got to the top we acted out our home-made drama, 'Be faithful'. Half the words were lost in laughter.

Later I wrote to Mama, then looked round the factory with Melitta. It's really worth taking an interest in, expending some thought on this world of machines. I find there's even a certain poetry about it. From the tiniest cog to the largest piston or wheel, everything is in constant motion, in restless action, particularly the looms. The shuttle flies so purposefully back and forth – even the smallest component has something powerful about it, and one admires the people who thought it up. – When Herr Lanner arrives, I shall ask him to explain it to me and write it all down.

Gretl and Melitta drove to Teltsch.

2 i.e. via Moravské Budějovice to Telč, 16 miles south-west of Jihlava in Southern Moravia.

Today there was something about Klimt in the paper – namely about his government commissions. Naturally everyone teased me dreadfully about him. If only people, other than me, would realize that they are deluded – even Kl. wouldn't dream of such a thing. Talking of his future projects, the last time I spoke to Kl., he said:

> The only thing that might prevent me {from completing them} would be marriage or insanity. At any rate, that would be the worst that could happen.

Sunday 26 June
In the morning, Gretl and Melitta drove to Teltsch. Meanwhile I wrote a setting of {Rilke's} poem 'Lehnen im Abendgarten beide' . . .[3]

Saturday 2 July
Finished reading Murger's 'Scènes de la vie de bohème', a delightful book, though not particularly moral.
Else and I go cart-riding every day. When I drive, the horses run much faster.

Wednesday 6 July
Took a long walk with Herr Lanner. This evening they teased me dreadfully about Klimt. I just don't know where they get it from. It's been like this ever since the unveiling of the Makart monument. – Frau Lanner said he was staring at me so purposefully that he never noticed her, although she was standing right beside me. Sometimes I looked across – & later, at the exhibition in the Prater, he said I never even looked at him!
Murger's 'Scènes de la vie de bohème', a delightful, racy book, although it's dreadfully immoral, is not made for the likes of us. Nevertheless it won my warmest sympathy. He describes artists' life in Paris, namely artists who founder and are destined to do just that – because of their mediocre talent and disreputable life-style. His depictions of grisettes and loose women are quite wonderful, yet innocuous. Of course, some scenes are pretty grim – the whole thing is unbelievably liberal and bubbles with humour. Mama is aghast that we're reading it! Goodness, I don't think anyone could ever be corrupted by a book – a good book, I mean, whether moral or immoral. Just consider {Goethe's} 'Kindred by Choice', a book which parents usually take pains to keep hidden – has anyone ever been corrupted by it? Certainly not. Only the French penny dreadfuls, which are

3 Orig.: 'Sassen im Abendgarten' etc. The poem, dedicated to Maeterlinck, is taken from Rilke's *Erste Gedichte* (1897), in the section entitled 'Advent'.

so badly written and have such a bad influence that they can contaminate any young boy or girl. I wouldn't dream of buying such a book, but would like to work my way through the classics from A to Z.

Wednesday 20 July
Yesterday and the day before I took to my bed – had a bad sore throat. I read all day: 'Die Waffen nieder' by Bertha Suttner (a splendid, serious novel), 'Tantchen Rosmarin' by Heinrich Zschokke (I'd expected more of it), 'Briefe aus Island', also by Zschokke (very agreeable), 'Die Nibelungen' by Friedrich Hebbel, a magnificent cycle of plays. But I have to admit that I prefer Wagner's 'Ring'. Much more poetic and much more to my taste. This Kriemhild, with her wild blood-lust, is a truly demonic woman – but how is Brünnhilde depicted (in 'Götterdämmerung')? Two women intent on revenge, but what a difference! – Br. never loses her femininity. For me, on the other hand, Gutrune ('Götterdämmerung') is a shivering, snivelling creature – in a word, unsympathetic. Hebbel's characterization of Brünnhilde is magnificent. The sense of loyalty which attracts her magnetically to Siegfried, his scorn for her and, after his death, her dreadful anguish . . . in truth, only a woman is capable of such feelings. – 'This silent love that *suffers everything*.' I also read 'Modelle' by A. v. Winterfeld, a delightful comic novel.
I got up again today, but still feel worn out.

Saturday 23 July
Yesterday I began and today I finished Alphonse Daudet's 'Fromont jun. & Risler sen'. A picture of Parisian lives and times. A magnificent book, hideously true, brilliantly narrated and utterly moving. When I got to the end, I sat motionless for at least ten minutes. I wonder whether Mama would have let me read it? I'm sure she wouldn't, and she'd be right too. – Why do I have to read about *such* evil people? And they really are disgustingly evil! With few exceptions.

Friday 29 July
In the morning: went cycling – wonderful.
Towards evening, all of a sudden: Klimt. Arrived unannounced. I caught my breath. – He stayed on. – Later Mayreder and Aunt Xandi. Mama

wasn't well and went to bed at 11:00. At 11:30 I threw them all out. –
Klimt was as charming as ever. Maybe he'll meet Carl in Munich and come
to Goisern with him.

Aunt Xandi was rude to Mayreder once again. I said I wanted to lose
weight, whereupon M. said:

  I'm happy with you just as you are.

And Xandi remarked, sarcastically:

  Oh, I'm glad to hear it.

[A real old bag!]

Secession (after Koloman Moser)

Saturday 30 July

Didn't get a wink of sleep all night – was so dreadfully worked up.

This afternoon: visited Herr Lanner. Beforehand I was at Mariahilf, where (at Herr L.'s) we met up with Carl. Together we went to the Secession, i.e. to the building site. There isn't a staircase yet, so we clambered up, over ladders and planks, to the highest point of the building. The rooms are beautifully proportioned, almost all with skylights. From the top you have a wonderful view over the Karlskirche and the future boulevards of Vienna. [I can't yet tell whether the building will really be so monumental, I fear rather the opposite.]

Unfortunately a small controversy has arisen amongst the Secessionists – architects vs. painters. There's a committee, namely, whose duty it is to monitor urban development on the square around the Karlskirche. Although in my opinion it's a purely architectural question, Klimt was elected (by the Secession) to represent their interests. Carl said it was merely a matter of form, as one person could achieve *absolutely nothing* against so many (one representative from the Academy, one from the Künstlerhaus etc. etc.). The most he could do would be to raise his veto and argue his case – but that wouldn't do much good. And now Olbrich (the architect of the new Secession) is so furious that Klimt has been elected, and not *he*, that he wants to resign. Altogether, the young architects consider themselves unfairly treated – which is absolute rubbish, as they've been favoured in every way, indeed often to their advantage.

One only need look at Olbrich – so handsome, such a dapper young dandy – to draw one's own conclusions, as I have: madly conceited, arrogant. What I've known for two years has suddenly become common opinion. I'm not as stupid as I look. – I'll be very interested to see how the controversy ends. It would be most unfortunate, now that the building is half-finished, if Olbrich were to withdraw. Carl is just laughing it off, taking no heed. –

As I said, we were at Herr Lanner's for lunch. In bed he looks weird – like a half-drowned rat. But he was very nice!

Sunday 31 July
Bismarck is dead. And so another of our heroes passes on, and nobody can replace them.

Yesterday Carl and I bumped into Grengg. As before, he was crazy about Zora [my parrot].

This evening Dr Sewald and Dr Lieser called on us and stayed until 1:00 a.m. After supper, Mama and I went to bed (Mama isn't well). The others played cards. Lieser might buy one of Carl's pictures. – Docterl[4] was there too.

At 5:00, Carl and the rest of us drove to Papa's grave in the Zentralfriedhof. The sun illuminated the bust from the side, and it seemed to me as if my dear, dear Papa was smiling at me, a strange, quietly transfigured smile. It moved me – I don't know why . . .

Tuesday 2 August
We left at 7:30 a.m. Dr Pollack accompanied us. At 1:00 we changed trains in Budweis and at 5:30 we reached Franzensbad.[5] The only acquaintances we made on the journey were two young girls, a woman (who looked rather poorly) and a man. Nomen odiosa sunt (I don't even remember them). We walked around in search of accommodation. Finally we took two rooms at Hotel Holzer. During dinner, at the hotel, we subtly contrived to get Mama to cry. It was long overdue! – I've long been meaning to say something she doesn't want to hear:

> We aren't children any longer – don't forget it.

Recently Carl gave us a lecture, during the course of which he said:

> You can tell your Mama anything – she's your best friend.

---

4 One of A.S.'s nicknames for Dr Pollack.
5 i.e. via České Budějovice to Františkovy Lázne.

That's all well and good – but a friend who threatens to slap your face every five minutes, whether others are listening or not – you don't say much to such a friend, can't say much, because you're *afraid* to. – How often have we been asked:

Why are you always so quiet when your Mama's there?

My secret reply would be: I'm afraid Mama will suddenly say, 'Don't be so cheeky – I'll slap your face' etc. I'm afraid of being crushed, of being put to shame.

We didn't elaborate on the subject, because Mama burst into tears, but I would have gladly told her the plain, open truth.

Wednesday 3 August
Franzensbad

I scarcely slept all night, because the man in the next room came in very late and made a dreadful noise shifting tables and chairs about.

Around 8:00 we went to Doctor Jakesch, whose wife is a friend of Aunt Laura. When she heard our names, she registered surprise, explained who she was, and soon we struck up a conversation. Then we went to look round town. It's quite nice – a typical spa. Snooty people, one hotel next to the other, but the streets are dull and lifeless.

At 12:00 we returned to the doctor. A pleasant, agreeable man. He tested our blood and diagnosed chlorosis in all three of us.

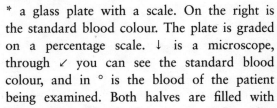

This is a terrific invention:

* a glass plate with a scale. On the right is the standard blood colour. The plate is graded on a percentage scale. ↓ is a microscope, through ╱ you can see the standard blood colour, and in ° is the blood of the patient being examined. Both halves are filled with water. You turn the regulator until the blood colour corresponds to that on the scale. He let me do it each time, because I have sharper eyes. The invention is by a Dr Fleischel.

I have 63 per cent red blood cells, Gretl 64 per cent & Mama 45 per cent, which is dreadfully low.

At the doctor's we bumped into the lady from the train, who was so nice. She was delighted to see us. The poor thing, she appears to be very ill.

Then we had lunch, after which I went straight to my room to do some writing. Gretel & Mama are in Mama's room. How I long to be alone!

{Sunday 4 September}[6]

To Dr Jakesch for a repeat of the blood tests. Gretl has 80 per cent against 64 per cent, Mama 115 per cent against the earlier reading of 45 per cent. I have 78 per cent against 63 per cent. One day before our departure.

Klimt had many things to tell me today. Anyone else would consider themselves committed to him. I know my artists better, but all the same I'm delighted: I've never heard anyone speak the way he does. But I shan't write any of it down – I don't think I'll forget it in a hurry.

6 Inserted into the MS of Suite 6 on a separate sheet, shortly before leaving Franzensbad.

Suite 7

Thursday 4 August
Franzensbad

We got up early and went to the spa. On an empty stomach the water tastes disgusting. But it's supposed to do you good. I'll have to try it first. It certainly did nothing to raise my spirits. I feel like bursting into tears. –

This morning, after the spa, Mama struck up a conversation about Klimt:

> Alma, I've been meaning to say this for a long time. It's not nice of Klimt to court your favour like this. – He's involved with his sister-in-law,[1] and even if he's really very fond of you (which seems to be the case), he has no *right* to behave this way – it's unscrupulous and abominable.

I said:

> Really? What business is that of mine?

To which she replied:

> He really likes you, don't deny it, but you're too good to be merely his plaything. That's why I'm telling you.

[I saw to it that I went to my room at the first opportunity . . .]

Later we went to the doctor, who prescribed us our diet – then to the *mineral baths*. Then home for an hour's rest.

After lunch I wrote letters, read and returned to the spa. Then a very pleasant stroll in the woods. – But I long for level ground, for far-off places – long to be free in my thoughts, feelings and senses!

After supper I went for another little spin.

Saturday 6 August

Took a steel bath.

'La vie de Jésus' is simply magnificent.[2] Renan challenges everything you learn at school under the heading of 'religion'. According to him, nothing

---

1 Emilie Flöge, actually the sister of Klimt's sister-in-law, Helene Flöge. Emilie Flöge, who was the model for many of Gustav Klimt's pictures, lived with him until his death in 1918. They never married.

2 When Ernst Renan's theological study *La Vie de Jésus* appeared in 1863, it was denounced

can prevent Mary from being Joseph's wife and Jesus their child, he changes the place and date of birth, laughs at the miracles – but says there will never be a loftier intellect, that Jesus surpasses all mankind. – He supports his arguments with statistics, and I can well understand this *particular* book being banned by the clergy.

This afternoon we took another little stroll. As my shoes were tight, I asked the others to go on ahead and sat down on a bench amongst the pine trees. – I do like being alone. I long for solitude.

Sunday 7 August

I can't understand why the Church has banned 'La vie de Jésus' [Renan]. Admittedly, the Church and the clergy are one and the same. – But I find the book can only be to their advantage, for in my opinion it's capable of converting the most obdurate of unbelievers. I used not to believe that Jesus had ever existed, but now I believe in him as the greatest *human* who ever lived. The book closes as follows:

> Except for Cakya-Muni, no man ever lived who so disregarded family life, worldly pleasures and everything transitory. He lived only for his Father and for the divine mission he was convinced he had to fulfil.
>
> But we, eternal children, condemned to inefficacy, who toil unceasingly and never reap what we sow, we bow before these demi-gods. They knew to create, to strengthen, to act – things of which we are incapable. Will such originals ever return, or will the world be content to travel further along the paths they have laid down, these boldest creative spirits of all times? We cannot tell. But whatever surprises the future may hold for us, Jesus remains unsurpassable. His cult remains permanently youthful, his legend provokes our tears, his suffering moves the finest of hearts; every century will loudly acclaim Jesus as the greatest son of Man ever to have walked this Earth.

That I find quite wonderful. It's *my* catechism!

Tuesday 9 August

Anniversary of dear Papa's death. They'd all forgotten it. I seem to be the only one to have remembered. But then – I believe nobody ever loved Papa more dearly than I. Particularly now. He is my constant refuge.

—

by the church. Though primarily an academic book, its 'mythical' account of the making of Christianity by popular imagination claimed the attention of a wide cross-section of readers. The German translation was published by K. Konegen, Vienna, in 1898.

Today I finished 'La vie de Jésus'. In my opinion it's one of the sublimest works of its time.

Friday 12 August
A few days ago I read 'The grey woman' by Konstantinos Christomanos. The play is madly immoderate, excessive! When read, it's all but meaningless. It tells of an unknown power that forces people to do the opposite of what they intend. The grey woman holds her child over a precipice and hangs on tight – but she lets go, and it falls to its death. The event drives her half mad – she becomes a shadow of her former self. Act I begins with a dialogue for a young married couple. – She's madly in love with him, but feels she can never fulfil him because she doesn't understand him. She's rather eccentric – wants to understand the flowers, but can't – which saddens her. They have a son, for whom they want to engage a nursemaid. The grey woman is recommended to them, and they take her on. She arrives – disaster! He'd been anticipating it all along and falls in love with her at first sight. But when she becomes the innocent murderess of *his* child (due once again to her inexplicable sensation), he becomes half crazed, falls at her feet, holds her tightly. Aglaisa, his wife, comes in, stark mad, sees them together, laughs, whispers, rejoices in her suffering – since it makes her beautiful – and rushes out with a shrill cry of 'Farewell' (the poet says it should sound like a glass shattering). Herself a flower with a broken stem, now she thinks she can understand the flowers. What happens next? Presumably she kills herself. But what about the others? It's all so obscure, so half-baked, one can distinguish not even an outline. Whatever he's trying to say is purely *conjectural*, he himself can't define it – the reader is left to guess. Naturally: the reader. A staged performance is out of the question. It's far too confused, eccentric and, at the same time, poorly written. Yet Klimt has provided the title page. That's really beneath his dignity!

Something funny happened to me today. As I'm not well, naturally I've not been taking the spa water. I was walking on my own towards the bandstand. I hadn't got far before I was accosted by the Polish woman we met in the train:

You're so beautiful, so sweet, so delightful! I've been admiring you all the time. No man can ever adore you as I do. – I have a great favour to ask of you: give me a photograph of yourself.

I replied that I had none at present but, as soon as I did, I'd send her one. She said:

I want to show it to a friend of mine, a certain Baron X. That could be
the making of your fortune.

I answered:

I shall never marry.

She:

Am I too late with my request?

We saw Mama approaching, and she took her leave. – If I can get a decent
photo of myself, I really shall send her one. But not on *that* account.

'One should not bewail the death of hope until it has been buried' (A.
Schindler).

p.m. Mama received a postcard from Carl announcing the death of Councillor Kühnelt.[3] It appears to have happened some days ago, for he
expresses surprise at not hearing anything about it from Mama. In the
evening we're simply too tired to ask for the papers. – All three of us were
out of town when the news was announced. Such a dear man, young and
healthy. For me this memento mori came at just the right time – just as I
was beginning to take a gloomy view of life. Now I have a new motto:
'Enjoy what the gods give you.' . . . Who knows whether I shall live to see
tomorrow.

Yesterday, when Dr Jakesch heard I was reading Renan, he said:

You should read 'The life of Jesus' by *David Strauss*.[4] It's incomparably finer.

Even if I don't believe it, I shall certainly obtain a copy. At present I'm
reading {Spinoza's} 'Ethics' (always worthwhile) and the 'Italian Journey'
– Goethe. It's strange: having read so much Goethe, I've grown so
accustomed to his wonderful style that nothing appears unfamiliar. I
can anticipate, even expect every turn of phrase. Apart from the 'Theory
of Colour' and a few philosophical tracts, I must have read everything of
his by now. I don't yet have the courage to read the 'Theory of Colour',
as I'm quite convinced that it's outdated. I'm familiar with his views on
painting from 'Poetry and Truth'.

---

3 Anton Kühnelt, railway engineer, died on 4 August 1898, aged fifty-six. Since 1889 he had
occupied a high-ranking position at the Ministry of Railways; in 1896 he was promoted to the
rank of Ministerialrat (under-secretary).
4 David Friedrich Strauss broke new ground in biblical interpretation by explaining the New
Testament accounts of Christ mythologically. In *Das Leben Jesu kritisch bearbeitet* (2 vol.,
1835–36; translated anonymously by George Eliot as *The Life of Jesus Critically Examined*,
3 vol., 1846), he denied the historical value of the Gospels and rejected their supernatural
claims, which he described as 'historical myth'.

Monday 15 August
Today – at last – we made the acquaintance of Baroness Pergler, who's staying in the room above ours, and whom we've been following like a dog eyeing its dinner. Fortunately it was she who took the initiative. Today the band played a very agreeable programme: between Flotow & Strauss, a piece from Grieg's 'Peer Gynt'. I usually go up close to the bandstand so as to follow the orchestration. When they'd finished, we turned round, and guess who was standing right behind us? The Baroness, tall and imposing, with her sister-in-law. She introduced herself and, while strolling home, we struck up a conversation. She appears to be a very pleasant young lady, and maybe this friendship will enable me to play the piano, for she has hired one & plays all day. Not wonderfully, but not all that badly either. Mostly modern operas or Wagner.

Wednesday 17 August
Overslept – Mama was finally woken by the noise of drumming from the bandstand. That drum, so deafening, was our salvation. –
The 'Italian Journey' is very fine – I've finished it. He doesn't actually write much about Nature, which is otherwise his main interest. For my taste, he writes too little about painting as well. But all in all it's a noble, well-shaped work of classical beauty. Yet Papa loathed it. He [really] venerated Goethe – so he must have had his reasons. He said it was hypocritical. – Well, it doesn't always strike one as entirely sincere, that I can feel.
The Baroness is quite a sportswoman – running, tennis, balls, picnics – and 'Cavalleria rusticana!' But she really is a nice young lady.
Tomorrow is the Kaiser's birthday, hence this evening there was a military tattoo. We went out onto the street and took the shorter route, which intersected with theirs. The procession approached from far off down the lane – which looked like a Gothic arch – and it looked just wonderful. At first we could see only the smoke of the torches, then the flames themselves and a jumble of innumerable faces. The crowd seemed vast, there must have been some three hundred people. – It looked really beautiful, also the sight of the flames shimmering through the branches – as we traversed the route. It was a perfect picture. The smoke, the surge of people – all lit in red or green – it was a picture. The Franzensplatz was brightly lit with lamps hung over the monument: the Kaiser's crown, all lit up with little gas lamps. On both sides were high poles with stars, and in front of the theatre the double eagle – all in gaslight. – It looked stupendous.

Monday 21 August
Dr Pollack has sent me 'Die Königin von Saba' (Goldmark), which didn't
do much to cheer me up, and 'Das Leben Jesu' by David Friedrich Strauss,
which made me jump for joy. – It was my particular wish to get to know
the book. Now I'd like to compare it with the Renan. – Dr Pollack wrote a
very kind letter on the subject:

> I agree with everything you write about Renan's 'La vie de Jésus'. It's a
> divine book, for it discusses the life of a divine man with an honesty
> worthy of such a man. – Truth is of God, and what is His can be no
> blasphemy. By depicting Jesus as the most human of men, Renan does
> nothing to diminish His divinity; He appears all the more divine: for
> the more human you are, the more closely do you resemble God.

I find that very succinct. –

Tuesday 23 August
Yesterday we went to see 'La belle Hélène' (Jacques Offenbach), a splendid, spirited operetta. We laughed ourselves half sick. Helena was pretty
well acted and sung by a certain Erna Fröhlich. Why is the work so seldom
played in Vienna? It's so melodious – delightful.
The theatre is old and very small but a real jewel. Mrs Fournier was there,
as well as the Baroness with her hangers-on. – In the intervals, we went
outside into the fresh air. The others did so too, and we had quite a time
of it. Johanna von Pergler and I walked round behind the theatre, where
all the actors and singers were gathered together – in makeup and with
Grecian costumes. It looked so quaint. A little further away stood the
orchestral musicians, and we had to run the gauntlet. But that didn't
matter – we enjoyed ourselves.

Thursday 25 August
I'm reading Renan and David Strauss and believe in absolutely nothing –
yet when I lie in bed at night – in the dark, so utterly alone – I can *feel* a
presence in which I can place *all* my trust, and I say 'Father'. Then I say a
short prayer – '*May everything turn out for the best*' – in which I place all
my hopes for the future, hopes which I would never confide to a living
soul. –

Friday 26 August
What I wrote yesterday seems completely illogical. By day I'm an
unbeliever, by night I believe in God. Very well – I don't believe in the God

dictated by the Church, who thrones amidst angels in Elohim, but I do believe in that *Being* of whom Spinoza speaks, that absolutely infinite Being, a substance which possesses those attributes of infinity that represent all eternal and everlasting existence.

God is Nature, and Nature is God. God is Destiny and the eternal substance, I would add – and every growing seed contains a drop of God's spirit – the essence of God – which that creature must retain, retain and multiply, that it may grow in His image . . .[5]

Wednesday 31 August
My nineteenth birthday.

I'm already an old fogy. I'm ashamed of myself – nothing achieved, nothing finished – and *so* stupid. When I see what others have achieved by my age, I'm aghast.

The event was celebrated in style. Mama gave me a cycling cape, cycling trousers, an umbrella and a hair-comb. In the afternoon arrived a gigantic fan and a huge bouquet of roses from Baroness Pergler and Frau Uhlemann. I rushed straight up to their room and hugged each in turn, squeezed the Baron's hand – and they wouldn't let me go. They were about to go to dinner, and we were all in the highest of spirits. After dinner the Baron ordered several bottles of champagne, and the first glass was downed in my honour. They were absolutely adamant that I should play, and in the end I did. For a while I played Wagner, with the Baron standing over the piano, then I struck up a waltz, everyone began to tap their feet to it, and soon all were dancing merrily. At 8:30 Mama came up to fetch us. We made ourselves moustaches with burnt cork. Frau Uhlemann grew frightfully boisterous, excited and – amorous. After all the champagne I was quite tipsy.

Monday 5 September
We left at 1:00. –

Today I wasn't in the mood for packing, so first I attended to all my other duties, called on people and paid my debts. As a result I can't find any of my things. – Frau Uhlemann and Frau Holzer gave us lovely bouquets.

---

5 Orig.: 1½ lines of dots.

We had to change trains at Eger & only had two minutes' time. It was such a frightful rush that my knees began to ache. The porter said to me:

> Your mother hasn't yet arrived, so I'll have to take the things out of the train again.

When we reached the compartment, Mama was there after all – but it was so late that the train had to wait, just because of us. You can imagine how the other passengers gawped out of the windows, and what a stir the whole thing caused.

In the evening: Munich. We strolled around a bit, then had dinner at 'Habsburg'. As I was getting undressed, I realized that I'd been unwell – and hadn't even noticed. The pain comes so often, I hadn't even given it a thought.

Tuesday 6 September

Got up early, bought Jugendstil postcards and sent them to the Perglers, Frau Holzer & Aunt Else. Then we hired a cab & drove to the Secession.[6] It's good, but the Viennese S{ecession} is better. Stuck has deteriorated dreadfully – pure commercialism! There's a Böcklin, 'The Keeper of the Secret', which by no means measures up to his best but is, in its way, unforgettable. A *wonderful* Alexander! Magnificent Meuniers. Dill is not to my taste – Klinger I don't understand – Uhde is, to my mind, cold and empty. Erler's portrait of Richard Strauss is very dashing – the pictures of young Zumbusch are ice-cold. Laermans I detest! Kalckreuth is uncommonly vivid, Habermann makes a fine effect with pastel colours – of Khnopff they have a tiny head, a landscape and an enchanting portrait of a child. At the sight of a picture by Eichler, I burst into uncontrollable laughter – simply couldn't grasp what the artist was trying to say. One of the painters came along and laughed with me – he couldn't understand it either. I was also taken with a charming earthenware mask by de Rudder. And there I go again, speaking of *my* opinion. – How can an inexperienced layman [like me] be so presumptuous as to form an opinion? But here, at least, I can write everything down – what I liked and what I didn't like. Maybe I don't put everything in my diary, but I do *imply* everything – my most secret thoughts – and if, years later, I'm no longer capable of 'reading between the lines', it will be just as well that things are only implied.

6 The Munich Secession, inaugurated in 1892 by Franz von Stuck, Wilhelm Trübner and Fritz Uhde, was the first institution of its kind to be established in Germany. Inspired by *Ver sacrum*, the Munich Secession published two journals, *Jugend* and *Simplicissimus*.

At 11:15 by train to Salzburg. At 11:00 we took a leisurely breakfast and almost missed the train. So far, on this journey there hasn't been a connection which we haven't almost missed.

After a hot but beautiful journey, we arrived in Ischl. By chance we met Carl, who had intended to come as far as Ebensee to meet us. Klimt and Hancke have returned to Vienna. So he's broken his promise. Admittedly he did say that if we didn't return to Goisern before September, he couldn't stay any longer. And then Hancke was an impediment . . . but it isn't nice of him, and he shall pay for it!

We have quite nice accommodation at the sulphur bath – although poor Mama has to share the attic with Mimi. But she doesn't mind. Mama can adapt to anything – fortunate disposition. I'm sorry to have left Franzensbad, and here I feel unhappy – so unhappy.

In later years, people will look at me and say, 'She must have been beautiful once – beautiful and carefree. But the glint in her eye has faded, she stares sadly into the void . . .'

Sunday 11 September

Goisern

The Empress is dead!!

Yesterday, disembarking from a boat in Geneva, the poor woman was stabbed to death by an anarchist [named Luccheni]. Carl has driven to Ischl to hear more news. – It's terrible. A woman who never harmed a soul, who never got involved in politics, who never got anything out of life but pain and anxiety, which had caused her to grow depressive. Fancy stabbing such a poor, broken woman! The man must have been mad. The whole Wittelsbach dynasty seems to be plagued by misfortune: last year the Duchess of Alençon lost her life in a dreadful fire, several others went mad, and now the poor Empress! All the jubilee celebrations have come to nothing – a dreadful loss for the people of Vienna.

Today is Mama Moll's name-day. She was so sad! – I wasn't allowed to go cycling, and I started to cry, so bitterly that the tears are still flowing. – I know exactly why I wept – the others can believe what they like.

Lunch with Mama Moll at the sulphur baths.

This afternoon: Gretl and I called on Frida. It's fair-time in the village, the villagers are happy and gay – unbelievably coarse feelings. I bought a large bag of gingerbread. On our way home a dreadful storm brewed up, stirring up so much dust that we could scarcely see each other. We took Frida along to the sulphur baths and fooled around like children.

This evening: the Geiringers called, and Fräulein Kohlberg sang the aria from 'Le Prophète' really beautifully.

Saturday 17 September
Cycled to Gosaumühle via St Agatha and Steeg. In St Agatha, Klimt is staying with his beloved sister-in-law. I hope they're having a good time . . . Today's outing was lovely. I rode right down to the water's edge and stared vacantly into the lake . . .
We met up with Mama and Gretl in Stammbach. – There we saw Girardi having high tea with his fiancée, Fräulein Ella Bösendorfer. How can one marry such a ghastly man? –
O Lord – something dreadful has just happened: without my noticing it, Carl looked over my shoulder and read the top lines of this page. So far he can't make much sense of it, but soon the penny will drop, and I shall be compromised and exposed to all the world. [He teased me throughout high tea.] That's just what I need! He asked me who the 'beloved sister-in-law' was, and *I* blushed to the roots of my hair . . . Dear God, how dreadful!
This evening the Geiringers came round, and Mama made wine-punch with peaches. It tasted quite wonderful.

Wednesday 21 September
Drove as far as Langwies, then got out. Mama and Gretl drove on to Ebensee. – I had a book with me and read. Half an hour later came Carl with Christine, and the three of us drove to Traunkirchen via Steinkogl & Ebensee. The road was wonderful – smooth as a billiard table – and the landscape indescribably beautiful.
On the way home I sat on my own (inside the buggy), reflected and fantasized. Christine quietly told me that it was gradually dawning on her that I was in love. If she'd only known that at the very moment I'd just got over it. I believe no power on earth or in heaven, no fiery eyes will ever make an impression on me again . . .

Wednesday 28 September
A letter from Rosa – she's desperately sad. It's all over. Adelso Campelle has written to tell her that a union is impossible. I feel dreadfully sorry for her – she has all my sympathy, poor girl! Maybe she'll be happy one day – I hope to God.
Today it rained all day. My favourite weather. It suits my mood!
Today, for the first time in ages, I practised seriously – three hours.

The Dreyfus appeal has gone through. How fortunate for France, that writers and academics can achieve such a reversal of public opinion. In Austria such a thing would never be possible, there's far too much pressure on the press from 'high places'.

Played 'Walküre' all evening. The 'Magic Fire Music' is unsurpassable.

Thursday 29 September
Carl left this morning. I don't think he was very happy. Rain – rain – rain . . .

[Read through and corrected. A.M.-W.]

Suite 8

Saturday 1 October

Goisern

Bleak weather! No question of going out. – Composed quite a bit yester-day. One of the themes should be of some use. All the others are rubbish. – Mama is unwell, her arm hurts terribly. – A very dear postcard from Aunt Else. Otherwise nothing new. All quiet!

Humans are such brutes! Even the most murderous, the most insidious of predators act unconsciously. Humans, on the contrary, act *consciously*. An animal relies on *instinct*, a human on *reason*.

A letter from Carl to Mama: in his eyes the Secession building has two faults, 1. the skylight construction makes too obtrusive an effect – that's not Olbrich's fault, but due to lack of money. The 2nd defect is architectural: the four columns which suspend the cupola are so massive that it appears dwarfed. Otherwise Carl is very pleased with the building. The galleries are delightful, as is the vestibule. The facade is said to be positively monumental. I'm sleeping badly – restlessly.

Wednesday 5 October

This morning: practised. This afternoon: a walk with Mama, namely to St Agatha. Mama asked a peasant woman if she knew where a family called Klimt had been staying. After a few minutes' deliberation, she said:

> I believe some young folk were living at the Schlossers', but I can't say for sure.

When we were alone, Mama said:

> So that's where Klimt 'nuzzled up' to his sister-in-law. You know, Alma, it was really abominable of him to make you such compromis-ing advances – considering that he's firmly hitched up. He was very attracted to you, but he's not a boy any longer and should have learnt to control himself. Mama Moll was disgusted too. She witnessed the whole business at first hand and heard the most scandalous things. Alma, I want you to promise me never to tell him of this, and never to behave as if you knew anything about it. –

I nodded in assent. But I can't promise that her rule will remain unbroken.
– I've already figured out exactly what I want to say. – And then . . . it'll
be difficult for me to hide my feelings, to listen calmly to extravagant
compliments and confidences without flaring up, without confronting the
miscreant with the entire truth. For I know – even if he's hitched up with
his sister-in-law, it's me that he loves.

This evening I played, and Mama sang along with me. It was fun, and *all* of
us were actually in good spirits.

Tuesday 11 October
We left Goisern in the morning and reached Vienna at about 6:00. – Quite
a pleasant journey. Some man stood in the gangway and stared at me all
the way. It was unpleasant: I was sitting with my back to him and couldn't
keep a straight face.

We arrived – but at the station no Carl. We got home – no Carl. We wanted
to go inside, but there was no key. So we had no choice but to sit patiently
at the foot of the stairs, reading 'Ver sacrum' and 'Simplicissimus',
and wait. The latest number of 'Ver sacrum' is definitely the weakest,
lacks ideas. Empty, dreadfully wishy-washy. With such a magazine, the
Secession lays itself wide open to criticism. –

Wednesday 12 October
First thing in the morning Carl took Mama and us two to the Getreide-
markt to show us the Secession building. I like it immensely. – Olbrich
hasn't entirely solved the problems – the building looks unfinished. But
when you stand in front of it, you're forced to admit that the facade
looks uncommonly distinguished. The gold, white and green make a
colour scheme of rare finesse. The bare walls are decorated with the
most curious of ornaments. Not to speak of the interior, which is simply
wonderful. I'm leaving space for some picture-postcards of the
Secession.[1]

Later we walked to Taubenrauch with Mama Moll, and ordered lovely
black velvet jackets.

In the afternoon: Dr Pollack. Oh I nearly forgot: we had the fright of our
lives yesterday. During dinner Carl started up a conversation:

1 ▶ Two postcards of the Secession building, one of them with a hand-written commentary:
'Olbrich. The 3 masks over the entrance-portal by Schimkowitz. Doors by O. after designs by
Klimt's brother.' Othmar Schimkowitz studied at the Vienna Academy, lived for three years in
New York, and returned to Vienna in 1895. He joined the Secession in March 1898.

You know, I've heard some strange new rumour about the Lanner girls. My heart missed a beat. I knew at once that he was referring to Else's secret, which Dr Pollack had been spreading so maliciously – the Burger affair. He ranted on: how could one possibly associate with such unrefined young women? It was too awful. – Today, fortunately, Dr P. told Carl that it was *us* who'd given the game away. So at least Carl won't pass it back to Herr Lanner. His reproaches were copious and justified.

Thursday 13 October
This evening: Carl had a committee meeting, then a conference with Hermann Bahr.[2]
Housework, nothing but housework. The odour of turpentine, dust, dirt, slovenly servants, discomfort – these are the joys of housework. To make matters worse, it's still raining, I can't even go out.
This morning we took our breakfast in a dark corner of the dining-room – couldn't move an inch because they were polishing the floor. At one point Carl had to raise his foot – otherwise they would have polished that too. It looked so pathetic, we just had to laugh.

Tuesday 18 October
This morning: we tidied up the little room. It looks entrancing. –
This evening: Dr Pollack. I played to him from 'Die Königin von Saba', and he was overjoyed. I can give him that pleasure as often as he likes, even if it's not altogether to my taste. The ballet music is quite dashing and attractive, but I played one of Assad's arias: it could have been written by any Italian hack. Just a vulgar potboiler. And as for Goldmark – it's the press that's inflated him into a big name.

Wednesday 19 October
Jour de vernissage at the Künstlerhaus[3]
We went on our own, as Mama didn't feel up to it – it was raining too

2 Returning from Paris in 1892, Hermann Bahr formed the literary group known as 'Jung-Wien', which used to meet at Café Griensteidl (popularly known as 'Café Megalomania'). Amongst its members were Richard Beer-Hofmann, Hugo von Hofmannsthal, Felix Salten, Arthur Schnitzler and, initially, Karl Kraus. From 1894 to 1899 Bahr was arts editor of the journal *Die Zeit*. His article 'Vereinigung Bildender Künstler Österreichs. Secession' appeared in the first issue of *Ver sacrum*. His villa at Ober-St-Veit (XIII., Winzerstrasse 22) was designed by Olbrich.
3 The exhibition at the Künstlerhaus, '50 years of Austrian painting', was organized as part of the celebrations to mark the jubilee of Kaiser Franz Josef.

hard. On the staircase we met up with Frau Fischel[4] (and the two girls), who asked if she could chaperone us. I neither assented nor dissented, but went in with her. We had to squeeze through the narrow corridors anyway. –

In the first room is Canon. To the right and left are about thirty of Papa's pictures, truly the finest. – In the next room we met Felix, who took us under his wing and showed us round the whole exhibition. We were overjoyed to be rid of the Fischels at last. We saw a series of wonderful Pettenkofens. In the fourth room: *Waldmüller*. I fell in love with one of his paintings, namely 'The Ruin at Schönbrünn'. It gleams like a precious stone – a wonderful, wonderful picture. I didn't so much care for the village scenes: not realistic enough and not in accord with modern taste. But he cuts an imposing figure – as forerunner of contemporary art, as forerunner, as *champion* of the Secession.

There are also some exquisite Makarts. First 'The Five Senses', then the 'Triumph of Ariadne', 'Cleopatra', wonderful fresco studies and portraits. I so like Makart's sumptuous reddish-browns. No matter how much the Secessionists rail or contemptuously shrug their shoulders, they have nobody to equal *him*. – The epoch of Pettenkofen, Waldmüller, Makart and Papa won't be surpassed that easily. Not by a thousand Engelharts and Klimts. Tempora mutantur.

This afternoon Gretl asked me if I could swear I wasn't in love with Klimt. I said:

> Yes I can.

That amounted to a solemn oath. *I really can*, and pride myself in being able to say so.

Sunday 23 October

Mikosd[5]

Alas, for us the days passed all too swiftly. On the first day Alfred took us for a wonderful ramble through the woods. It was divine! To our left ran a stream, crystal clear. At every step a motif. Dear God, if I'd been a painter!

---

4 The identity of the Fischel family is unclear. A.S. writes diversely of 'Uncle Fischel', 'Fischl' and 'Hartwig Fischl'. The Viennese address-books for this period include a painter, A. Fischel, and an architect, Hartwig Fischel.

5 An outing to Schloss Mikosd, country estate of the Zierers. A.S. writes of a train journey to 'Vath' via 'Adfad', but the exact location of the estate is unclear. 'Adfad' could be a mis-spelling of Arad (today in Romania), but in view of the relatively short distance travelled, it seems more likely that 'Vath' should be read as Vác, twenty miles north of Budapest.
▶ Picture postcard of Schloss Mikosd.

Friday 28 October
This morning: Fräulein Ella and I played 'Also sprach Zarathustra' by
Richard Strauss after Nietzsche. We played with the courage of the
damned. It's so unbelievable, difficult, crazy and confused, we hadn't the
slightest idea what we were playing. It *can't* be any good. Suddenly I felt a
very strange sensation in my stomach, as if I were about to faint. I stopped
playing, and confessed that I was unwell.

>   I feel just the same, said Fräulein Ella, but was too embarrassed to tell
>   you, otherwise I would have stopped long ago.

Gretl, who was listening, admitted that she'd been feeling unwell for quite
some time too. – The power of music, it transpires, extends as far as the
bowels. We laughed a good deal – but we do intend to keep playing the
Strauss until we understand it a little better. I came hurrying back with
'Tristan' – what a relief.
This evening: some Hungarians, occupied in the area with inspecting the
railroad, were invited in. Dreadfully vulgar – they did nothing but smoke
and drink. We withdrew fairly soon. It was just too tedious.

Thursday 3 November
Yesterday: typical All Souls' Day weather – murky, gloomy, foggy – Nature
mourning noble souls.

Saturday 5 November
I'm keeping everyone amused here. – Strange: at home I often don't speak
a word all day. This evening I was annoyed with Mademoiselle, who was
extremely tactless, and this morning five things annoyed me:
1. Carl has spoken to Frau Radnitzky about Epstein, and she asked him to
keep me on with her for another year, as she thinks that Epstein wouldn't
take me for just three months. That's all very well, but we don't even know
whether we'll be going to Italy. – And then, I'm nineteen, and at my age I
could at last embark on a course of serious study.
2. Mama has a bad cold and wants to leave.
3. The Secession is asking 5 fl admission for the opening day. That's the
height of arrogance. They'll see: the exhibition halls will be so empty, the
people will take fright.
4. and 5. We forgot a) Mama's wedding anniversary and b) Carl's name-
day. It looks as if we were ungrateful and thought only of ourselves.
Indeed, it doesn't only look like that, it really is so. – Phooey!

Friday 11 November
Vernissage of the Secessionist Exhibition[6]
Today, armed with fine new hats and jackets, we marched onto the battle-ground. It was so full, you could scarcely see the pictures. I greeted Klimt very calmly and politely. All our friends were there, a huge crowd of ladies, painters, bankers. Gretl and I did the honours.
This afternoon Mama came too. Carl's yellow picture has already been sold. I was engaged in a brief conversation with Klimt, when Mama suddenly called out:
Tell me, Alma, have you no pride? Shame on you.
Now it was my turn to be angry. First Mama says I shouldn't give the game away, then she doesn't even want me to go near the man – I find that utterly illogical. He noticed the change in my attitude, incidentally.
What's the trouble? You're quite changed, why are you behaving so strangely? etc.
Towards evening we began to have a whale of a time. Gretl and I were standing with König and Klimt, then we were joined by Bacher, then Olbrich, then Hoffmann. Finally all the Secessionists were gathered together, and we got up to the wildest pranks you could imagine. Klimt promised to fetch my fan. G. and I went to the Lanners'.
In the evening: Dr P. and Aunt Xandi. We drank quantities of champagne.

Saturday 12 November
3-fl day at the Secession.
Dr Loew, Moritz Meyer, Ernst Lanner, Mauthner von Markhof. *Today* I actually *spoke* to Klimt. I'm so happy . . . I consider him handsome and brilliant . . . I made a few insinuations. He must have understood them.
Pierre Lagarde's 'Sunset' is one of the loveliest paintings I know. I told Klimt as much, and he looked at me and said:
Do you really mean that?
I said yes.
I wouldn't have expected that of you: after all, you're not depressive . . . for my taste too, it's one of the loveliest pictures at the exhibition.
He came closer and said:
It's so disconsolate . . .
Ernst Lanner saw us home. Yesterday, at home, his father remarked:
The exhibition is very fine, but the loveliest exhibit was Alma.

6 Secessionist Exhibition (12 November–28 December 1898).

That doesn't say much for the exhibition.

My favourite pictures are Frits Thaulow's 'Evening Mood' – it exudes such an impenetrable silence, green, black – Ludwig Sigmundt's 'Old City' – finely coloured, amazingly delicate and filigree. Watercolours by Alt[7] – delightful and graceful, as ever. Krämer has some very lively watercolours on display. Carl's pictures look magnificent. One of my favourites is John W. Alexander's 'The Mirror'. It's unique. Fernand Khnopff's 'Deo Dei' and 'Incense' and Pierre Lagarde's '*Sunset*'. Zorn – terrific!

I can't summon up much enthusiasm for Uhde's 'Last Supper' or Henry Martin's 'Vers l'abîme' ('Towards the abyss') – some seductive hussy rushing down a steep precipice followed by the rest of humanity, with ravens flying overhead: the enticement of Vice. The idea is excellent, but the execution dreadfully coarse and unidiomatic – *in my opinion*.

Engelhart's contributions are very stylish. Klimt I cannot understand. I told him so too. Bernatzik's 'Fairy Lake' is extremely chic – commercialized. Two delightful items: a silk embroidery by Hélène de Rudder, 'The three Fates' and 'Washerwomen at the Well' by François Carabin. Charming! Simple. A little nude seated on a full wine-skin (as they have them in Dalmatia) – quite enchanting! The pipe at the bottom is the cord with which the skin is held together.

Sunday 13 November

Spent the morning at the Secession – full to bursting-point. Masses of friends.

Mama Moll to lunch.

This afternoon: Bertha. We lectured her on philosophy, which made her laugh a good deal. Then she took us in her cab, with Frau Hellmann & Gretl, to the Opera. We saw

Der Evangelimann.

The performance was superb, the acting and singing of Demuth and Schmedes noble and artistically perfect. I find the plot terribly moving: poisoned souls, poisoned lives and nobody to blame but themselves. A cheerless story which made me so sad that I couldn't even cry.

Back home, in bed, the tears began to flow. So unspeakably sad.

7 Rudolf von Alt was honorary president of the Secession.

Monday 14 November

This morning: to Labor. He doesn't look at all well, has blue rings under his eyes and a grey, waxy complexion. He stayed in Vienna almost all summer . . . poor man!

This afternoon: played act I of 'Der Evangelimann'. Then Mama went straight to Aunt Laura's, and we took a circuitous route to the Secession. There were over six hundred visitors and, incidentally, four pictures were sold. The building has an atmosphere all of its own – truly artistic.

Tuesday 15 November

This morning: Christine Geiringer and Narciss Prasch.

This afternoon: chamber-music at Frau Radnitzky's. We listened to a Beethoven quartet, then walked home. At 7:00 Herr and Frau Henneberg fetched us in their cab, and we drove to the Carltheater.

On the programme: 'The Geisha' by Sidney Jones, with a special guest, Mary Halton, as Mimosa. The operetta is delightful, but the highlight was and is Miss Halton. Such high spirits, grace and charm are truly rare. She has the sweetest little face and wears gorgeous costumes. One of them is white and covered with silver sequins. To match it she wears cornflowers in her hair – in act I poppies. They suit her perfectly.[8] Most English women are dour and rigid, but the graceful ones can't be outdone. The Mimosa-waltz is simply delightful, as is the Laughing-song.

Wednesday 16 November

This morning with Mama Moll to Habig, where we bought ourselves hats. They're very smart – but not as smart as my red hat.[9]
Then to the Secession, to ask Hancke how many visitors there were yesterday. The answer was gratifying: three thousand, and the police had to cordon off the building. Let's hope it goes on like this. Masses of pictures got sold too.

8 Caption on the drawing: {Mary Halton} 'as fortune-teller in act II'.
9 Caption on the drawing: My red hat.

In the evening: Dr Pollack. It was quite fun. As he told me, Dr Krasny said that I'd caused something of a sensation at the Secession on Sunday.

Today I finished reading Henryk Sienkiewicz's 'In vain'. The book is excellent and finely written. I shall never forget it – the search for identity, failure to find it, losses encountered in the process.

This afternoon Gretl and I went to the Künstlerhaus. I must have had a very good day, for without flattering myself I must admit that I caused quite a stir. Five young academicians chased after us through all the galleries, and everyone else eyed me from top to toe. Some very attractive paintings are on show, but my taste is more modern: I don't much care for retrospectives. Certainly I'm partial to Papa's pictures, as well as Pettenkofen's, Müller's, Makart's and some of Waldmüller's, but I wouldn't take Waldmüller's village scenes if they paid me. And Grottger, Koller, Danhauser, Matejka, indeed even Canon I find a crushing bore. I simply don't understand that kind of painting, while almost every picture at the Secession I understand and enjoy. I understand Papa's pictures too and am convinced that they will always be 'his own', always loved and respected.

I'm rather dreading the trip to Italy, not because of the landscape but because of the art treasures. I keep thinking: here the Sistine Madonna – there 'The Play of the Waves'. I shall always prefer Böcklin to Raphael, and that makes me a little fearful [no, no!!!]. My taste is too modern . . . I could raptly contemplate a Lagarde for hours on end. But although I tacitly respect the ability of Canon, Fendi etc., none of their pictures win my genuine affection.

Next Thursday there may be a dinner for the Secession. I shall be sitting between Jettel and Olbrich. The fine times of Aranjuez are over now . . .[10]

Friday 18 November
Lesson with Dubrot. We read Alfred de Musset's 'L'espoir en Dieu'. I feel moved to accuse the author of dishonesty: he says that the Christian faith – this faith of love – considers love a crime. But surely 'love thy neighbour as thyself' is the most beautiful doctrine of Christianity . . . How could de Musset say that love is frowned upon? Surely it depends on the kind of love he means. It's quite right to scorn *free* love, such as that which united de Musset with George Sand . . .

10 Opening line of Schiller's *Don Carlos*.

Sunday 20 November
Mama's birthday
Practised in the morning, dined alone at 12:00, then at 12:30 to the
Philharmonic. First they played the overture to 'Oberon', and brilliantly
too: Gustav Mahler conducted. Then came the torso of a B-minor
Symphony by Schubert, which is heavenly, and finally the 'Symphonie
fantastique' by Hector Berlioz. Really mad but wonderful. The last movement is a witches' Sabbath. Berlioz dreams he's being buried and that all
manner of monsters, witches and spectres attend the funeral. It's a terrific
movement – really spooky. The fourth[11] movement is amazingly loud and
– empty. All in all the concert was excellent. Orchestral music really is the
noblest – purest.

Tuesday 22 November
First lesson with Labor. I played him my song and the two movements from
my sonata. He said that all three were good, pointed out a few mistakes
and told me that the one minor-key variation with its constantly recurring
transition has fine details – quite by chance. He's right: I never do anything
well intentionally.

Thursday 24 November
It was terrific. The guests were the Hardys, with Lydia, the Fischers, with
Senta, the Engelharts, Gustav and Christine {Geiringer},[12] the Jettels, Uncle
Hellmer, Spitzer, Ernst and Hanna, Mama Moll, Gound,[13] Hoffmann,
Olbrich, Pollack, Moser and Klimt. Frau Jettel hadn't been invited, but she
came all the same. We were shaken rigid. But subsequently she was very
amiable – and quiet. I sat between Hoffmann and Olbrich. Before dinner,
Klimt looked at the seating plan, was offended that he wasn't sitting next
to me and asked me if that was of *my* doing. I denied it. I told him that he'd
be sitting opposite me, and he asked me to be sure not to forget it. He still
keeps the place-cards with 'Alma and Klimt' in his wallet. I firmly believe

11 Orig.: 'third'.
12 Gustav Geiringer, pianist, composer and voice teacher, and his wife, the actress Christine
von Bukovics. Before her marriage, she appeared at the Stadttheater (1880–1884),
subsequently at the Deutsches Volkstheater.
13 Robert Gound (from 1923: Gund), born in Seckenheim nr. Heidelberg, studied in Leipzig
and at the Vienna Conservatoire. Secretary of the Tonkünstlerverein from 1896, he was active
in Vienna as pianist and voice teacher until 1913. In 1898, his Symphony in G major was
awarded the Beethoven Prize of the Gesellschaft der Musikfreunde, jointly with Zemlinsky's
Symphony in B♭ major.

that Klimt is fond of me. If he's not, then he's the greatest sham on earth. If only I could speak frankly with him. I hope the opportunity will arise one day. He's such a nice man.

I talked a great deal with Olbrich, who's also a handsome fellow. I hope and believe that my initial impression of him was false. We fooled about like children. Spitzer sat in the next room, as there wasn't enough space. The other bachelors dined in the teaching studio. Spitzer got bored with the old people and came to join us. So I proposed that we, in corpore, should throw him out. They each grabbed one of the old halberds, and made for him. He ran hell for leather. Gound barked, Klimt crowed like a cock. Ernst is an accomplished grunter, so Doctor P. fetched him, and when he'd grunted his fill, we threw him out with the halberds. We had a whale of a time!

Later Gustav played the piano and everyone danced for all they were worth. Only Lydia didn't dance much – poor girl. I felt sorry for her. The Hardys then left, as did Jettel's Mama. Only the Fischers, the Geiringers, Gound, Spitzer, Pollack and the Secessionists stayed on. Pollack proposed one toast after another, then Fischer toasted Gretl and me. It was such fun. The tables looked wonderful. We had girandoles and, as centrepiece, a fruit bowl surrounded with flowers – and garlands, with which they later decked me out. On the table for the older guests, the centrepiece was Hellmer's water-nymph, also surrounded with flowers and garlands, and all the ladies had large bouquets of violets. Attached to each bouquet was a card inscribed with a little poem, which was passed round and signed by each guest in turn. We drank a toast of brotherhood with Senta.

Afterwards I spoke to almost nobody except Klimt. Hoffmann brought us a design and told us we should embroider it for Mama for Christmas.

Monday 28 November

This morning: wrote the exercises for Labor. Later Mama asked me to show her my songs. She liked them very much, and I liked them just as well – when sung with a beautiful, well-schooled voice.

This afternoon: to the Künstlerhaus, just to see Papa's pictures again. I shall never see them all together again, anyway. When I look at those paintings, it's as if I were talking to an old friend. Each one is a memory of my youth, indeed I saw them all in the making. How often did I watch him painting. I remember once joining in, in the garden at Plankenberg.[14] It was

14 In 1885, Emil J. Schindler bought a mansion at Plankenberg, nr. Vienna (between Neulengbach and Tulln). Here A.S. spent her early years.

a hot summer's day, and Papa was painting the vegetable garden on Rudolf's picture. I told him that a school-friend had asked me who my father was and what he did. 'A painter', I'd said, and I told Papa it was so strange saying that. He replied:

> You shouldn't have bothered to explain to her *who* your father is. If she doesn't know *who* the painter Schindler is, she doesn't need telling.

His words pleased me greatly, and they became imprinted on my mind. They reflect the pride of a genuine artist.

Later, towards evening, we went over to Flora's. Then I practised hard. In the evening: alone.

Tuesday 29 November

At Labor's. He gave me a good lecturing about 'time-wasting' and begged me to take things more seriously. I have to admit that he was right.

This afternoon: to the Gewerbemuseum – winter exhibition. There are some really wonderful things on display.

Then to Novotny: our embroidery will cost something like 25 fl. When I see Hoffmann, I'll give him a piece of my mind. But I think it'll look very fine.

This evening: to the Volkstheater – 'Circusleute'. We'd already seen it once. The play is good and was given an excellent performance. Particularly Tyrolt and Retty. We'd invited Rosa Kornblüh. She came, moreover, and was thrilled to bits. In future we'll take her to the theatre more often. It's such a joy to give pleasure to others.

Wednesday 30 November

This morning: to Geiringer for a voice test. He said I had a very pleasing, soft voice but that it lacked clarity, due to all the catarrh in my throat.

At 1:00: rendezvous with Herr and Frau Hellmann[15] and Gretl at the Secession. He said the most idiotic things, fit for the yellow press.

This afternoon: Ernst Lanner called (I was having dinner at the Hellmanns'). We danced a bit in the studio, Mama played.

This evening: C{arl} and M{ama} went to the Volkstheater, so we were alone. I composed a song to a poem by Wohlgemuth, 'Wie es ging'. Whether it's good or bad will be decided on Tuesday. Certainly it's very sad.

15 Paul Hellmann, industrialist. His family were close friends of the Molls.

Thursday 1 December
After lunch we were talking about the Lanners. I don't remember how the topic arose, but suddenly Mama said:

You don't have any pride whatsoever. You give yourself to all comers. Without saying a word, I stood up and went into the drawing-room. Did Mama have any idea of how deeply she'd hurt me? – She was referring to the Klimt affair . . .

If only I had *someone* to whom I could speak my mind. I live amongst strangers. If my dear Papa were here, I'm certain he would understand me. Gretl's way of thinking is entirely practical, and Mama . . . doesn't like me. Carl and Mama are both still too young to understand us, as they both think only of themselves. Carl invites all his friends, and Mama invites all hers, but we can't invite even *one* young man to call . . .

This morning: Herr Oberstetter.[16] He was formerly Court Kapellmeister in Berlin and now he wants to become a singer. A very good-looking fellow. Unfortunately a rabid anti-Semite. Maybe I shall have an opportunity of making music with him – that would be most agreeable. That fact that he's a frenetic Wagnerian should help establish a rapport.

This evening: orchestral concert with Marcella Lindh, supported by the violin prodigy Max Wolfsthal. Both are immensely talented, but leave the listener utterly cold.[17] – In the audience were Gretl Friedländer and her husband, Gustav and Christine, Egon Bloch,[18] Gutherz, Richard, Epstein, Spitzer, Pollack and our young belle from Franzensbad.

In the evening I was alone at home, as all the others had gone off for dinner together.

This evening there was a torchlight procession in honour of the Kaiser's jubilee, which is tomorrow. The Viennese are quite right to illuminate the streets: it's their way of thanking the Kaiser for all the stupid things he's done for them. His entire term of office has been nothing but a series of blunders, which he attempted to put right and, in the process, only made worse. Austria is not far from collapse. In truth, the Viennese are probably right to illuminate the streets . . .

16 Orig.: 'Oberstötter' – Hans Edgar Oberstetter, later director of the Music Academy in Rio de Janeiro.
17 Programme: Overture to *Don Giovanni*, arias by Mozart, Bellini and Félicien David, and Scottish folk-songs, sung by Marcella Lindh (soprano); Andante religioso (Vieuxtemps) and 'Souvenir de Moscou' (Wieniawski), played by Max Wolfsthal (violin); conductor: Hans Krenn.
18 An employee of the Nordbahn railway, Egon Bloch studied composition from 1895 to 1900 with Alexander Zemlinsky. From 1895 he was active as accompanist, from 1902 as conductor, and later as opera producer.

Friday 2 December
The Kaiser's 50th Jubilee
Carl has been awarded the Knighthood of the Order of Franz Josef. We're really thrilled. Of *all* his colleagues, only Strasser congratulated him, because he too has been awarded the Franz Josef Order . . . Eighteen words which serve to define the meaning of the word 'colleague'. If Strasser hadn't been decorated too, he would have said, 'This Moll fellow simply ingratiated himself . . .' If only all his dear friends could have heard, when the good news was brought to him, how he exclaimed:

It offends me that Klimt hasn't been honoured too . . .
Words spoken from the heart . . .

Saturday 3 December
I feel so awful. Nobody can imagine how I'm suffering – physically and morally. Today I'm completely down. Often I imagine that I shan't live long. I'm so dreadfully sad.

Sunday 4 December

Spent yesterday evening at the Geiringers'. It was great fun and went on until 2:45. We also had a wild dance. Oberstetter was there too – with his wife. This afternoon he sent me his waltz and a piano piece. Quite nicely done, but with no distinction. Apart from that, he made explicit advances and asked me to play duets with him. It was great fun! He's immensely capable. He told me he'd best like to divorce and then marry me. But I had to give him my word of honour not to let anyone into the secret.

We didn't get up until 10:45 – got dressed and went straight to the Philharmonic Concert. It was wonderful.[19]
As for Mahler – I'm virtually in love with him. Alexander Rosé sat next to us.[20] This time he knew who we were, and we recognized him from earlier too. He also looks amazingly like his brother, concert-master

19 Programme: Brahms, Symphony no 2, Dvořák, *Heroic Song* op. III (world première); Haydn, String Quartet op 76 no 3 ('Emperor') in Mahler's version for string orchestra; Mendelssohn, overture to Shakespeare's *A Midsummer Night's Dream*.
20 Alexander Rosé, violist, music dealer and concert agent, and Eduard Rosé, cellist, were brothers of the violinist Arnold Rosé, concert-master of the Vienna Philharmonic from 1881

Arnold Rosé. Alex Rosé has the most intelligent face
I ever saw. They played Brahms – a minor-key [*sic*]
symphony, Dvořák's 'Heroic Song' – terrific,
Haydn's Variations on the Kaiser Hymn and the
overture to 'A Midsummer Night's Dream'. I liked
the Dvořák best. It has drive and fire – magnificent.
Then the Brahms, then the Mendelssohn. The Haydn
took last place. I know I shouldn't say it out loud, but
I liked it least of all.

Monday 5 December
Carl has received over five hundred messages of congratulation. From
everyone I know.
This afternoon: Rosl – dressmaking.
Carl left this evening. First he's going to Dresden, then to Klinger in Leipzig. The latter doesn't want to exhibit 'Christ on Olympus' until later. That
upsets all the Secession's plans.

Tuesday 6 December
Labor. I didn't play him my new song, because he was in a bad mood.

[Checked in early January 1963. A.M.-W.]

---

to 1933. Eduard, a founder member of the Rosé Quartet, married Mahler's younger sister,
Emma, in 1898 and became principal cellist of the orchestra in Weimar. In 1902, Arnold Rosé
married Mahler's elder sister, Justine.

Suite 9

Thursday 8 December

This morning we wanted to go to the Zierers – took the magazines along and tried.[1] But Flora, Lili and Ernst met us in the entrance-lobby. We fooled around a good deal, then left. – Ernst is a dear, sympathetic fellow. They made caustic remarks about the latest number of 'Ver sacrum', and I had to admit they were right. From a literary standpoint it's an utter disaster. I'd so like to give Roller a piece of my mind – he appears to be off his head.

Sunday 11 December

This evening Olbrich, Hoffmann, König, Moser and the Oberstetters were our guests. |It was very entertaining| and lasted until 1:30. – At table I sat between Moser and Olbrich. Later I played Liszt's 'Les Préludes' with Oberstetter, then he played endless quantities of Wagner. He accompanied himself in the 'Magic Fire Music' and sang wonderfully. He played the 'Ride of the Valkyries' and the Prelude to 'Meistersinger' magnificently. Oberstetter begged me never to marry a Jew, saying:

Why don't you take Olbrich? (in his presence). He's handsome, young, smart – I'd give you my blessing right away.

Of course we laughed a good deal & didn't feel embarrassed in the least. I believe we shall always remain good fellows, but neither do I feel attracted to him nor he to me – not in the slightest. He's simply *not* my cup of tea, nor am I his.

Carl wanted to invite Klimt too, but *hadn't* seen him in recent days, so he didn't bother. Olbrich knew it and, out of spite, asked him:

Tell me, Klimt, are you going to the Molls' on Sunday too?

He replied, very pointedly:

I haven't been invited.

Whereupon O. replied:

For sure, you don't always have to go.

1 The Zierers (IV., Alleegasse 33) were close friends of the Molls, and their son Ernst had been acquainted with A.S. since childhood. A.S. refers here to the latest issue of *Ver sacrum*, the main theme of which was poster design.

Tuesday 13 December
What a day! On the Graben I lost my suspender-belt – something I can't abide – and had to vanish into somebody's front porch.
Then I got to Labor's . . . and was pleasantly surprised. Having stressed that I thought little of it, I played him my new song. When I'd finished, he said:

It isn't as bad as you think. It's quite attractive.

He could find no fault with it, and asked me to bring another original composition to the next lesson.

Do so as often as possible, he said.

I was so overjoyed, I flew rather than walked down the stairs.

Thursday 15 December
Composed a piano piece – entitled 'Vom Küssen'. I don't know whether it's any good, I believe rather the contrary.
This afternoon: to Fürst[2] to order a dress. This evening: Hancke and Dr Pollack at home with us.

Saturday 17 December
Frau Radnitzky. She was very satisfied, and gave me permission to learn Brassin's transcription of the 'Magic Fire Music'.[3]

Tuesday 20 December
This morning: Labor. I played him my piano piece 'Vom Küssen'. He was quite satisfied but said I'd crammed in too many themes in quick succession.

They'd provide enough material for several pieces. It would be better if you tried to derive various moods from just one theme.

He's right – even beforehand I'd sensed that the piece was somehow disorganized. I just didn't know why. He asked me to write another piece for the next lesson, and said that it was pianistic and playable. He liked the E-major theme best of all. He was charming today. We talked about 'Faust', and he was tremendously interesting.

2 The fashion designer Bertha Fürst, who owned a boutique at VI., Stumpergasse 15.
3 Only six weeks later, on 31 January 1899, A.S. played Brassin's transcription at a pupils' concert (cf. programme facsimile on p. 91). The composer-pianist Louis Brassin was a pupil of Moscheles. Of his *oeuvre*, which included two piano concertos, his best-known work was a transcription of the 'Magic Fire Music' from Wagner's *Die Walküre*.

Wednesday 21 December
I sat behind the door and heard Gretl complaining about me to Frau
Radnitzky. I feel so utterly miserable and lonely. Here, at home, not a soul
understands or loves me. Today, at table, Carl looked at me and asked:
  Tell me, A.S., what's the matter with you?
And my eyes kept filling with tears. Tears – the only friends that never
forsake me. If only I had a male friend or an honest female companion. I
can't talk to anyone. They consider me crazy or insincere – affected. Yet my
intentions are quite the opposite. Only one man understands me – or at
least understood me. And with him – I've simply lost faith in humanity.
Oh God, will it always be like this? . . .

Thursday 22 December
Composed a piano piece. But it's not quite finished. It's written in the spirit
of the classics, sounds at first much like Schumann, later like Beethoven,
but it's not plagiarized. Maybe it would be better to put a certain distance
between myself and Wagner. I'll be interested to hear what Labor has to say
about it!

Friday 23 December
Finished my Adagio.

Saturday 24 December
Dr Pollack has been promoted. He's been appointed secretary. We were
terrifically pleased. This evening is – Christmas Eve. I'm extremely tense. –
The lawn in front of our house is covered with snow – real Christmas
weather.
Each of us received twenty-four presents, including ten volumes of
Wagner's writings, fitted travelling bags and three dresses, pendants from
Mayreder, Hellmann etc. In a word: a vast amount. Spoilt. – And what
do we do in return? . . . Nothing!

Tuesday 27 December
Once again, Labor was satisfied. I played him my Adagio and my song
'Die Frühlingsnacht'.
  I must say, you're terrifically productive, he said.
I bring two works to each lesson, usually an instrumental piece and a song.
It gives me the greatest pleasure. But I wish I could make some headway!
That would make me so very happy.

Friday 30 December
Composed half of an Adagio, which follows the pattern of the Adagio from Beethoven's first piano sonata.

> Take exact note of the entire structure and write a piece of precisely the same kind [said Labor].

That's much harder than following your own arbitrary ideas. In every bar you have to be certain of following the pattern exactly. As a result, a good deal of individuality is lost. I'll be interested to hear what Labor says.

Saturday 31 December. New Year's Eve
I feel unwell, Carl is unwell, Mama isn't feeling too bright, and during the course of the evening Gretl got a dreadful pain in the side.
After dinner we played tombola ... Dr Pollack gave me {a picture of} Mahler, my beloved Mahler, with his autograph. It went on until 2:00 a.m.
Looking back on the past year, I can see that I remained unfulfilled, that I received much that gave me pleasure and gave little in return, that I cried and laughed a great deal & that the former was more sincere than the latter, that I was ungrateful to my mother ... and suffered for it. But there were also periods during which I was happy and contented. Such times will never return. They were the purest and most delightful of my life and will always remain so – Amen! ...

> Ring out, old Year,
> Let a new Year begin!

Not in a minor key but in the major, loudly rejoicing, exhilarated. Oh hope, sole saviour of humanity, enter our house, but not for me – I have no right to expect you – but for Mama and Carl. Smooth the wrinkle on their brow, fulfil Gretl's fondest wish ... and find a little time for me too. Let me find somebody who understands me instinctively & completely, whom I understand instinctively & completely, that our souls might flow side by side – that they might resound as *one* chord, as a beautiful harmony. O God, O Nature, eternal, great, mysterious, rich in love and life, grant me this *one* wish!

Thursday 5 January 1899
Composed a little song. I don't know if it's any good – but I like it and it
expresses my current mood fairly well. Text by H. Heine, i.e. a solid house
at which it's safe to open an account. I sang it to Gretl, and she stood up
and said:

> It's astonishing how you always manage to find a poem that cor-
> responds to your state of mind. I know you: anyone who hears your
> songs can feel what mood you're in.

It's true, I feel compelled to write songs only when they suit my mood,
therefore they'll never be any thigh-slapping folk-dances.[4] Never have I
written a cheerful song or a cheerful instrumental piece. I just can't!

Friday 6 January
O Lord God, give me the strength to achieve what my heart longs for – an
opera. It must be entitled 'Ver sacrum' and must express and glorify the
'struggle' of youth against old age. That would be my dream! The more
symbolism, the better. I wish I had the physical and moral strength to see it
through. I almost despair, yet my whole being strives to achieve this one
goal. Help me, divine power. I pray to you that I may suffer no defeat in the
battle against my weakness, against my femininity.

Saturday 7 January
In five minutes, I've just composed a little song, 'Ich wandle unter Blumen'.
I don't know if it's any good. All I know is that it's full of passion. The
whole thing is one chromatic run! It's crazy – it will probably give Labor a
pretty nasty turn.
Today: to the Secession with Carl. Were shown around by Roller, who
expounded some aspects of a picture by Rysselberghe. He's a pointillist.
Tremendously interesting! If he wants to achieve the effect of blue, he
juxtaposes yellow and green. In the one portrait of a lady the eyebrows are
green and the hair is yellow, green, red, violet and blue, yet the effect is

4 Orig.: 'Schnadahüpferln'.

absolutely natural. Roller much regrets not having thought of it earlier, because if now he imitates it, they'll say he's copying Rysselberghe.

I shall become a tram driver and give up painting for good . . .
Well, maybe that would be better for him and the rest of humanity.

Tuesday 10 January
Labor. On the way, I was followed by a couple of men. But I'm already quite an expert at giving people the cold shoulder. So all was well. And then . . . Labor. I played him my three new songs, and he said:

> There's talent there, I don't dislike them. – Wouldn't you like to hear
> them sung by a well-trained voice? It would be a good thing to include
> them in a Brandt[5] concert, and I wouldn't object.

I was overjoyed. Next week I've got to take along all my songs and play them to him. Today . . . my happiness is almost unclouded.
This evening: ball at the Wetzlers'.[6] It was terrific fun. Without flattering myself, I can assert that I was the prettiest and also danced the most.
p.m. Alfred Zierer sent us a wonderful bouquet of flowers and took us there with him, he also sat next to me at table. To my right was Dr Tersch. I danced mostly with Paul Altmann[7], Erwin Kuffner[8] and Alfred. Also someone called Neufelder, whom we once met at the Hellmanns'. The Bachrich Quartet[9] played throughout, and in the intervals we – five or six of the men and I – went into the little adjoining salon and chatted away very amiably. The only one who struck me as particularly intelligent was Neufelder. It went on until 5:00.

Thursday 12 January
Opening of the 3rd Secessionist Exhibition[10]
'Christ on Olympus' – monumental, grandiose, a little clumsy and austere, but great . . . Simply everyone was there. All our friends. We spent most of

5 The contralto Marianne Brandt sang at the Metropolitan Opera, New York from 1884 to 1888. From 1890, she was active in Vienna as a voice teacher.
6 Bernhard Wetzler (VIII., Trautsohngasse 6) was proprietor of the firm of B. Wetzler (manufacture of fruit conserves). He and his family were on friendly terms with the writer Arthur Schnitzler.
7 Paul Altmann, director of the firm of Elin A.G. (electrical industry).
8 Erwin Kuffner was the proprietor of a Viennese brewery.
9 Albert Bachrich, principal violist of the Vienna Philharmonic, was professor at the Vienna Conservatoire from 1869. He played in the Hellmesberger Quartet and, from 1884 to 1904, the Rosé Quartet.
10 Secessionist Exhibition (12 January–22 February 1899). The main exhibit was Max Klinger's gigantic canvas *Christ on Olympus* (approximately 30 ft wide).

the time with Fräulein Schlesinger,[11] whom we'd met at the Wetzlers'. It was most amusing. Klimt came up to greet us, and I responded like a block of ice. Unfortunately I soon gave myself away. He hovered around me, and finally I had no option but to be nice to him again. He's the most delightful person I know. Why should I deny it? Unfortunately I couldn't talk to him much, but the time will come. If only he were a little calmer . . . or had been . . . or I . . .
I feel so dreadfully lonely.

Friday 13 January
I'm terribly depressed. One song went completely awry. All my joy is gone.

Saturday 14 January
This morning: with Mama at the Secession. As we were passing the Künstlerhaus, we bumped into Klimt. He walked with us a little way, and Mama invited him to call on us. He reacted like a scalded cat:

> I would gladly have called long ago, but whenever I enquired after you, dear lady, they always said: she's not in the mood, very irritable, isn't receiving callers . . . so I couldn't very well drop in, could I?

Oh, what exquisite manners! When he mentioned her irritability, by the way, he looked me straight in my eye. I know he's insincere, but that he's also a coward came as a surprise. Life is full of surprises . . . especially with someone like that.
Frightful headache. I completely lack inspiration, but feel compelled to sit myself down at the piano. God give me strength, give me self-control. I'm so preoccupied, my mind is set on all sorts of things – except music. Although I'd dearly like to, I can barely collect my thoughts. I'm so unhappy. Thankless creature that I am. Usually I'm not troubled by things that others can understand – but today I am: the fear of losing my creative gift, my sense of melody. Dear God, it's the finest, purest, most wonderful thing I ever possessed. Don't take it from me, I beg you . . .

Sunday 15 January
At midday: Philharmonic Concert. It was terrific. First they performed {Beethoven's} F-minor String Quartet in an orchestral version. I missed the wind instruments etc. A quartet should be intimate, as it's actually house-music. Then followed the Symphony no. 1 in B♭ major, which was simply

11 Gerty Schlesinger, whose father was director of the Anglo-Austrian Bank. In 1901 she married Hugo von Hofmannsthal.

wonderful, then P. Tchaikovsky's '1812' ouverture solennelle. Very brisk and noisy, but little spiritual content.[12]

Tuesday 17 January
Labor. Today I played him all eight songs, and he said:
   A most respectable accomplishment . . . for a girl.
It's a real curse to be a girl, there's no way of overcoming your limitations. All the same, he liked them, and said that Frau Radnitzky should include some in her concert. That would be fine as far as I'm concerned.
This evening: concert with the Gewandhaus Quartet. Felix Berber (1st violin), Alfred Wille (2nd violin), Alexander Sebald (viola) and Julius Klengel (cello). We heard the Schumann A-minor Quartet and Haydn's G-major Quartet. We couldn't stay for the Beethoven, because we were invited to dinner at the Zierers'. Their ensemble was superb, and for the first time I really enjoyed a Haydn.[13]

Thursday 19 January
Dr Pollack here. I played my pieces to him and Carl, and Mama sang them. Carl liked them, but he wanted to make changes in almost every song. Pollack would like to give them to Rosé and have them performed in public. We'd like to drag Mama along unsuspecting. That would be lovely. All the same, I'm not the least bit interested in publishing my songs.

Tuesday 24 January
Labor. I played him my latest song, and he approved of it. Playing my pieces to Labor is what I would describe as 'dry cleaning'. Today he said:
   I'm expunging all the Secessionism, all the embellishment from your
   songs, because they shouldn't be only for the benefit of your painter-
   friends. All truly musical people should appreciate them.
Then I played him my two pieces for the pupils' concert, and he gave me some invaluable advice. Then he gave me a lecture on absolute music. He's the wisest man on earth.
p.m. composed a song, text by Heine. Then Dr Spitzeles[14] arrived. I played him several pieces, and he made pertinent remarks.

12 Programme: Beethoven, String Quartet op 95 (version for string orchestra by Mahler, world première); Tchaikovsky, Ouverture solenelle '1812' (first performance in Vienna); Schumann, Symphony no 1; conductor: Mahler.
13 Programme: Schumann, Quartet in A minor op 41, no 1; Haydn, Quartet in G major op 17 no 5; Beethoven, Quartet in E minor op 59 no 2; Gewandhaus Quartet, Leipzig.
14 Mock-Yiddish variant of 'Spitzer'.

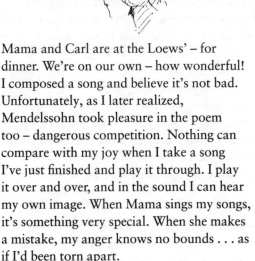

Mama and Carl are at the Loews' – for
dinner. We're on our own – how wonderful!
I composed a song and believe it's not bad.
Unfortunately, as I later realized,
Mendelssohn took pleasure in the poem
too – dangerous competition. Nothing can
compare with my joy when I take a song
I've just finished and play it through. I play
it over and over, and in the sound I can hear
my own image. When Mama sings my songs,
it's something very special. When she makes
a mistake, my anger knows no bounds . . . as
if I'd been torn apart.

Sunday 29 January
This morning: final rehearsal.
Lunch in Hietzing at Rudolf's and p.m. at Senta
Fischer's. It was exceedingly amusing. We drank a
toast of brotherhood with Felix, and he gave me a kiss *on the mouth* – and
a smacker at that. When I'm in such company, my pro-Semitic feelings are
really strained: they waver, but don't fall. Senta is pretty and sympathetic.
On Saturday evening we were at the Burgtheater: 'Fuhrmann Henschel'.
The play, by {Gerhart} Hauptmann, is gripping, moving, magnificent and
distressing. Sonnenthal wasn't good, but Witt[15] was simply magnificent.

15 Orig.: 'Witte'. A.S. confuses Lotte Witt, actress at the Burgtheater, with the actor Eugen Witte.

The Klinger picture is unique. Today I stood looking at it for half an hour.
I'm in despair. Yet another song came to grief. Although actually baffled at
my own behaviour, I was immoderately pleased with myself.

Monday 30 January
This morning: rendezvous with Senta and Mimi Wetzler. It was very
amusing.
This evening: Henneberg, Spitzer, Olbrich, Bacher, Klimt. I'm happy now
. . . now I know that Klimt loves me. Today he told me so. I reproached
him, with some justification, and – cast the word 'plaything' unto the
argument. He stood up and said:

> A.S., my child . . . what do you understand of all that? A plaything . . .
> in that case the game would already be over. If I intend to behave
> correctly just once, then let me. I positively avoid coming here. I often
> dream of you . . .

And all the rest . . . I had to believe him. Spitzer brought the new photographs along, and Klimt asked me to give him one. I said:

> It would be open to view by too many people.
>
> Not a living soul shall see it, he said.

Later we were standing at the piano, and he looked at my picture time and
again.

> A lovely girl. The man who wins her has much to be proud of.

[I replied:]

> Nobody shall ever win me.

Initially, as Mama and Gretl weren't yet ready, we were alone for a quarter
of an hour. We had something of a heart-to-heart. Now I know what he
feels, and I'm happy. He's the only man I ever loved and shall ever love. We
harmonize so beautifully . . . but then there's the 'other woman' . . . Today
I asked him straight out if what they're saying about him is true. He said
no, and it was patently obvious that he was lying. Why did it have to come
to this?
The evening was uncommonly pleasant and . . . enjoyable. Mama sang
my songs, and everyone liked them very much, particularly Olbrich – he
kept saying, 'Wonderful, wonderful', and asked me to work hard at my
composition. Klimt asked me:

> Where do you find the poems? They all have a bearing on our
> situation.

I also played the 'Magic Fire Music' and the C-minor Nocturne. The
Hennebergs were very kind. They're coming to the concert tomorrow.

SAAL EHRBAR
IV. Mühlgasse 28.

Dienstag den 31. Jänner 1899, Abends 7 Uhr:

Musik-Abend

zu Gunsten des Brahms-Denkmal-Fondes

veranstaltet von

Adele Radnitzky-Mandlick

mit ihren Schülerinnen

unter gefälliger Mitwirkung

des Fräulein **Josefine Donat** (Cello) und des Herrn
~~Adтом Stedbet~~, Mitglied der k. k. Hof-Musikkapelle (Violine).

Herr Fitzner sprang ein

PROGRAMM:

1. **Schubert** .... Scherzo B-dur. — Fräulein **Erna Chwalla.** *elend.*
2. **Schumann** .... Sonate C-dur, op. 118. —
   Baronesse **Louise von Weckbecker.** *mäßig — aber talentiert*
3. **Thieriot** .... Humoreske für zwei Claviere. —
   Fräulein **Else** und **Melitta Lanner.**
4. **Haydn** .... Sonate Es-dur. — Fräulein **Helene von Wöss.** —
5. **Brahms** .... Trio H-dur, 1. und 2. Satz. —
   Fräulein **Sofie Steingraber.** *recht gut*
6. **Chopin** .... Nocturne C-moll.
   Brassin .... Feuerzauber. — Fräulein **Alma Schindler.** *?*
7. **Schumann** .... Trio D-moll, 3. und 4. Satz. —
   Frau **Fanny Wengraf.** *gut*
8. **Brahms** .... Concert B-dur, 2. und 3. Satz. —
   Fräulein **Helene Schröth,** *gut*

Herr k. u. k. Hof- und Kammer-Clavier-Fabrikant **Friedrich Ehrbar**
hat in Anbetracht des Zweckes den Saal freundlichst zur Ver-
fügung gestellt.

Sitz-Plätze à 1 fl., **Entrées à 50 kr.** sind zu haben bei
Frau Adele Radnitzky-Mandlick IV. Margarethenstrasse 25.

Buchdruckerei: Wien. 1. Dorotheergasse 7.

Alma's added comments:
> Herr Fitzner {violin solo} took over at short notice.
> 1. Miserable.
> 2. Mediocre but talented.
> 3. Pretty good.
> 6. ?
> 7. Good.
> 8. Good.

Tuesday 31 January
As yet I'm not in the least nervous. What's {a concert} compared with my restless thoughts and emotions? A mere drop in the ocean.
My performance was very mediocre. I made a real hash of the 'Magic Fire Music' ... but was applauded very heartily and inundated with compliments. I listened to them all as from a distance, as if they had nothing to do with me.
All day yesterday I didn't give the pupils' concert a thought. It seemed so insignificant compared to my other worries. Yet music is my future.

Saturday 4 February
With Reininghaus to the Secession. It was uncommonly interesting to study the exhibits with him. For my taste, he looks at them too closely, and hence never really enjoys anything properly. In one of the Meuniers the head was too big, in another an arm was too short. When he points these things out, you agree with him, but this kind of art-appreciation is off-putting. When we got to the Klingers', he actually took a chair, stood on it and studied the brush-work with a magnifying glass.
The evening was pleasant, very quiet.

Sunday 5 February

This evening: with Rosa to the Paris orchestral concert, presented and conducted by Henri Rabaud and Max d'Ollone, with the pianist Miss Clotilde Kleeberg. They opened the programme with 'Wallenstein's Camp' by Vincent d'Indy, which I found all but outrageous. Then a Concerto in F minor by Théodore Dubois with the solo part provided by Miss Kleeberg. She commands a fine jeu perlé and has a wonderfully light, graceful touch combined with enormous strength. Then followed a Symphony in C minor by Camille Saint-Saëns, which was long and tedious, then Massenet's 'Scènes alsaciennes' – simply disgusting. Afterwards Kleeberg played 'Aurore' by Bizet, 'Passepied' by Delibes, a

Barcarolle by Fauré and 'En courant' by Godard. She gave one encore. Judging by the genre, it was probably Chaminade: coquettish, affected, Parisian. After a {further} piece, by Emmanuel Chabrier, we left. It's simply too tiring. Kleeberg I found captivating.[16]

Tuesday 7 February
Labor. I played him my four new songs, and he was delighted, as I could observe. We spoke of Chaminade,[17] and he said:
> Your pieces are better than hers. You're unaffected, at least, & you write as to the manner born.

Saturday 11 February
Composed in the morning, then to the Belvedere. Wanted to compose, but lacked all inspiration. I really must write a piece now, because I've found a motif that I simply adore.
The world is so inconceivably beautiful . . . so inconceivably sad, there's a smell of spring in the air, yet it's still only winter. Tell me, heart, when will spring come?
This afternoon: Prof Ludwig came to pass judgement on my songs. He concluded that I was very talented but lacked the necessary qualifications – counterpoint and all other such techniques. I know very well that he's right, that I haven't learnt about symmetry and that I approach matters too naively. He said:
> None of your works is simple-minded or naive. Your approach is ambitious, but that's where you're wrong. People are ashamed of writing naively. They know Wagner and Schumann and begin where those two left off [but without possessing their genius]. They probably know nothing of Beethoven before the 'Choral' Symphony.

He's absolutely right. Today there's no such thing as artlessness, it's a major deficiency of our age. He told me many things, but didn't mention the salient point, namely that I lack seriousness and make too little use of

16 Clotilde Kleeberg was noted as an interpreter of Beethoven and Schumann. Apart from the works mentioned by A.S. (she refers to the Symphony no 3 in C minor of Saint-Saëns), the programme included 'En courant' (piano solo) by Benjamin Godard, and Chabrier's *Gwendoline* Overture.
17 Cécile Chaminade started composing at the age of eight; at eighteen she made her debut as a concert pianist. Apart from an opera and a Mass, she composed primarily for piano. With the exception of the Concertino op 107 for flute and orchestra, her works are nowadays rarely performed.

my brain. Maybe that was on the tip of his tongue. I could sense it. Today
Gretl said to me:

> You know, the only man who'd suit you is Klimt. Only he could
> understand your feelings and your character.

Gretl, Gretl . . . angel of presentiment!

Monday 13 February

This morning: a row with Mama, but I felt totally in the right. She actually
struck me. If Mama thinks she can restrain me by resorting to violence,
she's mistaken. It just makes me defiant & stubborn. At such moments I
wish I were far away, far . . . away.

Tuesday 14 February

Today Kl. sent me this postcard.[18] It gave me much joy.
I'm still angry with Mama. We aren't talking to each other. I'd so like to
give her a piece of my mind, but I lack the courage.

I composed a good deal today – the sketches for
three piano pieces. One is already finished and
is, I believe, not bad. It has something gypsy-like
about it, which appealed to me. I'm curious to
know what Labor thinks of it.

This afternoon: Legler, Gretl and I took a
stroll in the garden.

This evening: at Dr Spitzer's. Kl. was there
too – Korpers, Gound and Klimt. Kl. had
to escort Frau Korper, which annoyed him
– and me no less. After dinner, Spitzer
and Mama sang my songs. They were
exceptionally well received. Even Gound
found them very attractive. Later he was
invited to play a paraphrase on my song 'Gib dich darein'. |It was simply
delightful.| Later Klimt sat beside me. I could sense he was unhappy . . .
and also believe he's fond of me, just as he knows I'm fond of him. He
asked me for my photograph –

> But with a dedication, he said. I must be able to distinguish it from all
> the others.

If only I knew how to go about it. He wants to give me his photograph

---

18 ► Postcard from the Rathauskeller, with coat of arms, signed by Klimt.

too – namely one of which he possesses only one copy. I replied, with irony:

Certainly, that's what I deserve.

And he retorted:

I should know better.

He told me he could sense that Mama was not particularly well disposed towards him, and therefore he didn't know if he could call without arriving at an inopportune moment. Later, as we went out to his cab in the dark, he said:

A.S., have you ever thought of visiting me in my studio . . . just you, on your own?

A tremor went through my whole body. I don't remember what I answered . . . He asked me to dedicate a song to him, and I said:

They're all dedicated to you.

Once, yesterday, he said:

Actually it's wonderful that we can't come together. Our feelings will remain unsullied – without regrets – and will leave nothing but beautiful memories.

I promised him, in case of marrying or dying, to send him my diaries.

In that case I shan't want them, he said.

But I'll do so all the same. Mama, observing that I was speaking at such length to Klimt, passed me several furious glances. In future my motto shall be: 'Grasp the opportunity'. It doesn't exactly correspond to the words on the blue envelope, but for me it amounts to the same thing.[19]

Wednesday 15 February
I literally didn't get a wink of sleep. It was only the third time in my life that I'd passed such a night, always when I was madly excited, and always in connection with Kl. Am I truly happy or, actually, deeply unhappy? I don't understand myself. But I think probably the latter. When I walk on the street, I can't recognize anyone. Everything is obscured by a <u>fine veil</u>, so impenetrable that nobody can tear it away.

19 Caption on the drawing: 'Wind'.

Sunday 19 February
For the first time I saw the son of my idol: Siegfried Wagner. He conducted
the overture to his opera 'Der Bärenhäuter'. The occasion will remain
indelibly imprinted on my mind. The resemblance to his father is quite
striking. The public was wildly enthusiastic, they threw laurel wreaths . . .
yet I don't envy him being the son of *that* particular father. They applauded
his name, his facial features. Nota bene . . . his music is neither epoch-
making, uplifting nor subversive. It's good, solid Wagnerian music . . . not
moulded by the hand of a Richard Wagner but by a young man of twenty-
six. Maybe in time he'll mature and proliferate. But although he bears the
name, he'll never be a Wagner.

The second novelty, 'Moorish Rhapsody' by Engelbert Humperdinck, was
dull at first, but improved steadily and ended well and effectively. Then
followed Kienzl.[20] Dull, dreary, empty. The fourth item was the preludes
to acts I and II of the opera 'Guntram' by Richard Strauss. He's decidedly
the most brilliant of the four, indeed, I believe, of all living musicians.
Mahler conducted and was received with demonstrative applause. Everyone had been *longing* for a true conductor. Mahler is a genius through
and through. Music has never pervaded me as it did today. Suddenly I
burst into tears. It's my wish – just once – to write a symphonic work.
Orchestral music is the clearest, noblest, purest of art-forms. And the
counterpoint, dear God!

Tuesday 21 February
p.m. Klinger and Klimt. I made the acquaintance of
Max Klinger
A reddish beard, reddish hair that rises from his head like flames, penetrating black eyes – altogether the appearance of a true artist. At one stage
Klimt came up to me:

You're a little reckless, aren't you?

And I said:

What do you mean? What have I done or said?

Well, the other day a model came up to me and said, 'Yer know, Mr
Moll's eldest daughter's in love with yer. Yup, she's even gotcha name
in 'er 'ankerchief. Th'only thing she doesn't like aboutcha is yer soft
shirts.'

20 The concert, with the orchestra of the Hofoper, included Kienzl's tone-poem *Don
Quixote's phantastischer Ausritt and seine traurige Heimkehr*. The first three works were
conducted by their respective composers.

I was flabbergasted. Who could have the nerve to propagate such lies? I'm appalled.

Mama was then collected from Mitzi Fischer's. Together with Reininghaus – who had vainly attempted to approach Klinger – his daughter, Carl, Uncle Fischel and Klimt, she left. The others went on ahead, Klimt and I followed. Unfortunately Carl sent us Uncle Fischel as chaperone, putting paid to any conversation. If only I could put paid to the whole affair.

Kl. told me that this particular model was a frightful chatterbox, and that in a few days all Vienna would know of it. Father, dear father, save me, or I shall be undone. If only Papa was with me now: I'd repeat every word in my soul to him, just as I always used to. – He would understand me, advise me, for he really loved me. But Mama and Carl . . . this afternoon they teased me about Kl.

Oh yes, we know all about that. It's O.K. A.S.'s soft spot.

And so on in the same tone. Papa would never have done that. If only he were still alive! I'd try to beautify his life with my music and my love.

Friday 24 February

12:30 lunch at Hotel Sacher. The Engelharts, Miss Troyfort (our host), Reininghaus and his daughter, Carl, Mama, we two, Dr Spitz,[21] Pollack and Klimt.

Klimt sat next to me for the first time in ages. He came up to me, I joined him, and so we just sat down side by side. Mama gave me a very strange stare. I was blissful, my neighbour likewise. We talked about the same things as last time – yet it was quite different. We've grown closer, even closer. What's it leading to? There'll be no end to it, no end. – No: the end would be despair. The day was beautiful! Beautiful. Gretl got tipsy [she kept shouting: 'In vino veritas'] and later confided to me that she was in love with Legler. I've known it all along, but I'm astonished.

In the evening: Prasch concert. I couldn't absorb it, I was too full of the day's impressions.

Saturday 25 February

This afternoon: to Coralie Legler. We played 'Tristan', and were both so fascinated that we fell weeping into each other's arms.

I sleep-walked all evening, until the moment when the door-bell rang and

21 Word-play on 'Spitzer' and 'Spitz' – point, sharp peak.

Klimt came in. Wagner was forgotten. I didn't talk with him much – but then, we have no need for words.

Tuesday 28 February

a.m. lesson with Labor. I was there for two hours. For a whole hour we talked about art, about progress and stability in art, about our contemporary musicians, such as Rückauf, Gound etc. He said:

> Nothing is more dangerous for a young talent than not allowing it to mature. For all young artists the example of Rubinstein & Goldmark should be held up as the direst warning – two such talents – ruined, because they didn't wait until they were ready. Rubinstein bestrewed us all with his spring-buds, but never brought forth fruit.

I said I was afraid that Gound would go the same way, to which he replied:

> He's already lost, sunk without trace.

Next year he wants to give me my first taste of counterpoint. That's a dangerous business. For greater talents it opens new vistas, but it smothers the lesser ones. I'd rather be crushed under the weight of knowledge than go on living in ignorance, 'protecting' a slender talent. I've become convinced that I shall never abandon Labor unless I'm so badly off that I can no longer afford it. Today he revealed his greatest ambition:

> You see (we were discussing 'Christ on Olympus'), most contemporary painters have more ambition than ability, they lack the means to fulfil their intentions. You know, ever since I can remember, I've always wished for an organ, but never had the money. I've given up all hope now – in the next world perhaps.

God willing, if ever I were really well-off – the first thing I'd do would be to buy Labor an organ. Then for myself I'd buy *Pierre Lagarde's* 'Sunset' and . . . nothing else would matter. One thing I do know: I'd support the arts wherever I could.

In the evening: concert.[22]

>   Cécile Chaminade
>   César Thomson

Actually the celebrated composeress doesn't deserve even the slightest mention, she's a disgrace to her sex. I'm only writing about her because *I*

---

22 Programme: Goldmark, Violin Concerto op 28 (soloist: César Thomson); Chaminade, Konzertstück for piano and orchestra op 40 (soloist: the composer); lieder (sung by Cécile Ketten); conductor: Hermann Grädener. From an early age, the Belgian violinist César Thomson appeared in concert-halls all over Europe. He was professor of violin at Liège from 1882 to 1897 and subsequently successor to Ysaÿe as professor at the Brussels Conservatoire.

was so bitterly disappointed. I said to myself: rarely do you hear of female composers, but here's an exception to support me – Cécile Chaminade – of whom I know almost nothing except the name. Now, after *this* concert, I know that a woman can achieve nothing, never ever. They performed her Piano Concerto op. 40 with orchestral accompaniment. I've never heard anything more hideous. With pipes and drums, a veritable monster-orchestra – and nothing behind it.

Oh yes: Goldmark's Violin Concerto [Thomson] wafted past as well. Labor is so right.

Thursday 2 March

Yesterday I wrote the third of my five pieces. Gretl liked it – but not unreservedly.

This evening: alone with Dr Spitzer. He'd come to rehearse my songs. He sings them all pretty indifferently and pulls funny faces all the while. At one point, I looked at him and almost laughed out loud. He laughed too, but didn't know what I was laughing at.

In the evening: Carl and I discussed Schumann and Schubert. Spitzer and Gretl were listening. Carl spoke of the sickly melancholy in Schumann songs, and I defended them staunchly.

> It's simply that you're passing through the romantic phase, during which 'love unto death' seems to be the highest ideal. Later you'll see things differently.

At this point I steered the conversation round to painting, particularly to Papa's, and contended that his work was imbued with the same melancholy as the songs of Schumann. Carl agreed, but here too he wouldn't accept the positive effect of grey. I said:

> My favourite picture is entirely in grey. Pierre Lagarde's 'Sunset'. If I ever had the money, I'd buy it.

Then Mama came in, and the conversation was over.

Last night, once again, I couldn't get to sleep. Many things went through my mind, and I concluded that I'd been bitterly betrayed all winter, namely by Kl. Everything he told me was insincere and simply reflected my own, deepest feelings. I do believe that he's fond of me, but whether he's as fond of me as I of him – no, absolutely not, otherwise he'd change his ways. He's leading me up the garden path, sometimes professing affection, sometimes quite the opposite. It's got to stop. I shall talk to him. It's in my nature to speak openly about such things. It'll be interesting to see him admit his divided loyalty.

Friday 3 March

I feel ghastly, have a dreadful pain all down the left-hand side of my head and face.

After lunch, Schmedes (the opera-singer, tenor) came to see me, and we chatted on our own for an hour in the dining-room. I'm open to anything new – well, today I met a man who unashamedly considers himself and his voice the most important things in the world. He's a dear man, and we conversed well – the sixty minutes prove the point – but I really provoked him, because that kind of conceit can in fact be quite endearing. I said I'd seen his debut at the Opera, as Siegfried, and told him how deeply moved the entire audience had been. I told him about the controversy that had broken out in the foyer between his opponents and his admirers.

> What did my opponents say? What didn't they like about my Siegfried? Were there opponents? Who were they?

With my back to the wall, I didn't know what to say, so I told him all kinds of fibs. After all, I had no choice.

> I {don't} understand why that should interest you so. Surely an artist should be impervious to public opinion. You really needn't worry about such things, I said

– a moral slap in the face, disguised as a compliment. He didn't dwell on the subject any longer. We spoke a good deal about the Opera. Naturally, he doesn't care for any of his colleagues, and he imitates them superbly, even if his stupidity makes you feel sorry for him. Anyone can see that it's nothing but professional jealousy. Just compare him with the painters and sculptors I've met – models of modesty and discretion. I've never heard a painter praise his own ability. Yesterday Schmedes spoke, quite calmly and without the slightest scruple, of his *talent*, in such a way that I can even accept it. You must remember that performing artists live *only* for the success of the moment and hence must strive for immediate acceptance. That doesn't apply to the visual arts. Today Schm. told me proudly:

> When Winkelmann sings, the box-office takings only amount to 1,700 fl, when I sing they rise to 2,500 . . . and then, when I sing, it's completely black backstage.

I didn't know what he meant. He explained: the crowd of admirers at the stage-door. He even takes interest and pleasure in {admiring} school-children – very sad. He did his best to persuade Carl to send me to Bayreuth. He'll be singing Parsifal, would even put a room in his apartment at my disposal. Hm – I declined the offer politely but firmly. At present he's learning 'Der Bärenhäuter', and he told me all about it. He'd already said

exactly the same to his wife and some other fellow – I was talking to
E. Bloch, but nevertheless managed to eavesdrop on the conversation.

> Oh, you can follow two conversations at once. Why don't you follow
> two people at once? I've been watching you for some time and
> observe, to my dismay, that you're incapable of it.

He told me the most awful things about Mahler:

> The poor man is so deeply in love (he laid much stress on this phrase,
> repeating it four or five times over in true Burgtheater style, as if
> addressing a large crowd). He keeps pinching her cheek and, during
> rehearsal, he kisses her repeatedly. All that smooching – it makes you
> sick.²³

Such words are scarcely designed to brighten a man's halo. But what do I
care about his personal affairs? It's the artist that I love. Schmedes is a dear
fellow. Later, when we were dancing, I danced only with him, and Carl
with his wife. Later I had another conversation with Bloch.

Saturday 4 March
This afternoon: Coralie Legler. I played piano duets with her.
This evening: Reininghaus, Docterl and Olbrich. I had a major argument
with Olbrich, and was appalled by his crazy notions. In his opinion, I
shouldn't study counterpoint:

> You have sensibility, you have ideas. What more do you need? You
> should break with tradition, cast away the old bunk, be modern,
> individual. You've got what it takes.

Vainly I tried to convince him that the main thing, from which everything
else follows, is technical ability. Typical Secession [in the wrong sense] and
[therefore] reprehensible. With such notions you don't get anywhere.

Sunday 5 March
Composed in the morning . . . really crazy, very modern – a curse on . . .
Olbrich – but not bad, I believe.
After lunch, the four of us were sitting together. Mama teased me about Kl.

> Well, A.S., if Olb. and Kl. were here, whom would you take? [You
> could subtly hint that he should break with his sister-in-law. I
> wouldn't object to that.

23 The object of Mahler's affection was the soprano, Margarethe Michalek. In the spring of
1900, he turned his attention to Selma Kurz who, in the interests of her career, refused his
offer of marriage (cf. Dési Halban and Ursula Ebbers, *Selma Kurz. Die Sängerin und ihre
Zeit*, Stuttgart-Zurich, 1983, pp. 88–90.)

Mama simply has no idea of the nature of our relationship, nor of what
kind of people we are.] I said:

Kl. of course.

But there will never be any question of that. I've long since given up hope.
When Mama talks about such matters, makes bantering, lightly ironic
remarks, it re-opens all the old wounds. It all means so much to me. It will
be my downfall.

Tuesday 7 March

Lesson with Labor. I played him my three piano pieces, and after the first
he said:

Nothing: just eccentricity and turbulence.

He liked the second one but wasn't satisfied with the third either. Yet both
the pieces he disliked are the outcome of deepest conviction. I stayed for
two and a half hours. He was wise and kind-hearted, as ever.

This afternoon I bought a copy of Liszt's 'Waldesrauschen', now I'm trying
to make a go of learning it.

Wednesday 8 March

This evening: assaut by pupils of fencing-master Barbasetti[24] in the
Kaufmännische Vereinssaal: fleuret, épée and sabre. Spitzer fenced with a
fleuret. The master of them all, without doubt, was Dr C. Müller. He's
handsome and moves gracefully. The whole thing is actually pointless. The
age of jousting and tournaments is long since past, and it's not a particularly healthy occupation either. What do you want? At least I've seen it
once, and I'm glad to know what it's about.

Thursday 9 March

You simply can't imagine what happened to me today, what I went
through. There was Frau Radnitzky's concert and, simultaneously, a concert of the Kaim Orchestra. I heard that the latter would be closing with
the Prelude and Liebestod from 'Tristan' and asked Mama to let me attend.
At Frau Radnitzky's I listened only to the <Breiner> Trio and a sonata by
Fuchs (the concert was very badly attended, and her playing, though clean
and assured, lacked temperament and strength) then I rushed to the
Musikverein as fast as I could. Through the cloakroom door, the first notes

---

24 Luigi Barbasetti was fencing master at the Consular Academy in Vienna from *c.* 1894; he
also ran a fencing school and wrote on the art of fencing and duelling. Amongst the
participants in the display were Hermann Bahr and Friedrich Spitzer.

I heard were 'Tristan'. I could scarcely suppress my tears, having to listen to *'Tristan'* behind closed doors. You simply can't imagine how I suffered: I'd been longing to hear it for a year, and now I could only make out the bare outlines. The conductor was Bernhard Stavenhagen. They'd changed the programme order and played 'Tristan' in the middle. Then followed a concerto for violin with orchestral accompaniment by Tchaikovsky – soloist Alex Pechnikov. Very lovely, but it gets on your nerves in due course. To finish: the 'Flying Dutchman' overture. A terrific piece. When you close your eyes, you can imagine a wild storm, with the sea surging and roaring. Tone-painting carried to the limits. It's wonderful, marvellous, the way the waves rise and fall, the endless, eternal sea.

Friday 10 March
Kl. called. Also here were Reininghaus, Mrs Troyfort, Richard, Dr Spitzer and Sackel. It was much the same as ever when Kl. visits us – I spoke almost only with him. He took the one photograph of me and put it in his wallet. I warned him that it was a proof copy and would easily smudge. To my astonishment, he put it straight back onto the table. Indeed I was offended. Such a cowardly, timorous thing to do. 'Let's hope nobody noticed that I'd taken it' – that's what must have gone through his mind. I felt sorry for him . . . and for myself.
Later I gave him Dettmann's fan, and asked him to paint something on it. He looked at it and said:
> No I shan't. I want to be on my own, not next to Dettmann. I'll make a
> new fan and paint it for you.
That made me wildly happy. If he really meant it, the way he said . . . perhaps he does care for me a little after all.

Sunday 12 March
Lunch with Hancke at Mama Moll's, and now it's late afternoon, early evening. A day I shall never forget. Mama Moll drove off to Hietzing, and we stayed behind with Mama. All of a sudden, she said:
> Children, come over here and sit down, I have something to tell you.
> Have you noticed anything? No? Before long you'll be getting a little
> brother or sister.
I looked at her – and burst into tears. Gretl laughed. As if in a flash, the future raced through my inner eye. Moll on the one side – Schindler on the other. Our dismissal, our estrangement from the family, our hatred of the intruder. I'd never experienced anything of the kind. I almost fainted.

Tuesday 14 March
Labor – last lesson. He was as kind as ever, and blew kisses with the tips of his fingers. We tried a bit of counterpoint.

This evening: at the Robicseks'.[25] Only Bloch and Blau were there. The latter took my lieder with him. I played my pieces and the general opinion was that they didn't sound as if they'd been written by a woman. We stayed until 3:30. Blau told me that I was madly flirtatious – that I'd first turned his head, but later taken no further notice of him. He's quite right: I'm utterly vulgar, superficial, sybaritic, domineering and egoistic!

Wednesday 15 March
In the evening: at the Hennebergs'. Kl. was there too. To begin with, I couldn't talk to him at all and had to listen to Herr Junker's feeble jokes. At table too – whether by accident or design – we didn't sit together. Instead, we engaged in continuous conversation with our eyes. Mama intercepted several meaningful glances – and told me so soon afterwards.

After dinner I accompanied Dr Spitzer in some of my lieder, after which the entire company betook themselves to the smoking-room. Kl. and I remained in the salon. I told him everything I'd been wanting to tell him, but it will lead to nothing. He's far too egoistic to venture out of his comfortable shell.

Later he spilt a glass of schnapps over my white dress. Frau Henneberg – as from today Aunt Marie – took me into the dining-room and fetched a glass of warm water. Kl. and Spitzer followed soon after. Kl. said:

Come, we'll do it like this.

He took my skirt on his knee, and himself washed the stain out of my petticoat. Both his legs and mine were hidden under the skirt, and inevitably they touched. Although I kept withdrawing – for I consider such behaviour vulgar – I did so with reluctance and was overcome by such a strange, sweet sensation [by the physical contact with the man I loved]. My goodness, what I'm writing here is madly sensual, but I've promised always to write the full truth – regardless of myself or my neighbours – so I'm writing things down that cause blood to rush to my cheeks. *There's nothing else I can do.*

Later we went up into the studio, and Kl. obtained our photographs from Spitzer. He's going to give me back Gretl's . . . heavens! Why do I have to be so fond of *this* particular fellow? – It will be my undoing.

25 Orig.: 'Robitsek' – the dentist Salomon Robicsek, whose practice was at I., Mayfeldergasse 5.

Even if he tried to persuade me a thousand times over that he's fond of me
. . . I simply [don't] believe him. Otherwise he would throw out his sister-in-law. But no: anything to avoid discomfort or disturbance. He's a man of habits. And at present he has the two of us – otherwise he'd only have the one. Thus for me the solution is decidedly unfavourable. Perhaps one day he'll regret it. Yesterday he said to me:

What would I gain by breaking with the past?
Can one love a man who's so unscrupulous? Yes, unfortunately. – Artists are rarely people of integrity.

Friday 17 March
Party and private viewing – at the Secession.²⁶ Klimt took me personally to look at his 'Schubert'. It's indisputably the best picture at the exhibition. Strasser is the most monumental artist I've ever seen. As for the rest, I'll have to study them first.

Saturday 18 March
Dance matinée of the Camera Club. Pretty dull at first, as there were speeches until 12:30. Then I danced with Altmann, Gareis, Kuffner, Comployer, Graf & Graf & Graf & abandon, and breezed through my first and only quadrille with Kl.
Today we talked everything over seriously, and he told me it would never be possible for him to marry me – that he was fond of me all the same. Never had we spoken in greater seclusion and solitude than in the midst of the dancers in that salon. Never had I felt sadder than in the inner circle of that waltz. Never. –
After that quadrille, we all went home. We were with Dr Henneberg – anyway, I couldn't have danced with anyone else.

Sunday 19 March
The postcard arrived this morning.²⁷ It's from Kl., and delighted me. My next volume will be entitled 'Italy' – if I get through today.
Could you imagine, he said . . . little A.S. – my wife?

---

26 Secessionist Exhibition (18 March–31 May 1899). The main attraction was Arthur Strasser's sculpture *Mark Antony with harnessed lions*.
27 ▶ Postcard from the Camera Club dance.

Suite 10

Italy
Live for the moment!

This is what a god looks like.
Rome, April

Sunday 19 March
This evening: at Mama Moll's.
The close of my diary {Suite 9} was an error: the postcard was not from Kl.
I wish I knew who sent it! I find it incredibly audacious.

Monday 20 March
To the Secession once again. Kl. not there, despite his promise. The
Hennebergs, Spitzer, Lanner – people who mean almost nothing to me.
This evening: to 'Zaza', a highly inept play by Pierre Berton and Charles
Simon. Odilon is terrific. In a box above us: Dr Krasny. I'm beginning to
loathe him. He simply has no pride. How often have I made it clear that he
means nothing to me, yet in his dog-like way he returns time and again.
With his prolonged handshake and searching stare, I find him quite
repulsive. If he comes to Florence . . . that will be the end.

Tuesday 21 March
Jettel to lunch.
p.m. Bacher, Uncle Fischel and Lackl. Pollack told me that Krasny was in
his office for a whole hour today – he also told me that the poor devil is
madly in love with me. I feel heartily sorry for him. Life is so strange: the
person you love always remains beyond your reach.
Humans are like flowers, they bend under the gentlest of spring breezes. If
the flowers are sturdy, they survive; if they're sickly and hypersensitive,
they're broken by the wind. Shall I be able to withstand the first spring
breeze? God knows, at present . . . better not go on. I wouldn't know
where to stop.
Tomorrow evening we're leaving Vienna . . . for Italy.

Wednesday 22 March
Venice
We left from the Westbahnhof at 9:00 p.m. – for Venice. At the station: the
Moll family, Dr Pollack and Legler. Never in my life had parting been so

hard. I cried in the compartment half the night. After all, I've buried all my hopes.

Around 2:00 p.m.: Venice. The first impression was unfavourable. Snow flurries – water without end – grey on grey. Rain, snow, black gondolas, cold and damp. You can scarcely imagine anything more depressing. Also a sore throat and a cold. We didn't see much, only the Doge's Palace, the piazzetta and St Mark's Square. In its moribund, melancholy yet lofty Byzantine splendour, it made me really depressed. A memento mori for all eternity.

Friday 24 March

Florence

The accommodation at Signora Vianello's was quite good, very simple, but at least we got some sleep. At 9:00 a.m. we took a vaporetto to the railway station and breezed off towards Florence. If you aren't already feeling utterly depressed, this grey city of lagoons makes you just that. The journey was wonderful. Morning mists swirled over the Canale Grande – everything lay before us, magically solemn and sublime.

One thing I should add: on this trip I've been flirting madly: on the train from Vienna to Venice and also on arrival, first with a young Frenchman, then with an Englishman and later several Italians. In my defence I can only say that all were young and handsome, and that the tedious journey and endless rain served to whet my appetite for adventure.

At 7:00 p.m. we arrived in Florence. Took two rooms at Hotel Stella d'Italia and strolled around the city. The cathedral, Florentine renaissance style, I found not nearly as appealing as the one in Venice. I find the style brutal yet small-minded: black-and-white striped marble. The whole thing lacks unity. We couldn't see much of the city, as it was too late in the evening. The streets are well-kept and Stella d'Italia [5 lire for a double room] is moderately clean. There's one patisserie on top of another, but in Florence they seem never to have heard of meat.

Saturday 25 March

Naples

At 6:00 a.m. we travelled on. It's still too cold in Florence. We made a brief stop in Rome and arrived in Naples at 6:30 {p.m.} First we were accompanied by a married couple from Brünn, later by two very intelligent and pleasant gentlemen, probably from Pest. Carl wanted to rent a flat, but had no success. He returned to us at the station and we drove to Hotel Bristol on the off-chance – one of the most elegant and expensive hotels in Naples, as we realized when they told us how much it cost. Hotel Bristol: 15 lire for a double-bedded room. Mama made a gesture of forbearance, sighed deeply several times and resigned herself to fate: 28 lire for two rooms. I feel awkward about it actually. Such hotels are made for braggarts – self-made men – not for simple painters and their families.

As yet, I can say nothing of Naples. In the dark I could only see the glow of Vesuvius and a string of city lights running along the water-front. More to follow tomorrow. The weather: rainy and cold.

Palm Sunday 26 March
Got up early and drove off with Carl in search of a flat. We landed up at Parca Margherita, Pensione Midi No. 2. Genuine Neapolitan side-streets – their earthiness and artless cheer we find quite delightful. Colour, noise, bustle, the joy of living. Truly: one should follow the example of this city and its poverty-stricken, contented inhabitants.

Naples is wonderful . . . and today there's such an atmosphere, such a scent in the hills, all around. The sea, boundless on several sides, so deep and beautiful, endlessly pulsing in noble repose. See Naples – and die, sink back, expire for sheer beauty and sanctity. Is there a more beautiful thought on earth?

After making countless enquiries, we found suitable living quarters. Then we drove home: everywhere palms and orange-trees – blue skies. The essence of Italy . . .

Before lunch, we walked with Mama along the riviera and the sea-front. It was really lovely.

At lunch, Gretl and I laughed so heartily that we could scarcely eat. Carl was the only man amidst a throng of women aged anything between fifty and ninety. One of them was so indescribably comical, gobbling away in a fashion worth describing in some detail [looked just like a rabbit].

After lunch, Gretl and I went onto the balcony to smoke, face to face with two old maids who had been sitting next to us at lunch and now also gone out onto their balcony. They looked at us in disgust and withdrew, shocked, into their room. Almost all the guests are stalwart Germans, whom one can truly describe as 'respectable citizens'. Lord only knows what they thought of us!

The whole area owes its strange appearance to the numerous pines and palms – two very similar types of tree, which offer little shade and have no particular purpose other than to be beautiful, a function which they fulfil to perfection. If every living thing were to make a point of being morally and physically beautiful, the world would blossom out.

This afternoon we went for a drive through the streets of Naples and up a hill, where we enjoyed a full panoramic view. It was singularly beautiful. We also passed through more 'typical' quarters and were astounded by the noise, the hurly-burly, the bright colours. One thing disturbed me though: the stereotyped regularity of the women's hairstyles. Every morning they all do their hair on the front doorstep. They wear it in a bun, combed to the side. One soon tires of it: it's too much like a picture by Blaas[1].

There are plenty of clergymen here, but they're less obstreperous than ours. Without giving themselves airs, they appear humble and kind-hearted.

Monday 27 March

This evening: at the Teatro San Carlo. What they played you can read on the programme.[2] This latest work of Mascagni's is a disgraceful hotchpotch. It overflows with bogus Wagnerism and lacks originality – impropriety bordering on frivolity. I've never been so bored. To crown it all, the claque roared persistently, and half of it was repeated. Every single aria – even the overture was encored. And that, of all things, was dreadfully inappropriate. The overture begins with the curtain already up: day breaks and the music swells but, unfortunately, doesn't grow any more edifying – just an empty racket ... Well, they'd scarcely reached the end before the fourth gallery started screaming and yelling. Civilization was thrown to the winds, it was as if one were witnessing the feeding of wild animals. They didn't need much prompting: in a trice, the spotlights were dimmed, and the sunrise began all over again. The more refined members of the audience, most of whom were foreigners, registered mild amusement. Had the drama created some semblance of reality, one would have been appalled at the lack of taste; under the circumstances one smiled, yawned and listened – with the same apathy as before.

1 i.e. the Austrian painter Karl Ritter von Blaas.
2 ▶ Programme of the Teatro San Carlo, Naples: Pietro Mascagni, *Iris*; with Nicoletti Francesco (Il Cieco), Karola Amelia (Iris), Colli Ernesto (Osaka); conducted by the composer (the opera was first performed on 22 November 1898 in Rome). Illica's libretto, based on a Japanese legend, was amongst the first to exploit the *fin-de-siècle* vogue for Japanese art. Mascagni later recalled, 'I gave *Iris* [...] at the San Carlo in Naples, in the presence of the Prince and Princess of Naples. Applause which never ended. All, all, all applauded. Up to that moment I had never seen similar enthusiasm. A real delirium – more than *Cavalleria*!' (from David Stivender, *Mascagni. An autobiography*, New York/London, 1988, 137). The introductory 'Hymn to the Morning Sun' is sometimes performed as a concert-piece.

The plot, which counts among the most vulgar of those currently taking the stage, abounds in brutal realism. In act II, for example, the heroine falls out of the window, and in act III we encounter her again, lying in an open sewer. Rag-and-bone men enter, poke her with their sticks and leave her lying there. At the end, I should add, the gutter is transformed into a garden of irises and the heroine into a withering flower. All would be fine, were it not for the mattress lying in the gutter, which becomes clearly visible in the glow of the lamps for the transfiguration-effect . . . But in *this* piece it can do no harm. All illusion was thrown to the wind.

We left before the ballet. The whole thing lasted from 9:45 until 12:30 a.m. Mindful of the proverb 'everything in moderation', we left the Neapolitans to their love of art, which must have gone on until 4:00, stopped at a beer-house, then went to bed. Peacefully, without a trace of agitation – just very tired – we fell asleep.

As for Mascagni: I wouldn't want to be in his shoes. At the age of twenty he was a deity incarnate, loved and honoured the world over. At forty – just an ordinary human being who's squandered his capital, lacks all sense of melody, all ability, yet thirsts for fame. Yesterday, going on stage with unseemly readiness and bowing to the claque with a foolish grin, I didn't envy him at all. I pitied him from the bottom of my heart. The foreigners laughed . . .

Friday 31 March

p.m. in Camaldoldi. We took the funicular railway as far as Vomero, drove for two hours to the osteria, then walked for thirty minutes to the pan-oramic vantage point. You can see the sea in a semicircle – in the far distance the islands of Ponza and Pozzuoli, all the little villages, all the islands of Naples – with perfect clarity. Everything lay under a grey haze, just as I like it.

In the evening I played the piano {to the hotel guests}. Mama sang one of my songs, then I played my three pieces. They went down really well. An elderly lady from England gave me a long talk, the gist of which was:

> Do keep on composing, won't you, my dear. Write operas and lieder, just as you please. Show the men that we women can achieve some-thing too. You've got what it takes.

Another guest, a very musical lady from Vienna, said to me:

> What I enjoy about your pieces, you know, is that, apart from origin-ality you also have a well-developed sense of rhythm.

My playing was also well received, many people complimented me on it.
Yet . . . what do I care?

Saturday 1 April

Capri

We sailed at 9:00 with a ship of the German Lloyd line, arriving in Capri at
12:00. 'Vedere Napoli e poi murire', the saying goes – in that case, they
should also say, 'Die, see Capri and return to life'. It's a veritable paradise
here. From our rooms we have a direct view of the sea, of the *open* sea . . .
p.m. went for a delightful ramble. Mama waited at one of the vantage
points, while Carl and the two of us clambered down to two Faraglioni
rocks on the sea-shore. It was incomparable. Down below we could see
nothing but the gigantic rock formations, against which the waves were
incessantly breaking. The pure grey colouring was wonderful. We clambered over the rocks like goats. I always adore being at the water's edge –
it's just a bit dangerous, which thrills me most of all. And I've always
preferred grey – it's the noblest, most picturesque of colours, and merges
with everything.

Easter Sunday 2 April

Had a fairly restless night. Woke up around 2:00, dreadfully agitated and
with frightful palpitations. When I opened my eyes, I was looking straight
at the moon, something I could never bear. I got up, went to Mama's room
and knocked on the door. It took Carl ages to find a light, during which
time I looked out of the window. The sea was quite silvery, the mountains
black. I was as if in ecstasy. Carl came out with the lamp, looked at me
from the side, approached me cautiously and spoke very softly, as if
waking a sleep-walker:

> Alma, what are you up to? Go back to bed. Why are you staring at the
> moon like that?

He helped me bolt the door, and soon I fell asleep. This morning he told
me I'd looked quite wild, and he was really frightened. What a crazy
woman I am.

This morning: a short stroll in the village. I can't stop thinking about the
nocturnal scene. It was so beautiful – the deep mystery of the water. Even
I could forget . . . perhaps.

p.m. to Anacapri. The view from the »summit«, across to Sorrento, was
beautiful. Mama and Gretl drove back down in the cab, while Carl and I
walked down with three men.

Tuesday 4 April
An evening in the theatre. They gave a tragedy, and we laughed ourselves half silly. The actors' facial expressions gave a fair idea of the plot. Felix was fast asleep, and during the next play, a little Pulcinella drama, Engelhart[3] dozed off. When it began, we nodded off too. In the end we beat a retreat.

Thursday 6 April
Left N. at 2:00, arrived in Rome at 6:00.[4]

Friday 7 April

Rome

Yesterday I spoke to Karlweis[5] about keeping a diary. He said it was good to get into the habit of reckoning up with yourself, but that one never confronts oneself with the whole truth, there's always an element of coquetry about it. Sadly, I must admit that he's right. In these pages I have often lied and glossed over many of my faults. Forgive me, I'm only human . . .
These postcards arrived in Naples. The sheep are Fischel, Krasny, Mayreder, Lanner, Zierer, Schmedes, Taussig, Pollack, Fellner[6] and (again) Krasny. I don't know who wrote the card, but whoever it was appears to be precisely informed about my friends. 🄰 signifies Joseph Olbrich, 🄱 could be Gustav Klimt . . . but might also be Carl Reininghaus. Let's wait and see!

Saturday 8 April
p.m., unfortunately, we had to move out of our beloved Hotel Germania [opposite me sits a young German: he looks uncommonly handsome and sympathetic] because Carl was so taken by the landlady at Pension Canisiana. We had a lovely corner-room – and now we have a dump. For this privilege, the two rooms cost 5 lire more.[7] We'd already discussed the

3 Several members of the Secession, including Engelhart and Haenisch, as well as the writer Karlweis and Felix Fischer, had joined up with the Molls at Capri on Easter Monday.
4 In the margin A.S. adds: 'Hotel Germania. One room, 2 beds: 8 lire.'
5 Karlweis (real name Karl Weiss), playwright and humorist, was a member of the 'Jung-Wien' group. He came under regular attack from Karl Kraus.
6 The architect Ferry Fellner cultivated the monumental style of Vienna's Ringstrasse. He collaborated with Hermann Gottlieb Helmer on several public buildings (banks and department-stores) in Vienna, and was known throughout Europe as a specialist in theatre architecture.
7 In the margin A.S. adds: 'Pension: 9 lire, room with 2 beds; Via Venti Settembre Nº 58: Pension Quisisano.'

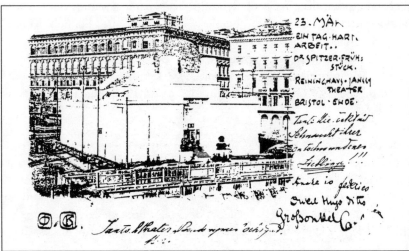

matter with Carl, but he lost his temper. So now we kicked up something of a fuss about the rooms. In short, Carl got very annoyed and bellowed:

You stupid cows, if you don't like it here you can go home.

Later Mama's eyes were red with tears. God in heaven, everything's happening just as I foresaw. Carl can feel his own child in the offing, and now we're merely an obstacle to him. The saddest thing is . . . we no longer have a home we can call our own.

On the open road I cried all afternoon. We were driving along the Via Appia towards the Campagna – but I took nothing in, I was so desperately sad.

During the past two months, Carl's attitude towards us has changed completely.

Tuesday 11 April

This morning: in the Lateran. Lovely sculptures, but not a patch on those in the Vatican. Then we looked at the churches, in which you can see very beautiful Byzantine mosaics. Art used to be more noble.

In Vienna a new magazine has just been launched, 'Die Fackel', edited by Karl Kraus.[8] A wonderful editorial about Julius Bauer and a very <u>stupid</u> article about Klimt, describing how Dumba became a Secessionist. It alleges that when he ordered the panels for his music-room from Kl., the latter was still a devoted pupil of Laufberger. But since then, he (Kl.) had 'learnt his Khnow-how' from Khnopff[9] and, to make the point, he'd become a pointillist. That was how Dumba became a Secessionist[10] – what a blockhead!

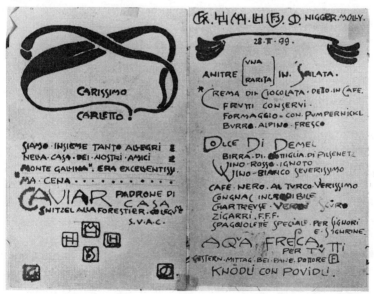

8 A.S. originally writes 'Die Flamme' and 'Felix Kraus' (the latter corrected by A.M.-W.).
9 'Es war ihm der Khnopff aufgegangen' – pun on 'Khnopff' and 'den Knopf aufgehen lassen' (to see the light).
10 Nikolaus Dumba's palace (I., Parkring 4) was decorated with numerous paintings by Makart and Klimt. He was also a collector of Schubertiana.

Yesterday a letter arrived from Kl. As far as bizarre handwriting goes, nobody can beat him.

In the National Museum. Beautiful bronzes once again: a kneeling athlete, Apollo and Bacchus, a girl's head in marble – delightful.

This afternoon: wandered around.

This evening: lots of fun.

Friday 14 April

Felix arrived very early in the morning to fetch us for an outing to Tivoli. From the railway station it's a half-hour's walk to the falls. A broad stream comes rushing down from high up and splits in mid-air into brilliant pearl-drops. The sun's rays cast a large, semicircular rainbow. It's so uniquely beautiful, so uniquely grey, I'd like to spend my life here. Solitary, unknown to all – and hence not unrecognized. Alone with a piano & myself – up there, on the rocky plateau, a hut. I know that I could create something that would bring me peace and joy.

I stood there a long time, don't know how long I would have remained, but Engelhart wrenched me out of my blissful dream. We were standing high up on the rocks, and far below was the grey, gleaming plane – for me that would have signified eternity.[11] I wonder whether I would have fallen to the depths of the water. Further down is the Sirens' Grotto. It's interesting too, but nothing like as beautiful as the falls.

At lunch I laughed so hard at Engelhart's pranks that I ached all over – does that have any bearing on the previous page?

In the afternoon: to the Villa d'Este and later the Villa Adriano. The kind of landscape that I adore – at every step you expect to find motifs of Böcklin. Earnest cypresses, silver-grey olive trees, agaves of rare perfection and brownish-grey ruins all around. The gardens of the Villa d'Este are blissfully beautiful. Long alleyways of cypresses, between which nestle fountains and old statues, and behind you, high on a stone terrace, the villa. The unkempt paths are covered with dark green moss. And behind you, again, lies eternity.

Saturday 15 April

Spent the morning at home. Rain.

p.m. in the Villa Borghese. Titian's 'Heavenly and earthly love': unique.

---

11 The Tivoli waterfalls are 354 feet high.

Everything else mediocre. There's a good Botticelli, but I don't understand it.

Sunday 16 April

High Mass at the Vatican

At 9:00 to the Basilica of St. Peter – a throng of fifty thousand people, the Pope (Leo XIII)[12] was slowly carried in – a yellow mummy, as if of wax. He gave his benediction. I was blessed in an entirely different sense – but more of that later. The crowd roared its enthusiasm, and the Mass began. When the Pope was carried out: the same demonstrations. I'm glad to have witnessed this ecumenical swindle.

And now the most important part – for me. We'd been sitting around for quite a time, when suddenly I spotted the young man who'd been sitting opposite us with a priest at Hotel Germania. He recognized me and greeted me. We exchanged long glances. We both turned our gaze towards the crowd, he looked back at me, I at him. And our gaze, which initially had been merely flirtatious, grew steadily deeper, sadder, desirous. Then our eyes veiled over, and we averted them as if by command. It went on like that for an hour. Mama was beginning to tire, and we looked for an exit, but it was impossible to fight our way through. So we had to return. The benches on which we had been sitting were taken, but all around us the benches were empty. Other people had evidently experienced the same thing, but couldn't find their seats. As I said, our seats had been taken – by my young German and the priest. His gaze, which, when I left, had betrayed regret, now revealed genuine delight. We were all standing on the benches, Mama and Gretl further forward, behind me my two friends. All of a sudden I could feel someone's presence: he was standing close beside me. Soon afterwards I heard the priest saying:

Hey, come over here, where I'm standing. There's a better view.

The view's terrific over here, replied my Hun.

You're stubborn today, said the other.

I had to smile. By now the Pope was standing on the other side. The priest called out:

12 Leo XIII (Gioacchino Pecci), who held office from 1878 to 1903, is considered to have been the founder of modern Catholicism. ► Extra page: 'The central stairway, which Christ is reputed to have ascended when he met Pontius Pilate, and at the head of which he stood as Ecce Homo, must today be climbed on one's knees. On the way up, for every step an "Ave Maria". But we saw that many people were cheating, sliding up two steps at a time. That made us laugh.'

Hey, let's see if the view is better further forward.

I'll stay here. You go on your own – said my German.

All right, I'll take a look, then call you over.

And the priest vanished into the throng. After a while he returned and took my neighbour with him. We were both really sorry. We exchanged glances, silently, but our dialogue was inaudible and sad.

I'd already begun to lose interest in the whole affair, when again I felt an indefinite presence. I turned round, & beside me – there he stood again. My face creased into a smile, and silently we rejoiced. Before long the priest finally managed to find a seat, and my handsome German – and he really was handsome – was obliged to join him. At the exit to the grandstand he hesitated. I looked at him once more, and our eyes betrayed deep sorrow. He went. I shall never see him again.

It's so strange: I never exchanged more than a few words with the fellow, yet we knew each other intimately – it almost hurts to think how I shall miss him! Perhaps God sent him to re-humanize me, to prevent me thinking of nothing and nobody but Kl. Indeed, I was so taken by that young man that it almost felt like love – yet I never even spoke to him . . .

p.m. to the races with Engelhart, Haenisch, Felix and Karlweis. We placed bets on two horses, but neither of them won. One of them came close to it, but fell. We were wildly excited. It made a lovely picture, the wide plain.

At the station we took a tearful farewell of our four friends, who are leaving tomorrow. Some Italian stared fixedly at me and afterwards followed me all the way back to my front door.

Shall I ever see my German again? Intuition tells me that I shan't . . . Dear God, if I go down the list – Rudi Horwitz, Theo Schumacher, Ernst Zierer, Klimt [!!] and now this smooth fellow, I'm horrified at myself. Shall I ever be able to be faithful [to myself]? Let me be honest for once: now that the Kl.-affair is over, or at least appears to be over, {I know that} he declared his love in all colours of the rainbow and – was just waiting to test me.

> I don't believe in your love. First I have to place my fingers in the open wound, he often used to say to me. First I have to see if your love is genuine and steadfast.

Words spoken by a man who has at least three affairs running simultaneously – i.e. the crudest lie imaginable. In spring I believed everything, because I trusted him like a god. Then came Franzensbad and the awful day on which Mama opened my eyes to Kl.'s life-style. I can scarcely bear to think of it. Initially I wouldn't believe it, but Mama was so persistent that I finally resolved to break with Kl. I met him again later, at the Secession. I don't know how it happened, but again he told me how fond he was of me, and again I returned his affection. It actually happened on the evening when he asked me to visit him in his studio. I knew everything, but let him invite me all the same. As often happens when you're in such a position, I was weak.

Then came the lunch-party at Reininghaus, the Henneberg dinner: we devoured each other with our glances, repeated everything over and over. At that time he also confessed to me that he was jealous of »Junker« and later he also said:

I can't bear to see you laughing with other people – yet I love the sound. Then came what actually was the most important chapter in this novel: the dance at the Camera Club which, for false shame, I misrepresented in my diary. The previous night I'd dreamt that Kl. had fallen out with his sister-in-law, woke up and went on dreaming – awake. I told Kl. about it during the quadrille – the one and only time I ever danced it and ever danced with him. We found a seat in a solitary corner, and I was determined for once to talk seriously to Kl. I told him about my dream. He smiled and asked:

And would that have improved the situation?

There's plenty of room for improvement, I replied.

He looked at me and said:

I see, so you're thinking of getting married. I'd always thought you weren't like other young ladies. So you're contemplating marriage, are you?

Thursday 20 April
Pisa
Arrived in Pisa at 9:30 p.m. I'm quite shattered. I'm obsessed by three figures: my young German, Lieutenant {Schulz}[13] and Klimt. The former is still foremost in my thoughts, but as we approach Florence, I again see Klimt's eyes and hear his voice. My mind is paralysed. Everything is in chaos!

Departure from Pisa 5:00, arrival in Florence 7:30. Accommodation at Hotel Helvetia – 11 lire per room with full-board.[14]

---

13 Lieutenant Paul Schulz, a guardsman from Cologne. He became acquainted with the Molls on Capri, and met up with them again in Rome. A.S. writes sparingly of him in her diary, but with his 'cheerful, dashing' manner (entry for 3 April 1899), he appears to have made more than a fleeting impression on her.

14 In the margin A.S. adds: 'Hotel Helvetia, Via dei Pescioni 2.'

Saturday 22 April
Florence
Lunch with Engelhart, Haenisch & Fischer, after which Felix left for home. We drove to the Prato, a delightful bois, where everything is green and fresh.

Dinner with Hofrat Burckhard and the others, then to Gambrinus – until midnight. Was great fun.

Sunday 23 April

Hofrat Burckhard was our guest at breakfast. I had a very unpleasant experience with him. After the meal he remained at table for three hours and, despite his brilliant conversation, we all began to feel drowsy. I stood up, Carl and Burckhard likewise. Suddenly he sat down, and I said to myself: 'O Lord, he's sitting down again.' The thought must have been written all over my face, for he promptly asked:

What were you just thinking? 'O Lord, he's sitting down again'?
Noticing that I was blushing, he continued:

Would you give me your word of honour that the idea hadn't crossed your mind?
I was dreadfully embarrassed and said:

No, that wasn't what I meant.
The answer was foolish, untrue and insulting. I still don't know what I should have said. For I can't give my word of honour to something that isn't true. N.B. the fact that I blushed betrayed me instantly. Later Carl told me that he'd felt just the same, and that such a question would have put him in just as much of a quandary.

This evening we bade farewell to Engelhart and Haenisch. The others, including Mama, went off to Gambrinus, while Burckhard escorted us home. Gretl suddenly stopped in her tracks and said:

Now we've gone too far.
Quite right: we'd gone down the wrong street. Her remark caused considerable mirth.

Monday 24 April

p.m. with Walter to the Museo Nazionale, where we met up with Burckhard. The approach is very attractive. Upstairs is a room of Donatellos, but they didn't make much impression on me. Of Michelangelo they have 'Bacchus' and a few unfinished pieces which, however, give little idea of his true stature. Then a room of della Robbias, exquisite things, mostly in blue and white. There are some wonderful animal sculptures by Giambologna. I was fascinated by wax effigies of plague victims – the bodies fresh and {un-}putrefied – although it turned my stomach. I actually imagined I could smell the stench of corpses – but it's all in the mind. Most of them have the stomach burst open, and rats gnawing at the entrails. That's art for you . . . realism!

Mama wasn't even allowed in. In her present condition, it could have given her a nasty turn.

p.m. at the Accademia. Michelangelo's 'David' leaves me cold. Botticelli's 'Spring' is superhuman.[15] There are also numerous Filippo Lippis, Verrochios and Peruginos, but I found none of them as immediately appealing.

On the way to the Accademia, Carl gave me a lecture and told me to keep out of Klimt's way. He put it very sweetly, but he doesn't know me . . .

Later we drove with Burckhard to the Cascine, where we cycled with him for an hour. It was delightful, and I felt almost entirely happy. The meadows, steeped in the rays of the sun, are a magnificent bright green.

Tuesday 25 April
Yesterday evening Klimt arrived. What more should I write?

This morning we went to the Palazzo Pitti. Of the thousand pictures, we liked 'La bella' of Titian, a van Dyck, a Rembrandt ['Old man'] and a Raffael ['Madonna del Granduca']. The rest is mediocre.

Lunch at Horace Landau's. He has some beautiful tapestries, a Rembrandt, Makart's 'Deadly Sins', delightful bronzes, a wonderful collection of books – altogether an immensely tasteful decor.

This evening: rendezvous with Burckhard at Gambrinus. Kl. is jealous of Burckhard. That amuses and saddens me. Lack of trust? Every morning B. brings us wonderful bouquets of flowers.

Spent the evening at Gambrinus. Talked at some length with Kl.

Wednesday 26 April
To the Campanile – wonderful view, then to the museum of Santa Maria del Fiore. The choir screen: ten reliefs by Luca della Robbia, four by Donatello. Then to the church of San Lorenzo with a bronze relief by Donatello, looked at the Medici Chapels with frescos by Benozzo Gozzoli.

15 It is unclear which picture A.S. means. The *Allegory of Spring* is housed in the Uffizi, while the most famous Botticelli at the Galleria dell'Accademia is the *Madonna of the Sea*.

Then the Michelangelo chapel, the Sagrestia Nuova – intended for the tombs of Lorenzo and Giuliano de' Medici.

p.m. in Fiesole. It was raining. Nevertheless, the view was beautiful. Kl. and B. drove with me in one cab, everyone else in another. Kl. was sitting next to me. When B. got out, he said:

Like a married couple,

and cuddled up closer. On the way home he was sitting opposite me, and our knees touched.

I couldn't sleep the night for excitement, sheer physical excitement.

Thursday 27 April

In Santa Maria Novella |we looked at St Bernhard.| The frescos of St John and St Philip by Filippino Lippi; then to another church, just to look at the altar, which dates from the thirteenth century. Kl. and I were standing behind the altar [where there were frescos of Ghirlandaio].

Well, at least we've stood behind an altar . . . , he said.

Then to the Uffizi to look at my favourite pictures.

Yesterday: a postcard from {Lieutenant} Schulz.

p.m. drove along the Viale dei Colli. It was quite exquisite.

This evening Burckhard left for home.

Friday 28 April

At lunch, Mama managed to steer the conversation round to the state of Kl.'s financial affairs, and we heard that he gets through quite incredible sums of money. On asking, we were told that five women are completely dependent upon him: his mother, his sister, his sister-in-law, her sister and a young niece. It's all well and good, but nothing is getting sold. Poor devil! I never felt fonder of him than when I heard of his domestic plight. At that moment I felt sorrier for him than ever and took a less optimistic view of our affair than ever before. Noticing my crestfallen look, he stood up and turned towards me with his back to everyone else. Quick as a flash, he pulled out the card, the place-card with 'Alma' written on it. He's still carrying it around! Despite my profound unhappiness, I had to laugh.

Saturday 29 April

This morning I went for another walk with Kl. and Carl. On the way home, Klimt told me more about his domestic situation: three sisters, one of them mentally unbalanced, his mother at times also off her head.

When he was twelve, he had to stay home for nine months because he had no trousers to wear. Once, at school, a watch was stolen, and for a long time he avoided his school-friends, for fear they'd think he was a thief. They all knew how poor he was. I found these stories of his early years terribly touching. He started painting by enlarging and colouring photographs.

Genoa

Left for Genoa at midday, changing trains at Pisa. Kl. was sitting in a different compartment and was furious at not being with us any longer.

In Genoa, towards evening, I was standing alone in my room. Kl. came in:

Are you on your own?

Yes.

And before I realized it, he'd taken me in his arms and kissed me. It only lasted a tenth of a second, for we heard a noise in the room next door. We went downstairs. That moment will remain indelibly imprinted on my mind. Halfway down, I turned round and went back up[16] again. It's indescribable: to be kissed for the first time in my life, and that by the only person in the whole world that I love.

In the evening we went for another stroll. When I came downstairs, Kl. came up to me and whispered:

Alma, my Alma.

Mama couldn't understand what was ailing me – I looked so dreadful.

Saturday 29 April

Spent the morning in the harbour.

p.m. to Nervi. Very lovely to begin with. We went sailing with Kl. Later I had a tiff with him. I was in the wrong, and he wouldn't even look at me. In the evening we made it up, but it's not the same as before.

Monday 1 May

Verona

This morning I brought Kl. his blouses. He held me and kissed me again. We were both terribly agitated. Later he stood behind me and said:

There's only one thing for it: complete physical union.

I staggered and had to steady myself on the banister.

At 6:00 in Verona.

He returned to the subject once again:

16 Orig.: down [!].

If two people are united, their happiness is assured. God won't object either.

I resolved to give him an answer. In the evening, on the stairs, I asked him for a copy of 'Faust' and said:

From this book I take my code of behaviour: 'Do no favours without a ring on your finger.'[17] There's nobody I'm more fond of than you. But that – not yet.

The graves of the Scaligers are most interesting. Didn't get much pleasure out of them.

In the train, Kl. told me further stories of his joyless childhood, and I felt heartily sorry for him. He also told me of his plans for new pictures – dear God.[18]

[The worst is over! A.M.-W.]

17 Goethe, *Faust I, 3695*: 'Tut keinem Dieb / Nur nichts zulieb / Als mit dem Ring am Finger.' – 'No robber take, when love he'd make, but with a wedding ring!' A.S. quotes the line again in Suite 13, 4 August 1899.
18 cf. Suite 16, 8 March 1900: at this time Klimt showed A.S. his first sketch for *Philosophy*.

Suite 11

I was born to be lonely –
and loneliness is my destiny,
for I feed off my own thoughts . . .

BOTTICELLI: INCORONAZIONE DELLA VERGINE

Wednesday 3 May

Venice

Today Kl. said:

> I'm not supposed to show the slightest affection for you, but I can't help myself.

This morning: St Mark's. Upon entering: grey with a shimmer of gold – on closer inspection: wonderful mosaics. The building is finer than St Peter's, uniquely mystic – moved even me to religious sentiment.

Today I received a dear letter from Labor and a postcard from Schulz.

p.m. drove to the lido. Spoke at length with Klimt. He may be fond of me, but he offended me with his brutal behaviour.

In the evening: went for a stroll.

Thursday 4 May

This morning: Aunt Mie walked around with us, then we drove to the Giardino Pubblico for lunch. Yesterday Kl. asked me for the picture with the bear, and today I gave it to him with just the word 'Genoa' on it. He was absolutely delighted and said:

> So you've bought two copies of yourself, one to take home, the other to leave behind, one for yourself and one for the whole world.
>
> Both for you, I replied.

And our eyes met in a sad, penetrating gaze.

p.m. we were at Dr Henneberg's for high tea. I didn't sit next to Kl. – neither then nor at dinner. Henneberg has two friends here, Herr Kuhn and Dr Posselt, who plonked themselves down next to me. Already at dinner, Kl. was muttering venomously, and later, on the way to St Mark's Square, he suddenly barred my way, seething with rage and trembling with agitation.

> I've brought you something nice – something very nice: there – take back your photograph . . .

At that moment Carl happened to arrive, and he had to put it away again. I clenched my teeth and nearly fainted. Everyone repaired to Café Florian, and Kl. started whispering:

Alma, what have I done? I'm so ashamed.

Softly I replied:

Give me back my picture.

I wouldn't dream of it, he said. You didn't take the blindest notice of me all afternoon. I can't bear it.

As we were leaving, I deliberately kept beside Carl. Kl. pursued me doggedly.

Let's make it up, Alma, let's make it up . . .

We arrived home. Carl came up to me and said:

I know everything now. I know about your relationship. I know how close you already are. Tomorrow I shall speak to him. I find it disgraceful. Alma, tomorrow we must talk, you and I.

I went to bed, I don't know how . . . lay all night open-eyed, thinking of nothing but that I should softly open the window and throw myself into the lagoon. Although I've contemplated suicide often enough in the past, compared with the mood I was in last night, it was a mere bagatelle. Everything was so far away: Vienna, my former life, Carl's words and this one, dreadfully brutal action. I was preoccupied by this one event, motivated as it had been by boundless love and boundless jealousy. And below, the incessant murmur of the grave, dark lagoon – so inviting for disconsolate lovers. And yet one clings to life! Had it happened that same night, I wouldn't have lived to see the following day. –

Friday 5 May

This morning Kl. came and, with raised hands, begged forgiveness. Carl drove with me to the station, alone, and what I had been dreading yesterday evening now followed: he asked whether I had a relationship with Kl. and what he'd said about the future. I remained silent, merely replying that I hoped for nothing.

Listen, Alma, if I were absolutely certain that you'd be happy with him, I'd give up my painting and take over the Miethke Gallery.[1]

---

1 Gallery Miethke in the Dorotheergasse. In a prolonged inter-Secessionist controversy between a Klimt group, which included Auchentaller, Bernatzik, Böhm, Kurzweil, Moll, Roller and Otto Wagner, and a group led by Josef Engelhart, the Miethke Gallery played an important role. Moll, who was its artistic adviser, attempted to establish a close collaboration with the Secession, but the Engelhart group, fearing a loss of commercial independence, was opposed to the idea. In 1905, finding themselves in a minority, Klimt and his associates resigned from the Secession.

Then, on condition that he freed himself from his sister-in-law, I'd be able to support you more generously. But even that I don't believe, because I believe brutality to be his second nature. And that, for you, with your sensitive disposition, would be most regrettable.

I had to agree with him. Yesterday evening I became aware of his tendency to brutality. For him the highest expression of affection is a firm pinch in the arm. I also think he'd be madly jealous. And that, for me, with my spirit of freedom . . . my will to freedom . . . ! Carl begged me to tell him how far our relationship had gone, and said:

I shall talk to him this afternoon. But if you don't tell me how things really are between you, I shall make an utter fool of myself.

Carl, I beg you, say nothing. I'll talk to him myself.

After a while, he said:

Very well, this afternoon you should tell him that the affair has got to end, that people are already beginning to talk – that's the truth – and that anyway it will lead nowhere.

I gave him my word, and the conversation was over. I could scarcely take in my surroundings. We met the others outside St Mark's.

You made a fine mess of things yesterday, I said to Kl. Carl was watching the whole business, but I didn't betray you.

For the rest, I took a fairly reserved attitude towards him. He came up to me and said:

Alma, don't be angry. I couldn't sleep all night. I felt as if I'd killed a little child. You had no choice in the matter. Won't you let me see you, talk to you any more?

p.m. we sailed around in the lagoon. The sky, reflecting my feelings, was grey and black. Kl. was sitting opposite me, his eyes begging forgiveness. I felt awful, everyone complained about my pallid complexion.

{in the margin:} a.m. to the Doge's palace. Made no particular impression. Much gold, little noblesse.

In the evening: concert on St Mark's Square. Before dinner, Kl. said:

I'm not allowed to sit next to you, but do look my way from time to time, won't you?

I did so. His eyes, those eyes, such an ocean of love. In the turmoil, amidst the throng, Kl. stole up to me unobserved.

Keep a place in your heart for me, Alma, just a tiny one.

I told him:

Klimt, it's got to stop. Everyone's talking about us, it's got to stop.

Yes, he said, it was stillborn.

Don't be jealous any longer, I said. You know how tremendously fond
I am of you. Even if I don't speak to you, you can trust me, for you
know that I love[2] *only* you.
He said:
   But not {just} for now, Alma. I want you to love me always.
   For ever, I replied.
We lost sight of each other in the crowd, but met up again near a pillar. I
said:
   And you, will you always cherish your love for me?
   Alma, he said, I've been struggling with myself for two years. I
   shouldn't, but I have no choice. Alma, dear Alma, would that I'd never
   set eyes on you . . .
I bade him farewell and said:
   Keep my photograph as a remembrance of me and the wonderful
   times we had together. Despite everything, I feel something almost like
   happiness: we love each other. Even if we can never be united, our
   souls meet in a kiss.

Saturday 6 May
Kl. is behaving very correctly, neither walking at my side nor sitting next to
me at table.
This morning we walked to the church of S. Giorgio, where there are
frescos by Carpaccio, and very beautiful ones too.
Kl. left at 2:00. Previously we had a lunch with Asti at the Cavaletto. He sat
far away, but time and again our eyes met. A heaven opened in our gaze.
Later, drinking a toast, Kl. and I locked arms. When everything had
quietened down, I said:
   Kl., we drank a toast of brotherhood. That may not be.
I held out my glass, and we toasted each other alone, gazing long and
intently into each other's eyes. Then he had to go and fetch his luggage.
Softly he said:
   Farewell, Alma . . .
We remained seated. Later everyone toasted me. Mama said:
   I wish something special for you.
Carl said to me, quietly:
   I drink a toast to your prudence, dear Alma.
He squeezed my hand hard and looked at me trustingly. Maybe it was all

2 A.S. had always used only milder forms of endearment, such as 'gern haben' and 'lieb
haben'. Here, for the first time, she expresses herself more directly, with 'lieben'.

the sympathy – I can't say for sure – but suddenly tears welled up in my eyes, and I had to fight them back.

Then we all went off to buy Kl. farewell presents. Nobody in the world is more spoilt than he, which partly explains his egoism. They gave him sweets, wine, flowers, sandwiches etc. Then the moment arrived for me to shake his hand, for him to look at me for the last time. I felt the ground trembling beneath my feet, the whole world darkening before my eyes. All of a sudden I could feel just what – whom – I had lost.

Beneath my window, while I write this down, soldiers are marching across the bridge – the band is playing. Up here death in the heart – down there life. Carl drank a toast to my common sense. If only he knew what a trial it is [has been] for me. Since the train left the station, everything for me has grown empty, pale and desolate. Everyone is being touchingly kind, they can sense my anguish.

p.m. on the lido. The sea is wide, but how small it seems compared with my suffering . . . And not being able to cry!!

Sunday 7 May

In the morning: to Chioggia by steamboat. A truly dear little place, in some respects more genuine than Venice. Brightly coloured sails, light reflected off the canals, girls wearing white veils, hustle and bustle.

Reininghaus told me a few things about his wife. I feel sorry for him. Why does a man who has everything – money, healthy children, joie de vivre – marry a woman who drives him crazy? Wherever you look: nothing but misery. And now I have my own cross to bear.

This evening: concert in St Mark's Square. People are so childish. They all have to push and shove, rush about and draw attention to themselves. I went with Dr Spitzer, and we both remained calm and collected.

Monday 8 May

Sun, why do you wake me? Why? That's how I felt yesterday, that's how I feel today, from now on that's how I shall always feel. The romance of my life is over, all spiritual energy is spent. That's just what the Empress meant: at some stage every one of us dies a secret death. Two days ago, at 2:00 p.m., I died secretly. A leave-taking from life and for life . . .

Aunt Mie said:

> It's strange: whenever Alma is with Klimt, she's always gloomy. As if his shadow had fallen on her and silenced her laughter.

She was right. – When I laughed with others, it annoyed him. And with him

I *couldn't* laugh – what grounds would there have been for merriment? When he was gone, my spirits soared. At least, I made them soar – and I know how to act. When Klimt was leaving Venice, I said I could no longer hold back my tears.

Just dissimulate, you know how.
But this time he was wrong.[3]

Tuesday 9 May
a.m. by gondola to the Riva. I was sitting in a gondola alone with Reininghaus. And he asked me indirectly whether . . . well, more or less, whether I'd wait for him. I gave no answer.
Left at 2:00 p.m. – travelled until 7:00 a.m.

Wednesday 10 May
Vienna. How sad I am to be here. The closer I am to him geographically, the greater the distance in my mind.
Letter and sheet-music from Oberstetter. On the latter he wrote, 'To my brilliant friend Alma – a souvenir of H.E. Oberstetter.' A most attractive ballad.
Saw Mahler.

Thursday 11 May
An episode just occurred to me that I haven't yet written down. In Verona I asked Kl. for his copy of 'Faust'. Mama was there. He fetched it. Suddenly he turned round, {took back the book} and removed something from it wrapped in paper. He said they were letters. He came back and returned the book to me. That evening, while I was reading, Mama came into the room:

Well, today you almost got to see the letters from his sister-in-law.
The following morning Kl. asked me:
Did anybody see what was inside my book?
I shuddered.

They were the lilies of the valley you gave me in Florence. I couldn't think of a better place to press them on the journey – than in 'Faust'.
I believed him, and still do. I didn't ask him about the letters and, considering the honesty of our relationship, he wouldn't have had to make excuses.

---

3 The entire passage from 'Aunt Mie said' to 'he was wrong ' is written in block capitals.
▶ Interspersed within the passage: twelve picture-postcards of Venice.

And anyway: he's far too awkward with words to think up so sophisticated a lie on the spur of the moment. Inwardly I rejoiced.

I'm only writing this down to prevent it being forgotten, and because the contrast between suspicion and truth was so striking, so pleasurable for me. One should always take note of the few pleasurable moments in life – there aren't many.

Friday 12 May

Today my pleasure is gone. Mama aggravated me so much that I had to cry. She won't let me go out on my own any more, for fear that Kl. might waylay me somewhere. So I'm deprived of my freedom as well. Poor Kl. has a vast amount on his hands just now, finishing off various commissions. Do they really think he'd loiter about in someone's front porch, like the gardener and the art mistress? You only need to know something of his character to realize that such behaviour goes against all his principles. It's more than I can stand. What misery![4]

Towards evening, Mayreder and Herr and Frau Prasch arrived. The conversation didn't interest me. I went into the garden. The moon was shining, hence it was sad. Standing on the terrace, suddenly I began to pray. I don't know to whom I prayed or for what. All I know is that I wrung my hands, wept and kept repeating the words, 'Father, I love you.' Never in my life have I prayed more fervently. I was so dreadfully sad. If only I had *someone* in whom I could confide. But I have no friends, neither male nor female. No friendship. And I do so long for love – for <u>unselfish</u> love.

Saturday 13 May

A storm is brewing – my limbs are heavy as lead, and disaster is looming. Such a wind outside my window. The crown of the walnut tree heaves to and fro – its branches softly creaking. The blades of grass on the lawn sway and scatter – as if moved by an invisible comb – the air carries the rushing sound to my ears, into my dear, pink room, to the confines of my chaste children's room. How often, fruitlessly, have I wished to escape it? Fruitlessly: for the time being, I shall not be getting married. It would be the most unscrupulous course of action imaginable. It would mean betraying the man to whom I gave my hand – betraying my heart, my entire person. For my person is no longer my own. And if another man really loved me, he wouldn't be able to bear the thought.

---

4 ► Letter from Labor, written with a special typewriter for the blind.

Frequently, in Florence or Genoa, Kl. would approach me. Without resisting, I'd let him come, as behoves a woman who can weep for sheer joy. Kl.
would ask:

Have you any regrets, Alma?

And always I would reply:

None. I am yours, therefore I have no rights over myself.

The phraseology may seem somewhat Jesuit in tone, but the idea made me
happy, it ennobled me.

Sunday 14 May

This evening: Fischel and Mayreder. Lili spoke of Kl. in reprehensible,
unprincipled terms. And I, when I think of him – I can find nothing to
reprehend.

How brilliantly observed is Gretchen. The song 'Meine Ruh ist hin': every
word is truth – every word awakes my sympathy.

Now it's over – all over.

Monday 15 May †

And now I know what life is. Now I know what it is to be betrayed.
Yesterday Carl spoke with Kl. In a cowardly manner he beat a retreat,
betrayed me, admitted that he'd acted without premeditation, proved
himself a weakling. Now I know what it is to be disconsolate. He's
betrayed me. I cannot write for tears. Mama spoke with me. Yesterday Kl.
went to see her and asked:

Are you very angry?

And Mama replied:

Yes, very angry.

As he was leaving, he begged Carl time and again:

Don't hold it against me, I beg you, don't hold it against me.

And that from a man who for me was the finest on earth. – God in heaven, I
betrayed my own family to avoid exposing him, and he – I simply cannot
grasp it. The first time I ever loved a man – must it be? He gave Carl his
word of honour to break off the relationship. Certainly he has no option.
When I saw him going into the studio with Carl, it was clear what was
going to happen. Why do I have to go through *all this*?

Carl came, kissed me and said:

Listen, Alma, does it really affect you so deeply? Wasn't it just a
diversion on your part, nothing more? Try to forget him. You can
still be happy.

I have only one thought: he abandoned me without a struggle, betrayed me.

Carl and Mama are both being very kind to me. Mama wept at the idea that I wouldn't trust her. And I – cannot speak. My heart, my whole heart belongs to him, that I cannot sacrifice. I can write no more and can at present not bear the company of others. I hate them.

I *simply* don't believe it! Klimt, Klimt, what have you done? You had no right, you had no reason. Did he confess to everything – even the two kisses in Genoa? Did he reveal my holiest secret? My love is gradually turning to hate. Why do I have to go through all this?

This morning: to the Prater with Hofrat Burckhard, where I met Kurzweil and his wife.

Yes, why all this? What does joy mean to me now?

Carl has just been to see me again. He wants to talk, to discuss everything in detail. And I simply *can't* speak to anyone. He said:

> Look me in the eyes, I know you can. You have nothing to reproach yourself for. I know everything. He told me everything. I would have preferred you to have told me, not him.

If only I could run away – far away. Not that I'd be ashamed, in heaven's name. And even if I weren't as innocent as I am, I wouldn't be ashamed, for I did everything for love's sake. But I'd like to run away, to banish all these false, evil people from my sight. I trust nobody. –

He betrayed me! He never truly loved me. That would be impossible! – Actually it was Lili who brought me to reason.

> What is life? she said. A comedy. And what lies behind it? Nothing.

Very well then, let me experience all the joy and suffering that a human being is capable of experiencing – and not shorten my life by a second.

Wednesday 17 May

I can compose no more, can no longer practise. The blood stagnates in my veins, my throbbing passion is spent, sensibility has given way to pathetic insipidity. Where then could melody be born? Can fire issue from a spent crater?

It's curious: on Sylt, immediately after the death of my dearly beloved father, I was almost mad with pain. Then, already during the funeral, came a phase – to my shame I have to admit it – in which I accepted everything calmly, composedly, even serenely. And now my thoughts are with him almost daily, hourly I wish him near me. I love him more than when he was alive and mourn him perhaps more than ever, or rather: only now do I mourn him really deeply. Indeed I often feel the maddest desire to speak, to lament, to seek comfort at his side – comfort which certainly would have been forthcoming.

And now: on Monday 15 May, the day I chose to mark with a big cross, & on Tuesday, I was almost mad with grief. But today everything has receded into the distance, as if it were a stranger's story, and I know that a time will come when I shall weep for him daily, hourly, a time when I shall come to realize the true measure of my loss. That will be in Goisern. For here, where everything is in constant flux, I can often forget my misery. But at night, in bed, I think things over – and pray – for him, for the man who for me was the finest in the world – and betrayed me.

That's the nature of – woman!

Thursday 18 May

While rummaging in old papers, Mama found a book of my old drawings and poems. Carl looked at it and realized that I have considerable talent for drawing. He even asked me to make him the odd drawing, but then I began to practise, and lost my temper.

Carl said he hadn't slept all night on my account – and yet I'm expected to put a brave face on things.

It was at the lido. Kl. and I were standing on the beach, down by the water's edge, watching the sea. Gretl joined us and – how the conversation arose I don't remember – Kl. said that Gretl could learn a thing or two from me, about music for instance. And softly he added:

  And kissing.

He said it in jest. But as he spoke he looked into the dim distance. And as I'd had enough of him for the time being, I went back to join the others. He followed soon after:

  Why so silent? Think of a melody, the one you invented in the train between Genoa and Verona.

  No, I said, I've written that melody off. I've dismissed it. And apart from that, you know very well why I'm so silent.

A little later we were standing together on the sea-front again, and he said:

  Genoa – that was lovely. Now it's past.

  Yes, I said, that was *our* best time.

  And now, Alma, do you really want to erase all memories of it? Do you want to deprive yourself of them? Although you knew exactly what I was going through – that I took everything at least as seriously as you. You could feel me trembling. You know me, you know I often make irresponsible remarks, and that afterwards I immediately regret them.

I know, I said.

And my thoughts turned to the day of our first kiss – to the atmosphere, which was anything but frivolous. We were engulfed in dark silence, and he kissed me with such force, with such a frisson. It was so sad, we were both close to tears. It was almost a kiss of benediction. A kiss with which he begged me never to love another man and with which I gave him my promise – plied my troth. And we rejoiced. The joy of the second kiss was greater: it was longer, and only then did I comprehend it. That kiss fulfilled a physical instinct. It had to happen. For both of us it was the most natural thing in the world. I felt that I had been born just to experience that moment. That moment, for which I had longed for two years, and for which I shall yearn for the rest of my life. God in heaven!

It was a spiritual union, we held each other, pressed each other. We *both* knew it was the last time, and once again we felt the sadness and gravity of the moment. Now I know what a kiss is: neither a diversion nor a trifle, but a union of the spirit and the lips. Once a man has kissed you, you are his for eternity.

Friday 19 May

This morning: Rosa. In Florence, Kl. told us he'd travelled with a lady who knew Carl, but was all but ignorant of the existence of Gretl and myself. Although he shrouded the whole affair in mystery, we didn't pay any further heed to it, for it appeared unremarkable, one of those pieces of odd gossip. Well . . . today Rosa arrived:

Are you angry with me?

But no, why should we be?

I shared a compartment with Klimt en route to Bologna.

Really? We had no idea.

Rosa answered:

I would have expected you to recognize me from his description of the journey to Bologna. My dears, that was a trip I shall never forget!

I shan't recount the exact story, except that to begin with Kl. fixed her with a stare, and that later he struck up a conversation. She was happy to have a living soul to talk to. And then there were a few little coincidences. They were talking about the Secession, and Rosa said that her favourite pictures were the ones by Klimt, whereupon he introduced himself. Then she said:

There's a family staying in Florence just now, a family Moll.

That's funny, he said. They're the very people I'm going to see.

Then came tunnels. Rosa was sitting far away from him and could feel him sidling gradually towards her. She did her best to move away. He was breathing heavily, his eyes aglow, red in the face. Never in her life had Rosa seen anyone in such a state. All she could think was – I must get out. And in Udine she did so.

It was pure lechery – lust for a stranger. And he couldn't even see her {face}, for she was heavily veiled. Animal lust for the next best woman. Well really! And that on the way to see me! Every woman, it appears, excites his appetite. No! Today I found him truly repulsive.

It was just as well that Rosa hadn't told him her name, and that she'd professed not to know us. For Mama would have heard that she'd been to Bologna to visit her lover and, considering her complete ignorance of the affair, would have censured her behaviour and perhaps even forbidden us any further contact. It's also just as well that Kl. didn't molest her. It gives me some idea of his appalling lechery. And that might heal my wounds. My God, if only it could.

As he was getting out, he said:

> You had no need to be afraid of me. After all, I'm a friend of Herr Moll!

He kept repeating those words, as if to win her confidence. But his eyes told another story, and Rosa was downright afraid.

What a world! Never again can I be happy.[5]

Saturday 20 May[6]

Recently Carl said:

> After all you've been through with Kl., you can't possibly be fond of him. I know you: you're proud. I'd be sorry if you disappointed me.

Carl, dear Carl, do you know what it means – to be in love? Do you really believe that I'd be capable of suddenly purging my heart of a friendship

---

5 On the same day, Klimt wrote Carl Moll a long letter in which he apologized for his conduct. Although A.S. was now almost of age, his letter reads as if Moll had accused him of child-molestation: 'Forgive me, dear Moll, if I have caused you grief. I beg your dear wife to be so kind as to forgive me. And Fräulein Alma, I'm sure, won't find it difficult to forget. Let's hope that time will heal the wounds . . . I really am dreadfully sorry about everything that has happened.' The complete text is published in *GoR*, pp. 473–476. In *AtB* A.M.-W. changes the year to 1897, i.e. three years *before* her coming-of-age. Her allegation that 'Klimt kept trying to approach me' (p. 17) is also inaccurate. It was she who later often considered returning to him, and he who took care to avoid any further direct contact (cf. Suite 16, 7 February 1900).
6 ▶ Small, underexposed photograph in a decorative frame, showing a group of seven people. To the right, in the back row (scarcely distinguishable): Klimt.

that endured for two years? You have no idea of women, nor of human nature – nor, above all, of love!

Today I started composing a Fantasia. As motto I chose:

> I was born to be lonely –
>
> and loneliness is my destiny,
>
> for I feed off my own thoughts . . .

It's Kl.'s motto – hence mine as well. It's not easy to translate the feelings these words arouse in me into music, indeed it's impossible. But I feel the urge to try – the urge!

Then I started on a cradle song to send to Mama in August. At the time of writing, however, I feel little inclination to finish it, for my thoughts turned to the idea that for us the little brat will signify – a loss. Well, perhaps I'd best abandon it.

Once, in Florence, we were all taking a nap, Kl. and Walter. My hair was dishevelled, and Mama said:

> See to it that you do your hair.

Kl. asked me if he could take out the hairpins. I said yes, and he started pulling them out, gently and carefully, one by one. Finally my hair was loose and fell over my shoulders like a cloak. Kl. moved back, as if in holy awe. Then he came closer, ran his hand caressingly over my head and stroked my hair with uttermost devotion, so gently, so softly, yet so firmly. Over my head and down through my hair, again and again – so sweet.

Later, that evening, he said:

> I would have loved to burrow my hands in your hair. I'm so fond of hair, and yours is soft and beautiful. But I didn't trust myself.
>
> Why not? I asked.

And his eyes implied that otherwise he would have lost control of himself and done something foolish.

This evening: rendezvous with Felix Fischer and his family. Olbrich was there too, and down there {in 'Venedig in Wien'} we met up with Hoffmann and Moser. First they performed an operetta, 'Der Leutnant zur See' – a tasteless farce and completely plagiarized.[7] For the most part, the costumes were poor, but there were eight pretty girls who were smartly dressed à la Moser. They wore freely flowing garments of pale green crêpe

---

7 'Venedig in Wien': an area in the Kaisergarten of the Prater (Vienna's largest amusement park), built in 1895 and decorated in Venetian style, with shops, restaurants, cafés, champagne-pavilions, wine-bars, beer-houses, a concert hall and diverse theatres. The famous big wheel, the only attraction to have survived, was added two years later. 'Der Leutnant zur See' was composed by Louis Roth.

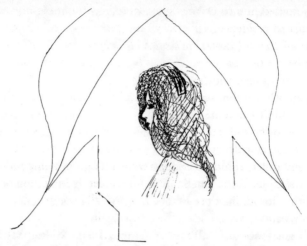

and to the left and the right, in their hair, large marguerites. Their tights were black, with pantaloons of green crêpe. The latter were on display most of the time. There were smutty jokes, but they were inoffensive.

Olbrich paid me a sort of homage. We were getting into the gondolas, and I was courteously invited to sit in the 'grandee' gondola. That did little to cheer me up. Olbrich noticed it and promptly came into our boat, although it was already full. With my eyes I expressed my thanks. He looked me straight in the eye and – I didn't avert my gaze. Well really, Alma, what a flirt! But today I liked him.

We took a ride on the big wheel, went twice down the water-chute, saw the Icarian games and watched La Tortajada dancing. I made sure to watch the latter with Moser, who's a specialist in such matters. Her dancing is madly passionate, her singing dreadfully vulgar. Felix stood us a round of champagne, and I drank three glasses straight off. I had quite a job pulling myself together. We rode in the gondola too, but nobody was really in the mood. At 1:30 – a.m. – Aunt Mie, Senta & Wally drove home. Olbrich, Hoffmann, Moser and Felix were with us, and we decided to visit a coffeehouse. At first Carl didn't agree, but we persuaded him and strolled, with me on Felix's arm, all the way from the Prater to Café Secession, where the interior decorations are by Auchentaller.[8]

I was walking with Olbrich. He's such a dear, sensible fellow. The Duke of

8 Joseph Maria Auchentaller was professor at the Academy in Munich from 1893 to 1895. He returned to Vienna, where he remained until 1901, before settling in Grado on the Gulf of Trieste. He was responsible for the design and presentation of numerous Secessionist exhibitions. For the 7th Exhibition (8 March–6 June 1900) he designed the poster.

Hessen has invited him to Darmstadt, where he's founding an artists' colony. As artist in residence, Olbrich would be given free accommodation and a salary of 6,000 Marks. He'd take Hoffmann and Moser with him – that would be a blow for the Secession! I did my best to dissuade him, but against my better judgement. And Olbrich said:

Look, an offer of that sort comes your way only once in a lifetime, so why shouldn't I take it? I'm young, love to read, to play the piano, I enjoy life to the full. Here I don't get a moment to myself. And in the long run interior decoration won't satisfy me. In Darmstadt I'd have peace and quiet, could do exactly what I like. I'm going up there in a few days' time. If the sun shines and I meet sympathetic people, I'll stay. If it rains and the people are cold, I shall take the next train back to Vienna and never mention the affair again.

I'd be really sorry about Olbrich. My reactions to him are really strange. First I disliked him, then I came to like him. Then he published his article in the 'Bauzeitung' and I detested him, and now I like him again. It'll be interesting to see when I change my mind again. The look in his eye is affectionate, candidly open.

Tuesday 23 May
a.m. with the Lanners to the Secession.[9] Kl.'s paintings are indisputably the finest on display. I spent a long time looking at them and thinking about his artistic standing. His 'Schubert' is wonderful, but in those surroundings I would have preferred to see Schumann. Schubert sits at the piano, surrounded by ultra-modern young ladies singing. The whole thing bathed in dim candle-light – hence in fact alien to Schubert's melody, which is so primary and healthy. It's Schumann's music that's the more sickly and ultra-romantic, hence also the more modern.

Wednesday 24 May
Once, in Venice, we were standing on a bridge, staring into the black canal (it was night-time), in front of us the magnificent arch of the Bridge of Sighs. We were leaning on the parapet, Kl. standing at my side, the others further off. Suddenly I could feel Kl.'s fingers pulling, tearing at my collar. As I was leaning on the stone, the neckline tightened. Before I could realize

9 The 4th Secessionist Exhibition ran a few days longer, i.e. until 31 May 1899. Klimt exhibited *Schubert at the piano* and *Nuda veritas*. Also on display were paintings by Moser and, for the first time, Ferdinand Andri, as well as gold mosaics by Olbrich and Alfred Roller's mosaic sketches for a recently completed church in Breitenfeld.

what he was about, everyone moved on, and we had to start walking too, but further behind. As was his wont, he pinched my arm, whispering:

Silly girl, Alma, I could have put my hand on your heart – easily.

A cold shiver went through me, my heart missed a beat. He wanted to feel my breasts! Or did he want to see how fast my heart was beating? The former would have been lechery, the other love – unfortunately I'm *sure* it was the former.

Towards evening I walked into town. It was raining hard. I walked boldly into a shop and said I wanted 'Faust', the Reclam edition. The salesman smiled at me and said:

Did madam venture out in such frightful weather?

I gave him a look he won't forget in a long time. Who on earth did he think I was?

Now I shall carry 'Faust' with me always. Kl. *always* has his copy with him. The more you read the book, the better you like it.

I must confess to one thing more, one final confession: whenever Kl. and I sat opposite each other in the buggy, we always moved our legs up close. A gentle pressure from time to time, we'd look at each other and enjoy at least a brief moment of happiness. We always tried to sit opposite each other. Once, in Padua, we did so, and Mama was sitting beside me. Had she noticed? I don't know – but suddenly she said:

Alma, move up closer to me, there's no room for Kl.

Both of us assumed an expression of utter innocence, but that was the end of it. It was the last time.

I loved him and strove to be utterly his. If at the time we'd had the chance, I would have given myself to him unreservedly. God had other plans for me. Today I'd no longer do it.

Thursday 25 May

Goisern

We left Vienna at 7:00 a.m. Ernst and Doctor P. were at the station. The day was quiet. Mama slept almost all the way {with her head} on my lap. I read 'Oedipus' by Sophocles, then 'Einquartierung' by Henrik Herz and 'Es war einmal' by Holger Drachmann. The latter appealed to me most. It's a folk-tale comedy with delightful, fine, robust humour. The poetry of 'Oedipus' leaves me unmoved. Of course it's magnificent, monumental, but it doesn't touch the heart. And as for the comedy 'Einquartierung', the less said the better. It's modest, quite amusing, but singularly uninteresting.

Friday 26 May

Have just finished Sudermann's 'Der Katzensteg' and am still under the spell of this wonderful book.[10] Rarely have I experienced such brilliant characterisation. There's a strange, wild passion in it. I like it more than I can say. If anybody wants to know me, let them read 'Der Katzensteg'. How I'd like to be as full-blooded as this Regine. Utterly and entirely human!

Priests – scum of the earth! Our landlady here has an eight-year-old son suffering from severe tuberculosis, in fact they've already given him up. Today the priest came round, and in plain words he told the little fellow:

> Listen, you're going to die, you have no further hope. Resign yourself to God's will and be comforted.

Since that time, the boy's been sitting in his room, crying, refusing all food, utterly disconsolate. What a cur of a priest! For the sheer pleasure of inflicting pain. If I knew him, I'd give him a dressing-down that he wouldn't forget in a hurry. Poor child! I don't care for children, but I'd never ever do a thing like that.

p.m. Mama, Gretl and I took the footpath to {St} Agatha. Mama got tired, and I said she should return home with Gretl while I walked on alone as far as the Hallstättersee.

> No, said Mama, I won't let you walk on your own.

That was more than I could take. Furious, with tears in my eyes, I turned back. The older I get, the less freedom I'm given.

> I can't bear it, I refuse to be held on a leash – etc.

Mama said there might be drunks on the road:

> I'd be too afraid for you.

Just leave me in peace! I'm twenty years old and know perfectly well how to look after myself. Or are you afraid I'd do away with myself? After all, you know me best. Even if you can't read this, I'm telling you straight out: if it came to that, I'd do it, even if a hundred men tried to stop me. Set your mind at rest – if ever I found myself at the edge of a sharp precipice and felt truly disconsolate, no God could stop me.

Saturday 27 May

I dream of him every night – and when I wake, I feel happy and doubly sad.

---

10 ▶ Four postcards of Traunkirchen and Bad Ischl. Hermann Sudermann, a leading exponent of poetic realism, was one of the most popular dramatists and novelists of his time. The title role in *Heimat* (1892, better known as *Magda*), was performed by Sarah Bernhardt, Mrs Patrick Campbell and Eleonore Duse. *Der Katzensteg*, his finest novel, was published in 1890.

This time I was at an exhibition again, and our meeting was unclouded joy and happiness.

I take my morning walks with 'Faust', just like Kl. And, curiously, I'm beginning to see things through his eyes. I have his eye for colour, and constantly perceive his shapes and forms – not the ones he's already created, but those he'd be capable of creating, his characteristics. I can perceive and combine just as he does, and my perception is finer, more felicitous than that of those who aren't inspired by him, who don't enter into his colourful fantasy world of dreamy-grey.

Fog becomes rosy, the snow glitters, every dewdrop is a pearl – yes everything flickers, glows, sparkles in the light. Who said that there can be no happiness? But where, how, what? No matter how often you ask, I have no answer. But this morning, I don't know why, I feel moved to happiness . . .

A little boy was standing on the road. A railway engine roared past close by, and he watched it pass. When it was out of sight, he hopped onto the railing and stared longingly into the distance. What was he longing for? A big city, riches or – in a nutshell – life? You *un*suspecting angel. –

Sunday 28 May

Today I finished reading Sudermann's 'Frau Sorge', a very fine, grey book. I don't entirely understand it, because the hero is such an incomprehensible character. I'm too much of an egoist for that, but it's beautiful – and very earnest.

I've just got home. I walked down the salt-water gallery[11] from Goisern. Alone – alone with 'Faust' and my misery. Maybe it's not good that I so often walk on my own, for I think only of him. I torment myself with futile questions, with cruel joy I torture my soul, standing and gazing up at the mountains. Now and then I take out my book and absorb myself in it. I have no other thoughts.

People who see me must think I'm mad. Once today, standing on a bridge, I suddenly realized that I was muttering to myself. I stopped at once – and had to smile.

Alone, just leave me alone! I feel happiest when I just stand on the banks of the Traun and stare at the white foam on the waves. Then I feel so utterly solitary. And in my solitude I feel blissful.

---

11 Orig.: 'Solenleitung': salt mined in the caves above Hallstatt was transported in liquid form along wooden channels to refineries in Goisern.

Tuesday 30 May

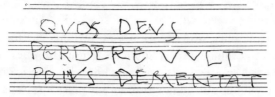

Kl. wrote these words[12] in the train between Genoa and Verona. An empty scrap of paper – but what memories hang on it. At the time, Mama and Carl had fallen asleep. I had manuscript paper on my lap and was composing. It was tremendously amusing.

Once, in Nervi, we went sailing, just with Kl. He was holding on to the sail behind my back. Involuntarily I leaned back, and suddenly I was lying in his arms . . . Gretl didn't even notice. She kept laughing incessantly, and the merrier she grew, the more firmly Kl. grasped my neck. It was an idyllic hour. Afterwards we had a tiff about some trifle. I was in the wrong, and for the rest of the day Kl. stayed with Mama & Carl. That was a sad ending. As a result I came to loathe that dump and even forgot our hour of bliss.

That evening Kl. came up to me and said:

    Well, did you have a good time this afternoon?

    Don't be angry, I said, I can't understand what made me say such horrid things. I regret it now.

And everything was in order again. So many hours of happiness are destroyed by waywardness – never to return.

Friday 2 June

Yesterday we brought a book and some toys from Ischl for our sick little boy. How gratefully the poor mite smiled. My heart bled at the sight.

Saturday 3 June

Worked hard at a composition. It's a song that I began yesterday and revised today. It's not exactly cheerful.

For me, the days are always too short, even though I'm already on my feet by 6:00 a.m. This morning I cycled to Goisern, from there to Steeg and

12 'Quos deus perdere vult, prius dementat' (Sophocles, *Antigone*, 620). Literal translation of the Greek original: 'To him whom the gods have ordained to suffer, evil seems good.' The Latin version, quoted by Klimt, differs slightly: 'When a god intends to destroy someone, first he corrupts their mind.'

then home. But the days are running away with me. If only I could maintain this steady pace. Who knows what conflicts, what experiences lie ahead of me?

Now I'm content. I live with my memories. For myself I have no further hopes. I wish for nothing – except Bayreuth. The account is closed – a little too early and too abruptly. But then, I was born on a Sunday. Who knows, perhaps one day I'll be able to laugh about my present state.

Suite 12

Sunday 4 June
Yesterday evening at 8:00 *Johann Strauss* died. In my opinion an absolute classic and the greatest musical genius to have lived. I genuinely mourn him. Such effervescence, such grace and elegance – words cannot define the essence of his waltzes. For me he stands beside Schubert and Brahms, he *was* a classic.
a.m. completed a song: 'Hinaus'.
p.m. cycled to Steeg. A farm-worker, who didn't know that you should give way to the left, rode straight into me. We both came crashing to the ground. Nothing happened to him, and I survived with a few grazes. I started cursing and swearing, and the poor fellow kept repeating:
     I beg yer pardon, lady.
In the evening I was feeling cheerful, so I played one waltz after another.

Monday 5 June
Last night I dreamt that Gretl and I had gone to London on our own, and everything was so unbelievably clear that I thought: this is exactly what London must look like.
Currently I'm playing 'Parsifal' and studying it very carefully – I wouldn't want to miss any of its beauties. It's heavenly.
Composing hard again, this time a song in slow tempo and strict form. It should be finished by tomorrow.

Tuesday 6 June[1]
Mama and I have just returned from St Agatha. On the way she had much to say about Kl. – but only vile things. I could weep.
     Alma, he never really loved you – never.
A few days after the row in Vienna, he wrote Mama a letter. The poor devil reproached himself for everything, but what did he do wrong? Is it his fault that I love him more than anyone in the world? He was weak *too*, that was

1 ▶ Letter from Else Lanner, and dried flowers.

his only mistake. But surely I was the weaker by far, and it's I who deserve the sounder thrashing, for he never duped me, never left me in any doubt that he couldn't marry me.

Why then did he go so far? We both knew that such an opportunity would never arise again, both knew we'd never belong together. The tacit agreement was: live for the moment. He was in love with me, after all, and missed no chance to prove the point. For me it was the same: I was aware that time passes, and knew I'd never love anyone more than him. The moment was opportune, I wanted to love him, wanted him to return my love and to feel it . . . And I felt it all right! Wonderful memories, to cherish for the rest of my life.

I loved him from the day I first set eyes on him. If all this had never happened, I'd still be longing for him. But now I'm calm and composed. I long for him no more, for I know I'd reached the peak, a point beyond which I would never have been able to go. [He was *very* ill and would never have been able to marry me!]

What, then, did he do wrong? He restored my sense of repose.

Mama added that in his family insanity is the rule: his mother was mad, his sister too – and one day he'll go mad himself.

Just look into his eyes, Alma, there's something crazy about them.

I must admit that she's not entirely wrong. And he himself told me he was convinced that he'd go mad.

At dinner: Mama gave me a compassionate look – suddenly I burst into tears. There's nothing more frightful than pity.

Although I'm unhappy and always shall be, I don't ask *compassion* of anyone.

Wednesday 7 June

A letter from Rosa, telling me that her father won't allow her to visit us because our cookery isn't kosher. Today I wrote in reply – a letter which I intend her father to read. I made several pointed remarks about Judaism, about her father's fanatical standpoint and how it incurs anti-Semitic sentiment, about intolerance and other such things. It will, I hope, make its effect.

A letter from Lili, in which she argues that in human beings animal qualities keep rising to the surface. She seems to have drawn her conclusion from the case of Rosa, who married young. After all, it's pretty unfair to say such things about a sixteen-year-old girl – particularly if they're only based on a single experience.

Friday 9 June[2]

Since yesterday evening I've been wondering: what if I were at death's door and were to write to Kl.? I don't know why, but I can't take my mind off the idea. If for a moment I stop talking, my thoughts promptly turn to that letter. It would start like this:

> Klimt,
>
> You are unworthy of me! Before I die, I want to tell you so openly and honestly. I am just as much an artist as you are, I have no need to look up to you as if to a god. And I have the great advantage of having truly loved you, while you merely played with me. I know perfectly well that there was a time when I appealed to you. But the fact that you fell back into the arms of your sister-in-law proves you weren't serious about me for a moment. And already on the way to Florence you had the nerve to accost a young lady, who felt so intimidated that she got off the train at Udine. That alone serves as proof that for you the whole thing was just a joke.
>
> I was foolish enough to believe it to be more than a joke, and for that I have been amply punished.
>
> In reward for my boundless affection, you surrendered without a struggle, betrayed me. All I can bequeath to you now are beautiful memories, for which you have me to thank, and my diaries. Read them, and you will know me better.
>
> Farewell – farewell for eternity!
>
> Yours, yours, yours
Alma

If I were dying *now*, that's roughly what I'd write. For the future, namely, I can guarantee nothing. –

Is my love genuine? Let me cast it out. It's nothing but unnecessary ballast, time-consuming and nerve-racking. It's time to put paid to such folly. I've already suffered enough on that account. I have no desire to go on with it. Take courage, Alma. You must find the energy, self-confidence and pride to tell yourself: 'I shall wash this fatal passion out of my hair, shall forget the most wonderful hours of my life or simply look back on them as something experienced by strangers.' I want to forget *everything* – and prove that I can survive perfectly well without him. Yes, I shall do my best to find someone I really like, and who likes me. I want to marry, and my spouse's happiness shall prove that I'm perfectly capable of exuding goodwill and

---

2 ▶ Two postcards from Goisern.

cheer. I was born on a Sunday: I can do it if I wish. Good luck doesn't just
fly in through the window.[3] It has to be won and deserved.
All hail to me!

Sunday 11 June

Recently Mama and I were in Gosaumühle. At the table next to ours sat
an actor from Ischl with six actresses and the director, Miss Wild. Their
conversation – I never heard anything of the kind. They talked, ridiculed
everything with such cynicism and at the same time such naivety. I was
shaken rigid. One of the actresses had lost her husband a few months
before. She kept talking of her 'dear departed husband' and laughing – so
loud that Miss Wild kept putting her finger to her painted lips to calm her
down. It must be impossible to grow up in such surroundings and remain
good and honest. One of them said:

> My doctor told me I shouldn't ride a bicycle, but even in Vienna I
> rode on the hard pavements. Admittedly I was standing up over the
> saddle . . .
> Well, said the actor – putting on a woman's voice – my doctor didn't
> tell me not to ride my bicycle . . . except when I . . .

And he looked bashfully under the table. To make matters worse, they all
broke into loud, uninhibited laughter. I was really annoyed at myself for
getting the joke: I blushed and looked away. They noticed it and could
scarcely conceal their mirth.

Rosa wrote to say that her father was staggered by my letter – nobody had
ever told him anything of the kind – and he only hoped he could talk to me,
so as to prove I was being unjust. I shall ask Rosa to bring my letter with
her, then copy it or paste it in.

Monday 12 June

A letter from Bertha, a card from the four Perglers and one from – Paul
Schulz, 'a souvenir of unforgettable days in Rome'. Unforgettable, huh!
That they were, but the good man contributed precious little towards
them. I shan't answer – there's no point.
p.m. Ernst and Hanna.
This evening: Meistersinger!
At present I'm dismembering Mozart's first sonata in F major – like a
chicken. Am taking the greatest pains, and want to compose something
along the same lines. It'll be tricky, but should do me good. The third song

3 Orig.: 'Das Glück fliegt einem auch nicht wie ein gebratenes Hendel in den Mund' – luck
doesn't fly into your mouth like a roast chicken.

that I began here, 'Nixe', still awaits elaboration. It's a curse: time is just running away with me.

Wednesday 14 June

I've just finished reading a book by Sudermann, 'Geschwister'. It consists of two short stories, both very vividly coloured, of which I was particularly taken by the second, 'Der Wunsch'. It's about two sisters who both love the same man. *He* returns the love of the one and marries her. But Olga, the younger sister, has the stronger personality. His wife doesn't come up to his expectations. Martha, who had always been delicate and sickly, dies in childbed. During her illness Olga cares for her, and for a moment the thought crosses her mind: 'I hope she dies.' On this wish, this dreadful callous wish, her happiness founders. Already during the year of mourning he begins to love *her*, and later he asks for her hand. She rejects him, but the lie nearly kills her. A week later, nevertheless, she's lying in his arms & the following night she poisons herself. In penance. The writing is magnificently tense. The book is still whirling around in my head.

Rain is falling, it's foggy and grey.

Thursday 15 June

It's raining . . .

One evening Mama Moll was walking with us along the Kaltenbachstrasse in Ischl. We came to a magnificent house situated in a beautiful garden. The terrace extended down to the street, so that you could see clearly into the middle room. It was brightly lit, and to one side sat a good-looking old lady with snow-white hair, visible to us in profile. Dressed all in black, tall, and still able to sit upright, she was improvising at the piano. We watched for a long time. All the while she gazed at the ceiling, smiling sadly. 'What can she be thinking and playing?' I asked myself. The melody appeared to flow calmly but sadly – we couldn't hear it. What was she lamenting? What did she still desire of life?

I know very well that when I improvise all sorts of things go through my mind. The music comes out according to my mood. I think of the past and simultaneously make wishes for the future.

How lovely it would be if an old person were to compose the story of their life: the innocence of childhood, first love, passion, the joy of mother- or fatherhood, stories of children, softly echoing their own youth, the approach of old age, purification of the spirit, calm, sublime contentment – the whole interwoven with the fight for existence, which towards the close would slowly fade. It would be lovely, even lovelier and psychologically more interesting than an honestly kept diary.

I wonder what that old lady was thinking? Perhaps she was recalling her dreams of youth and how they'd been fulfilled. Who knows? It was so strange. –

This morning I walked along the salt-water gallery to Goisern. It was wonderful, uniquely beautiful. I was alone with my 'Faust'. Often I hesitated – and was genuinely stunned by the beauties of Nature. Man is not worthy of appreciating Nature, which explains why only few people are capable of doing so.

Monday 19 June

Wrote the fair copy of my first piece – the dickens of a job. Then wrote to Lili. I explained to her something of the nature of love – based on my experiences. I told her I could only ever marry a man if I felt a primeval urge to kiss him, if – when I longed for him – I felt the primeval urge to be his. But I didn't mention the most important point, namely that you can only feel that way once in a lifetime – and that in my case it was all over. Dear Lili, you're so young! You know so little of love – so fortunate.

p.m. Mama and Gretl drove to Ischl, and Ernst, Christine, Gustav and I cycled for two hours to meet them on their way back. I wasn't feeling very well, and my throat was inflamed from the ear down to the chin, but I went with them all the same. The outward journey went absolutely smoothly. Ernst fooled around a good deal and tried to persuade me to follow suit – but he doesn't know me. Once he fell off, but fortunately he landed softly, and everything went without a hitch. Having met up with Mama in the forest of Lauffen, we turned around. Ernst performed a few stunts, for which he deserved a good hiding. He may be thirty-three, but at heart he's still a little scoundrel and will never change.

We took high tea in Lauffen, then remounted, allowing the buggy a good head-start. Ernst cycled off in pursuit, tearing along like a madman. Christine, Gustav and I followed at a more sedate pace. We soon caught up with the others: Mama's buggy had come to a halt, and Ernst was leaning on a railing at the road's edge, his knee bleeding. In front of him lay his bicycle, wrecked beyond repair. There's a sharp curve, and a fiacre had been approaching at full gallop. Ernst, who was riding directly behind Mama's buggy, probably tried to ride between the two vehicles. He won't admit it, but there's no other explanation: if he'd stayed behind Mama's buggy, it would have shielded him. To cut a long story short, the horses ran into the bicycle, Ernst pushed the latter away with his foot and grabbed one of the horses around the neck. After a few paces, he lost his grip and fell to the ground, rolled over three or four times and lay there in a heap, severely dazed. It was a miracle he didn't end up under the fiacre, as his bicycle had. Then he got up, still groggy, and steadied himself on the railing. Meanwhile Mama had got out of the buggy and was terribly agitated – in her condition a dangerous thing. That was the first thing to enter Ernst's head.

Anna, don't worry . . . everything's going to be all right.
His first thought had been neither of his injury nor his bicycle but for Mama. With this small gesture and those few words he proved himself by far the finest of our honourable friends. We were genuinely impressed. He may have cheated at school, may seduce other women and betray Hanna, but those few words made up for everything.

How did Hanna react to the news? Christine and I rode in front of the buggy. Gustav and the wrecked bicycle, in the buggy, caused quite a stir, as everyone thought it was he who'd had the accident. And there he sat, in his blue shirt, with Mama and Gretl, looking truly crestfallen and bemused.

We arrived at the Pitz villa and old Frau Dahner came to meet us. We told her the whole story, describing in the darkest shades of black the perils that Ernst had been through. Then we called Hanna. But although she was aware that something had happened to Ernst, she'd gone to her room to change her skirt. A little later Ernst himself arrived, suffering from shock and exhaustion. He called for Hanna. Several minutes passed. At last she appeared:

I – had – to – put – a – hat – on – first, she said slowly, just like that.
Then she went over to the bicycle.

For heaven's sake, just look at the bicycle! she moaned.
Ernst was standing beside it, pale, his knee still bleeding. She didn't take the slightest notice of him – the bicycle had cost so much money . . . We were shocked to the core, and Mama shouted angrily:

Never mind about the bicycle. You should thank your lucky stars that Ernst is all right. He could have been killed.
She looked at him, then at his knee, and burst into lamentation. But it cut no ice with us. Hastily we got ready to drive home: in our eyes, this touching family scene had turned rather grotesque. Now I can also understand why she doesn't come up to Ernst's expectations. He's warm-hearted and young – very young, perhaps too young. Hanna is older, and fish-blood courses in her veins.

Which reminds me of Gretl. Sadly, she's just the same, moreover she lacks rhythm. When we play duets, I get furious, and in real life it's the same thing that irritates me: her lack of rhythm. Rhythm is not only the soul of music, it's also the key to a person's heart. Whether passionate or melancholy, every temperament has its individual rhythm. But what about Gretl, who has no temperament whatsoever?

Tuesday 20 June
This morning Carl arrived with Legler. Now I know that Gretl is in love with him. That alone would be something, but *how* does she love him? Their conversation is utterly inane and they never communicate with their eyes.
Kl. always used to say of me: 'She laughs too much and cries too little – that's not love.' But what would he have said of Gretl, who neither laughs nor cries, but with her brown eyes just gazes indifferently at the surround-ings, smiling and frowning by turn? I always used to say to myself: she has a secret that she's hiding from me, I shall take her into my confidence. But now I know that she never had a secret! She's quite fond of him, would take him just as he is – and will too. But she'll never show affection for him, because she'll {never} overcome her inhibitions. Alas, dear Gretl, you have no idea of the measure of fortune – and misfortune – there is on this earth. Now I'm certain I'd never take her into my confidence, because she'd never understand me. I wonder: will she ever make anything of her art?
Today I feel terrible. My stomach is aching badly, my cheek is badly swol-len and, to make matters worse, I'm dreadfully depressed.

Tuesday 27 June
Carl and Legler left yesterday evening.
It's raining today. Lunch at Christine's.
p.m. to Ernst's. Gustav was great fun, Hanna deathly boring. Once again it became clear that it's the lady of the house who sets the tone and puts her guests at ease. Christine is kind-hearted, an excellent housewife, and in her home you always feel comfortable. Gustav is fun, but nothing com-pared with the exuberance of Ernst, for instance when he calls on us. But within his own four walls it's as if he'd been struck dumb. Hanna's stupid-ity and slow-wittedness weigh on everyone like lead. It was a relief to get away.
Ernst saw us home. On the way, I walked on ahead with him, and we

talked about art, starting with Klimt and later touching on most modern painters and architects. We spoke mostly of Klimt, because for Ernst he's the hardest to understand and for me – the easiest. We tried to reach a consensus. Ernst has only a smattering of education, and his conversation is larded with platitudes, but I'm fond of him and, if it doesn't last too long, I enjoy chatting with him too.

Today, once again, I composed a good deal.

This evening I started reading Zola's 'Rome'. I find it uncommonly interesting, particularly the descriptions of streets and palazzos. I can almost see them, and half-forgotten memories well up in my mind.

Don't feel at all well today.

Tuesday 27 June

The first movement of my sonata is almost finished. The task gave me the greatest satisfaction, but was also hellishly difficult.

the first subject

There are three main subjects and two or three subsidiary ones. The first subject leads naturally to a countersubject, which usually opens in the dominant.

It's raining, raining, raining!

Friday 30 June

It's morning, and I feel sad, very sad. I'm thinking about what I've lost – happiness that will never return. My happiness? |My Klimt.| Where have my thoughts led me?

Give me peace – oblivion!

It was a beautiful day. This evening everyone came round for dinner. It was terrific. We distributed the parts and read 'Götz von Berlichingen'. I've rarely laughed so hard. If Goethe had seen our distinguished circle, how we disparaged his 'Götz' and laughed at the sublimest passages – and I joined in . . .

Once again Ernst was awful. He does his utmost to make physical contact with me. I find his lechery repulsive. I made it clear to him and told him so in no uncertain terms.

Tuesday 4 July
This morning: Ernst. I played 'Tristan'. It aroused his passion, so much
so that he took a chair and threw it at the lampstand. Yesterday I was
playing the piano, and Rosa all but burst into tears. It's not the first time
that my playing has moved someone to tears, and it won't be the last
time either. Those tears reflect my anguish, deflected towards others by
the lightning conductor of my playing, so that I myself feel them less
intensely.

Wednesday 5 July
Rain!
p.m. long walk to Ischl. Halfway there, I refused to go on, for the path
was muddy and unpleasant to walk on. Ernst was furious, Aunt Dahner
sympathized with us, and Rosa went along too. I was wearing low shoes –
confounded recklessness on my part – and the water was running right
through them.
So the three of us turned back. We had a really great time. Of course we
chatted away about Italy and, after high tea in Lauffen, we walked home at
a leisurely pace. The others got back late in the evening, soaked to the skin.
I think we got the better part of the bargain.
Ernst brought me Pushkin's 'Onegin' and a bottle of perfume. He's a good
chap: he'd lost his temper with me but brought the things all the same.
In the evening he stayed with us till late, then walked home across the
meadow, which was shrouded in fairy-like mists. Will-o'-the-wisps lit his
path. –

Thursday 6 July
To the village, later in the day, with Ernst. On the way we argued about
the highest ideal of beauty. I supported the theory – which I have from
Kl., who convinced me of it – that a handsome man is more pleasing to
the eye than a beautiful woman. Ernst disagreed, and I tried to convince
him. The question can *only* be resolved in Rome, where you see all those
exquisite marble figures, the Capitoline Venus and many, many others –
then the Apollo of Belvedere, Hermes and the knife-sharpener. Only then
can you see how much more beautiful and noble the male physique is: the
exquisite proportions, the smooth line of the hips. You can see hips and
breasts – unattractive protuberances as a rule – and discover that if
they're smoothly curved and well-proportioned, they really can be beautiful, even if in real life they don't look that well. Why should women be

more beautiful than men? After all, that's *never* the case with animals: whatever species you examine, the males are decked out with more finery – hair, feathers etc. – than the females. With humans, it's the beard that makes all the difference. Female physique is softer, sleeker, more cat-like, but the male is more muscular, nobler, more imposing, altogether more godlike.

Why is our judgement so strongly biased towards women? Because one sex is so strongly attracted to the other, and it's the men who cast judgement. One thing is clear: female perfection is beautiful, but male perfection is even more beautiful. And what is beauty? A person is beautiful if every part of their body perfectly performs the functions for which it was intended. Certainly, if a person is entirely healthy, if their hair, skin, eyes, ears and everything else are completely healthy, then they are beautiful. Beauty is a pretty vague concept. I wouldn't know how else to discuss it.

Returning to the subject: after a woman has given birth, her beauty fades. After the first child, her skin loses its smoothness, her figure its perfection. A man's life remains uninfluenced by such events. He ages slowly, and his body shrivels up, but so elemental an experience – one that wrenches every muscle out of position, can turn a woman grey in nine days, shake her to the core – such a thing he never experiences. Do men have even the slightest notion of pain and suffering? Women already grow accustomed to physical pain during their childhood.

Friday 7 July
High tea at Ernst's. It was quite amusing. Yesterday, particularly!
On 23 June the whole clan was in Hallstatt. I stayed home as I had ear-ache and stomach pains. When they returned, they told me that Mahler was there too, indeed that they had spoken to him. They recounted even the tiniest details.
And then, the day before yesterday, this postcard arrived . . .[4]
One further thing: they told me they'd sent me a postcard and that Mahler had signed it. Gustav {Geiringer} allegedly gave it to the waiter, but the card never arrived. So the day before yesterday Gustav told me the whole story: not a living soul had ever set eyes on Mahler, the whole thing was pure fabrication, a pack of lies. At my cost the story had kept them *heartily* amused for two whole weeks. Anton Geiringer arrived here a few days

---

4 ▷ Humorous postcard from Mahler (reproduced in *GoR*, p. 49).

ago. On the way, in Ischl, he met Dr Boyer, who was on the point of driving to Aussee to see Mahler. They let him into their little secret, and he passed it on to Mahler, who, just for fun, really did write to me. The whole thing was arranged very cleverly, and I'm delighted about the postcard. All the same, this little prank showed me just how frequently and adroitly people lie.

Saturday 8 July
Today: letter from Carl. Olbrich has definitively accepted Darmstadt. That's a blow for the Secession. What if Moser and Hoffmann go too? If our youngest and most talented artists are invited to Germany, who will remain? The Germans are crafty: if they attract people from all over the world, give them titles and distinctions, pay them lavish subsidies – then Germany will become great and powerful, and unity will win through. And the Austrians? Instead of urging the ministries to use every means at their disposal to keep them here, they let their best people go without a murmur. You wretched bureaucrats, pack of uninterested sluggards, have you no eyes to see or ears to hear? Don't you see how Germany is flourishing? Don't you know what a tragedy it would be for Vienna to lose its young artists? Don't you realize that Austria is paralysed by red tape, by legal restrictions? Our country is being devoured by wolves, while our odious neighbours, the Germans, are flourishing!
They're paying Olbrich {a salary of} 1,000 Marks – just for going there to work – and here they scorn him. I can scarcely say how I feel for him – both as man and artist. It's a crying shame!
Composed today, started new piano pieces. Would like to make a group of four or five depicting my experiences in Italy. I'll give it the title 'Italy' and want to work in an Italian popular song. Italy – just original popular songs and sentimental ballads. I'd want the popular song treated not seriously but ironically. I'd also like to harmonize it cleanly, absolutely smoothly, as an expression of classical antiquity. Then, later, modern Italian art: frolicking, dashing, rousing, passionate, but without reason, without depth – trite and smooth like the Italians themselves. And dirty!

Tuesday 11 July
Started a new piece.
p.m. to Gosaumühle with Hanna, Christine, Gustav and Ernst. Actually we all planned to go to Traunkirchen, but Hanna had visitors, and the

weather was changeable. That's why we only drove off towards evening. As we intended to drive only as far as Steeg, I didn't take a jacket. We took high tea in Gosaumühle, and I was sitting bathed in sweat, without any covering. I was afraid that the longer I stayed, the greater was my risk of falling ill. So I asked them to let me drive home. Alone. They all protested:

No, Alma, stay here. We'll fetch you a shawl, and everything will be all right.

By the time the shawl arrived, it was too late. I broke into shivers and felt a stabbing pain in my back and shoulders. Hanna wanted to stay put, but Christine, Gustav and I drove on to Hallstatt. All I was concerned about was getting warm again.

We were just leaving Gosaumühle, when Mahler rode towards us on his bicycle, behind him an old woman, followed by his sister and Rosé. I cycled past quick as a flash. The Geiringers dismounted, the others too. Mahler asked if this was the road to Hallstatt. Christine said it wasn't, and offered to show him the way. By this time I was riding more slowly. They caught up with me and said:

Mahler is following us.

He soon overtook us, and we met some four or five times. Each time, he struck up a conversation. Shortly before Hallstatt he dismounted. We were pushing our bikes, and he started up another conversation, staring hard at me. I jumped onto my bike and rode off into the distance. The Geiringers were angry: they'd wanted to introduce me, and he was expecting it too. Judging by the way he looked at me, he appears to have perceived the connection between myself and the postcard – which I found most embarrassing. Anyway I feel absolutely no urge to meet him. I love and honour him an artist, but as a man he doesn't interest me at all. I wouldn't want to lose my illusions either.

We picked up Hanna and Ernst in Gosaumühle, and rode home. Hanna was dismounting on every incline, and Ernst got so angry, so irritable, that when he joined us, you could actually see his pulses throbbing.

In Mama's room he almost cried, he was so angry. They joined us for dinner. I felt sorry for Ernst. He's so agile, energetic and young. She's so immobile, tedious and old. He told her as much too.

Friday 14 July
On Tuesday I received a telegram from Hofrat Burckhard announcing himself for the coming days. We're still waiting ... If he comes, I'll be delighted.

Monday 17 July
This morning: at Ernst's. Then with Burckhard: twice to St Agatha and back.

On our walk, Burckhard went on ahead with us two, and we talked all the way about Goethe. A serious discussion with a man of such intellect is for me one of the real pleasures of life. We spoke above all about 'Faust', and he explained several things in Part II. The symbolism of Euphorion, for instance – antiquity and the Middle Ages give birth to the Renaissance. Or the designation of the 'Mothers' and much, much else I hadn't thought about. B. isn't particularly fond of Goethe's prose, which he finds dated, over-cultivated and effusive. But the ballads are simply magnificent: 'Der Gott und die Bayadere', 'Die Braut von Corinth', 'Der Fischer' – all the more pity that {the latter} is so weighed down with symbolism. Isn't everything self-evident, explained by its own virtues, by Nature? Some strange and mysterious instinct draws him downwards. Is there any need for symbolism?

Which reminds me of Fernand Khnopff. At the time, we were walking in the Prater, and he told me:

> It's strange. When I put something incomprehensible into a picture, it's usually because the form and colour interest me and because it just happens to fit in. Then my friends come along: 'What is that supposed to mean?' And they rack their brains for an interpretation, finding so many ingenious explanations that I feel quite proud of all the unarticulated ideas concealed in my pictures.

Symbolism!?

Tuesday 18 July
p.m. cycled to Hallstatt with Burckhard. Mama and Gretl in the buggy. On the way we scarcely spoke. When we arrived, B. mixed a punch-bowl of peaches, a bottle of vintage wine and two bottles of Heidsieck Monopole. We drained it to the last drop and became frightfully merry. Before Mama and Gretl arrived, B. and I visited the museum. There isn't much to see, and after the punch we were all teetering around, noticeably tipsy. The son of Jäger (the singer) is staying there again – one of the handsomest men I know.

We flew back home. When you've had a drop or two, there's nothing better than a cycle ride. At the same time, we conversed very seriously about Wagner's writings, Hanslick and Mahler. As we were passing Heuberger's house, he remarked:

Let me tell you a secret: Heuberger wants me to write a text for an operetta. But I'm simply too lazy, and haven't got anywhere with it. I do have an idea, which has a certain similarity to 'Faust' but tends the opposite way. The prologue would play in hell, where the devils hold a meeting, recount their triumphs and spur each other on to new conquests. They emerge from the underworld to prey on lawyers, barristers etc., whom they encourage to evil deeds. But in the end they're forced to admit that they themselves have been duped, for humans are even more perfidious than devils. It's a good subject for an operetta.

Suddenly Burckhard said:

Would you like to compose the music? It would encourage me to work at it.

I was overjoyed, for I feel *certain* that it would go well! At any rate, it was his way of expressing confidence in me. Unfortunately I feel little urge to write an operetta, I strive only for opera. To write an opera and experience its successful first performance – that would be utter bliss. I long for fame and success.

Nature! Heart! Life!

God!

The one and only!!!

Suite 13

Off to Bayreuth! Off – in quest of happiness!
Alma!

Tuesday 18 July
Yesterday Mama received a letter from Carl, asking her to let us go to Bayreuth. My joy knows no bounds. Each of us will get 100 fl, and we have an absolutely free hand to do as we like with it.

Thursday 20 July
7:00: Aunt Alma, Gretl and I took the buggy to Hallstatt. It was magically beautiful – fresh morning air over the mountains and the lake, in tones of grey which all but merged. We caught up on enough gossip for a year. Nobody was overlooked – except Kl. Poor Auntie was quite exhausted.
11:41: Mama, my poor, dear Mama, left for Vienna. I was terribly loath to see her go. Who knows if I'll ever see her again?
One thing offended me deeply: it was a farewell for life and death, but Mama just went on chatting with Mama Moll and the others. Leaving at such a worrying time, we should mean more to her than all the others together. I told her so too.
With tears in my eyes, I cycled through the village, Christine and Gustav right behind me. The latter invited me over and spoke very kindly to me. Dear God, he has no idea what a state I'm in!
We no longer have a home we can call our own!
If all goes well, the child will deprive us of our mother's affection – as is already partly the case. If anything goes wrong, the outcome will be disastrous. Wherever I look, there's no hope of rescue – except marriage. Must I marry – Krasny, perhaps, or Schulz or . . . ? I simply don't know who else. Considering that I love just *one* man and shall love him for eternity. All the others – ugh, they fill me with horror.
Then a third snag: who or what can lead me out of this labyrinth? Only death! That would be the salvation for us all. But how? Time will tell!
p.m. cycled to Hallstatt.
I've just got home. We had dinner in the Ramsau, and walked home by moonlight – full *moon*. Having drunk a good deal of beer, I was initially in very high spirits. But then I saw the sad, white face of the moon and calmed

down immediately. By the Traun it was so beautiful, I was rooted to the spot. The water glittered and glimmered, alluring and coaxing, as it flowed playfully down the weir. I longed for one thing: to jump in, never to re-emerge.

Versinken, ertrinken,

Unbewusst, höchste Lust.[1]

When I got home, I made myself comfortable in an armchair on the ver-anda, and sadly, wearily contemplated the horizon: the mountains vague in a silver haze, the skyline undefined. Only close by – leaves bobbling and shimmering in the light. On every smooth surface the moon made its presence felt – as a silvery line.

Dear God – if only I had someone to talk to, someone to embrace me, a heart to love me, a soul to understand me. Never! I see something of my future, and can sense the present: nobody will ever really know me.

Friday 21 July

Beauty? Firstly, Nature. Then mankind, though related. Finally, the works of man. Earth, digested by the worm, returns as earth in new guise. The art of mankind is Nature: mankind consumes it, digests it and regenerates it in new guise. Eternity – παντα ρει. One thing flows from the other – from the seed of one human body the next arises. *All* returns to the earth and all is restored to new *life*. This is implicit in the concept of the transmigration of souls, as expounded by the ancient Egyptians.

It's evening. Once again we went for a stroll, once again the moon was shining. It was extraordinarily interesting. The sky wasn't clear, and all the clouds had gathered around the moon. There we stood, waiting for the yellow disc to force itself out of its bed of thick fog. As the edges of the clouds grew brighter, the moon began shining transparently through them. Brighter, ever brighter, until finally the disc rose triumphantly into the empty, clear air. What a phenomenon, what unfathomable glory! We mortals see you, marvel silently – and long for you!

Saturday 22 July

This morning: cycled to Ischl. A few minor incidents on the way.

p.m. went for a beautiful long walk, played 'Parsifal'.

Full moon! It's so beautiful outside. All alone, I leaned out of the window. Everything glimmered and shimmered in the light, and I was overcome

---

1 'To sink, to drown, oblivious, highest joy' (Wagner, *Tristan und Isolde*, act II).

with longing. I thought to myself: what would you do if Kl. were standing out there? My only thought: jump down. Come what may! His for eternity! Often – how often – have I forgotten all about it. But then the moon rises, only to refresh my memory, to bring tears to my eyes, a lump to my throat, to hold me in its spell, just as a great master transfixes his sycophantic retinue. And here I stand, hands clasped together – figuratively speaking, for nobody can see me – weeping compulsively. For I have lost everything: my father, my Klimt – and now I am about to lose my mother. The three people who constituted my world . . . I feel so wretched, more than I can say . . . so lonely and abandoned. And yet I must put on a cheerful face, for I'm known as cheerful Alma, smart, high-spirited Alma! But deep inside me, how do things look? I haven't composed a note for a week. I can find neither inner nor outer repose.

Give me peace, sleep!

Death! – Cessation!

Sunday 23 July

As ever: a bright summer morning and a short walk with 'Faust'. Then composed a little but, unfortunately, with no particular compulsion.

This letter from Mama has just arrived.[2] It's immensely sweet-natured, therefore I'm putting it in here. I'd so like to be with her. Imagine: to be so far from your mother at a time like this!

p.m. wrote to Mama and then to Paul Schulz – I wouldn't want him to forget me entirely. He sent me two postcards, and I didn't answer either of them.

I've just finished this drawing of a spa-town belle, and I'm putting it in here because I find it appealing.[3]

Did nothing but lounge around all day. It's so dull here. And the moon has changed too – deathly boring!

Tuesday 25 July

To the village with Gretl. On the way back we had a serious conversation about the forces of Nature, the sun, the moon, man and the universe.

As knowledge and intellect grow, and old beliefs are cast aside, we become increasingly aware that we shall never know anything, that we are powerless. What does the moon look like? [A region of dormant volcanoes.] What is the sun? A chaos of burning gases that vibrate, producing light,

2 ▶ Six-page letter from A.S.'s mother, dated 22 July 1899.
3 Caption on the drawing (p. 172): 'The hyena'.

or a burning mass of lava which is gradually cooling down and will end up, just like the earth, as a planet? Will it cool still further and become a <u>moon</u>? Will that be the outcome of our actions? A moon, a world without life, without warmth, frigid, rigid? The greatest works of man destroyed, forgotten? All of us – forgotten? Mankind is so terribly small and ineffectual. Why do we create? What are we? A molecule in the universe. What is the universe? With the help of science we shall come to understand something of creation, but then the end will follow. I'm convinced that science will transform us into demigods, but before we realize it, <u>the end will follow</u>. And the same process will begin on the sun, which by then will have cooled down, and on countless millions of other suns circling in the universe. The further science advances, the further art will decline.

'Ver sacrum' – holy spring: don't be deceived. It's only a brief flowering, they'll never equal {the art of} antiquity. In those days people were so naive and moral – moral, because they had no sophisticated motives but simply followed their instincts; naive, because art was young, young and inexperienced. But today art is an ageing tart who was once good-looking and, with the help of cosmetics, hopes to get hitched up with a 'new spring'.

As knowledge and sophistication grow, true art gradually declines. When did art reach its highest point? When it was at the service of religion. And why? Because belief was genuine, and creation an act of devotion. The artist felt <u>God</u> within him and created for God[!!!]. And today, does anyone really believe? No: we are all enlightened. The religion of our time is symbolism. But it cannot compare with the high-mindedness of former times, one senses the untruth, the lustrous veneer. The artist no longer believes in what he creates. |The last believer was Wagner.| We reach back to the earliest ages, falteringly repeating the words of antiquity, for we no longer speak their tongue. And so it will go on, until art – once lofty and divine, now laid waste and desecrated – is engulfed in a sea of eccentricity.

After dinner I improvised in the dark and – don't ask me – suddenly I felt the urge to smash the piano, not out of anger, but in frenzy. I had no idea what I was playing or doing. All around me was chaos, from my fingers issued chaos, within me everything was *chaos*. At that moment I would have been capable of killing somebody, not for revenge, but in frenzy.

Around me the darkness came to life: I heard footsteps and started playing 'Du bist die Ruh', closed the piano – and now here I sit. For *once* let me pull myself together, for *once* let me get drunk, for *once* let me compose something that satisfies me, for *once* let me kiss until I go mad, *just once* let myself go entirely, and experience that bliss which ends in death. Would that I had done so! I would no longer be alive. But I was timid and sensible. And so here I sit, vegetating, getting nothing out of my paltry existence. My motto, 'Live for the moment', is disavowed. And my energy, my raging passion, what will become of them? They wither away, nobody has reaped their fruit.

And suddenly it's evening. My early spring, my childhood, was sunny, my spring beautiful and uplifting: my spring was Italy. My summer has been forfeited. I'm nineteen years old, and it's already autumn.

Why, why on earth did I ever meet you? Why? You, my misadventure! You, my god!

Thursday 27 July

p.m. two packages: one from Ernst, with a large bottle of perfume and a letter – such a wanton rascal – the other from Dr P., with writing paper embossed with Mahler and Siegfried Wagner. Really terrific! The latter gave me far greater pleasure. With Ernst I can't help thinking: now he's in debt and all for my sake. His wife knows nothing about it, he's doing it <u>in secret</u>. Very awkward.

Saturday 29 July

p.m. at the {Munich} Secession. Mediocre display and the pictures not quite up to standard. Stuck is miserable. Then to the Vereinigte Werkstätte: quite interesting.
p.m. Gallery Schack: the most wonderful pictures I'd ever seen: Böcklin, nothing but Böcklin! 'Sea idyll', 'Italian villa in springtime', 'Shepherd's lament' – at any rate, those three are the best.[4] The latter not so recent, a little heavy-handed but thoroughly poetic. The 'Italian villa' is a nature study, true nature – unfathomable how he captured it on canvas.
Wagner, |Böcklin,| Goethe! The greatest naturalists ever to have lived.

Sunday 30 July

Left Munich in the morning, arrived in Bayreuth at 2:30. {In the margin:} Lodging at Frau Emil Mühl's, Richard-Wagner-Strasse 21: 8 Marks.
A pretty boring little place. Took a look at Villa Wahnfried. Lilli Lehmann here. Gretl unwell – stomach pains.
In the evening: Hotel Sonne: a real low dive. Else Lewinsky here.

Monday 31 July

Before breakfast: with Gretl to Wahnfried and the Hofgarten. The latter very dull, reminds me of the spa gardens at Franzensbad. I liked Wahnfried better than yesterday.[5] So far, the streets are deserted, just a few English ladies, a few pert mademoiselles – mostly people who are only here because it's in vogue. How I long to hear the first bars of music. I can scarcely believe I'm actually in Bayreuth.
This evening we talked about unstable characters, and Aunt Mie said:

---

4 In 1901, Böcklin's *Sea Idyll* was purchased by the Austrian Ministry of Education for the Moderne Galerie at a cost of 80,000 Marks. It was the main attraction of the 13th Secessionist Exhibition (1 February–16 March 1902). The correct title of the second painting is *Idealized Spring Landscape*.
5 ▶ Two postcards from Bayreuth (Villa Wahnfried and the Festspielhaus).

You have a good deal of energy, Alma,
    but sometimes it's self-destructive.
I hope so, I replied.
Suddenly her tone became more serious
and, extending a hand to me, she said:
    I value you, dear Alma, more than
    any other young lady I have ever met.
And Hugo added:
    Yes, I've never met anyone quite like
    you.
I was close to tears. They were with us in
Venice, hence they know me a little. Dear
God, I don't deserve it! If they had some idea
of my inner turmoil – so sad! Gretl wasn't with us.

Parsifal[6]

Burgstaller not *particularly* good, Ternina excellent.
a.m. with Gretl in Wahnfried and the Schlossgarten. Schmedes and Fräulein
Goldenberg here. At 3:00 began the pilgrimage {to the Festspielhaus}.
For an hour we scrutinized the public. Around 4:00, four heralds
appeared and played the 'Grail' motif. We all trotted up the primitive
wooden stairs and entered the auditorium. Didn't recognize a soul. The
seats terraced, in amphitheatre fashion. Quite a rumpus of expectant
murmurs. All of a sudden: the auditorium goes dark, a dreadful rumbling noise as everyone folds down the wooden chairs, then expectant
silence.
The first note – my spine begins to tingle – and then, immediately, one
stimulus after another, one rapture after another. Such wonderful power
and passion, such true poetry. My heart was in my mouth. I listened,
looked – listened as if in a dream, looked as if blinded – another sphere.
Heaven opened before my very eyes.
In my dream I could hear the curtain fall and see the final chord, I could feel
the end! The lights went up, everyone started pushing and shoving, and
before I knew what had happened, we were outside again, incapable of
thought or action. Uncle Hugo forced a glass of champagne down my
throat. It helped: I almost came to. And so it went on during the two
subsequent intervals, although I was so excited and actually already too
tired.

6 ▶ Printed cast list from the programme for *Parsifal*, with Aloys Burgstaller in the title role
and Milka Ternina as Kundry.

The day will remain indelible in my memory – inconceivable that a mere mortal could have created all this. Happiness does still exist, then . . . for me too . . . Today I became fully aware of the fact.

Tuesday 1 August
a.m. at Wagner's grave, but as I'm an impious wretch, I remained unmoved. Lunch at Bayerlein: Schmedes was sitting opposite us, but I gave him no opportunity to greet us. If he can't come over, I don't need his greeting. Since yesterday morning, someone else has been following me – a very picture of a man! As we were leaving the restaurant, Schmedes got up and walked towards the door. My stranger did the same, and the two coincided and met. I followed it all with my eyes – for I can see without looking!
P.M.

Die Meistersinger von Nürnberg

To see 'Die Meistersinger' for the first time at Bayreuth – that was my wish. It's been granted – and was a complete success. Never again will so much vitality, heart and soul, gaiety and genius come together. 'Die Meistersinger' – the work is so rich in human emotion that it becomes divine. I wasn't as excited as yesterday, but today too I could sense that <u>life is beautiful again</u>.
Van Rooy was splendid, Sistermanns poor, Eva – Frau Kernic – delightful, Friedrichs terrific. But my new hero is Ernst Kraus![7] He's handsome, has a powerful voice, is capable and has enthralling stage-presence.
We had dinner in the {Festspielhaus} restaurant, where we were given seats downstairs, and (whenever a singer arrived) we would rush over to the

window to join in the ovations. Afterwards we moved upstairs, facing the table at which Cosima and Siegfried Wagner were sitting with all the performers. That was a scramble [great joy!]. I immediately started making eyes at Ernst Kraus, and quite emphatically at that. He was happy to return the compliment. Once we even surreptitiously drank a toast – enthusiasm excuses everything!
During the intervals, my stranger had been devouring me with his eyes, and

7 The cast included Anton van Rooy (Hans Sachs), Anton Sistermanns (Pogner), Beatrice Kernic (Eva), Fritz Friedrichs (Beckmesser) and Ernst Kraus (Walter von Stolzing).

once, when I was very late returning to the auditorium, he'd arrived later still.

Now my young stranger was sitting opposite me at the same table. And

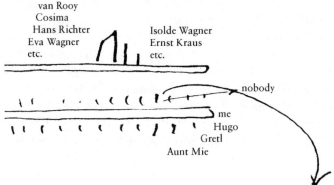

later, when a few seats became free, he promptly sat down next to me. I had to smile! Very discreetly we entered into conversation – nobody noticed. Aunt Mie said:

Look, that's Eva Wagner sitting next to Ernst Kraus.

No, I beg to differ, that's Isolde, piped up my stranger all of a sudden. Not wishing to let the moment pass unexploited, he pulled out his visiting-card and gave it to Uncle Hugo. Being rather shy, the latter was nonplussed, to say the least. But Aunt Mie was the personification of amiability. They talked about Rotterdam. He's Dutch,[8] and Aunt Mie said she was travelling to the Hague and Rotterdam. Dead certain that we'd be going too, he beamed with joy!

Cosima stood up and, in a soft, almost inaudible voice, started speaking. All we could make out were the words 'mother', 'greatest joy' etc. Suddenly she raised her voice and said resoundingly:

And to my son Siegfried, who enjoys the high privilege of bearing *his* name, I therefore ask you all to raise your glasses. All our hopes rest on him. He is the light of my old age. In my son Siegfried I place my trust. Herr Richter knows how much his birth meant to me.

(Richter had all the while been holding Cosima's hand under the table. At these words he kissed it.)

To my son Siegfried!

A roar of approval went round the room. At the sound of her plain, sad voice, everyone was moved to tears. Only later did we realize that every

8 ▶ Visiting card of C.M.H. Minderop.

word was horribly calculating. 'My son Siegfried' is her own discovery, she it was who forced him into the limelight. And such proclamations, instead of helping him, are merely detrimental to his career.

Uncle Hugo ordered a bottle of champagne and, to the accompaniment of Herr Minderop's stories of Rotterdam, his home-town, we toasted each other time and again.

The cab was waiting for us at the door. Gleefully and in a loud voice I said:

It's me you've to thank for making his acquaintance.

Only then did I realize that he was leaving the restaurant directly behind us!

Addio, mio amico!

Friday 4 August

In the train I read 'Gottesfriede' by Peter Nansen. After all I'd heard about the book, the slant he takes is clear, but the heroine remains a mystery. A discussion with her future husband serves to define her character: she is consumed by the wish to bear him children. I don't care for children at all, and my concept of 'love' differs radically. Yet there was a time when I myself fervently sought to sacrifice my virginity to become a mother, to bear his child. And at that time he bullied and begged me:

Alma, it's no use, we must come together in *total* union.

And I replied:

No robber take, when love he'd make, but with a wedding ring!

Lord knows, to utter those words was the hardest task I ever faced: my love for him was boundless, utterly devoted. My only wish was to be his, body and soul, for ever.

I'm certain I would have been the happiest woman in the world – then. And now the unhappiest. How grateful I am for my steadfast character! In Genoa, nothing would have been easier than sleeping with him. Gretl is a sound sleeper, our bedrooms adjoined, the doors didn't creak, and Mama's room was on the other side of the corridor. But somehow I felt: this is forbidden – and not just because I'm well brought up. I wasn't ashamed of going into his room, of kissing him and letting him kiss me, but I knew Kl. too well. What would have become of me?

Perhaps I would have been blissfully happy, and he probably would have married me. Under the circumstances, if I'd reached the peak of happiness with him, he wouldn't have been able to reproach me for my misconduct. Things turned out better, but I can never be entirely happy and joyful.

Sunday 6 August

Hansl died at 6:00 this morning. The poor little boy never had anything from life – only pain and suffering.

Fearfully I whisk away every fly that settles on my hand, for fear it may be carrying toxins from the corpse. The unendurable smell of death, the candles and flowers. What is death? An abrupt cessation of all bodily functions, the moment when the blood ceases to circulate.[9] But how, why, for what reason?

The death-struggle began yesterday at 2:00 p.m. This morning he emitted a protracted scream, and it was over. That poor child was spared nothing. Is there no justice? No! What harm did that child ever do? He just lay there on his cushions, a pale, suffering martyr. I'm certain: there is no afterlife. So he had nothing from life, nothing at all!

This morning: with Christine and Gustav in Gosaumühle. Christine gave me a lecture: I should get married.

> Listen, Alma, you're at the height of your beauty, you're in demand, you can choose whoever you like. Make your mind up! Don't miss your chance! You're so bone-headed! You've set your heart on one man, and now you don't care for any other. And you aren't making the slightest effort to meet people. It's not right! You'll come to regret it! Yesterday we had a visit from a man whose sister was really gorgeous. But she's no longer young, and frightfully unhappy. In her youth she fell in love with some fellow who didn't care for her. And now, at thirty, she's cheerless and embittered. And I thought of you, Alma, and how frightfully choosy you are – and stubborn as well. Snap out of it!

In Gosaumühle we dismounted, and Christine said:

> My uncle (Dr Bukovics) would love to meet you. He kept asking me, 'What does Burckhard's latest flame look like?'

> What, I said, Burckhard's? Who on earth put that idea into his head?

> Well, Burckhard admitted as much to Hermann Bahr, and he's terribly worried that B. might do something foolish.

I had to smile. What nonsense people talk before the day is out. Christine advised me against it, by the way, saying that B. was too old and too volatile. But he's a brilliant fellow, if you ask me.

---

9 Orig: 'ein Zerreissen der Herzadern' – literally: 'a tearing of the heart-arteries'.

Wednesday 9 August
This telegram just arrived:
> a sister[10] blue-eyed black-haired hale and hearty greets alma gretl and granny stop all well

Oh what joy! Another girl! Yet another poor, unfortunate creature on God's earth! I could weep.

My dear, dear father died exactly seven years ago today, and today this little mite comes into the world. There's something grey and symbolic about it. I'm so sad, I just can't stop myself crying.

Thursday 10 August
Today I wrote to Mama but, much as I'd like to, I could find no warm words for my *stepsister* – I simply avoided them. I commiserated with her for her suffering but didn't mention the cause. I can't act against my better judgement. I cannot and will not! Carl will be offended: it's *his* child I'm insulting!

We two are so much richer: in our veins flows the blood of a genius, while Carl . . . may be capable and hard-working, but he'll *never* attain the rank of a true artist. Indeed, apart from Olbrich, there isn't a single genius in the whole Secession. Engelhart apes the French painters, above all Roll. Klimt indirectly copies Botticelli, although he doesn't actually know his work – he imitates Burne-Jones, who in turn imitates Botticelli. And the others . . . hard-working artisans. Only Olbrich is self-sufficient, he alone has the *self-confidence* of a true artist. He should be able to make something out of his life.

Wednesday 16 August
Mama sent a bottle of Moet & Chandon and a pair of gloves.
This evening: 'The Geisha' with Mary Halton.
Apart from the fact that Mama Moll bought us clasps, the climate remains unchanged: our barometers still point to storm.

Thursday 17 August
Have been reading Zola's 'Le ventre de Paris'. A very good book, except that it betrays too much of the author's intentions, i.e. it's too tendentious. He constantly plumbs the depths of human misery, and eventually the reader becomes insensible to it.

10 Maria Anna Alma Margarethe Moll.

Friday 18 August
The Kaiser's birthday. What do I care!
I haven't heard anything at all of Klimt. Carl hasn't mentioned him in any of his letters, so of course I've heard nothing.
Everything I've just written is untrue! Lies, insincere! I'd been thinking of him, started to write, and wrote things that are untrue. Only a few lines, but I think it necessary to revoke them, for this book should not contain a *single* untruth – not one.
Of course I should like to have him here, at my side ... but as soon as he's gone – to his sister-in-law – he means nothing to me. It's strange: although I'm so dreadfully jealous, The thought of him in the arms of his beloved is not objectionable to me, nor do I feel any hatred, neither for him nor for her. To me, from that moment he simply ceases to exist. When he's with me, I love the real Klimt. When he's gone, I love a dream-vision. It has his dear eyes, speaks with his voice, bears his name – but it isn't him.
If today they told me he was dead, I'm quite sure it wouldn't affect me in the least. Indeed, when I imagine things that others dread, I remain dry-eyed. Most people will find this inexplicable, but I repeat here in a firm and steady voice: my love for Klimt is utterly loyal, truer than anyone else's. And even if I marry ten times, I shall always love him – despite everything that happened. I love him more than my own life.
If he were to come to me today and say, 'Alma, do such and such for me and do it for *love's* sake' – even if it meant my death, I would do it unhesitatingly. But if he died, I couldn't weep. Especially if he'd been with another woman, it would be no concern of mine. But if he were to pass away in my arms, I couldn't live a moment longer.
And now, when I see him again, I shall have to put my nose in the air, envelop my heart in a shield of ice. I don't want him to know what anguish he's caused me, I don't want anyone ever to know what I've been through. The day – May 15 – on which my illusions died: how ashamed I am of the tears I shed, tears shed in the presence of Mama and Carl. For they betrayed the fact that I was madly in love. How ashamed I am! Nobody should ever have realized what I was going through!
O God, show me the way, show me a path to happiness, that I may be able to make others happy. Show me a path to oblivion, that I may forget my joys and my sorrows. For until my memory is blurred, until my beautiful recollections have faded, I shall never be happy. And that can never be!

Saturday 19 August
Spent the whole day reading Flaubert's 'Madame Bovary'. I'd been expecting more of it. I find it totally outmoded, the individual characters
undefined. For me the heroine is utterly incomprehensible. Is she flighty,
cowardly and base, or just *common*? Apart from that, Flaubert is rather
long-winded and loves to digress. In a word, the book failed to inspire me.

Sunday 20 August
We had an opulent lunch, at which the Moet & Chandon that Mama sent
for Gretl's birthday was drunk out of beer-glasses. We had nothing but
praise for Mama's brilliant idea.
All the same, I felt utterly miserable. After lunch we all slept awhile, then
we laid our plans and afterwards I had a stand-up row with Gretl. For me it
actually ended in tears. One thing about Gretl is that she never really
expresses a genuine opinion, and at table her Jesuit attitude did me great
harm. I just wanted to make that clear to her. How did she react? Stopped
her ears and uttered the most infamous, false accusations. I tried to reply,
and she stopped her ears. You want to say something, and nobody listens:

that's something that makes me
seethe with rage. Apart from that,
it's Gretl who's the coward. I told
her as much too.
Later the others went out. Alone
in the house, I finished my second
Italian piece. What's it about? It's
a dream – a dream of rash
indulgence and fugitive happiness.
Klimt, my Klimt!
Much that I used not to understand
is now clear and settled in my
mind. Much that I formerly
didn't dare think, or that I used
to dismiss as wishful thinking, I
now perceive as reality. I'm so
grateful to the author of this
article for the pleasure he has
given me in discussing a subject
of such importance.
Goethe – how far ahead of his time he was! In those days, nobody ever

dreamt that protoplasma could be created in a laboratory, but with the concept of the homunculus Goethe clearly foresaw it. When, how and who? How many generations shall pass before the riddle of creation has been solved?

Monday 21 August
And now, my dear diary, I've *betrayed* you. It happened when we were leaving (at the station). I said to Gretl:

Gretl, take the keys from the chest of drawers.
I hadn't noticed Mama Moll, who was standing nearby. Suddenly she said:

You can give them to me. I'll lock them away for you.

No thank you, I said, we always carry them with us.

Oh, but surely you don't want to drag such a weight around.
So she took the keys and locked them away. My heart missed a beat: you, my poor, dear diary, you were in there too. Were you opened? Did someone discover my innermost secrets, poke their nose into my soul? I have no idea. Have impious fingers touched pages which only you, my Klimt, were supposed to turn? When we left, I felt quite sick, but could do nothing without arousing suspicion. For me my diary was sacrosanct: how could one do such a thing? I can't believe it!
We arrived home and hurried noiselessly upstairs in the hope of catching her in flagrante. But no – there she sat, calm and collected, knitting . . . knitting!

Good evening, children!
Later, watching her carefully, I asked her for the keys, but she didn't bat an eyelid! It's all a pose! Pah!

Tuesday 22 August
First thing in the morning: to the station, hoping to find the roses that Carl had promised us – but in vain.
At about 11:00 there was a sudden hullabaloo on the staircase, and Carl and Ernst Moll made a grand entrance. We were thrilled to bits! There was much to discuss with Carl: as Mama Moll doesn't object, the baby is to be baptized into the Protestant faith. Not much other news. We'll be returning to Vienna on 9 September. I can't wait to get away.
For lunch, Mimi brewed up a lousy bowl of punch.
This evening: Carl and Ernst went back {to Vienna}. Carl dropped a hint to the effect that Burckhard is involved in some juicy scandal. I'd be very sorry if it's true.

Thursday 24 August
This morning: climbed the Tressenstein. Rather strenuous, but the view made up for it – you can sea the lake at Alt Aussee, and as far as the Grundlsee.

This afternoon: Dr Putz gave a lecture on philosophy. It was immensely interesting, and I realized that I know next to nothing about philosophy, particularly about [the significance of] logic, psychology, ethics, aesthetics and metaphysics. It was fascinating.

Poor chap: one of the most brilliant minds, but what a position – teacher at a finishing school for girls.

p.m. rowed out in the boat. Paul was in a boat following us, with Miss Cook and Otto, and vied with some stranger, who had a very lovely voice, in singing every imaginable Wagner motif. Gretl and I disembarked near the Hellmanns' mountain hut, which is very picturesquely situated on a green slope overlooking the lake.

This evening: at Dr Sternlich's. We made music. He played, I played. Later we even danced – a wild, Bacchic dance.

Friday 25 August
This morning: to Gössl. I overslept, and therefore didn't find time to go to the loo. Anxiously I got into the boat, anxiously I stepped out on arrival. We had breakfast, and I, silly goose, was too embarrassed to . . . From there fifteen minutes' walk to the Toplitzsee, in a wonderfully bleak and isolated position. I was beginning to feel dreadful. It took us a further half-hour from there to the Ranftl mill. There's a pretty waterfall, but I couldn't enjoy it.

    Gretl, you've got to help me, I implored.

She knew exactly what to do. The two of us walked, ran on ahead, with the others following. Gretl called:

    Paul, I beg you, don't follow us. Just go to the jetty. We've forgotten
    something in Gössl.

We ran as fast as our legs could carry us. Sweat was pouring off my brow. An indescribable, dreadful sensation. Gretl had no idea how to help me. The pain brought tears to my eyes. At last a house hove into sight – I'd already seen it from afar:

    Come Unto Me All Ye Who Are Troubled And Heavy Laden.

We caught up with the others, happy and gay: Gretl said she'd forgotten her purse. Paul and Conrad Mauthner took a quick dip. We got home at 12:00.

This evening the moonlight was wonderful, the lake silvery – almost a Böcklin picture.

Sunday 27 August
p.m. called on Frau Magg, whom we know from Abbazia. I was asked to play. They gave me the 'Well-tempered Clavier' and asked me to play. Naturally, I had no intention of doing anything of the sort. They begged me, and finally, reluctantly, I sat down and struck up the 'Magic Fire Music'. Frau Magg was quite taken aback. She turned to Gretl H. and asked:
> What on earth is that?
Now it was Gretl H.'s turn to look astonished: the good lady had never heard of it. Later I played Beethoven's first violin sonata with her son Paul. Somewhat crestfallen, we set off home. One thing I shouldn't forget: she showed us round the house, which was very simple but extremely tasteful: the walls full of engravings, none of them as poor as the ones here, for example; the bedrooms entirely of white-wood, darker wood in the living-rooms, also some old inlaid chests.
Afterwards I went to the villa and finished my song. It isn't my worst.
p.m. thirty guests, including the Maggs. Paul Magg has *never* been to a Wagner opera. Poor chap! It was quite fun. Irene Redlich is a very nice girl. I played the Schumann Concerto and the Andante and Variations with Mrs Boas. It went pretty well, and I was lavishly praised, the applause was thunderous.

Tuesday 29 August
This morning: a letter from Helene Brückner (enclosed here). Later Dr Egger,[11] Frau Magg, Frau Sternlich and Paul Magg. The latter is so strange. They all came over to rehearse the Mahler symphony, which they played in a version for two pianos, eight hands. It sounded hideous – a potpourri of Wagner operas.
Afterwards I played the Schumann Concerto with Dr Egger. But his playing is pretty mediocre, and he missed every entry. Afterwards, Gretl told me he'd been gawping at me all the time, which is why he kept coming in late. When he said goodbye, he looked deep into my eyes – singularly deep.

11 Regierungsrat Friedrich Egger, departmental director at the Austrian National Library. He participated in the activities of several literary societies, including the Goethe-Verein, of which he was a committee member.

Thursday 31 August

My twentieth birthday. Summing up the past year, I wrote on 31 December: 'The year included a period during which I was happy, entirely happy. I'm convinced that I shall never experience greater happiness.' But I did – Genoa! What did I know about happiness? A single word from him, a searing look, was enough to move me to transports of joy.

Now I know what it is to find happiness and lose it again. I can't imagine any stronger emotion. I refuse to accept what Kl. kept repeating to me in Verona:

> There's no happiness on earth greater than that of two people united – physically.

That I refuse to accept! For then happiness is dragged through the mud, reeks of lechery. I know – during that twilight hour in Genoa I possessed him completely! Body and soul! Completely. But the joy was pure, and my memories of it will remain eternally pure! Why then should I stifle this feeling of eternity, why degrade myself to an animal?

God knows what hideous, oppressive memories I would otherwise have cherished of my dearly beloved, of that marvellous experience.

God, I thank you from the bottom of my heart for having rescued me. Above all I have to thank my mother, who taught me to distinguish between Good and Evil. My inner voice, my instinct, fearing no retribution, steadfast in heart and soul, told me: 'This is forbidden.' In Genoa it was those words that prevented me from doing something which – had it not led to my death – would have been cause for eternal regret.

And yet I loved you, and love you still – my Klimt!

Suite 14

One day follows another. Nothing improves,
nothing gets worse! All is dull, grey, sad and dead.
The more one thinks, the worse things become.
A ray of light glanced my way, but only glanced.
There is no hope, none at all. –

Friday 1 September
Started a piano trio yesterday, but I'll have to leave it for now, because my knowledge of stringed instruments is too shaky. I'll have to learn a bit about them in Vienna first.

At Grundlsee, the day before yesterday, I pulled out one of my molars. First I loosened it with a finger, then I pressed it inwards with a nail-file, causing the gum to turn blue. Finally I took a piece of thick twine and pulled at it until it fell into my hand. I should add that I took frequent pauses, during which I considered calling the whole thing off. Only the fear of a swollen jaw and even greater pain persuaded me to keep at it. It hurt like mad, and blood flowed profusely. But it gave me the inner satisfaction of prevailing over myself. It's not easy to pull out one of your own teeth, especially if it's scarcely loose. Every yank signified a fresh battle with my own nerves. But I'm glad to be rid of the brute.

Saturday 2 September
p.m. in Gosaumühle. Walked back.

Have just finished a novel by Hermann Bahr, 'Die gute Schule'. It's frivolous in the extreme, but unprepossessing and not boring in the least. The fight for art and sexual conquest – futile struggle! His chosen hero is no artist, indeed in the end he becomes just an ordinary fellow. Why then does he present him in all these phases? We live with his fears and his desire for fame and artistic success, and in the end he's merely a poseur – a fashion designer with delusions of artistry. That hurts!

Love never cheats. Art, above all, never cheats. And Bahr shouldn't cheat by thinking up non-existent situations. For that reason, no matter how much I enjoyed it, I can't take the book seriously. It achieves nothing! When I read them, some passages of incredible cynicism annoyed me greatly. And there's no doubt about it: reading obscene books can do great harm. For I know that I never experienced anything like the physical thrills of his smuttier episodes.

Sunday 3 September

At a concert, someone once said to me:

> I've scrutinized all the faces in your row, and I must say that yours was the most composed. Your eyes reveal a startlingly classical personality – a clean conscience.

And today? A year has passed since then.

This evening I let Gretl and Mama Moll go into the dining-room on their own, and stayed behind to play the piano in the dark. All the time I could feel the presence of Kl., he simply *had* to be there. I could even feel his beautiful hands. I was playing on my own, but cried so hard that I had to stop. No tears ran from my eyes, I was weeping silently, leaning my head on the piano. Fortunately nobody came in. I could just imagine him in the room. It was dark, nothing was clearly distinguishable, but I could feel his presence, his breath! He really was here! He leaned over to comfort me:

> Listen, Alma, keep calm. You know that I love you, it's just that we can never be united. Alma, my Alma!

I stood up and I was calm.

Why do those wretched people meddle in my affairs? Why do they have to tear open my old, dear wounds? After all, it isn't long ago that I lost everything, barely four months!

Tuesday 5 September

Last night: read in bed till late: 'Villa Falconierei' by Richard Voss. His style is quite delightful. He describes springtime in the Campagna: Rome, with all its colour and heady sensuality. The characters are well defined but not very convincing.

At any rate, I read till late, and as I opened the window and snuffed out the candle, day was just dawning. The stars were pale and motionless. My room felt so confined. Unspeakably so! Away, away! But not to Vienna, where I'm to be confronted by an infant whose parents love each other. No, out into the big, wide world – Italy, Corfu.

We had such a lovely house in the saddle of the hills – two hours from Kérkira. On one side you could see the Adriatic, on the other side the Ionian [Aegean] Sea. I can still remember a terrific storm (I was eight years old). We were standing on the street leading to the house, and the sea was a mass of silver. Above it black clouds, penetrated here and there by moon-light. It was exquisitely beautiful.

Or the century-old olive trees, hollow, so that three people could easily sit inside them, and the wonderful grey of the leaves.

Close to our house was a rocky incline, and high above it a waterfall. Everywhere it formed little pools, on the brink of which bloomed the sweetest flowers. In January Gretl found the first violets there. Later everything was a-bloom with wild hyacinths.

The people in the area were awful thieves. We always had a big crate of pictures by the front door. They even pilfered things from the church. We also had some magnificent bronze candlesticks. The papas stole them and sold them to us. This papas – he would wash his robes in the puddles on the street, and had no bed of his own, not even of straw. He simply lay on the bare stone.

I could go on telling stories and writing all night, it was so wonderful [& so sad!]. Once a group of twenty people came to visit us. They were all on horseback, and I clearly remember a beautiful lady with a tight-fitting blue riding-costume and, in each buttonhole on her breast, a tiny bouquet of violets.

How lovely it was to stand on our hill and look down to the fort, built far out into the sea. It was far off in the grey sunlight, etched against the blue of the sea. I can still see everything as if it were yesterday. And yet the time has passed – passed for ever. Corfu was beautiful!

Few people of my age, I believe, have seen as much as I. For even then I saw everything with the eyes of a painter. After all, our dear father was there, and would point out every beauty to us. If only he were alive today. I'm convinced I would have developed quite differently. He was the only person whose love for me was genuine and selfless. Already then! How would it be today, now that I understand him?

Wednesday 6 September

Today was a day the likes of which I have seldom experienced. I cried all afternoon. We called on the Geiringers to say goodbye, and out of the blue Rudolf suddenly mentioned that the baby was to receive a Catholic baptism. At first I thought he was joking, but soon I realized what diabolical disdain lay at the root of it all. These outsiders all knew about it, but we didn't. Rudolf laughed.

Well, aren't you Catholics too?

Yes, worst luck, I almost shouted.

Mama Moll was deeply offended at what I'd said.

That's enough, now. Let's go.

And we went. I was crying so hard, I could scarcely stand.

You may have got used to the idea that your mother only does what you want, but when it comes to their child, after all, those two can do what they please. It's not your child. It's no business of yours whatsoever.

She's right: it's none of our business. I asked everyone to keep to the road, and took the footpath across the fields. I found a bench, sat down and cried as I had *never* cried before. This is the end.

The day on which Mama told us she was expecting a baby, that very day ... that very moment, I could foresee everything. 'Children, I've got a new toy now, you should get married. And keep your opinions to yourselves, it's none of your business. You're strangers now, strangers in my house!' Tomorrow, I know, there'll be presents for us. Give me strength, my soul, to refuse them, to conserve them for a more opportune moment. I don't want any presents from people who've betrayed me. Everyone knew about it except us. Indeed, there was no need even to tell us, because it's actually none of our business.

My eyes are so sore, I can scarcely see! In my heart I felt as if I were being torn forcibly apart. *How* can I love my mother, if she abandons us for the sake of another child? We mean nothing to her now – we're just in her way. I'm well aware of the fact but, for heaven's sake, I can't marry a man I don't love.

When we get to Vienna, I'll ask Mama to give me the small sum of money that I can call my own, and then I'll move out. But where to? I'm too sensitive to be alone amongst strangers. Every indelicate gesture makes me wince. I simply *can't* believe that motherly love could evaporate so quickly, is it not an inexhaustible stream? I can write no more, my eyes are too sore. *Never* have I been so upset!

Thursday 7 September

Departed at 12:00 noon, arrived in Vienna at 7:00. Legler, Ernst, Hanna and Carl at the station. Gretl drove with Legler in the cab, Carl with me. He said:

> You're such play-actors.
>
> What? I said.
>
> You can't fool me. This evening, the cat's going to be let out of the bag.
>
> What on earth do you mean?
>
> Well, Legler has made a clean breast of it: this evening, he and Gretl will announce their engagement.
>
> What? I screamed. And she hasn't told me about it?

Tears began to stream down my face. Then I brought up the subject of the baptism, and later we talked about Legler's artistic standing. I said I was convinced he'd never be a heaven-storming genius. He'd be an artisan – diligent, discerning and competent – no more than that. Carl agreed, saying that I was far harder to please than he was. I expect more of life, and I *am* more. Although too much apathy is not good, they make a good match. Apathy plus apathy equals – more apathy, and . . . well, I say no more. That's the end of Gretl, as far as I'm concerned. Time may heal wounds, but the scars remain. The fact that she kept secret the most important decision of her life proves that she never really loved me.

This evening they celebrated the engagement. She takes such a callous attitude towards him: I feel sorry for him.

Friday 8 September

Yesterday evening she came to me – I'd gone to bed early – and begged my forgiveness.

Look, you know that I love you more than anyone in the world.

You haven't exactly proved the point, I replied.

And I turned to the wall and said no more.

Now she's sorry and would give anything, anything to make it up. But it's no use. She's a stranger to me now.

a.m. Olbrich came to fetch us. We drove with him to Mödling, where we looked round the villa he's built for Max Friedmann.[1] I'd never imagined that Olbrich was *so very* gifted. The villa is a jewel from top to bottom. Everything breathes *one* artistic spirit – every lock, every detail has been attended to with the greatest affection. This is a man of stature – and he impresses me! The dining-room is decorated entirely in lighter colours, the bedroom in cyclamen, the smoking-room[2] in green, everything extremely comfortable. I also played the piano a little. I'm exceedingly taken with Olbrich. Any time after tomorrow, he might be summoned {to Darmstadt} . . . And then he'll be gone – we'll have lost him!

This evening: Ernst and Hanna.

Saturday 9 September

a.m. unpacked everything & arranged our room. Gretl didn't help, of course. As for the rest, I feel desperately lonely. And Gretl . . .

This evening: with Aunt Alma to 'Götterdämmerung'. That's life for you!

1 Max Friedmann, industrialist and politician, owned a machine-tool factory.
2 Orig.: 'Herrenzimmer' (lit. gentlemen's room).

Music, my hope, my strength, don't abandon me, as the others have abandoned me. At the Opera I was moved to tears. Will there ever be anything to match it? Can there be? Such mastery combined with *such* freedom.
On the way home: spoke with Aunt Alma about Kl. She *loathes* him. She *curses* him. I cannot.

Friday 15 September
This morning: in town with Gretl and Wilhelm, then to Gerstner[3] with Wilhelm's sisters. Then composed. Gretl is delighted with the song 'Einsamer Gang' (Leo Greiner). I consider the poem very fine, and I have, I believe, caught its atmosphere pretty well.

Saturday 16 September
Yesterday Mama said to me:
> Alma, give me your photograph with the bear. I know you've given one copy away, but the other five . . .

So Klimt has even betrayed my photograph. How can *one* person be so beastly? Every word pierces me like a dagger. I haven't forgotten him. I can't.
a.m. rendezvous with Legler's sister in {Café} Demel. As I was busy composing, it was most inopportune. Rosa was there too. She's had to provide a doctor's certificate guaranteeing her virginity. Poor girl.
Later: composed, embroidered, wrote.
This evening: the Geiringers. Gretl offended me deeply. They both asked me to stay with them awhile. I did so. After a while, Gretl said:
> It would be much more fun if we were alone.

I left at once, was close to tears. I'm not wanted!
This evening I played my songs to Carl and Mama – the five new ones – and they were very taken with them.

Tuesday 19 September
There's so little to write about just now. Life is monotonous . . . {but for a few} bright spots. This evening:

Die Walküre

with van Dyck, Sedlmair, Reichmann. Sedlmaier terrific, v.D. a real ham, and also vocally flawed. The opera is heavenly. Every note, every bar is a revelation. Unfortunately Ernst tried me sorely with his advances. He kept brushing my knee with his. He disgusts me.

---

3 Court Imperial patissier (I., Kärnthnerstrasse 6).

Wednesday 20 September
On Sunday I composed a new song (text by Leo Greiner),[4] then 'Tränen-kinder' and, today, 'Ich will den Sturm'. Working very hard.

Friday 22 September
Tonight I dreamt I was 'engaged' to Kl. How stupid the word 'engaged' sounds in connection with Kl., with his name. 'Klimt' and 'engaged' . . .
But my dream was even more absurd: he'd won a big prize in a lottery, used the money to pay off all his womenfolk, then married me. Nothing could be more idiotic, it's even absurder than the biggest prize of all. And in my dream I wasn't even particularly happy.
This evening: 'Siegfried'. Schmedes and Mildenburg terrific. Of the whole tetralogy, 'Siegfried' is the one I like best. The music is the most rugged and Teutonic, full of true heroism. The first and third acts are my favourites. Even the text is wonderfully, magnificently Germanic in conception. No Jew can *ever* understand Wagner. I was in such raptures – the world might have ended – and I wouldn't have noticed.

Sunday 24 September
a.m. telephoned with the Secession, spoke to Hancke. Then over the Ring to the Schwarzenberg gardens. Wondrously beautiful . . . reddish brown leaves on the ground. Unhappy people, constantly hesitating and moving slowly on, bewailing their misfortune. Autumn has come.
This evening: 'Götterdämmerung'. It was uniquely beautiful. Schmedes and Sedlmair unsurpassable. The close of the prelude and the scene on the Valkyrie's rock are so sublimely passionate. If Gustav G. ever again pro-pounds the idea that Wagner only understood the dirty, sensual aspects of love, I shall laugh in his face. People don't realize *just* how great Wagner really is.

Saturday 30 September
We shudder: what kind of ministry do they want to create? First they said it would have Czech and ecumenical characteristics (a disgrace for Austria), and now they say it will be a ministry run by officials. If that happens, and Departmental Director Hartel is appointed Minister of Culture and Educa-tion, well . . . It would be terrific![5] Carl, if he pestered him long enough,

4 A.S. copied the Greiner text into her diary on 15 September 1899; on 20 September 1899 she wrote the opening lines down again, but later deleted them.
5 Wilhelm von Hartel, classical philologist. As Minister of Education he was instrumental in

could win him over entirely for our cause: a modern gallery. In Germany all but the smallest towns have their own gallery of modern art. In Austria there isn't one. And Carl would be appointed director. Dreams! Reveries! Today the news was that Wittek[6] has to go, and that Liharzik[7] will be Minister of Railways, as Hartel has turned the post down.

This morning: I gave Gretl {Hellmann} her first piano lesson. I'm her real teacher now. Shall give a series of eight lessons at 6 fl.

Then: private view at the Camera Club.[8] A few very good exhibits. Henneberg: a landscape; Kühn:[9] a landscape; Craig Annan:[10] portrait; Perscheid:[11] portrait of Max Klinger, which is the best. Altogether sixty items. Rubber-plate imprints work well with landscapes, but have no future in portrait photography. And yet these people have devoted an entire exhibition to rubber-plate technique – sixty items in all – and apart from four or five pictures, it's rubbish. It's hardly likely to cause a stir. Spitzer has three portraits on display – Frau Ries, fencing-master Barbasetti and Klimt. I didn't know anything about it. It was an indescribable feeling to look into his eyes for the first time in three months. Such a sweet facial expression, and his mouth – his mouth! I can feel it: my life long, I shall cling to him. I can't free myself. I'd always thought I'd banished him from my thoughts, but whenever I see him or his picture, I'm compelled to laugh and cry for the joy of seeing him again, just once. I love him. I see no other way!

Today I put on a pretty good show: I went along and looked {at Klimt's picture} with an indifferent expression – and my heart was leaping for joy. Spitzer was there.

—

opening Austrian universities to women, advocated the presentation of a literature prize to Arthur Schnitzler (despite strong anti-Semitic opposition), and supported Klimt in the controversy surrounding his mural paintings for Vienna University. In 1902 his proposal for a Gallery of Modern Art won the approval of the Kaiser; it was opened the following year.
6 Heinrich Ritter von Wittek, Minister of Railways from 1896, was a close friend of A.S.'s father (cf. *Mein Leben*, pp. 17–18).
7 Franz Liharzik, secretary at the Ministry of Railways since 1896, was influential in the areas of tariff regulation and tourism.
8 During the summer, the Camera Club had moved into new premises (III., Lagergasse 3). Its first exhibition opened at the Gewerbemuseum.
9 Chr. Heinrich Kühn, an honorary member of the Camera Club, started work as a photographer in 1888 in Innsbruck. He invented the technique of multiple rubber-plate printing.
10 The English photographer James Craig Annan and his father, Thomas, both came to Vienna in 1888 to study the technique of heliogravure.
11 Nicola Perscheid was active as a photographer in Leipzig from 1894.

p.m. saw Felix for the first time in two years. A nice old gasbag.
This evening . . . Burckhard. Yet again. I rather liked him today.

Sunday 1 October
I can't live without him. Looking at his picture yesterday, I realized it
again. All my joy of living lies in the two words 'Gustav Klimt'. Without
him, everything appears a sombre dream. But if I see him again today, I'll
have to ignore him. The face – there's something very moving about it. I
stood aside, only glancing at it from time to time and thinking to myself: on
that mouth I kissed him, with those lips he kissed me. Into those eyes I
stared long and deeply, with those eyes he drove me crazy. The most beautiful eyes in the world, sparkling greenish-grey. With those hands, those
dear hands, he held me firmly, hotly, passionately, those hands took complete possession of me. I could never bear anyone touching my face, but he
could run his fingers round my mouth, cover my eyes. He could do what he
pleased!
And *all* is lost.
This evening: 'Lohengrin'. I hadn't heard it for a long time, and now I was
hearing it after the Ring. That hurts. All the same, there are wonderful
things in it. Mildenburg, as Ortrud, was magnificent. Also very good were
Sedlmair and Winkelmann, with whose wife we spoke before and after the
performance.
p.m. Rosa. I told her what I thought of her squalid love-life.
This evening: Fischel. We were with the Hellmanns.
While listening, sometimes I'd close my eyes. I could see his picture. I
sought it and thought: 'If only he were here!' To soak in the music with me,
to delight in it with me. For whom do I otherwise enjoy?

Monday 2 October
And they say you shouldn't trust in intuition? Yesterday I was longing for
his picture, today I have one! Gretl H. came round:
      I've brought you something nice.
She showed me a package wrapped in tissue paper, and pulled out this
picture.[12]
      Do you want to keep it, or shall I take it with me? she asked impishly.
      Well, since you brought it along, you can leave it here, I said quietly.
I could scarcely contain my joy. I'm so delighted to have something,

12 ▷ Photograph of Klimt.

something of him. Now I no longer need strain my imagination to picture his dear features. Gretl has no idea what endless joy she has given me. Klimt, my Klimt. Mine for eternity.

Olbrich, Hohenberger,[13] Moser, Klimt. Olbrich next to Klimt. If I could, I'd cut out his dear, dear picture, so that I could see nobody but him. But it won't be necessary: where he stands, I see nobody else.

Gretl is unhappy. She was in love with Max Neumayer, but last Sunday he got engaged. She cried a lot, but I told her it was just a youthful prank and wouldn't last. So off she went, a little comforted.

It's evening. I've just taken another long look at that sweet picture. He's a thousand times more beautiful than me. And a genius!

Today something gave me great joy. Frau Radnitzky came and said:

> Listen, Alma, I've spoken to Labor and asked him if he'd mind if I included your lieder in one of my chamber-music concerts. He said he wouldn't mind at all, on the contrary, he'd be delighted.

And I . . . I'm delighted too.

And now here I sit, it's 11:00 p.m. and I'm writing my last, dear memories into this sacred book.

Tuesday 3 October

Today I have my first Labor lesson. I'll be interested to see what he has to say.

I played everything to him: 'Hinaus' is too long and too much a piano piece. 'Qual' is unhealthy, has a bad melodic line, and the text is too silly for words. 'Der Morgen' is good, except that the modulation to A♭-major is unnecessary. 'Einsamer Gang' has very good ideas. The sonata movement is good, and my courage in tackling it is remarkable. The Etude is dull.

> Well, Fräulein, let me tell you something: you have a very fine talent. We might be able to make something of you. Watch out that it doesn't go sour on you.[14] That's how things are: your environment is detrimental to you. Your life of luxury. You should be poor, forced to earn a living. And then the Secession, the detrimental influence on you of all those young, immature artists.

He's right. I admit it a thousand times over: he's right. My environment is

---

13 Franz Hohenberger returned to Vienna from Paris in 1893 to collaborate with Josef Engelhart and others. Having accompanied Adolf Fischer, a specialist in Oriental art, on a journey to Japan, he succeeded in persuading him to loan his collection of woodcuts, scroll paintings and handicrafts to the Secession for their sixth Exhibition.

14 Orig.: from 'you have' to the end of this sentence in capital letters.

my death. If only I could make a reputation for myself: that would be the fulfilment of my dearest wish.

A fairy-tale

Once upon a time there lived a young, beautiful child who loved a proud, flighty painter. For a short time he treated her like one of his toys – then he put her aside. But the young girl was endowed with artistic ability – in music, And when her parents would no longer let the blond, handsome man enter their house, she thought, 'I do not want to see him, but I would like him to hear me. I shall let him see the most attractive side of me.' So she sat herself down at the piano and played and played . . . But the uncouth fellow simply leaned against the wall – and wept.

After all these years, we're supposed to give up our dear room – for the infant. It's all happening exactly as I feared. –

Friday 6 October

. . . And yet another disappointment. Gretl Hellmann would have loved to take piano lessons with me, give up her teacher and study really seriously. And I'd been heartily looking forward to it too. Just how much I'd been looking forward to it only became clear to me today, when the whole thing was called off. Today, namely, she wrote to say that her Mama didn't want it, because we're intimate friends, that we know each other too well to take it seriously. I'd spoken to Frau Radnitzky about it, had prepared a schedule for the whole winter, had really been looking forward to it – and now . . . With every fresh disappointment I grow more discouraged, more silent. Everything I undertake turns in my fingers into thin air. It's enough to make you despair. Will *everything* fail?

I wept.

Saturday 7 October

This morning: composed a short song. When I sang it to her, Gretl wept. The brief introduction is very meaningful:

It's intended to signify a major disappointment. It's the motto of my life, the sempiternity of my existence.

This evening: Gretl H. She wants to set everything straight.

Saturday 14 October
This morning: Frau Radnitzky. I spoke to her fairly sharply about the singing of my lieder. Freistätt would be fine by me, very much so. For her taste she's too Jewish.
This evening: Gretl H.'s first lesson. She'd practised like mad. She also played the studies etc. well, except for the Schumann . . . If someone plays without feeling, can you funnel feeling into them? I played it through to her once. She was enthralled, but then she imitated my playing – like an exercise, as before, but more sloppily. That wasn't what I was intending.

Sunday 15 October
This morning: the Angerers.
This evening: 'Mignon'. I'm so happy! I consider it a major step forward that I now *realize how* awful this opera really is. Thomas's graceful ditties and sentimental dirges leave me unmoved. I hear nothing but appalling capriciousness, a lack of proficiency and a loused-up text. I hear nothing but a mishmash of genuine French chansons. The whole thing reeks of the Dreyfus affair.
Mignon was sung by Selma Kurz, on whose account we'd chiefly gone to see it. She promises well. Lovely voice, poor acting. Madame Saville as Philine I found annoying. If you've ever heard Marie Lehmann, you should never listen to anyone whose technique is still so utterly underdeveloped. Naval as Wilhelm Meister was good but affected.
Why didn't this wonderful opera plot fall into the hands of a *German* musician? How can some shallow Frenchman understand our feelings? Poor Goethe – if everyone were to read you like Ambroise Thomas . . .
Today I was walking down the street, alone, and a young man kept following me. I gave him a dirty look. He sent his servant over, who asked me to look in tomorrow's edition of the 'Neues Wiener Tagblatt'. I told him where to get off.

Tuesday 17 October
Yesterday morning, Narciss and Anna Prasch. I complained that I still hadn't a clue about orchestration, and N. said:
　　Go to Heuberger.
As if someone had thrown pitch into a brazier, his words kindled a fire in my mind, for at the time it was already ablaze. That was just it – go to Heuberger. I rushed to Mama, who agreed.

All right, Aunt Prasch, make sure to tell him straight away.
Pure bliss . . . And then Carl arrived. I told him the whole story.

Why do you act first, then ask me when everything's been decided?

Decisions like this can't be rushed. You'd do better to go to Fuchs.
And Carl is right. So we hastily wired Aunt Prasch.

Thursday 17 October
Labor. He liked 'Ich trat in jene Hallen', but not because it was by Ibsen.
We started on the various clefs. I asked him about orchestration, and he
said:

Counterpoint first.
And, once again, Labor is right.
Labor was terribly sweet, and we talked a lot about Papa. Maybe I'll make
a name for myself after all. Just take things seriously, seriously.

Monday 23 October
a.m. Olbrich with a Herr Weidenbusch. A smart fellow. He'd come to see
Papa's paintings. I'm very fond of Olbrich. Unfortunately he doesn't return
the compliment. I believe he's firmly hitched up. But I really like him. Alas,
poor girl!

Tuesday 24 October
Labor. I played him the final versions of my songs (the ones to be
performed at the chamber-music concert), in case any mistakes in the
harmony needed correcting. After hearing 'Einsamer Gang', he said:

A curious piece. But that doesn't matter: it's good.
This evening:

Tristan

The opera of operas. With its continuous ebb and flow, its mad passion and
boundless longing. Longing for something that exists but which we cannot
recognize. Wagner had a presentiment of it! I love this work as much as my
'Faust'. There too one finds this longing for the unknown, for things we
can sense but *never* recognize. Here we have the two greatest geniuses,
united in one thought-process.
Counterpoint is dull as ditchwater. I was struggling to find an upper voice
for a chorale, and Labor drove me nearly mad with his constant 'Go back.'
It reminded me of 'The magic flute'.

Wednesday 25 October
I've just been playing Tristan, act I and act II, up to his entrance. This immortal work thrilled me so deeply, I was almost moved to tears. Only *one* opera exists in the whole world: my 'Tristan'.
And while I'm dying of passion, Gretl is sitting in Carl's room, copying recipes out of cookery books . . .
Spent the whole day at the Hennebergs'. Gretl is learning to cook – while I play 'Götterdämmerung'. Uncle Hugo brought me home. Two really cultured, dear people.
Yesterday I talked to Labor about modern education. Why are boys *taught* to use their brains, but not girls? I can see it in my own case. My mind has not been schooled, which is why I have such frightful difficulty with everything. Sometimes I really try, force myself to think, but my thoughts vanish into thin air. And I really want to use my mind. I really do. Why do they make everything so terribly difficult[15] for girls? That would be a goal for women: women's emancipation will never be possible, unless their minds are systematically trained, *drilled*. He was forced to agree with me.
Dear God, is there a place for me on this earth?

Tuesday 31 October
Labor. He was highly unsatisfied.
      Well, if this is the best you can do, you'd better give up.
I felt miserable.
This afternoon: to the Zentralfriedhof with Carl.

Wednesday 1 November
This evening: with the Hellmanns to 'Tannhäuser'. Winkelmann magnificent, Sedlmair not good, Ehrenstein[16] – as usual – disgusting. But the opera really *is* beautiful. And this Wagner is a fine fellow. He knew: the old church-music style[17] would be of no use {to him}. Only then would it be possible to emphasize the passion of the drama. Nothing ventured, nothing gained! The overture and the chorus at the end of act II prove that he was right.

---

15 Orig.: 'leicht' (easy), altered by A.M.-W. to 'schwer' (difficult).
16 The soprano Luise von Ehrenstein, previously active in Berlin, sang at the Hofoper from 1889 to 1901.
17 Orig.: 'Rosalien' (sequences).

Thursday 2 November

Yesterday, before going into the theatre, we had a stand-up row. I overheard Carl saying to Aunt Laura:

The children deserve a box on the ears for that – etc.

I was so disgusted by his way of speaking that I burst noisily into tears. Never have I heard anything more hideous. For me, from now on Carl is just air. Sometimes I really hate him. And Mama said:

Don't be so silly – I mean you, rather. Gretl has *nothing* to do with it. And don't forget all that Carl has done for you!

She considered herself entirely justified – letting oneself be insulted out of gratitude. For me the concept of 'gratitude' doesn't exist! Nor do I acknowledge the concept of 'filial piety'. I honour the shade of my father, because I loved him, not because I feel in any way indebted to him. Am I indebted to anyone? I would say: *never*. Parents bring their children up because the state obliges them to. For the same reason they give them food and clothing. Whether they treat them well or badly usually depends on their financial status. As a rule, parents try to bring their children up as well as they can. Why? 1) because for the parents every child is a plaything; 2) because they prefer their plaything to be bright and red-cheeked, rather than pale and stupid; and 3) because all parents love to show what *they* can achieve. Only parents can take responsibility for having brought their children into the world. In the final analysis, the love they display is often motivated by pure egoism. They love their children because they are their own flesh and blood, in their children they love themselves. Hence it's quite natural for children to feel an obligation towards their progenitors, but it can and may not be expected of them.

To return to the subject of so-called filial piety: why do I have to stand before Papa's grave in the cold for three minutes every year? After all, I cherish his memory constantly. The strangest thing is that you generally find these two qualities, which are usually a mere pose, in 'worthy citizens', something that in my eyes means little else but 'idiots'. Some people deny themselves their biggest chance in life, so as not to impede their fellowmen. Admittedly, by making others happy, some people are allegedly happier still. But I find that unnatural. Only by enjoying life can people truly love and live. That's why I detest people who squander their lives and give them to others. The others have no need of such gifts.

Enjoy life – you only live it once.

This evening: I played a good deal of 'Walküre' until, half dead from excitement, I *had* to stop.

Sunday 5 November
To the Philharmonic:
> Overture 'Euryanthe'
> Mozart: 'Jupiter' Symphony[18]
> Beethoven: Symphony no 5 in C minor.

I must honestly admit that during the Mozart I got frightfully bored. I felt it wasn't exciting but merely long-drawn-out. Times have changed. Nowadays nobody wants such hyper-naive themes. Our ears are spoilt by Wagner, Liszt etc. The Beethoven aroused my sympathy. His music is entirely modern and intelligible. In Mozart I miss all the qualities needed for absorbing oneself in an artist's character and works ... love, understanding, interest. Everything.

Tuesday 7 November
Labor. My exercises were better. We had a long, long talk. Mostly about Beethoven and Mozart. Labor might even be able to talk me into loving Mozart.

Wednesday 8 November
At Aunt Mie's. Once again they both radiated heartfelt warmth.
This evening: alone. Mama said to Carl:
> See to it that you're at the Secession whenever the children are there. I'm not keen on them wandering about on their own.

Afterwards I went to Mama and said:
> It's very sad that you still don't really know me. If I can't protect myself, Carl's protection won't help me either. So far, I've always succeeded in protecting myself, and in future I shall always do so too.
> Yes, but what would you do if Kl. were to approach you?
> Mama, I know exactly what I have to do.
> I don't want you even to clap eyes on him.

---

18 Orig.: 'Symphony with the closing fugue'. On 14 November 1899 Max Kalbeck wrote in the *Neues Wiener Tagblatt*: 'Herr Mahler has studied the dossiers of our classical composers and, in Beethoven's above all, has found not everything to be in order: here an insignificant marking of expression that has been overlooked, there a characteristic idea that has been ignored – ideas that have suffered generations of misinterpretation. [...] Having recognized these faults, it was Herr Mahler's intention to rectify them. Thus in the C-major Symphony the unsuspecting listener experienced several surprises, not all of which were agreeable. Following the performance with a score, however, it transpired that what might have been taken for arbitrariness or high-handedness on the part of the conductor was in most cases a defensible interpretation of the composer's markings.'

Carl came into the room. How stupid it is of Mama. She really doesn't know me at all. But I do want to see him, and I shan't shrink from his gaze. I shall stand there, motionless, and engrave his picture on my heart – indelibly.

Friday 10 November
This morning: worked hard at my violin sonata.
p.m. at the Leglers'. Played act I of 'Götterdämmerung' with Coralie. Silly me – for then I went to
The flying Dutchman
I must say: I never left an opera-house more bitterly disappointed. That wasn't Wagner. This was someone who, unknown to himself, had borrowed ideas from his contemporaries. You notice the immense influence of Meyerbeer and the Italians. Some passages do reveal his individuality, e.g. the overture and the spinning scene (which isn't entirely beautiful, for instance in the ugly entries of the four, repetitive verses of the ballad). Above all, when it comes to depicting the sea, his music becomes great and magnificent. Even then, he already had a feeling for Nature.

Saturday 11 November
This evening: D'Annunzio's 'La Gioconda' with
Eleonore Duse
I've never seen a more beautiful woman or a greater actress. Every movement she makes is the epitome of classicality. Every word she speaks sounds like music. She is unique and great. She must *be*. And never mind Schiller's unkind words: 'Dem Mimen flicht man {die Nachwelt} keine Kränze'.[19] Lilli Lehmann – Eleonore Duse, opera – tragedy: two immortal heroines. This was an evening I shall never forget.
All the Jews of Vienna looked to see how la Duse wept.

Tuesday 14 November
Opening of the 5th Secessionist Exhibition[20]
. . . and Klimt wasn't there! But everyone else was. I'm sorry I didn't see him. I would have liked to test my strength.

---

19 From the prologue to *Wallensteins Lager*: 'Posterity does not crown an actor's head with laurels.'
20 The 5th Secessionist Exhibition (15 November 1899–1 January 1900) was dedicated to graphic works and associated media, chiefly by so-called 'corresponding members' of the Secession from London, Paris, Munich and Berlin.

Burckhard was there, and I asked him why he hadn't called on us for so long. He said:

> Because I've had an immense amount to do all along, and hence was in a bad mood. I've only been calling on people I didn't care for, so that I could work off my bad temper on them.

> You must like us *very* much, I replied.

That aside, I like *him* very much. What a wonderful fellow he is. I tried to draw him out on the article in 'Die Fackel',[21] but he professed to not having read it. He can tell that to the birds. I'd like to meet the man who hadn't read a newspaper article that slung mud at him. Surely he'll want to read at least *what* they have to say.

All our friends were there – I know most of the names by heart – a big, big crowd. I can't say anything about the drawings, because I haven't yet seen them all, and wouldn't wish to pass ill-considered judgement.

---

21 *Die Fackel*, no 18, end of September 1899, p. 21: 'As Herr Burckhard, formerly director of the Burgtheater and currently Hofrat at the Court of Civil Law, once brought a theatre to its knees, he is considered a capable lawyer. This quality might also perhaps explain the inept style which he recently demonstrated as contributor to *Die Zeit*. Having offered such abundant proof of his literary incompetence, Herr Burckhard would be well advised to leave it at that.'

Suite 15

The past crumbles – times change,
and from the ruins blossoms forth new life.

Tuesday 28 November

Labor.

I'm in a dreadful state. I just can't say how sad I am. And the saddest thing of all is that I have no real idea of what's happening, For the first time that I can recall, I don't know what's wrong.

It's evening. Everyone loves but *once*, and I'm not sure: this love burgeoning within me – is it sincere, or is it just another of those short-lived enthusiasms? The kind that have flickered up even after Klimt?

Sunday evening: the first uncut performance of 'Die Meistersinger'.[1] Olbrich came to fetch us. On the way over, he told me he hadn't slept all night, and that my dancing on Saturday had displeased him. Sat with Aunt Mie in her box. I'd invited Burckhard up for the longer interval. And he came. Spitzer and Ernst Moll were there too. It was very entertaining. Olbrich took no part in the conversation, however, remaining seated on his little stool behind the curtain. Afterwards I asked him why, and he said:

After that wonderful quintet, I just can't make small talk.

I like him all the more for having said that.

Then we had dinner in Hotel Bristol. He doesn't care for me, I care for him. I laugh at all the adorers whose love I can't return. But now I know what it feels like. –

Wednesday 29 November

This evening: house-warming party at Spitzer's: Aunt Mie, Uncle Hugo, the Engelharts, Hoffmann, Olbrich. So this was the first time we'd visited Spitzer in his new Olbrich house (bedroom, dining-room, music-room). The bedroom is white with light-grey accessories – rather too virginal for Spitzer but wonderful in its way. Its simplicity and ingenuity are well-nigh

---

1 Having opened the traditional cuts, Mahler's performance lasted fifteen minutes longer than usual. There were also new sets, built in the Bayreuth tradition, and the entry of the Guilds and Masters in act III was re-staged.

astounding. The drawing-room[2] remains as it was – the old furniture really hits you in the eye. The dining-room and salon are blue. A peculiar, haunting blue, like a Wagner motif. Also finely detailed. The piano is enclosed within wooden boards,[3] creating a rather theatrical impression, with tall candlesticks to the right and left, and with laurels as stems. It sounds rather muffled.

At table I sat between Engelhart and Hoffmann. Olbrich sat opposite me. I was angry with him and exchanged neither a word nor a glance. Once he wanted to drink to me. I pretended not to understand.

After dinner, they absolutely begged me to play the piano. I did so. Only a screen separates the dining-room from the music-room. I went in, Olbrich too. We closed the screen, and I said:

> I've got a bone to pick with you: I told you something for *your* ears only, and you passed it on.
> Impossible, he said.
> The dream, I said.

He laughed:

> Dear young lady, that was pure folly. On Sunday I was in such a bad mood, I simply had to annoy someone.

Well – I soon forgave him. Sat down. Began to play 'Forest murmurs', moved on to the 'Magic Fire Music' ('Siegfried'), then 'Meistersinger' and 'Walküre', finally 'Tristan', of which I played the 'Liebestod' right through – and well, as I was told. O. was sitting beside me, the two of us alone in a closed room. He couldn't keep his eyes off me. Then Mama sang my three lieder, 'Gleich und gleich' and 'Ich wandle unter Blumen'.[4] Everyone liked them, particularly O. In his opinion my work deserves greater recognition. I promised to send him all the lieder I thought were good. Already today I'd given him a copy of 'Einsamer Gang'.

He has wonderful eyes. Sometimes our eyes meet and cannot part. I peer deep into his soul, he into mine. –

Engelhart was in terrific form, altogether the atmosphere was most agreeable. Good-natured, unconstrained. Olbrich is hugely interesting. In many respects he reminds me of Wagner – his immense pride, immense vanity,

---

2 Orig.: 'Herrenzimmer' – presumably not the Turkish-style smoking-room mentioned in Suite 16 (26 February 1900).

3 Olbrich had a penchant for piano design. In his house in Darmstadt, an upright piano, played from the adjoining upstairs room, was embedded into the wall of the living-room (see Plate 13). He also designed *Jugendstil* grand pianos for several German piano manufacturers.

4 Evidently A.S. means three lieder *and* the two other songs.

immense self-assurance. Also the dogmatic way in which he expounds and defends his principles, both verbally and in print. Also his versatility and proficiency, which can really get on one's nerves. I'll be interested to see how he develops.

Today I told him I couldn't see him designing monumental buildings. That, he contended, was actually his greatest strength, but as yet he'd been in no position to prove it. Later I told him I considered him the most talented artist of the Secession. He was visibly delighted.

This afternoon we again visited the Hennebergs. Aunt Mie said she could now understand Mama saying that Burckhard had a mad crush on me. Maybe it's true – maybe not. At any rate, it doesn't interest me greatly. Olbrich is the only man who can impress me.

I've just been reading through my old diaries – Venice and the ensuing fortnight in Vienna – and I don't know whether I should be pleased that I set all my feelings down on paper or not. They seem so foreign to me now. Is it a crime that I'm now growing fond of someone else? No, I'm too resolute to waste my life unloved, like some Ritter Toggenburg.[5] Or am I just talking myself into this new love? In a word: I long for Olbrich and, if he were here, I'd take him straight away. But he isn't – that's the trouble!

Friday 1 December

Olbrich has gone. I must admit that I'm already hankering after him. What a man! Today I told him that he reminded me of Richard Wagner, both as man and artist. I also told him why. I said I considered that the interior and exterior of a house corresponded to the score and libretto of a music-drama. Until now, architects designed the facades of buildings, but entrusted the interior design to the taste and ability of carpenters. Until Wagner, opera composers wrote the music, but depended on librettists for the text. Wagner brought the whole work into equilibrium. His maxim was: outside and inside – beautiful, distinctive.

As for Olbrich: so far I know only his librettos – but they are so vocal, so great, that I expect the most beautiful music-drama of him. A 'Siegfried', a 'Tristan'. And he's still young. I told him all this – but also that I resented his well-nigh petulant vanity.

Today he came to have lunch with us. At first we scarcely exchanged a word. At table it was the same. Not until the black coffee had been served

5 'Ritter Toggenburg': Schiller's ballad tells of a knight who returns home from the Crusades to find that his betrothed has taken holy orders. He builds a hut close to the nunnery, living – and dying – just for an occasional glimpse of her.

did we speak. Mama went off to look to the infant. Carl was talking to Ribarz[6] and Spitzer, and Gretl kept wandering in and out. We felt singularly relaxed. Sitting together on the sofa, the room filled with blue cigarette smoke, we talked . . . and talked. So sweet. I can scarcely say how much I liked him again today.

At Spitzer's, I'd brought him the 'Einsamer Gang'. And today he told me he'd already played it through, had found some things very difficult, but liked it very much.

At the moment of his departure – about 8:00 p.m. – I sat down at the Leglers' piano and played the 'Liebestod' as I'd never played it before . . . so beautifully! Everyone was enraptured, kissed me and looked sad. I felt I'd never played more beautifully in my life – and never shall again. With every note I was recalling my lost friend – Olbrich. Why then? It seems appropriate.

Half a year has passed. I love another man – with renewed fervour – as if with a sacred, morally purified fervour. Is it unjust? Just *once*, physical union – that was what I felt with Klimt. With Olbrich I wish for physical union my whole life long.

Which love is the purer?

Saturday 2 December

Yesterday morning: at the dentist. Robicsek didn't see me himself, unfortunately. I was treated by his assistant instead. It hurt like hell. When I came out, I felt like doing away with myself. Whom did I see? Aunt Mie. I was really delighted by the chance encounter. –

Two days ago I composed a song in just ten minutes – Heine. Not bad, I hope. And today I feel so dreadfully lonely . . .

Uncle Fischel finds Olbrich infuriating, considers him lacking in originality and imagination. Poor chap – he sees himself as a misunderstood genius. But actually he's nothing of the sort.

Sunday 3 December

This morning: called on Bertha. Then on the Ring: met the Lanners. It started to snow, so we took refuge in the driveway of the Grand Hotel. Soon afterwards someone walked past, turned round, approached us: Schmedes. Frau Lanner said:

> You know Fräulein Schindler, don't you?

6 Rudolf Ribarz had been professor of floral painting at the Kunstgewerbeschule since 1892. Like A.S.'s father, he studied with A. Zimmermann.

And he:

>   Oh, what a surprise.

We celebrated a joyful reunion. The Lanners went home. We and Schmedes walked a little further along the Ring, then home. Schmedes is dense but amusing. This evening he's singing Froh in 'Das Rheingold'. He said:

>   An awkward role. You stand around on stage all evening and don't get
>   anything decent to sing.

I teased him about his visit to Ostend. They say he behaved scandalously. Quite right too – you're only young *once*.

This evening, for the first time:

Rheingold

I like it very, very much. Already the opening: forty-two bars with an unchanging harmonic basis – a fine idea. And the water, the rise and fall, the whoosh and roar. In my mind's eye I could see and hear the water. I'm convinced I wouldn't have liked the opera half as much if I didn't know the other parts of the Trilogy so well. But like this it's interesting, you can find the origin of each motif, sense its gradual approach.

Schmedes looked around in search of me, found me and nodded his greeting. I was delighted – my goodness, I'm so terribly superficial and vain. Afterwards we dined with the Hennebergs, who'd also been to the Opera. Spitzer came too. It was quiet – someone was missing!

Tuesday 5 December

Labor. Thoroughly dissatisfied with my exercises. But he liked my new song, 'Aus meiner Erinnerung erblühen'. Later another young lady arrived and with him she played four-hand variations by Saint-Saëns. No warmth, no feeling – but *solid* musicianship.

Wednesday 6 December

Yesterday evening: the Sewalds. Today: to Aunt Mie's.

This evening to

Siegfried[7]

I rate it as highly as 'Tristan'. It's so wonderfully great and youthful. Schmedes was brilliant. Teutonic, boyish. A guest, Lieban, was terrific too.[8] Sedlmair was in top form. The forging scene. The Wotan-Erda dialogue.

---

7 A.S. missed the performance of *Die Walküre* on 5 December 1899.

8 À propos Lieban's Mime, Debussy wrote in 1903 of an interpretation 'in which the art of the singer and of the actor attained such a perfect and rare balance that one did not know what to admire most.' (Debussy, ed. F. Lesure, *Monsieur Croche et autres écrits*, Paris, 1971).

Forest murmurs. The Magic Fire Music, incomparably finer than in 'Die Walküre'. And the closing scene:

Yes everything, everything.[9] Every word, every note. A miracle!

Friday 8 December
This morning: practised hard. For the first times in ages.
This evening:

Götterdämmerung

It was wondrously beautiful. Schmedes and Mildenburg phenomenal. A few minor triumphs:
I. Siegfried and Isolde Wagner were in the director's box. That was very nice. Gretl Hellmann said:
> I do wish he'd look our way, but so far he hasn't.
> We'll see, I said.

I began staring sporadically up at him. After a while young Siegfried shifted his gaze and gave us a long, long stare. I should add that little of it was directed at Gretl H. During the interval we saw Dr Briesemeister, who sang Loge on Sunday, in the foyer. Afterwards Siegfried looked over to us with a smile, only then did he take his seat.
II. Schmedes recognized me and greeted me from the stage with a smile.
III. Walking through the cloakroom, we saw Frau Goldenberg in conversation with Frau Schmedes. Gretl was behind me. A little later she came and told me that Frau G. had said: 'That's Schindler's daughter.' I was delighted: I know her, and I find her beautiful. And she knows me, and she finds me beautiful.
And 'Götterdämmerung' *is* beautiful.

Sunday 10 December
Midday: Gesellschaft concert.

'Lucifer'. Oratorio by Benoit[10]

Soloists: Naval, Gura, Musch, Katzmayr, Körner.

---

9 A passage from the closing duet of *Siegfried*. The accuracy of A.S.'s notation leaves much to be desired.

10 In 1867, the Belgian composer and conductor Peter Benoit founded the Flemish School of Music (from 1898: Flemish Conservatoire) in Antwerp. His *oeuvre* includes four stage-works, but he was primarily a composer of sacred music. *Lucifer* (1865) was the first of five oratorios.

For an oratorio the whole thing's a bit too theatrical. Naval sang splendidly, Gura likewise. Naval, the better-looking of the two, got the most applause.

This evening: Fischel and Spitzer. I got very annoyed with Spitzer. He's so utterly stupid, unintelligent.

Monday 11 December
Worked hard at a new violin sonata.
Spent the evening at the Zierers'.
p.m. with Gretl at the Secession. From the standpoint of artistic individuality, my favourites were B. de Mouvel, Leistikow,[11] Hoffmann, Roll – and Klimt. What these people have to offer! Extraordinary. Morin is very interesting too, but I'm not as fond of him. There's a magnificent group (sculpture) by Bartholomé,[12] 'Love's grief', and some fine drawings by Orlik, Jettmar and Stöhr. Apart from some even finer pastels, there's a splendid bust by Roll: a woman, proud and imperious, her head held high, but her lip curled meaningfully into a smile.

The presentation is ingenious: the large hall has been transformed into several smaller ones, which for an exhibition of graphic art is highly appropriate. Everything is intimate, white, chaste. The right-hand annexe is dominated by Böhm's glass windows. Indescribable. A forest, with trees and leaves. The colour effects are so brilliant, they remain in your mind long after.

Tuesday 12 December
Labor. I was there a long time. Again we had a long, heated discussion about Wagner.
p.m. composed a good deal. The violin sonata gives me great pleasure.
It's the coldest day in three years: 11° below zero. Men and horses have frozen beards. With their spiked barbs they don't look particularly attractive. But at least the trees do. There's nothing more delightful, more charming, than fresh snow, covering every branch, every rooftop – such a sight is so sweet, so enchanting. I can scarcely see my fill. How it glistens!

11 Walter Leistikow played an influential part in the founding of the Berlin Secession in 1899.
12 The sculptor Paul Albert Bartholomé was a so-called 'corresponding member' of the Secession.

Thursday 14 December
Dental appointment, as often at present.

p.m. Gretl Hellmann. On Saturday she was introduced to Mahler, and now she was singing his praises. But what she told me I found rather less appealing. Evidently he trims his sails to the wind. It was at the Goldbergers'. He kept praising up the Jews to the detriment of the Christians. He actually made so bold as to claim that the public had rejected Rubinstein's *wonderful* work 'The Demon' merely for reasons of religious belief. Honestly, that's going too far! Firstly: the opera public is mostly Jewish anyway, secondly: the opera is said to be long but almost devoid of interest. Fancy putting such ideas into the mouths of the Jews, especially if you remember that they see themselves as a persecuted race. She went on in much the same manner. But it's so trivial, I shan't bother to write it down.

As for Richard Strauss, he shares Labor's opinion, except that Labor is more tolerant. He says: 'R.S. is one of our most talented young musicians, but he squanders[13] his vast ability by eschewing melodic line, and concentrates instead on the magic of orchestral colour. It's a crying shame.' Mahler asserts flatly, 'I don't understand him.' But such a rejection is too categorical: Richard Strauss is a mighty 'sounding heart'[14] but unfortunately he's hedged in by false principles. I find him immensely interesting. In my opinion his F-major Symphony[15] is outstanding.

This evening: first Krasny, then Mayreder. Once again, K. was insufferable. I was playing to Gretl – 'Siegfried'. Krasny came over and asked if he'd come too soon. I replied:

You always come too soon.

You can't give a clearer answer than *that*. He left soon afterwards, thank God.

Earlier: Lilli Lehmann. As ever, she was uniquely pretty, sweet and kind. When she arrived, Gretl and I were playing 'Siegfried', and making rather a hash of it. We weren't together. I was busy taking her to task when the door opens and in walks the greatest soprano in the world. I told her we were playing 'Siegfried' and she said:

I'd never have recognized it. To me it sounded like a child tinkling about.

They took her to see the infant, and Mama said Carl was so crazy about the child, he'd always take his colleagues to show them.

---

13 Orig.: 'verschweindeln' – a portmanteau word, comprising 'verschwenden' (to waste) and 'Schwein' (pig).

14 Orig.: 'tönendes Herz' – derived from 'tönendes Erz' (sounding brass).

15 i.e. the Symphony in F *minor* op 12, composed 1883/84.

And you expect that baby to grow up to be a respectable young lady? She said it more sweetly than you could imagine, with real authority. When I look at her in profile, she drives me crazy – her eyes so black, her nose so fine and dainty, her mouth, her teeth. Yes – she's uniquely beautiful – something special.

Saturday 16 December
This morning: first to the dentist, then lesson at Frau Radnitzky's. I'm learning the 'Emperor' Concerto now. When I play Beethoven, I always feel as if my soul were at the dry cleaners, and that the ugly black stains caused by the impurities and nervous traumas of Wagner were being removed.
Played the second part of act I and the whole second part of act III of
Siegfried
Gretl was in ecstasy.
Baroness Bach[16] was listening in Frau Radnitzky's studio. Afterwards she said:
　　You play Wagner very well.
A little later, I told her I was a pupil of Labor's, and she said:
　　I wouldn't have taken you for one.

Sunday 17 December
At present I'm in an almost indescribable state, between living and not living, awareness and unawareness. It's the fault of the schnapps – and a pair of fiery eyes.
Reininghaus to lunch.
This morning: Philharmonic concert.
　　L. Spohr: Overture to 'Jessonda'
　　Brahms: Violin Concerto
　　(Violin: {Marie} Soldat-Röger)[17]
　　Beethoven: 'Pastoral' Symphony
Beethoven is the Michelangelo of music, great and powerful. Because of its unbroken calm, I'm not so keen on the first movement of the 'Pastoral'. The second movement, on the other hand, 'Scene by the stream',

16 Baroness Leonore Bach was a friend of Brahms and an accredited interpreter of his music, notably of the solo soprano part in *Ein Deutsches Requiem*, which she sang at the work's first complete performance. Her daughter, Maria Bach, was a composer.
17 Marie (or Maria) Soldat, a pupil of Joseph Joachim; in 1899 she married a lawyer named Röger. She later founded the celebrated, all-female Soldat-Röger Quartet.

is delightfully appealing – but a little too long. But the fourth[18] is great and powerful. When I closed my eyes, I could see the lightning flashing and hear the thunderclaps. It's the most magnificent interpretation of elemental violence, of the forces of nature, of conflicts in the soul of man. Beethoven: the hero of absolute music – Wagner of opera. These two extremes will one day be united in *one* work of art. Both *equally* modern, both *equally* great. Both true to their individual principles.

Today, as I said, I don't feel quite responsible for my actions. You know what it feels like![19] One doesn't know what one is saying – but actually one does.

This evening Richard, Uncle Fischel and (again) Reininghaus. The latter bet me four bottles of champagne – which the two of us would down alone – that I'd show him my diary. Both ideas – showing him the diary and drinking *alone* – are rather curious. I don't quite know who he thinks he is. I'm quite fond of him – but no more than that.

With Fischel I had another violent argument about Olbrich and Hoffmann. Now he's calling me his 'bone of contention'.

Wednesday 20 December

Have made my peace with Wilhelm.

Composed a good deal, but more with the mind than the heart. I wasn't very inventive, but it didn't work out too badly. I only hope Olbrich comes soon, for then it would go that much better. He always stimulates me so strangely. After he left Vienna, while still entirely under his influence, I wrote 'Einsamer Gang' – perhaps my best song.[20] And now, after the evening at Spitzer's, in just *ten* minutes, I wrote a song entitled 'Aus meiner Erinnerung erblühn'.

I'm so ashamed of myself. On St Mark's Square Kl. asked me:

> Alma, you'll keep a tiny spot in your heart for me – for ever – won't you, Alma?

And I replied:

> For ever.

Kl. laughed softly & repeated:

18 Orig.: 'third'.
19 Orig.: 'Kennt ihr das Gefühl!' – i.e. as direct speech.
20 A.S.'s memory is short here: 'Einsamer Gang' is first mentioned on 15 September 1899 (Suite 14), and was presumably composed a few days earlier. But Olbrich did not leave Vienna, as A.S. herself records, until Friday 1 December. Presumably the song was composed under the impression of the news that he was leaving, rather than as a reaction to the event itself.

Just a tiny spot.

He really understood women. He didn't demand my whole heart. He knew: sooner or later it would belong to someone else. And at the time I was so self-confident, so full of my great love, that his words grieved me. And I was so dreadfully fond of him. A passion can only be banished by an even stronger one or, as Spinoza says, an affect . . .

We've just been counting up my youthful flames: Hermann Rieser, M. Winkelmann, Walter Bopp, Theo Schumacher, Rudi Horwitz, Ernst Zierer – but what followed I didn't say.

I also recalled a few amusing episodes. In Goisern, for instance: Rudi H. and I were courting, and Gretl was getting on our nerves. A *fitting* opportunity presented itself: he said he had a pimple on his nose: would Gretl bring him a pin so that he could prick it open? Off she went. We were delighted at his cunning ruse. R. said amorous things to me and, under the impression of his words, our faces glowed.

In Hamburg came the Schumacher flirt. Once, just to tease me, he put a big stone in my bed – and I was having my period. On another occasion the same youngster, in search of a kiss, chased me down a dark hotel corridor. I ran and ran, until I came to a locked door. I banged into it, and Theo was able to reap his reward. – From inside we heard a long-drawn-out 'Oh'. When we were leaving, he asked Mama's permission to write to me. And he really did – his letters were unremarkable, moderate, *official*, but he always included { – } little postcards of a less official nature. One of his scribblings began with these words:

> To you, my dear Alma, I must needs unburden the love-pangs of a
> parturient heart.

And so on, in the same style. In those days I used to take it all so seriously – today I think differently of my beaux. So many recollections: how old I already am!

Sunday 24 December

This morning: Hofrat Burckhard. Such a nice man! Then the Legler girls, then – I can write no more. Even after so many years, opening Christmas presents always makes me feel pleasurably excited.

I'm putting the postcard in here, because it's really cute and dashing.

Twenty-eight presents: a chinchilla fur, a skunk fur, blouses, writing paper, a green handbag, vocal scores of 'Siegfried', 'Rheingold' and 'Die Götterdämmerung', six pairs of gloves, books etc., etc. Really lovely, beautiful things.

Friday 29 December
Just now I'm avidly reading

Beyond Good and Evil
The Genealogy of Morals
Nietzsche

I must be honest and admit that there's much, very much that I don't come anywhere near understanding. But sometimes you find maxims, confessions of faith, so beautiful that they stick in your mind.[21]

Saturday 30 December
p.m. Flora Berl, Ernst Zierer, Moser and – Olbrich. Something pleases me *so* much that I almost regret it. We were talking about my 'Einsamer Gang', and he played a chord progression by heart. I was delighted – still am.

Sunday 31 December
We're still in the old year – 10:30 p.m. – so a few hasty words:
What has the year brought me? Many lovely things and many sad experiences. I don't want to grumble. Everything that happened, I observed consciously and even provoked. I'm not ashamed of anything I said or anything I did. There are a few things I would wish for, but I shan't clothe them in profane words. I bear no grudges, feel no hatred. Nobody means *so* much to me that they could arouse *such* feelings in me. I love one man. Although I found him, did I learn by my mistakes? That's how it will always be. I also have no hope for the future.
Around me everything looks dismal. I'm in everyone's way, a burden to everyone, and nobody loves me. Where then could hope spring from? I long for much and hope for nothing.
That's how things are – and I'm twenty years old.

21 At this point, A.S. copies the entire section 41 from Part Two ('The free spirit') of Nietzsche's *Beyond Good and Evil* into her diary. The passage – it begins, 'One must test oneself to see whether one is destined for independence and command; and one must do so at the proper time' – is written in block capitals throughout.

Tuesday 2 January 1900
Yesterday Walter Bopp gave me Houston Stewart Chamberlain's book on Richard Wagner. It's magnificent, with many beautiful photographic plates and facsimiles, also copies of scores, drawings, caricatures by Menzel etc. I was terrifically pleased. I was less pleased that it was Walter who gave it to me, for I have a funny feeling he'll soon be standing on our doorstep. Well, it's easy enough to say no.

This morning: Labor. He was angry with me for not going to Rika's this evening, and groused about it all through the lesson. My sonata isn't bad – but it isn't good either. At least, not as good as I'd imagined. The styles are all jumbled up. The opening is simple, later it becomes ultra-pseudo.[22] In a word, it simply has no form. *For now* I'm to stick to lieder. As for me, I'd prefer to start on a symphony right away.

Thursday 4 January
Gretl Hellmann called.

This evening: to Dr Spitzer's. Max Friedmann and his wife, Mie, Hugo and Olbrich were there.

I'm so very sad! I'm not sure – do I really like O. so well, or is it just wounded pride? In a word, O. spoke almost exclusively to Frau Friedmann. He also appears to be afraid of me. When I was accompanying Spitzer, he didn't go to the piano with us like last time. And every time he made as if to talk to me, she would call him. To me it seems their friendship is *very* close. I'm really depressed – none of my wishes seems ever to come true.

Now I know. He's in love with her. And she's small, cute and superficial, loves to talk about things she doesn't understand – I don't care for her at all. We scarcely exchanged ten words. I'd been so looking forward to the evening. Tomorrow, however, he's coming to us: I shall remain utterly cold and indifferent. My heart is frozen over. Yesterday evening I realized that nobody will ever love me, ever understand me . . . to think that someone should prefer an insignificant little mannequin – to me!

22 Orig.: 'ultra-verlogen' – probably a word-play on the catch-phrase of *fin-de-siècle* Vienna, 'ultra-modern'.

I'm strangely fond of him. The thought of him pierces my heart [as if with a knife]. I'm convinced that he already feels my love for him. Yesterday, in company, he addressed me several times. I didn't look at him, but simply looked into the void. Finally he took his leave. I said nothing, turned on my heel. Whether he comes tomorrow is all the same to me. As far as I'm concerned, he's dead, as I've always been for him. I'd like to cry, but can't. I have no more tears.

What should I do now? Music? What can a dumb woman like me achieve? – Nothing! I lack application. My head is full of other, *silly* ideas. Save me! – Save me from my new disease.

Nirvana! – Death! –

Apart from accompanying Sp., I didn't play a note yesterday. For whom was I to play? For Olbrich I no longer can. At other times I played only for him. I've lost a grip on myself. Feel apathetic about everything. Whether he comes tomorrow, I couldn't care. I hate him and love him. I hate him, because he let me be caused such offence. I wonder if he realized what he's done to me? –

Saturday 6 January

Mama has a slight cold, and therefore put Olbrich and Spitzer off. Now he'll forget about me altogether. Today I've been pondering: if he'd loved me, would it have brought us happiness? I pondered the question for some time.

My problem is that I observe everything *so* closely. I noticed that Olbrich isn't entirely unaffected. I noticed how he revelled in Frau Friedmann's empty flattery. I noticed – once again – that he's insincere. *Despite all that*, I'd take him on the spot, for everything else about him is impressive – and liberal. As for these few small matters – dear God, everyone has their faults. He has his. I have mine. You have to put up with that. But what's the use . . . He just doesn't love me!

Wilhelm has just left. I'm not particularly sorry to see him go.

Something else is making me so dejected that I have to cry. I have no choice. I'm not to be envied. I just hope my stupid tears don't give me away. He'll never be mine. Just a diversion. I must try to take my mind off him.

Carl sent the cancellation to the studio, but Olbrich hadn't been there all day. And so it happened that suddenly, at 7:30, he was on our doorstep. Gretl and Carl had driven to the station, and I was pacing about in the dining-room with my Nietzsche, unsuspecting. He came in and gave me the book, 'Ideen von Olbrich',[23] that I'd long been wanting. I was overcome with joy! One thing though: I'm convinced he knows how deeply he offended me the other day, and that he brought the book more or less as an apology. I asked him to write something in it. He got out a pencil and . . . put it away again.

What should I write for you? Nothing is appropriate!
What did he mean by that?
I led him into the dining-room. Mama came in and read him the passages I'd underlined. He liked them all. Mama went out. We were alone. Now and then Bertha came in to put things on the table. I sat facing him, like a stranger – the experiences of the other day have clearly shattered my trust in him. Feeling the need to say something, I began:

I don't really understand how you . . . oh, why should I be telling you all this? It's not up to me.
He looked at me and said:
I know exactly what you're trying to say.
I believe him.
[He said:
Just you wait, this evening we'll find we agree on all sorts of things.
But that wasn't the case.]
He began to sketch out my room on the Hohe Warte. He's so handsome. Such lovely eyes. False teeth, unfortunately. But he's as chic as chic can be. I would have liked to talk a little longer, but all the others came in, and for me that was the end of it. Although I'm convinced he only values me as a friend and feels not a trace of affection for me, his gift gave me inordinate pleasure. I do wish it hadn't served to raise my accursed hopes, though. He stayed until 11:45.

Monday 8 January
I'm dead beat today. Can't compose – nothing. Just turning things over in my mind.
p.m. Spitzer, Mie.
This evening: composed. It went marvellously, I had all kinds of ideas. And then the door opens: in comes Mama with a book, sits down. Not long afterwards Carl. My good mood down the drain. That's where I wish myself and the whole world, I'm so annoyed.

23 *Ideen von Olbrich*, a collection of Olbrich's drawings and sketches with a preface by the art critic Ludwig Hevesi, was published in Vienna in 1899.

Oh to be alone, to have a bit of money, to be independent – how wonderful that would be! I have no choice but to cry. After dinner I went quickly upstairs, happy to have the living-room to myself, to be free, to be able to compose. Then along comes Mama – and stays. I was just beginning to feel, 'Now I can.' And now, an hour later, I'm sterile. Mama said:

You should be glad that you're not in my way.

What a woman! Elbows her way through life. I went into my room and cried.

Tuesday 9 January

Happy. Labor was very satisfied. Even though he disguised the fact, saying:

Blind hen . . . seed of grain . . . but the chicken's gifted!

I was overjoyed. Now I'm composing a song-cycle, 'Schilflieder', after Lenau. Very tricky. Somewhat uniform.

p.m. Aunt Laura and the Zierers' French teacher. On Sunday we've got to go to Lili's. They're throwing a ball for young people. A frightful bore. I loathe all such functions. Always the same.

Thursday 11 January

p.m. Gretl Hellmann for a lesson. It looks as though she's lost the urge for regular practice.

Because Röntgen was playing the Schumann C-major Fantasy, which I'd never heard played by a concert pianist, I bought tickets for the Messchaert concert. Gretl's cab was an age arriving, so we took a cab ourselves, and drove to the Bösendorfer-Saal. Arrived late of course, the concert had already begun. But we were astonished to hear the sound of fiddling, which appeared to be emanating from several instruments. Gretl fetched a programme: 'Soldat-Röger Quartet'. We'd mistaken the date by a whole week. What to do? Fetch our jackets from the cloakroom and make for the exit, tails between our legs. Do we take a cab? No, 1 fl was already down the drain. We'll walk then! And that in the filthiest of weather, snow and ice. Soon I could feel a tickle in my throat.

As we arrive home: a fiacre at the door. A visitor: Hofrat Burckhard. I was delighted. I told him the whole story, and he said:

You're making it all up. Anyone could say that.

We started making plans for next winter. Carl would like to go to Palermo, Mama to Capri, and I to Ceylon. Burckhard said my suggestion wasn't so stupid, and that he wouldn't have expected it of me. I started making impudent comments, the conversation grew somewhat familiar. He asked Mama's permission to go South with us, as butler, to which I replied:

No, as bed-warmer.

Embarrassed silence . . . Everyone felt compelled to take the edge off my remark but, no matter how hard they tried, the situation became increasingly uncomfortable. That amused me. I also came up with the following remark, which wasn't as vulgar but just as cheeky: I know that he dislikes Krasny, and as I also have an aversion to the fellow, our opinions of him tally. I said:

This fellow Krasny, you know, he always turns up in the evening and stays to dinner. Recently I was so beastly to him that he left.

That was going rather too far, for Burckhard himself always turns up in the evening and stays to dinner. Carl fumed . . . Burckhard laughed.

One thing I've noticed: if the conversation is playful, his wit is a match for anyone's. If we turn to more serious, artistic affairs, he says nothing. Particularly when it comes to painting. That's wise of him – I believe he isn't particularly well informed on the subject.

Friday 12 January
Frightfully tired! Sore throat.
p.m. Lili and Ernst. Later Baroness Bach came along and played piano duets with me. She played well and with spirit. A very talented woman – and pretty too.

Saturday 13 January
I got undressed – and suddenly I felt as if I were disgorging some slimy object. It hardened rapidly, only to melt again. I grasped it in my hands – it was nothing but a pair of blue eyes, blue eyes! I held the shadow in a stranglehold, thrust it from me. It cried out:

I am your child – yours and Klimt's. More than once in your imagination you have conceived me – and now you deny my very existence.

It was as if everything was happening, was being said, in the distance, from outside me. I was alone. And I became terribly sad, had to cry. In truth, how often did I see myself as Kl.'s wife – blessed with his child, joyful, inconceivably blissful. For it was *his* image that I had created. How often have I dreamt it – asleep and awake. And now the thought comes and indicts me. All the same, I love the thought.

Sometimes I think I'm going mad. –

All being well, we should be spending the whole
of next winter in Sicily. Perhaps that would be
my salvation, spatial and mental salvation from
everything . . .

Tuesday 16 January
This morning: Labor. The work I brought was
good.
This evening: lecture by Dr Lichtwark in the
Gewerbemuseum.[24] For the first time in ages I
saw – Klimt. And again I feel: this is the man
whom Nature has eternally and uniquely
predetermined for me. I know every muscle of
his face, I know his whole personality. We were
standing with Aunt Mie. He came over, paused,
bowed and walked on. And I had to look on,
couldn't even shake his hand, had to let the dearest,
sweetest of men walk by as if he didn't know me.
What use is self-deception? In truth, I love nobody but him, and him I shall
always love. Everybody said I looked so pale. Is that surprising? The last
time I saw him – and today. How much lies between.

Thursday 18 January
Gretl came for a lesson. Such a nice girl. We three young ladies sang
through an entire volume of Schumann lieder. Downstairs sat Hoffmann
and Bernatzik, discussing how to arrange the studio. Tomorrow there's a
party for thirty-six guests – not ours but the Secession's. Carl has placed his
studio at their disposal, and now they plan to decorate it with tapestries
etc. etc. We're not invited, of course – thirty-six men and three women! But
we hope for a few visitors. Shall I see Klimt? Will he come? My beloved!

{*Friday 19 January*}
p.m. we helped to lay the tables. The studio looked magnificent. They'd
borrowed tapestries and Empire furnishings from Otto Schmidt, the tables
were laid with traditional Viennese crockery. We watched all the guests
arrive – Klimt came too. To begin with, we stayed outside. Then Hancke
brought us this card, Moser brought us another, on which he'd drawn a

24 Alfred Lichtwark, an influential aesthetician and patron of the arts, founded the Hamburg
Kunsthalle in 1868.

picture of one of us peeping through a chink in the door. Hoffmann brought Mama the fourth card.[25]

Everyone took their places at table. We went into the dining-room, and the Bachrich Quartet started playing lively Viennese dance-music. Burckhard and Mama came upstairs to fetch the punch-bowl. Hoffmann came too, and brought us whole trays of sweets. Moser came, also Auchentaller (to whom we were introduced), List and others. We were still in the anteroom, where the wine was being poured out. We had a good view into the studio. Absolutely incognito. I could see Klimt. He could see me too. Auchentaller looked over to us and said to Hoffmann:

> I say, she's pretty.

Immediately afterwards he asked to be introduced. Stayed with us. Moser and Hoffmann kept returning with fruit and sweets. More people joined them, more and more. In the end they all begged to dance just one waltz with us. We tiptoed into the dining-room, rolled back the carpets and danced for all we were worth.

Suddenly Carl: he'd forbidden us to come downstairs. We ran into the »office«. The others grabbed Carl, lifted him up bodily and carried him out. We, meanwhile, made ourselves scarce. Upstairs was Hofrat Burckhard, with whom we later went back downstairs.

Back into the little antechamber. Time for the speeches. Engelhart greeted the guests, particularly Lichtwark. Lichtwark responded, expressing the hope that this new trend in Viennese art would hold sway for years to come (his speech was neither persuasive nor eloquent) and that within a decade a new Viennese style would arise, that could vie with Paris. Hofrat Stadler,[26] spokesman for the Government, responded warmly and amiably. Hermann Bahr rose to his feet and launched into a diatribe of fifteen minutes' duration, repeatedly beating his breast etc. – He also derided bureaucracy and public taste. Everyone was furious at such lack of tact, all the more so when Hofrat Stadler ostentatiously stood up and left. He said to Carl:

> You know, I should really have responded, but I didn't want to spoil the fun.

Everyone was annoyed, but not for long. Soon all was forgotten. Our little chamber began to fill again, Burckhard was still standing next to me. Hancke came in:

> Oh, pardon me,

25 The cards are reproduced on pp. 231–2.
26 From 1898, Friedrich Viktor Stadler was employed at the Ministry of Education, initially in the section responsible for technical colleges and high-schools, later in the art section.

Do come in, dear Hancke, said B. You can stand between us if you like, you still won't be able to separate us.

Hancke went out, dreadfully offended. Outside we could see him rushing around behind the laurel bushes. Angry, jealous? Ha-ha. Klimt came towards us, but kept a slight distance. List said:

No need to be shy, dear Klimt. Do join us.

Klimt approached and shook hands with him – then made off. From outside the door he threw me a rose. He aimed badly: the rose hit the lintel and fell to the floor. He laughed, went over, picked it up, played with it, then threw it back into the antechamber. It landed at my feet. Lenz picked it up, and I stuck it in my hair. Kl. saw it and smiled [a wicked, frivolous smile]. More and more people came over to us, even Lichtwark and Otto Wagner.

L: Please, Fräulein, just one dance.

I'm not allowed to.

Finally, after much pleading (he kept saying, 'I'll take full responsibility'):

You'd better ask Carl. By the way, do you have any idea who Carl is?

Everyone laughed heartily.

But of course. I shall ask him.

While he was out of the room, Otto Wagner asked me:

Please, Fräulein, would you care to walk round the studio with me? Give the other guests something pretty to look at, just one round? –

I: Carl doesn't approve of my going in there.

This time the laughter was hysterical.

Well said, young lady – marvellous!

He: But with an old man like me – fifty-six years old!

I: You know, age makes no difference.

He: But I'm a grandfather.

I: Not even then.

Lichtwark came back:

Well, Carl has given us permission, but only in the dining-room, where nobody can see us, not even he.

So we all repaired to the dining-room. Lichtwark is an excellent dancer. Then a pause. We all went upstairs, Burckhard too. Earlier, because he was intercepting all the eyes Kl. was making at me, he described himself as 'the wall'. And I have to admit that the love of my life has deteriorated to a mere tease. I was simply flirting with him. Tant mieux!

Well, my 'wall' hadn't missed a thing, neither Hancke's fury nor Klimt's . . .

You know, I said, some of these people hate you.

Yes, I know it. Already in Florence . . .

In other words: he knew my secret. I explained everything with my eyes, with his eyes he indicated that he'd understood. Together we went downstairs. Before that, Kl. saw me:

Where on earth is Burckhard?

Upstairs with us.

Tell him to come downstairs! – and he pulled a face.

I shook hands with him again and said:

Good night.

In the corridor, B. and I had a long talk. He told me a bit about my character:

You're not stupid, you know. You follow your common sense, but you're also an emotional person, and within you the two qualities are in conflict.

Yes, but usually my common sense wins through.

Mama called. Hohenberger and Lenz had dressed themselves up à la japonaise, with lampshades on their heads etc. They were executing a Japanese dance and having a whale of a time.[27] Moser was with us all along.

Finally it was time to go to bed and, a little squiffy, we all went upstairs. It was 3:00 a.m. The others dispersed at 5:00. I'm so happy that everything turned out as it did.

After the Lichtwark party, I still believed: Klimt – only Klimt. But since this evening, when I spoke to him again, I've returned to earth. His behaviour is childish, his smile vulgar. He has no business to smile at me. And throwing the rose – that was entirely inappropriate. The latest news, incidentally, is that he's having an affair with Rose Friedmann, that old scragbag.[28] He takes what he can get. No: yesterday, already, I could feel: it's over. All over! The closer he came, the more remote he was. His cool reserve used to drive me mad, {now} his penetrating stare disgusts me.

Yes, it's over. All over. –

27 In the 1899 edition of *Ver sacrum*, vols. 4 and 9 both included essays on Japanese art (Ernst Schur: 'Der Geist der japanischen Kunst', 'Das Theefest am Hakone-See; Zur Werthschätzung der japanischen Kunst'). Amongst the Secessionists, the subject of Japan was at this time extremely topical.

28 Orig.: 'Scharteke'. Klimt painted his magnificent, but little-known portrait of Rose von Rosthorn-Friedmann in 1901.

Sunday 21 January
Engelhart was wonderfully sweet and amusing. At all cost they wanted to drag me inside. Klimt's first glance was one of regret. I returned it too. But later his expression became bolder, cheekier. Quite right too.

Today Gretl told me that while Moser and I were dancing – alone in the dining-room – Klimt was watching from outside. I was tickled pink by that. I can only say: it's his fault that I no longer take the whole thing seriously. I wouldn't want to waste another thought on him. Let him be buried – for ever. Let him be numbered amongst my dead, my beloved dead. Never shall I think or say a word against him. I repeat: for me he is sacred.

And so we come to the end of a romance that lasted three years. And what an ending – ha! I've lost three years of my life. But I shan't despair, for despite the terrible times I went through, Kl. made me happier than anyone else ever will.

It was my first, great, beautiful love. –

Amen!

Koloman Moser's invitation card for the banquet given by the *Vereinigung Bildender Künstler Österreichs* (Vienna Secession) on 19 January 1900, with the signatures (top left to bottom right) of: Josef Maria Auchentaller, Ferdinand Andri, unidentified, Wilhelm List, Kolo Moser, Josef Hoffmann, Friedrich König, A. Lichtwark, Otto Wagner ('A toast to the lady of the house'), Hermann Bahr, Dr Max Burckhard.

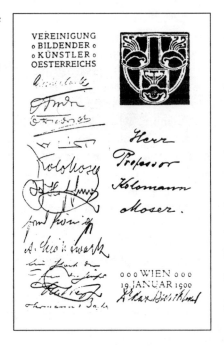

'One of us peeping through a chink in the door' – drawing by Koloman Moser, with signatures of Moser, Hancke and König.

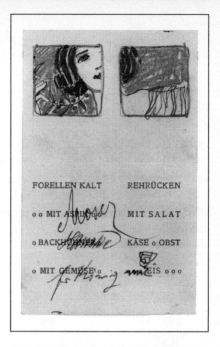

Drawings by Friedrich König

'Flowers – but wild flowers' –
drawing by (?) Josef Hoffmann

Suite 16

... once again a slender hope
slips through my fingers ...

Sunday 21 January
Lunch at the Hennebergs' with Director Lichtwark, Hoffmann, Bernatzik and Moser. It was rather fun. Lichtwark was unbelievably rude to me. We were taking black coffee. He loves Bach and Beethoven, and I couldn't do him the honour. Instead I played Schubert, then Wagner, to which Lichtwark kept saying 'Good night.' Then Mama sang some of my lieder – including my latest, 'Stumme Liebe', to a text by Lenau. They went down rather well. Lichtwark said:

I wouldn't have thought you capable of it.
Who does he think I am? Altogether I wasn't particularly taken with Lichtwark. He made polite remarks, but that was all. I was offended.
Then we were at Flora Berl's. Hoffmann has triumphed. His dining-room is delightful. The hall too, let's say the anteroom. Auchentaller is good. But Olbrich . . . the music-room is too cluttered for music, too obtrusive, too pompous. The bedroom, though conceived in the grand manner, is shabby and unrefined. The mauve is disturbing to start with, then the exaggerated arches – uncomfortable, unpleasant. A showroom, but not fine enough for that. I was sorry: I'd expected better things of Olbrich. He's made a complete mess of it. Could it be that he isn't coming up to expectation?
Bernatzik is a dear fellow. He can remember me even before I was born. He said:

You'd prefer to have Klimt or Olbrich sitting in my place.
I looked at him, stupefied . . . Why, of all things, those two? Especially considering they have absolutely nothing in common. He replied:

If one is blessed with instinct and powers of deduction . . .
It's strange.
Meanwhile Hofrat Burckhard had called – I was so sorry {to miss him}. By the way, unbelievable rumours are circulating about him. A married couple named Süss is getting divorced – because of him. He takes what he can get. Just what I'd do!
Bernatzik liked the silhouette of my hair falling down my back so much, he couldn't stop talking about it.

Tuesday 23 January
Played Labor the new song, and he said it was one of my best, a good song. Although I already knew it, I was very pleased. Technically speaking, I've made no progress – I'm so *mindless*. Keep making the same stupid mistakes. I can well understand him losing interest in me. – I'm so terribly superficial, I hate myself for it.
Why am I so lonely? I feel so abandoned.

Wednesday 24 January
At the Hennebergs'.
Yesterday p.m. I called on Prof Epstein junior. Old Frau Epstein was there too, and invited me to the Sauer[1] concert. I accepted, albeit a little unwillingly, then we went to call on Pollack, whose apartment has been redecorated by Hoffmann.
Hoffmann is wonderful. Such elegance yet such simplicity, all for 1,200 fl. Two rooms, the entrance lobby, service rooms – beautifully done – the dining-room in green, the bedroom in red. Exquisite fitted cupboards, adorable armchairs – the forms and colours are delightful.
In the evening I went to the concert with old Frau Epstein. I must say, I find a whole concert of piano music most unsatisfying. He played:
> Sgambati: Piano concerto
> Weber: Konzertstück
> Chopin: Piano concerto {no. 2}

All with orchestra. I didn't know any of it. The Sgambati is phoney, thin and threadbare, lacks substance – leaves without a branch. An appurtanance. I liked the Weber and Chopin on the whole, but I simply don't care for piano concertos. The orchestra plays a beautiful, melodious introduction, then the virtuoso springs into action, rushing up and down the keyboard with ape-like dexterity. The noise grows ever wilder. The harder he hits the keys, the more you realize what a miserable instrument the piano really is. Wood – nothing but wood! And Sauer thrashed it so mercilessly that after the first piece it was completely out of tune. Prudently, a second instrument had been made ready, and now they wheeled it on to meet its fate.
I love passion. I love power and strength. But like this – broken strings and split hammers – and a man with hair flailing down his back and across his forehead in rhythm to the music – I find such 'virtues' appalling. He

---

1 i.e. Emil Sauer, the celebrated concert pianist.

finishes his brilliant solo, pulls out a handkerchief, mops the sweat from his brow, throws back his head, leans back on the stool and fixes the audience with a stare: 'Look how wonderful I am.' The public is taken aback, thunderstruck. For heaven's sake, is that art? To my mind, a virtuoso is on the same level as a trapeze artist. No higher! By no means does he approach that of a real musician.

This evening: Brahms–Schumann recital with Johannes Messchaert and Julius Röntgen.

Messchaert sang 'Feldeinsamkeit', 'Über die Haide', 'Versunken', 'Todes-sehnen' and 'An die Nachtigall' of Brahms, and Schumann's 'Mondnacht', 'Schöne Fremde', 'Auf einer Burg' and 'Frühlingsnacht' really beautifully. They're all elect, God-given pieces. Wonderful – uniquely beautiful. I didn't care for Röntgen at all. He played the two Brahms Rhapsodies op 79 and Schumann's C-major Fantasy. I was appalled by his playing. He changes tempo too violently and too abruptly. Moser and Simandl[2] were there too. It was endearing to observe Moser listening with rapt attention.

Thursday 25 January
p.m. Gretl Hellmann, later Fräulein Freystätt, who's to sing my lieder on the 2nd. She has a lot of temperament and a big voice, but little brain. –

Saturday 27 January
At 3:00 comes this ass, Breithut,[3] and pesters me into sitting for him for an hour. And his style is so dreadfully coarse. Soon my features were perpetuated on paper in academic, Jewish style. Don't ask me how. Carl came in, pointed out a few significant errors, and soon he took his leave.

This evening: Dr Franz Servaes, art critic of the 'Neue Freie Presse'.[4] A very agreeable man. His judgement is probably not very individual, but if he lets himself be taught and guided, that won't be necessary. In some cases I prefer that to obdurate dogmatism. –

On Wednesday {I'll be going} to the Secession with Aunt Mie:

5th Exhibition: 'Japan'[5]

2 Franz Simandl was principal contrabass player of the Vienna Philharmonic and a professor at the Vienna Conservatoire.
3 Peter Breithut, a pupil of Edmund Hellmer, specialized in medals and pendants. He was known above all for his portrait pendants.
4 Orig.: 'der Neuen Frechen Presse' – 'New Brazen Press'.
5 *Recte* 6th Exhibition (20 January–15 February 1900). Koloman Moser was responsible for the presentation of a wide range of Japanese handicraft objects, woodcuts and scroll

Tuesday 30 January
Labor. I played him my lieder for the last time. He gave them his blessing.
Moser dropped in – made a rough sketch for my carnival mask.

Thursday 1 February
The weather is beautiful and spring-like, and I keep asking myself: am I in
Vienna or back in Rome and Naples? Often I can feel the spirit of the South
in and around me, making reality doubly grim. I long for Italy! I love the
sea, the cypresses, the olive-groves. And here I sit, in this ghastly dirt-heap
which, to strangers, I call 'my beloved Vienna'.
This morning: final rehearsal at Frau Radnitzky's.
p.m. As the detailed sketch hadn't arrived, Gretl and I drove over to
Moser's. Passing through a dingy entrance hall, we climbed the equally
dingy stairs to the apartment. On the doorbell we read:

—

paintings. While Japanese art stimulated the Secessionist ideal in various ways, public
reaction to the exhibition was meagre: there were only 6,200 visitors, as compared to 22,300
at the 5th Exhibition.

Theresia Moser, financier's widow.[6]

Shyly I rang the bell. A woman in a threadbare cardigan opened – she so resembled Moser that I instantly recognized her as his mother. I asked after him – he wasn't at home. A dowdy young girl appeared – his sister. I could see behind her into the front room, which also served as the kitchen. It was fairly sordid and, above all, dreadfully shabby.

We were glad to leave. – On the chilly stairway someone called:

Please, ladies, just a moment.

The sister came rushing downstairs, apologizing profusely for not having told the truth: her brother was indeed at home but, because he was unwell, she usually told people that he was out. Hearing that it was us, he got very annoyed. So she begged us to come upstairs again.

There we found Prof Hoffmann. We passed through the untidy entrance lobby into a very simple room. The walls were spruce and whitewashed, but everything else was very plain and, again, very shabby. Moser greeted us, his face swollen, and promptly disappeared to look for his necktie, leaving us with Hoffmann and Moser's sister. Soon he returned, and hastily prepared a detailed sketch, which we immediately took to the dressmaker. – It's sad to realize how spoilt we are. Back in the cab, we talked about it. For us, the least sign of poverty is sickening, repulsive, disagreeable. I'm quite sure, even if I had just as little money, I'd decorate my home quite differently – more pleasantly, more elegantly. My wonderful childhood is to blame, my upbringing which taught me to appreciate beauty. Or is that hereditary?

Just imagine this girl's joyless youth – she can never go out of an afternoon or an evening – just imagine the joyless youth of all such poor, *respectable* girls. I feel heartily sorry for them. They get nothing from their childhood – no sunshine on which to look back. If you grow up in poverty, your later life can never be entirely unclouded. You can see that the whole Moser family knows the meaning of – hunger ... And such people – smell so funny.

Later I said to Gretl:

You know, Christians are actually pretty malodorous.

We both laughed heartily down our noses at everything we'd seen. Truly these people are honest and respectable, yet they're poles apart.

I couldn't love a man who'd grown up in such surroundings. Yet who knows what it's like at Klimt's? Less respectable, maybe. But less shabby?

6 Orig.: 'Ökonomswitwe'. Koloman Moser's mother Therese (*sic*) lived at III., Stanislausgasse 5. In 1901 Moser moved into a new villa on the Hohe Warte.

My visit to the Mosers' gave me much to think about – much. I caught a glimpse of a different world.

In the evening: Bernatzik. A dear fellow.

Friday 2 February

p.m. my first appearance at one of Frau Radnitzky's chamber concerts – I played well. Schumann's E♭-major Quartet. My partners were Frau Steeber, Frau Radnitzky and Fräulein Donat. Fräulein Freystätt sang my lieder. She made a complete mess of one of them, but the others were quite good. They were well received.

After I played, Prof Epstein came to me and said:

> Haven't you ever played in public before? You should play professionally.

I most certainly should not, but what does he know . . . Then came Labor. He kissed my hand three times. Epstein, whom he congratulated on his grandson, said to him:

> You know, it isn't hard to have a grandson. To have such a wonderful pupil is much harder. –

Etc. etc.

I arrived back home. The decorations on the head-piece for my carnival costume looked like a large flower-basket. So everyone helped bend them into shape, and they looked really lovely. I went inside, found Gretl at the door – she didn't have the courage to go in on her own. We entered the salon arm in arm.

At first I was dreadfully shy. I didn't know who to talk to. Then I grabbed Dr Bilk, with whom I was vaguely familiar, and Altmann, who recognized me immediately. Kuffner and Engel too – almost everyone recognized me by my ears.

Now comes the best part of it. 'Come, Schmedes', I said, and promenaded with him. I couldn't talk to him much, so I asked him to escort me to table. He agreed, although he hadn't recognized me. I also invited Altmann and Dr Bilk, then made haste to unmask. Schmedes was watching. –

Dinner was served. I spoke only with him, afterwards we danced together. His wife started casting furious glances. Lola Beeth[7] came up and spoke to me:

> I wouldn't have recognized you, young Schindler[8] – so beautiful, so tall.

7 Having begun her career in Berlin, the soprano Lola Beeth sang at the Hofoper from 1888–1895 and 1898–1901.
8 Orig.: 'Schindlerin'.

Just then Frau Schmedes swept past.

What's the matter with her?

Oh, she's jealous.

Of whom? Of you?

I had to laugh.

That's just like her!

Come, Schmedes, dance with me.

He was clearly in two minds about it. Finally we danced pertly into the
little reading-room, where we found a seat. Paul Horwitz was sitting there.

Why are you giving me such dirty looks, Schmedes?

he said, and pestered Schmedes terribly. Finally he went off. In the doorway he turned round and said:

Shall we be friends again?

We laughed and laughed – and every time we struck up a conversation,
Paul stuck his head in the door.

Suddenly Frau Schmedes appeared, with young Baum, and sat down opposite us. Our conversation faltered – Schmedes has no idea of wit or repartee. We got up and went into the adjoining room. Scarcely had we settled down, before my friend's wife and Baum followed us inside. Schmedes began to laugh out loud, and I feared there would be a scene. I left him to his fate, and went onto the dance-floor. He'd invited me for the cotillon. It began, but there was no sign of him. I found plenty of other partners. Finally he appeared for the flower presentation:

Do please excuse me. She wouldn't let me.

Baum came too – she really wouldn't let him. Later I heard that she'd made a scene in the smoking room. Poor devil. –

Since he asked so nicely, I accompanied him to the buffet. Suddenly Baum appeared, saying she'd sent him to keep an eye on us. It was so stupid. In the meantime we had a heart to heart. I said, sneeringly:

You, the freest of the free – Siegfried the hero.

He said:

Yes, I can cope with the larger dragons but not the smaller ones.

He told me that last month everything was set for a divorce – he would have been given custody of the child. His wife had already moved out, but she returned and pleaded with him until he took her back, out of the goodness of his heart, as he maintains, and, as I maintain, out of sheer stupidity.

But it won't last much longer, he assured me.

They say she nags him outrageously. About anything and everything. Before they left home, she'd said:

If Alma Schindler is there, you're not to dance with her.

And he obeyed her to a tee: apart from dancing with her, which he had to once or twice for the sake of appearances, I was his only partner. He said:

I'd love to know what you'd be like as a married woman.

I'm sure I'd enjoy it.

But I believe you'd be too much of a flirt.

Isn't your wife just that?

No, he said, my wife does nothing of the kind.

Is the Zasche story true or not? And if it is true, doesn't he know about it or does he just not want to know?

Heavens yes, it could all have turned out differently, he sighed.

He pleaded with me to tell him at what hour I generally go for my daily stroll. Then he said:

That one time, at the Geiringers', you really jeopardized my position.

> All that bickering at home, you understand, and then you. But tell me
> honestly, didn't you rather fall for me – then?

As I didn't want to say, 'No, dear friend, you were too good to be just a
playmate', I said nothing.

From time to time Gretl Hellmann came up to us:

> My dears, everyone's talking about you.

This time I didn't treat him like a playmate, incidentally. It's just that I
preferred his company to anyone else's, because he was the best-looking.
And really, I do like him. His wife's jealousy made the whole thing more
stimulating, of course. It redoubled the pleasure – for him and for me.

Maybe I put our hosts in an embarrassing position – but I had a wonderful
time.

Schmedes was sitting beside me, and the youngsters who introduced
themselves asked to be introduced to him too.

> Almost as if we were already married, he said.

Wednesday 7 February

This morning: to the Hagenbund exhibition.⁹ – Konopa mediocre,
Bamberger good, Hejda inventive. I liked Kasparides. Eckhard too. The
latter somewhat coarse.

Mie and Hugo came too.

Then home with Uncle Hugo in the Stadtbahn – via Meidling. Out of 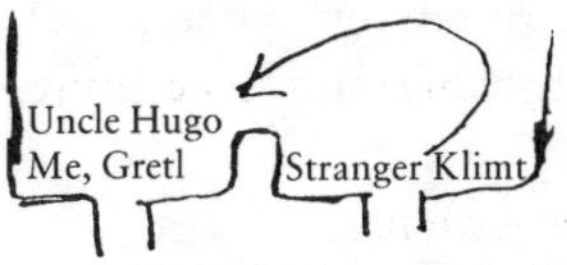
curiosity. At some station or other Klimt got
in. The blood ran to my head. He greeted us,
shook hands and sat down a little way off. After
a while he stood up and started talking to Gretl:

[Diagram labels: Uncle Hugo / Me, Gretl / Stranger Klimt]

> How's the carnival going?

G.: We're scarcely invited anywhere.

He: That's a great shame – looking at me.

I said not a word. Uncle Hugo also took little part in the conversation –
being obliged to keep out of it, he looked pretty foolish.

I was very galled, for I still love him as much as ever. I felt it when he came
in, felt it as my heart began to pound, as my joy overflowed. He's the one

9 The exhibition concentrated primarily on landscape painting, with works by Franz
Jaschke, Rudolph Konopa and Eduard Kasparides, and pictures in other genres by Heinrich
Knirr, Gustav Bamberger and Wilhelm Hejda. The latter, who was acclaimed by the *Neue
Freie Presse* (7 February 1900) as 'doubtless the finest native talent on show at the
Künstlerhaus', also exhibited sculptures, polychrome reliefs, impressionistic landscapes and
three larger paintings, *The Lions of Mars*, *Salvation* and *St George*.

appointed for me. No matter how often I try to repress my memories of him, time and again, with renewed ardour, they pervade my feelings. A glance in his eyes suffices. If I haven't seen him for some time, I can perhaps deceive myself into believing that I no longer love him. I could perhaps persuade myself, or let myself be persuaded, that I loved someone else. But when I see his dear face, all my dissimulation and feigned disinterest crumbles. My soul thrills to him, I desire him with every fibre of my body. I long for him as for a saviour, a deliverer, my only redeemer! Were I to have met him alone – today – I could vouch for nothing.

I have no respect for constancy, none whatsoever, for I know from experience that only lack of courage stops a girl taking the decisive step. And I – coward that I am – I looked away when he came in, stared out of the window, instead of sating my eyes on him, for the first time in ages and for a long time to come.

What would actually prevent me from going to him in his studio and making a full confession – living life to the full just *once*? An idiotic fear of discovery, of unpleasant consequences. Not for moral reasons, no – *merely* out of fear.

But actually that would be the obvious course of action – my ideal.

I'm convinced he believes I've long since forgotten him. That grieves me too. I want him to know that I love him – now and for ever and ever!

What is the meaning of morality, what is morality? Tradition. A feeling handed down from one generation to the next. Surely everyone should strive to imitate Nature, to abandon themselves to those they love [of the opposite sex].

A woman must subordinate herself.

A man must rule.

I don't give a damn for morality. It simply doesn't exist – it's something with which you are brought up, an illusion drummed into you. I loathe all sermonizers – and all morality. For I love Nature. And morality is unnatural.

Freedom – that's what I long for and can never attain. O spirit of complete freedom, O Übermensch, you don't yet exist, your day is still to come. Let that day dawn! O day of great wisdom, O day of freedom, of complete freedom: even if I never live to see you, I greet you at least from afar – as champion of spiritual freedom – of the great future.

Friday 9 February
Aunt Xandi just told me she'd seen Klimt with a lady in the Favoriten-strasse. That's all the same to me, I couldn't care less. Could it be that I don't love him as much as I thought? – No sense of jealousy or envy – nothing of the kind, only one sensation: he's right. He's young, let him enjoy himself.
Today I struggled in vain to compose. I feel completely vacant, lack all external stimuli. It's hopeless.
p.m. first to the Hardys – to apologize. Then to Bertha Meyer, who's become so stilted, so inane. Then to the Zierers – actually to Bertha. Her apartment had an enlivening effect on me. They're nice people too. Both Bertha and Flora already knew about the Schmedes affair. I believe it isn't over yet. –

Sunday 11 February
This morning: at home. Ernst called.
At midday: Gesellschaft concert
    Bruckner: Mass in D minor with chorus
    Mozart: Serenade in D major
    von Zemlinsky: 'Frühlingsbegräbnis' with chorus
The Bruckner failed to impress me. It overflows with beautiful ideas but it's also flawed. I was particularly irritated by the way the movements ended. The way he terminates phrases abruptly, in both chorus and orchestra at once, doesn't appeal to me.
Mozart I'm not yet ready for.
Zemlinsky: quite original – very Wagnerian. Phrases such as

are incorporated[10] – verbatim – with the greatest disrespect. The whole thing seems a little immature – the orchestration is magnificent. The man himself cuts the most comical figure imaginable. A caricature – chinless, small, with bulging eyes and a downright *crazy* style of conducting. It always makes a comical effect when composers conduct their own music, because they always want to draw *too* much out of the orchestra, more than necessary.
p.m. at Felix Fischer's with Irma O. and Helene Egger. The former very chic

10 A leitmotiv from Wagner's *Ring*. In Zemlinsky's *Frühlingsbegräbnis* no such phrase occurs.

Gesellschaft der Musikfreunde in Wien

unter dem hohen Protectorate Ihrer k. u. k. Hoheit der durchlauchtigsten Kronprinzessin-Witwe Erzherzogin
STEPHANIE.

Sonntag den 11. Februar 1900, Mittags halb 1 Uhr, im grossen Saale:

Drittes ordentliches

GESELLSCHAFTS-CONCERT

unter der Leitung des Concert-Directors Herrn

Richard von Perger.

Mitwirkende:

Fräulein **Mathilde von Hochmeister**, Concertsängerin.
Frau **Gisela Körner**, Concertsängerin.
Herr **Ferdinand Marian**, k. k. Hof-Opernsänger.
Herr Dr. **Josef Meyer**, Opernschüler des Conservatoriums.
Herr **Georg Valker**, Mitglied der k. u. k. Hof-Musikkapelle (Orgel).
Der **Singverein**.
Das **Gesellschafts-Concert**.

Zur Aufführung gelangt:

1. A. Bruckner . . . Messe in D-moll für Soli, Chor, Orchester und Orgel.
   (II. Aufführung in den Gesellschafts-Concerten.)
2. W. A. Mozart . . Serenade in D-dur für Orchester (Köchel 320)
   (I. Aufführung in den Gesellschafts-Concerten.)
3. A. v. Zemlinsky . „Frühlingsbegräbnis" für Soli, Chor und Orchester.
   (Manuscript, I. Aufführung) unter persönlicher Leitung des Componisten.

Dieses Programm 20 Heller.   Texte auf den folgenden Seiten.

Mittwoch den 14. März 1900, Abends halb 8 Uhr:

Drittes ausserordentliches Gesellschafts-Concert

unter der Leitung des Concert-Directors Herrn **Richard von Perger.**

Zur Aufführung gelangt:

J. S. Bach . . . . Chor mit Orchesterbegleitung „Schleicht spielende Wellen" aus der
                    Geburtstags-Cantate für August III. (I. Aufführung.)
Kaiser Ferdinand III. . . . . . . Madrigal für gemischten Chor mit Begleitung (I. Aufführung.)
R. Schumann . . . . Musik zu „Manfred„ mit verbindendem Gedicht von F. Körnberger. —
                    Declamation: Herr **Josef Kainz**, k. k. Hof-Schauspieler.
                    Der **Singverein**. — Das **Gesellschafts-Orchester**.

Karten zu 6, 5, 4, 3 und 2 Kronen

sind für die p. t. **Stifter, Gründer** und **unterstützenden Mitglieder** vom 13. bis 27. Februar reservirt;
der **allgemeine Verkauf** beginnt am 1. März 1900 ab in der Gesellschaftskanzlei an Wochentagen täglich
von 9—12 und von 3—5 Uhr.

and pretty, the latter chic but frightfully affected. They teased me dreadfully about Olbrich. Felix Fischer showed me a letter he'd sent them from Darmstadt and said:

> It's all here!

What exactly? I asked.

> Well really, Alma. At the wedding we all noticed the way he was looking at you, as if he was completely afire.

Felix said:

> We'd like to bet that you'll marry him.

All right, I said, I accept.

> If you win, he said, I give you a kiss, and if I win – you give me a kiss.

All right, I replied, I'll accept that too.

It would be but a small sacrifice for such a prize. They could demand anything of me in return for such a guarantee. But I have no hope, no longer dare to hope. Him of all people. They just don't know what they're saying. Such a brilliant fellow. Either he'll remain single – or he'll find himself an utterly stupid wife. That's how things go. You only have to take a look at other celebrated artists.

In the evening: Hancke and Hoffmann. Hancke disgusts me with his doggy eyes, so faithful and forlorn.

Dear God, my thoughts keep returning to Olbrich. How lovely it would have been if I had met him first, him and not the other. Maybe he would have liked me. But now: Olbrich has a mania for cleanliness, and he can see straight into my soul, he can see stains that can no longer be washed away. I'm no longer so young, so pure. I have shuddered, trembled for another man, was half crazy for sheer worry and anguish. Perhaps I can never again experience such unclouded happiness. And he knows it, senses it. I also dropped a hint about it once – and if now he were to ask me exactly what happened, I'd tell him the whole, unadorned *truth*.

Monday 12 February

This morning: Hellmer. He said:

> I could say of myself: I am happy to be alive and to know that other people are aware that I am alive (Michelangelo).

Then he told me that the Academy has awarded Klimt an Honorary Fellowship. It still needs to be confirmed by the Ministry and by that arch-booby, H.M. the Kaiser. Klimt deserves it – he's our leading artist, a true genius. I revere him as an artist and love him as a man.

Erwin Kuffner came to invite me to a ball. I shall probably accept, and cancel Baroness Odelga.

p.m. Baroness Bach came here to sing some of my lieder – it was really wonderful.

She said:

> Do you know what I recently said to Count X? 'You know, if I were a man, she's the only girl I could fall head over heels in love with, and I'd marry her on the spot.' –

This evening I played the Norns' scene and the closing pages of 'Götterdämmerung'. I still haven't got over it. It's so wondrously beautiful. How I'd love to play to Olbrich – on his own – lots of Wagner. How lovely it would be. He with his enthusiasm and I with mine. Two souls that could completely harmonize – and yet will never be united.

In the morning I composed a piano piece, or rather the opening of one. I don't think it has much future. It didn't come from the heart. I'm so empty, burnt out, and unless someone stimulates me, I have no idea where to find new life. I've been unproductive for quite some time. No wonder. Olbrich is in Darmstadt. Klimt has vanished – and when I do see him, he offers me almost no stimulus. I just can't talk to him. And neither Franz Hancke and Kuffner nor Schmedes or the like can give me what I need. Even Burckhard, whose intellect, wit and good humour have often stimulated me, has made himself scarce. His wife died, and due to him two marriages are on the rocks. His hands are full – one has to have the grace to forgive him.

Tuesday 13 February

Anniversary of Wagner's death.

This morning: Labor. I spoke with him of the enduring quality of generosity and the certainty of its being manifested. He disagreed. First vehemently, later more quietly. I said:

> Generosity always wins through.

He: I don't believe it. Someone always has to give things a jolt to set them moving. In the case of Beethoven, who worked in solitude, it was the aristocrats who offered him a pension, allowing him to survive without worrying about his daily bread. Wagner had no need of that. Schumann once said of him: 'He'll pull through. He has all the pluck you need.'

I disagreed:

> I'm convinced that something really first-rate can't go unnoticed.

1 *l to r* Alma with her mother, Anna Bergen, and her half-sister, Gretl

2 Josef Labor, Alma's first composition teacher

3 Karl Kraus 1900

4 Gustav Klimt 1903

5 Max Burckhard

6 Koloman Moser

7 Josef Maria Olbrich

8 Hermann Bahr

9 Josef Hoffmann

10 Alexander (von) Zemlinsky 1898

11 Poster for the first Secessionist
Exhibition *Gustav Klimt* 1898

12 Josef Maria Olbrich: Living-room of his house in
Darmstadt, with piano let into the upper floor

13 The Vienna Secession 1898

14 Villa Moll on the Hohe Warte 1901

15 Portrait of Marie Henneberg *Gustav Klimt* 1901

16 Alma at the Banqueting Table *Carl Moll* c.1899

17 Gustav Mahler with his sister Justine

18 Alma 1899 ('the picture with the bear')

19 Silver casket for Alma Mahler *Koloman Moser* 1902

I think it can, he whispered.

Then it's not capable of survival.

Maybe it is – and he smiled meaningfully.

All of a sudden our discussion had moved from the general to the specific – to his own artistic existence. And without admitting it, we were both aware of the fact.

> You know, for that one needs – (he placed his hands squarely on his hips). If you haven't got that, you'll be quashed, devoured by other, more powerful personalities. High-minded people used to lend a helping hand, nowadays it's the press that's supposed to take responsibility. But no honest person would want to place himself in the hands of that rabble.

During the conversation his face assumed a strange, transfigured expression.

That's how I imagine a martyr must look. And indeed he is a martyr, a martyr for his art. I felt so sorry for him today. What has he had from life? Little recognition, little affection and – little money. And yet he said, boldly:

> If I were born again, I'd still want to be an artist.

I don't consider him monumental or revolutionary, but he's a fine artist, highly intelligent and genuine. For me, there's something singularly touching about him. –

p.m. played all of act III of 'Tristan'.

This evening: 'Tristan'.

I've just got back from the theatre. I'm writing this on my knees. No greater victory has ever been won for art, nothing is more sublime than 'Tristan'. It's the Song of Songs of love. The greatest work of all art and of all times. I'm in such ecstasy, I actually dread the thought of writing – I shall stop.[11]

'Tristan' is the work of God. –

---

11 The paragraph is written in a shaky, well-nigh illegible hand.

Thursday 15 February

p.m. Gretl Hellmann. Such a dear girl.

There's much gossip about the Schmedes affair. Some lady said to Mama today that it would be advisable to cheer me up a bit, I was so disconsolate about Schmedes – this in confidence. Mama was dumbfounded.

Spitzer wrote to say that Olbrich will be arriving on the 19th[12] – that's to say, on Monday. I feel an unbelievable sense of joy. And yet I have no hope whatsoever.

This evening I composed – a rhapsody. Every day something new, but nothing gets finished – what a quandary! Gretl told me that Mama had the idea of getting {Selma} Kurz to sing my lieder.

Friday 16 February

All morning and p.m. until 4:00: at Spitzer's, having my photograph taken. p.m. Frau Hardy. Mama committed an error of tact: she let the Kurz idea out of the bag. I was so angry that I left the room. I hate such premature gossip.

Sunday 18 February

At midday: the Nicolai concert

    Choral Symphony

    Beethoven

I was overwhelmed, particularly by the second and last movements. The chorus was superbly well-trained, each singer totally committed. It was exquisitely beautiful, dramatic and gripping. The experts assert that Mahler made many changes to the scoring.[13] As I only knew the work from playing it on the piano, it didn't bother me. The whole thing has such a majestic glow, one is dazzled and forced to close one's eyes. Silent in admiration, I'd like to absorb this superhuman music with every pore.

Before the concert, we went to the Künstlerhaus to view the pictures being sent to Paris. The exhibition wasn't open to the public, we had personal admissions. The Genossenschaft[14] cuts a poor figure. Their best picture is definitely Hirschler's 'Scene on the Acharon'.[15] The Secession is in good

---

12 Orig.: '17th'.

13 Mahler's radical retouchings were almost unanimously condemned (cf. Suite 21, 27 January 1901); after his death they were adopted by a few of his disciples and associates, notably Schoenberg and Zemlinsky.

14 i.e. the artists of the Künstlerhaus group.

15 Eduard Hirschler was principally known for still-life paintings. After completing his art studies, he learnt the weaving trade and took over his father's textile factory.

form. Their crowning glory – naturally – is Klimt. He's contributed 'Pallas Athene', the pink portrait and a new, unfinished giant picture for the University.[16] He's wonderful, liberally minded, both as man and artist, enviably liberal.

Carl's two new pictures look quite good, but in Paris they won't exactly cause a stir. – A picture by Hörmann[17] deserves mentioning. New portraits by Krämer,[18] a 'Vagabond' of Engelhart's – amazingly vigorous but coarse, brutal. I can't mention everything. Our gallery will look wonderful.

p.m. we wanted to hire an open carriage and drive to the Prater, but they were all taken, and *sorely distressed* we went home.

In the evening: party at the Leglers'. It was very entertaining. I spoke almost exclusively to Dick and Hassmann[19] (the painter). Later with Wolanek. I like Hassmann. Maybe he'll join the Secession – he's sorely tempted.

I lectured Wolanek severely, told him he should at last do something for himself, try to achieve something – not just fritter his time away on the dance-floor.

It was quite fun.

Thursday 22 February

p.m. Hohe Warte, on the site where our house is to stand. It's in the backwoods. May I never live to see the day on which we move there. –
We'd arranged that Olbrich should meet us on the site. But by the time we arrived, he'd already left. So we looked round the Villa Stifft[20] on our own and, to be honest, I didn't like it at all, maybe because I was so dreadfully resigned and actually not in the mood for looking at houses.

I believe there's no more effective way of displaying disdain. Had I really imagined that he liked me? That was sheer madness. I arrived home all but speechless.

16 With 'pink portrait' A.S. presumably means the *Portrait of Serena Lederer* (1899); the 'unfinished giant picture' was the controversial *Philosophy*.
17 Theodor von Hörmann. On four occasions, the Künstlerhaus refused to exhibit his work (as was also the case with Josef Engelhart). He therefore formed a breakaway group, which eventually grew to become the Secession. At the opening of the 1st Exhibition in 1898, the Secessionists laid a wreath in his honour.
18 Johann Victor Krämer was a founder member of the Hagenbund; in 1897 he joined the Secession. The 11th Secessionist Exhibition (1901) was devoted entirely to his work.
19 Karl Ludwig Hassmann studied at the Vienna Academy; subsequently he was active in Munich.
20 The merchant banker Alfred Stifft, who married the daughter of Felix Fischer in November 1899. Olbrich had recently refurbished the interior of his villa.

This evening, at home: Hoffmann, Moser, Spitzer and Olbrich.

Olbrich stayed for some time in the entrance lobby talking to Mama and Carl – I didn't join them. Later I diverted myself by chatting to Moser & Hoffmann. To me Olbrich was just air. But as that didn't seem to bother him, I grew more friendly, and at table I spoke almost only to him. – Why is it always my fate to like people who don't give a damn about me? What did we talk about? Nothing but trivia. We exchanged glances, as before, but clearly I mean nothing to him.

I was standing with Moser in front of Papa's Tulln picture, of which he spoke with remarkable respect and affection. His only criticism was that it was too detailed – for that reason he much preferred the sketch hanging beside it. But it's beautiful and up to date. – He promised to make me some needlework designs.

Hoffmann is the least intelligent, Olbrich probably the most.

All in all, the evening put me in a really foul mood. I couldn't get to sleep, kept turning things over in my mind.

Saturday 24 February

Got up very early and went for a walk in the garden with 'Faust'. –

p.m. Gretl Hellmann.

Dinner at Spitzer's. Kurzweil and his wife, Monk, Bahr and Olbrich there too. The evening will remain unforgettable. I came home – never had I felt quite so <u>disconsolate</u>. I was madly in love with Klimt, and I still love him. He was unattainable. *Apart* from him, Olbrich is the only man to whom I would give myself. Not so much out of love, but for common-sense reasons. Until now I had set my hopes on him. Yesterday I saw them crumble. –

Spitzer told me I wouldn't be sitting next to Olbrich at table, and as he said so a look of deep regret flickered in his eye. I sat between Hermann Bahr and Kurzweil – both nice fellows, the one frivolous and witty, the other good-natured and honest. Olbrich sat diagonally opposite. He scarcely bothered to look my way.

Afterwards I was pestered into playing the piano. I did play – but entirely without flair. I began with a piece of my own. Olbrich sat next to me on the stool, and was very taken with 'Stumme Liebe'. I told him I'd made a copy of it for him. He asked me to send it to him, and I was on the point of saying, 'Come and fetch it tomorrow', but couldn't – he's leaving in the morning . . .

In conversation with me his manner was so unbelievably indifferent, it

made me so sad. I'd give ten years of my life if he were to grow fond of me!
– It's no use struggling. That won't change anything.

Mama and the two of us drove home at 1:00 – the others stayed on.

I hardly expect to see Olbrich again before next autumn. – Who knows what might have happened by then. Maybe he'll get married. But to whom? Someone inferior to him in every respect.

Monday 26 February

This evening: at Spitzer's. I went with the greatest disinclination – and had a wonderful time. Spoke almost all evening with Alexander von Zemlinsky, the 28-year-old composer of 'Es war einmal'. He's dreadfully ugly, almost chinless – yet I found him quite enthralling.

I began:

> Just imagine – I'm one of those old-fashioned fuddy-duddys who haven't yet heard your opera.

He replied:

> Well – get a move on, otherwise you won't get to hear it. You never can tell how long it'll stay in the repertoire.[21]

We took our seats at table. To my one side sat Dr Hans Fuchs, son of the deceased Kapellmeister,[22] who found Spitzer's Turkish smoking-room more attractive than his modern rooms, which, in my eyes, disqualified him from the start. To the other – Zemlinsky. Naturally I spoke only with him.

First we talked about Schmedes – and became so abusive that Zemlinsky said:

> If we can think of someone with whom neither of us has a bone to pick – we'll down a <u>glass of punch</u> in their honour. –

After a while we did indeed think of somebody: Gustav Mahler. We drained our glasses. I told him how greatly I venerated him and how I longed to meet him.

> Why don't you make an appointment with him at his office? He'd be terribly pleased.

I wouldn't mind if I did. We were more or less rapturizing over him, when suddenly Dr Fuchs turned to us and said:

21 Zemlinsky's opera *Es war einmal* . . . , based on Holger Drachmann's eponymous folk-tale comedy, was first performed on 22 January 1900 at the Hofoper, with Mahler conducting. It ran for twelve performances

22 Johann Nepomuk Fuchs, who was Zemlinsky's composition teacher at the Vienna Conservatoire from 1891 to 1893.

Mahler is a scoundrel.

We were both flabbergasted. And in a quiet, sad voice he poured out his tale of woe:

My father hated him as long as he lived. He took years off his life. –

Yet I know perfectly well that Fuchs died of blood poisoning. Some people even claim that his son was to blame for it. It all struck me as unspeakably infantile. All the same I fell silent. And Z. said softly:

You've gone all quiet. Has Fuchs dampened your enthusiasm for Mahler?

No, I replied, on the contrary.

It's common knowledge that their hostility was motivated by egoism. Fuchs had set his hopes on the directorship, and was furious that an outsider had been engaged, and one, moreover, who ousted him from his conducting post. I never experienced a worse conductor than he. Like a cart-horse. All of a sudden he'd set off at a canter, waving his stick with great fire and temperament – but not for long. Then he'd settle back to his customary trot. Scarcely a performance ran smoothly.

His brother, Robert Fuchs – the composer[23] – was there too. With the Nicolai concert, he said, Mahler had ruined his reputation. That's simply preposterous. Then he told me a few stories about Papa – whom he knew – and a few trifling anecdotes about Bruckner and Brahms. Mahler was fourteen years old when he came to study with him, and already then he was dreadfully impertinent. On the whole Robert Fuchs did not impress me as being a great artist. With every word he apologizes, so to speak, for being alive. His voice is soft and insignificant, he doesn't move with the times and has no self-confidence.

At table Zemlinsky asked me softly:

And what do you think of Wagner?

The greatest genius that ever lived, I replied casually.

And which work of Wagner's is your favourite?

'Tristan' – my reply.

That so delighted him that he became entirely transformed. He grew truly handsome. Now we understood each other. I find him quite wonderful. I shall invite him to call.

For me the evening wasn't wasted. – It was a taste of life.

23 Robert Fuchs was Zemlinsky's harmony and counterpoint teacher from 1889 to 1890.

Monday 5 March
This evening: Burgtheater

Agnes Jordan

by Georg Hirschfeld

with Reimers, Zeska, Witt, Hohenfels, Sonnenthal and Wilbrandt.
I enjoyed the play. And it's very sad. About a poor, disillusioned creature
whose life ends in bleak resignation. And so unloved. – I don't know, I
believe my life won't turn out much different.
Afterwards to Bertha Kunz. Met Moser, Hoffmann, Auchentaller,
Bernatzik. It was quite nice, quite amusing.

Tuesday 6 March
Labor. I hadn't given much thought to anything, and he said:
    It's stupid of me to teach you at all.
And he's right – I can't be taken seriously.

Thursday 8 March

Opening of the Spring Exhibition at the Secession[24]

Klimt's 'Philosophy' amazed me. He sketched it in the train between
Verona to Padua, and discussed it with me at the time. Now that I see it – it
appears so unfamiliar. But it's beautiful – beautiful. So beautiful, that most
people don't appreciate just how beautiful it is. A symphony of colours,
unparalleled. And actually not a painting.
Most of the time I went round with Khnopff. I'm immensely taken with
him.

Friday 9 March
At the Secession again. Khnopff was there too. I was with him most of the
time. – I said:
    I'm sorry that my French is so poor.
    Please don't keep saying that. It's just not true.
    You are too kind.
    I'm not kind – he replied.
    That's just as well, because I detest kind-heartedness. Usually it
    amounts to <u>stupidity</u>. I'm not kind-hearted either.

24 The 7th Secessionist Exhibition was presented by Adolf Böhm. On display were paintings
by Carl Moll, Josef Engelhart and Friedrich König, but these were overshadowed by the final
version of Klimt's *Philosophy*.

I can see that, he said.

How – why?

And he pointed to his eyes.

He's building a house near Brussels, by the way. – A strange fellow. There's something unlifelike and unearthly, something transfigured about him. A strangely veiled expression in his eyes. And his mouth remains firmly closed. The embodiment of silence. I love to look at him. He told me he'd been to the museum. I asked him about Klimt's spandrel pictures. He was immensely taken with them. I told him I preferred them to what was on display here. He agreed, saying this was no longer painting.

It's atmosphere! A ∿ but not a picture. – But I mustn't talk about it, for I have the same weakness.

But you are much more original.

I hope so.

Indeed Klimt has learnt much from him. Viewing the Toorops, I again told him that he'd been wonderfully imitated. That pleased him. –

All of this in French. I managed quite well. I can understand everything he says, wants to say – keeps to himself. For he's a walking secret. –

Saturday 10 March

This evening: party at the Conrats'.[25] It was terrific.

I was wearing my white crêpe-de-chine dress, which looked classy and really beautiful. I made my entrance. Frau Conrat came to greet me, and led me through four rooms full of strangers. But I wasn't in the least apprehensive. In the last room but one sat Madame et Monsieur van der Stappen[26] and Monsieur Khnopff. I was ushered to a seat next to van der Stappen, and they asked for silence, as a piano quartet by Dvořák was being played in the next room. Then Fräulein Kusmitsch, Pacal and two others sang the Zigeunerlieder.[27] It was delightful, and particularly pleased the foreign guests. Fräulein Kusmitsch sang an aria from 'The Taming of

---

25 Hugo Conrat, a merchant of Hungarian origin and honorary treasurer of the Tonkünstlerverein, and his wife Ida (I., Wallfischgasse 12.). They had three daughters, Erica, Lilli and Ilse. Erica Conrat later married the art-historian Hans Tietze (their portrait was painted in 1909 by Oskar Kokoschka); Ilse was a sculptress, whose works included the Brahms monument in the Zentralfriedhof.

26 (Pierre) Charles van der Stappen, sculptor and medallist from Brussels. In 1883 he was awarded a professorship at the Brussels Academy, of which he later became director.

27 Hugo Conrat translated the texts of the *Zigeunerlieder* from the Hungarian for Brahms. The soprano Karoline Kusmitsch sang at the Vienna Hofoper from 1898 to 1902. Before taking up singing, Franz Pacal was a violinist; he was a lyric tenor at the Hofoper from 1895 until 1905.

the Shrew'.[28] She was exquisitely dressed, and made an immense impression upon van der Stappen.

Later, Khnopff came and sat down next to me. The doors to the two next rooms were thrown open, and the band struck up a lively waltz. Monsieur v.d. Stappen {danced} with Frau Conrat, Herr Conrat with Frau v.d. Stappen, Khnopff with me.

In the last room stood ten girls who all happened to be dressed in Austrian national costume – Bohemian, Hungarian, Bosnian etc. etc.

Zemlinsky had greeted me earlier. He told me he'd spent some time looking through my music and had a few things to say about my song. He couldn't tell me more, because I was sitting between Khnopff and Fräulein Kusmitsch. Eating was tricky – we were pushed and shoved from all sides. Concert-master Grün[29] was there too and introduced himself. Of critics: Kalbeck and Schönaich.[30] –

There's too much of a crush here.

Khnopff gave me his arm, and we went into another room. I told him that for me he was a secret walking the face of the Earth –

Le secret qui va sur terre.

He asked me why I felt that, and I told him that his eyes and his mouth were sealed – that they spoke, but said nothing. An impenetrable wall of iron sealed off his soul from the outside world. He agreed, and said he was glad that it was so.

Incidentally, I am often sad.

I know, I replied, one can see that. –

In the smoking-room, a lady said to Madame van der Stappen:

Ah, que Madame Khnopff est belle.

She came over and told us. We were all there together – Khnopff, Zemlinsky and several other men – and I laughed heartily at the silly remark.

It was time to dance. Khnopff didn't dance. I said to Zemlinsky:

Why haven't you spent more time with me?

28 *Der Widerspenstigen Zähmung*, comic opera in four acts, music by Hermann Goetz, libretto by J.V. Widmann and the composer, first performed at Mannheim in 1874.
29 Jakob Grün, a violinist of Hungarian origin. Although Mahler favoured Arnold Rosé, Grün served as concert-master at the Hofoper from 1868 to 1909. For thirty-two years he also taught at the Vienna Conservatoire.
30 Gustav Schönaich, music critic of the *Wiener Allgemeine Zeitung*, and an enthusiastic Wagnerian.

Fräulein, you're a dreadful flirt. You know just as well as I do that it
was impossible to get near you.

He was right – the men were hovering about me like midges round a
lamp. And I felt like a queen, proud and unapproachable, exchanged a
few cool words with each in turn. The rest of the time I spent with
Khnopff and Zemlinsky. Countless people introduced themselves – it
was a veritable triumph. And since I was chaperoning Madame van der
Stappen – in whose honour the party was given – I was the centre of
attention. The talk was only of the van der Stappens, Khnopff and
myself. –

Later I had a long talk with Zemlinsky on his own. Before long, however, Khnopff was sitting opposite us with Fräulein Leinkauf, one of the
best-looking girls. Zemlinsky told me that he was extremely impressed
by my song, that I have real talent – and other things too. I said that he
and Khnopff were the two major attractions for me. He didn't believe
me.

Fräulein, if I weren't so sensible – you could easily turn a man's head.
Suddenly he grew serious.

Fräulein, can I ask you something, it's a serious matter for me. I'd like

to dedicate a song to you – no, more than that – a whole volume of
lieder that's going to be published soon. May I dedicate them to you?
Would you accept?

I was overwhelmed with joy. Fancy making such a request, and with such
deference! I gave him my hand. I was thrilled to bits.

Khnopff came to ask if I was enjoying myself, saying it was cooler in the
next room. But I stayed with Zemlinsky. He's a dear fellow, and I do like
him so. – He's as ugly as sin!

Two strangers kept hovering around. For one of them I coined the name:
the hairless one, for the other: the Prince of Arcady, because he just stood
there with a wistful expression on his face. I was much amused by a certain
Baron Hahn who played endless extracts from a ballet that he'd been
composing for ten years. Everyone spoke derisively of him. In the end I
introduced myself – as an enthusiast for his music.

I left at 3:00. It was a wonderful evening. Zemlinsky and a Fräulein
Hoffmann[31] took me home in the Conrats' cab.

At the start, while I was sitting with Khnopff – and Zemlinsky appeared –
the former said:

Oh comme vos yeux brillent. –

And Zemlinsky kept saying:

I simply can't resist the idea of abducting you from Khnopff for a few
minutes.

It was terrific! Basta!

Tuesday 13 March

Labor. He tested me in various ways, and I hadn't entirely forgotten what
I'd learnt.

Well, at last the penny seems to have dropped. I could never see you
actually grasping things. You know, I shall turn you into a kind of
musical homunculus. Since natural processes don't work, I shall
force-feed you.

He was in a very good mood – my dear, fatherly friend!
Zemlinsky has cancelled for Friday. I'm offended.

31 Possibly the sister of Rudolf Stefan Hoffmann, who was at that time studying composition
with Zemlinsky.

Wednesday 14 March
This morning: at Mie's.
Lunch with Spitzer in his apartment. He'd invited van der Stappen, the two
Conrat girls and Zemlinsky.
Zemlinsky is a dear fellow. He played me the 'Tristan' prelude. Won-
drously well! He asked me not to breathe a word about the {dedication of
the} lieder. –

[Corrected in January 1962. A.M.-W.]

Suite 17

Many a star used to
shine in my heaven.
All are fading!

Friday 16 March[1]
This evening: the van der Stappens, Herr and Frau Ribarz,[2] Prof and Frau Zuckerkandl, Gretl Hellmann, Khnopff, Moser, Hoffmann, Spitzer, Pollack.

It was more fun than usual. I talked to Khnopff almost all evening. At table he told me he'd never met a girl more flirtatious than me, which made me fume. I feigned annoyance. He may be right, but I'm unaware of it. Then I played 'Tristan', Prelude and Liebestod – maybe not as well as when I'm alone, but with feeling and altogether – not badly. Madame van der Stappen kissed me twice. Everyone came over to congratulate me.

Khnopff trotted out a poem he had written – and asked me to set it to music.[3] It's very atmospheric, and I find it interesting. I took his pencil and followed the words as I translated them. He took the pencil and kissed it. Frau Zuckerkandl came and said:

> She's good-looking – that's bad enough. She's a brilliant pianist – that's infuriating. And on top of it she composes – it makes you sick.

Before the dessert I sat with Khnopff, and he, who knows and loves every note of 'Tristan', showed me his favourite passages. Fifty-six bars[4] before 'welcher König' is a passage at the sight of which his eyes dilated. He dug his fingernails forcefully into the vocal score and shouted like a man possessed. Suddenly he said:

> I must stop, otherwise I'll get depressed, and that wouldn't be appropriate.

Why that particular passage, I don't understand. – It's the moment where the King approaches – wedding music interwoven with a few sad notes of denial – one knows that the outcome will be fatal. It's wonderful,

---

1 The first half of this entry was originally included in Suite 16.
2 Since 1892, Rudolf Ribarz had been active as professor for floral painting at Vienna Technical College. He was a fellow-student of Emil J. Schindler.
3 ▶ *Viviane*, poem by Khnopff ('Sous l'ombre verte du Boscelinde').
4 *Recte* 116 bars.

wonderfully beautiful and lonely, but in 'Tristan' there are other passages
which are more deeply sad. Directly after the love-draught in act I:

 – Khnopff wants to make a free translation of these
two notes into colour. Of Tristan only an arm – of her
perhaps just the face – but all expression concentrated
in that face – all the torment, pride, love, hate, every nerve-fibre a-tremble.
One of the most exacting tasks an artist could set himself. –
A few years ago he wanted to transform act III of 'Tristan' into colour. But
while he was working he became afflicted with nervous fever, and couldn't
bear to look at the picture any more. He was so carried away by his
emotions.
At table, Hoffmann asked me to tell him what I'd like, and he'd design it
for me. I asked him for a bookplate.
    But Moser would probably do that better.
Hoffmann will design a typeface and have it cast for me. Moser brought
me his photograph.
The evening was quite wonderful. Khnopff I absolutely adore. His calm,
earnest manner and his sagacity are most impressive. He's building a house
– the dining-room is to be fitted out entirely in white marble – and he said:
    Even from a distance it must be clear: only Khnopff could live here.

Saturday 17 March
I'm mad today – feel impelled to laugh and cry, and don't know why.

Sunday 18 March
At midday to the Philharmonic. They played:
    Haydn: 1st Symphony[5]
    Weber: Konzertstück
Busoni played like a god –
then Liszt's Mephisto-Waltz for the scene in the village-inn from Lenau's
'Faust'[6] and Goldmark's 'Frühling' overture – completely Jewish, tainted
music. I liked the Liszt – there's passion in it. But the laurels went to
Haydn. Old papa Haydn. –
This afternoon: to Frau Radnitzky's. I played Rubinstein's E♭-major trio. It
went like the wind.
This evening: ball at Witteks'. Irritating at first. Carl and I didn't know
anyone and just stood around. Then I was introduced to a Baron Weber,

5 Actually the Symphony No 103 in E♭ major.
6 Busoni probably played his transcription of the orchestral version, published in 1904.

and Baroness Heimberger, who I'd met at the Taussigs', came and renewed our acquaintance. Most enjoyable was the table conversation with Baron Banhans and Dr Eisel – we talked mostly about the other guests, but that's the best fun of all.

Afterwards we visited the Zierers. Gretl Hellmann said:

Alma, Khnopff has been talking to Helene Gottlieb all evening.

That's all right, I said, let him.

And I spoke scarcely a word with him for the rest of the evening. Danced crazily and left him to Fräulein Gottlieb. Now and then he came over, but I didn't have much to say. Why should I?

Monday 19 March

Dinner at the Conrats'. I scarcely spoke to Khnopff today. I'll show him. I can survive without him. Van der Stappen said he would have liked to sketch me, I had such a fine line when dancing.

I spent almost all my time with Zemlinsky. A dear fellow. Later I played Lanner waltzes with him four-hands.

Khnopff said he was expecting a sad reunion in London with an ex-fiancée who's married now. He said it was his fault: she loved him so much, she couldn't stand him flirting with other women. And he told her:

Well, that's how I am, and I have no intention of changing my ways.

The only consolation, he said, was that with him she would have been sadder, even less content.

I'm in such a state of nervous agitation – I had to stop composing. I believe I'm going out of my mind. Don't know what's happening – I hate, I love . . . Let me die. – I was writing a song: 'Meine Nächte' – I couldn't go on. If only I had someone to embrace, to kiss – to kiss to death – let me love *just once* – enjoy life *just once* – and then die. I can't go on vegetating like this. I must experience life. *I must.* I feel the urge to fall at someone's feet and give myself to them body and soul. There's too much zest in me. Klimt, my beloved, come to me – if you come now, I am yours. Or should I write and just go to him?

p.m. Percy Miles. I've no idea what I played. In my frenzy I composed something – that's all I know.

Tuesday 20 March

This morning: Labor. I shall never make a proper contrapuntalist, I don't know how to use my head.

On the way home I bumped into Schmedes on the Kärntnerstrasse . . . and

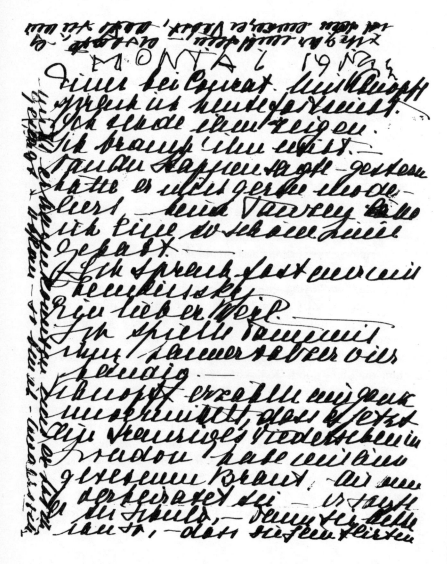

pp. 266–7: facsimile of the entry for Monday 19 March 1900

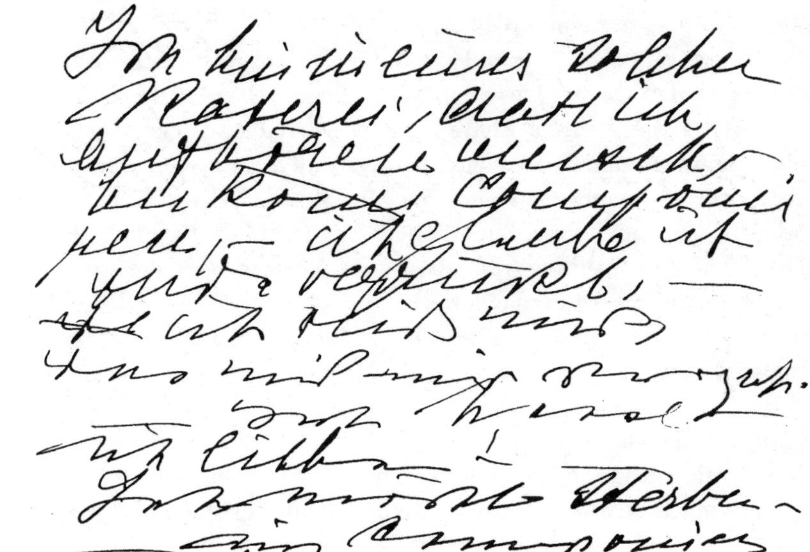

he saw me home. Tomorrow it'll be everybody's secret. He told me they were on the point of getting divorced. My name was mentioned at the solicitors', but in no sense detrimentally. Simply: he, Schmedes, had danced with a girl named Alma Schindler, whereupon his wife made a scene in public. Nothing to besmirch my name.

I'm so very, very fond of him. He has devoted, loyal, sweet eyes. He was really thrilled to see me. This evening he's singing Loge for the first time. If I'd known, I would certainly have gone. He offered me a ticket – next to his wife. I declined politely. We chatted amiably all the way home. Lots of my friends saw us together. – Tomorrow Mama and Carl will hear about it, and it'll come back to me. But – nobody can undo what's done. I like the fellow! There's something fresh about him. Maybe something stupid too! Ça ne fait rien.[7] He's fun to talk to.

p.m. I composed. The song is terrifically difficult, but the poem is full of atmosphere, which had to be retained. –

Wednesday 21 March
This morning: Khnopff, alone, for two hours. We fetched schnapps, and he felt very much at home. Then I played 'Tristan' for quite a while. It's a pleasure to play to such an expert as Khnopff. He knows and loves every note of 'Tristan'.

In the afternoon: in town. Met Alfred and Ernst Zierer. The latter insignificant but pleasant.

In the evening: Pollack.

Composed a lot. –

Thursday 22 March
On Tuesday Schmedes sang Loge for the first time, and Khnopff said he'd never heard so magnificently conceived a Loge. All in all, the performance sent him into ecstasies. He'd never experienced such an ensemble, neither as regards staging, singing or orchestral playing.

Carl has sold three pictures at the Secession, thank heaven. At last we can rake something in. Last year was meagre enough. –

p.m. at the Secession. Khnopff was there – asked us if he can call again before he leaves.

Dinner at Felix Fischer's.

---

7 Orig.: C'est fait rien.

Friday 23 March
With the Hellmanns to 'Siegfried'. I'm simply knocked off my feet. Such consuming passion. And . . . Schmedes! He was so good. If he was here now, I'd be capable of anything. – I'm simply bowled over. The music is flabbergasting. And the Siegfried was as well. He saw me! –

Saturday 24 March
What was the matter with me again yesterday? It's just as well I wrote something down. At least I can see what pure abandon and passion do to you. And I was serious – deadly serious. Today I can laugh about it, even if Schmedes, wretched man, still makes the blood run to my head.
This is the most beautiful opera – apart from 'Tristan'. Such joie de vivre, such youthfulness. And the passionate ending carries you away. – After 'Siegfried' I'd be capable of anything! But unfortunately – nobody wants me. I simply would have loved to give Schmedes a kiss for his performance – for his singing, acting and handsome appearance! – I do believe he'd have accepted it!!
Khnopff came into our box. He was in ecstasy. He'd never heard such a performance of 'Siegfried' anywhere. And, in all seriousness, neither had I. The orchestra, the singers surpassed themselves. How lucky I am!

Monday 26 March
Just got home after 'Götterdämmerung'. Looked into the orchestra pit all the time and followed the part-writing – except when Schmedes was on stage. Once again, his acting and singing deserved a kiss. And he looked wonderful!
The work is everlasting.

Tuesday 27 March
This morning: row with Carl.
Then Gretl and I called on Aunt Mie.
Then to town. Happened to see the funeral procession of Dumba, the parliamentarian.[8]
I was a little annoyed with Schmedes. He'd told me he'd be there again today. I walked across the Schwarzenbergplatz, a little downcast. Suddenly I saw Schmedes and Dr Winter coming towards me. Winter hastily made his excuses. I felt awkward, because it made our meeting look like an

---

8 Nikolaus Dumba died on 23 March 1900 in Budapest.

assignation. Actually that's more or less what it was. – Gretl was a bit of an embarrassment to S. He escorted us home. Told us a few titbits from the Opera. Yesterday, during the performance, he boxed Pacal's ears. In act II, Siegfried has a high C, which he always leaves out. Pacal, who was standing behind him, opened his mouth – as if to sing it. When they went backstage, P. laughed inanely.

> You shouldn't laugh like that, my dear P. Don't kid yourself that you
> could sing that high C.

P.'s retort:

> You blockhead.

Schmedes gave as good as he got, and boxed his ears so soundly that P.'s helmet fell off.[9] Pacal will probably be fired. –

We talked about the Hellmann ball, and how stupidly his wife had behaved. Then he said:

> If I were your husband and I'd spent so much time talking to another
> woman, I'm convinced you would have been even more angry than my
> wife.

Actually he's right. I'm jealous by nature.

He was very handsome again today. Altogether, I'm very fond of him.

Finally he looked at me and took a regretful farewell. I said to myself: 'Next Tuesday' – and see no reason why I shouldn't go.

In the evening: Hennebergs, Hoffmann – quite nice. In truth: I long for Schmedes to kiss me. God forgive me.

Wednesday 28 March

Yesterday evening I must have been out of my mind once again – or drunk – or what know I. I'm not ashamed of what I wrote, but it does sound rather strange. –

Yesterday I talked to Hoffmann about style in the arts. He agrees with me, more or less. – Labor's opinion differs.

Zemlinsky I now loathe. He didn't come to the Hennebergs' yesterday. And Spitzer told us that he boozes whole nights through. If he prefers that to the companionship of artists and artistically minded friends, that's all right with me. And I'd taken such a liking to him. What a misfortune! When a young fellow makes a success of something, he finds himself

---

9 A.S. seems to have misrepresented the scandal. The incident could only have occurred in act III/ii of *Die Götterdämmerung*, for there is no other high C for Siegfried in the opera; at that moment, however, Siegfried is alone on stage. And Pacal, a lyric tenor, was not directly involved in the performance at all.

surrounded by parasites, who ruin his good name, often for life, with their toadying. Few can cope with that. And Zemlinsky seems to be very susceptible. –

Thursday 29 March
Yesterday p.m. I was at the Wittgensteins' for the final rehearsal of the Baumeyer concert, which opened with a clarinet quintet by Labor. It wasn't very exciting. To me it made the impression of a tricky mathematical problem, carefully worked out. I can summon up little enthusiasm for such cerebral art. –
This evening: with Frau Conrat, Khnopff and Dr Horn in the Conrats' box for a performance of Zemlinsky's 'Es war einmal'. On the whole I liked the opera quite well. Some passages are too strongly influenced by Wagner. But he's still young and will find his own, personal touch. He does have one. I didn't much care for the Prelude. Act I was quite good, but I liked act II best of all. It's dramatic and well shaped. In the first act there are too many scenic and linguistic fireworks. That leaves me cold. Kurz, Schmedes and Hesch were very good. Schmedes was a picture, and sang magnificently.
Afterwards we all went round to the Conrats'. Khnopff asked me in what form I'd like Schumann's 'Faust'. I replied, boldly, 'The full score.' But perhaps I won't get it at all. Meyer from the orchestra was there too, and we talked about almost nothing but Wagner.

Friday 30 March
Yesterday p.m. Madame van der Stappen. She told us that Khnopff had been wandering around for days on end, pondering whether Helene Gottlieb or I was the more beautiful.
p.m. Gretl Hellmann. I received a very dear letter from Zemlinsky.
This evening: the Baumeyer concert.[10] Listened to the Labor again . . .
In the evening: Reininghaus. Such a nice, sensible person. Spitzer was there too. One could hardly say the same of him.
The Klimt hubbub still isn't over. The professors are on the warpath.[11]
I composed a good deal today, and now I want to write a cycle. One of the

10 Chamber-music concert in the Bösendorfer Saal, with Richard Mühlfeld (clarinet), Marie Baumeyer (piano), Marie Soldat-Röger (violin), Alfred Finger (viola) and Wilhelm Jeral (cello). Apart from Labor's Quintet in D major for piano, clarinet, violin, viola and cello, the programme included piano music by Brahms, Graun, Piccini, Domenico Scarlatti and Mendelssohn, and works for clarinet and piano by Schumann and Brahms. Marie Baumeyer was noted above all for her Brahms interpretations.
11 Seventy-eight professors lodged a formal protest against the hanging of Klimt's

songs is about pregnancy, a distasteful subject, which no poet – I'm convinced – has ever handled more beautifully.

Tuesday 3 April

The day on which I usually see Schmedes. I arrived at Labor's. He was in Laibach. How was I to pass the time? I went onto the Ring and saw – Mahler. I'm very taken with him . . . Christine was walking beside me. He greeted her, looking at me all the while.

I got to the Heugasse early, around 12:30 – last time he'd been waiting there at 1:00. I don't care, on the contrary: the affair must be brought to an end. What's it to lead to? . . . There was a time when I felt genuinely, erotically attracted to him. That's over, thank God.

This evening: with Conrat at the Tonkünstlerverein. Nothing but Brahms. Afterwards we all stayed there for dinner. To my right sat Heuberger, to my left Meyer. In a few words, the latter professed his profound admiration for me – let's say: love. And while he was in full flight, I suddenly interrupted:

Did you hear that Pacal is leaving the Opera?

He, namely, happened to be sitting opposite me. Meyer was stupefied.

> Fräulein, you obviously have experience in dealing with situations like this. I've never seen anything like it. The way you changed the subject, so casually. I congratulate you, Fräulein, on your expertise.

I had to laugh. Meyer asked permission to escort me home. But I replied that I'd be driving.

> Look – you can see that my intentions are not dishonourable.
>
> Yes, I said, that's what you think – and that's what I think. But I don't know if other people would see it that way.

He didn't answer: very offended.

Zemlinsky wasn't there, worst luck. Only his two friends, Wolff[12] and Schoenberg. Wolff is dreadfully unkempt. Later he was talking to Heuberger, just behind me. Suddenly Frau Conrat said:

> Just look at his hair. I rather fear that W.'s head is a breeding ground for little beasties.

———

Philosophy in the main hall of Vienna University. In reaction, on 28 March, members of the Secession laid a wreath in front of the picture.

12 The composer and pianist Erich J. Wolff, who was primarily self-taught. During 1901–2 he was Zemlinsky's assistant at the Carltheater. His *oeuvre* includes incidental music to Hofmannsthal's *Der Schüler* (lost), sixty posthumously published lieder, a violin concerto and a string quartet.

I moved hastily aside, and from a safe distance we laughed heartily at the poor devil. – If only I could get him to take a hot bath!

Someone bumped accidentally into Schoenberg – right there. That was enough to provoke a duel, with Meyer as referee. Altogether – apart from the fact that the distressing word 'lice' was mentioned once too often – I had a most entertaining evening.

Most of them are artists – and musicians at that, of whom I have so far little experience.

Saturday 7 April

I'm sitting in the train to Pest – travelling alone.

First I read 'Victoria' by Knut Hamsun, and now I'm looking out of the window. The route follows the Danube. The river is wide and grey. Here and there I see fields torn asunder. They're building a railway-track, a road. To me it looks as if the earth were bleeding. Wherever paths and roads have been laid – those are slashes in the skin. And where a hillside has been blasted away, a gaping wound is left. Humans hate the Earth. They love only themselves – everything else they subdue – they desire everything for themselves. And instead of tenderly stroking the womb of eternal being with their hands, they scratch it open with their fingernails. Their nails are black and encrusted with blood. And the Earth avenges itself.

I arrived at 2:00. Laura and Lili Hirsch at the station.

We drove home. The city looks dirty. To the right of the house is a large yard, to the left the stairway, all rather insignificant and new-rich. My room is quite nice – somewhat unwelcoming, but that doesn't matter. Frau Hirsch sat at table in her night-gown, he was constantly wheezing. Typically Jewish.

The journey was uneventful. A couple of people were loafing around outside my compartment, but I gave them a dirty look. That did the trick. This evening to the Opera: 'Hunyadi László' by Ferenc Erkel.[13] Arányi in the title role, etc. etc. The opera is written in the Italian style – but not bad, I believe. It's effective on stage, particularly the closing scene. A singer named Pewny was the best. She has a well-developed coloratura but over-acted horribly. To me it was quite clear that the work is overrated. Since it was sung in a foreign language, I scarcely understood the music. When

13 ▶ Playbill of the Royal National Opera, Budapest: *Hunyadi László*, after a play by Lörinc Tóth. The opera was first performed at Pest in 1844; radically revised and newly orchestrated, it was revived in 1878. Today it counts as one of the most popular works in the Hungarian national repertoire.

Duse is on stage, although I scarcely speak a word of Italian, her gestures and facial expressions communicate the beauty of the play to me. But an opera is neither fish nor fowl. It's a weird concoction of music, gesture and language, which an outsider can scarcely grasp. Never did the art of theatre strike me as more inane than this evening at the Opera. All the greasepaint, the fervour, the passion . . . but why? – Do I know? What concern of mine are the pain and joy of these people? For me, they and their history are a closed book.

Thursday 12 April
This morning with Aunt Laura and Albert Hirsch, the twenty-year-old son of the family, to Parliament and the Palace of Justice. Both buildings grand but rubbishy.
In the evening: guests at home. – Miki (Dr Surány), Schönherr (a music-fan), Magda {Mandello} and her husband, a Herr Baumgartner and a cousin of Mandello's. I talked a lot with Mandello and Schönherr. I didn't play, but talked, mostly to Miki. He's a dear chap. Told me he'd been here so often during the past days because of me. He also said he knew that I liked him. –
And, by Jove – he's right.

Friday 13 April
Yesterday p.m. Frau Hirsch gave me a belt and handkerchiefs from Paris.
a.m. at Mandellos'. Met Miki on the way home. He accompanied us. Various women passed by, and his comments were rather too indelicate for my taste.
Waiting for us was Carl Ellenberger. He gave me a delightful pendant, an enamel Easter egg with a little diamond and, inside, three smaller, golden pendants. – It gave me such joy.
This afternoon Miki came round, and we all walked up the Blocksberg. On the way up, I lost Ellenberger's pendant. I was so sorry. Miki and Albert Hirsch searched for it a long time. From the summit, the view over Pest was really delightful. –
Dr Surány was standing next to me and couldn't take his eyes off me. He said:
    The two of us together would make *one* reasonable person.
We crossed the Danube in a steamboat and sat down on the bank. Suddenly it started to rain . . . He and I walked on ahead.
    Fräulein Alma, I have a request to make. If you are as unprejudiced as

I believe, you won't be angry. And you can't throw me out, because
we're on the street: Would you give me your photograph? . . .

I was embarrassed and said nothing.

So you're not as unprejudiced as I thought . . .

I replied:

Look: that's asking more than you can imagine. I don't do that kind of
thing.

He said:

Think it over.

That's the trouble with such a bathing-resort affair – that's how I'd
describe this one too – you strike up a friendship, like each other and never
meet again in your life.

I regret it. –

Saturday 14 April

In the morning: packed.

Miki came for lunch and brought Lili and me a gigantic gift box, full of
Kugler candies. Albert and Magda gave me lots as well. At table, Miki sat
beside me. Softly he asked:

Have you thought it over?

I smiled softly but said nothing. He got out his wallet, and I knew straight
away: he's looking for his address. Out of the corner of my eye I saw him
take out his visiting card and roll it up inconspicuously into a ball.[14] That's
for me – I knew it. Mandello came with violets. Miki said:

Show me your violets –

took the bouquet from me and gave me the ball of paper. I felt terribly
embarrassed, held it in my hand for some time, then finally put it into my
bag. Softly he said:

You may be inexperienced, but you're quick on the uptake. You knew
immediately what I was getting out of my wallet . . .

I'm determined *not* to send him the picture. It's not my style. I did it just
once – and that was with a picture from Genoa.

I really like Surány immensely – really. He's a Jew. But what difference does
that make, actually . . . ?

Left Pest at 1:00. A Herr Singer (from the 'Neue Freie Presse') travelled
with us.

Back home. Everyone is being very nice to me. –

14 ▶ Card (without address!): 'Nikolaus Surány wishes you a pleasant journey.'

I shall only miss one friend in Pest. But it's all over, finished.
– It was a sweet dream. –

Tuesday 17 April
At Labor's. They rehearsed his quintet again. I find it *terribly* boring.
He {Zemlinsky} wrote this to me today.[15] I can't blame him for going to see
his opera. After all, it's his first-born.

Thursday 19 April
Reininghaus to lunch.
This evening: Tonkünstlerverein.[16] Zemlinsky sent me tickets, but as
Reininghaus had announced himself for the evening, Mama didn't want to
let me go. And there was nobody to escort me.
p.m. Gretl Hellmann dropped in. And it occurred to me: what if Mama
allowed us to go together, Gretl and I? It was only speculation. Summoning
all my audacity, I outlined my plan to her. She seemed half-inclined to
accept, and went away. She'd hidden the tickets somewhere. Frantically I
searched for them, found them & decided to go, even if Mama wouldn't let
me.
The coach was meant to come at 7:30. At 5:00 the coachman rang to say:
Frau Hellmann was sitting inside, waiting for Gretl. I threw myself into
evening-dress and ran outside with Gretl. The two Mamas stood side by
side. Finally they assented. We were overjoyed.
Arriving fairly early at the concert-hall, we took our seats in the first row
on the left, where the young artists always sit, and, sure enough, J. Wolff
soon appeared. We chatted away gaily. He said:
    Z. wasn't at the Conrats' yesterday.
That pleased me immensely.
    But you knew already?
    No.
    You know, I do believe that you and Zemlinsky have some kind of
    compromise . . . don't deny it. And I know what it is, too. I'm no fool.
Zemlinsky arrived soon after. He came over to me and spoke to me at
length. Fräulein Guttmann[17] was sitting behind him. He didn't greet her –

---

15 ▶ Postcard from Zemlinsky: 'If you would be so kind, come to the Tonkünstlerverein on
Tuesday evening: nice programme.'
16 Programme: Josef Suk, Serenade for strings op 6, conducted by Zemlinsky; lieder by Erich
J. Wolff; Robert Fuchs, Andante and Capriccio for strings, conducted by the composer.
17 Melanie Guttmann, daughter of a shipping agent from Brno, took voice lessons with

although she's supposed to be his fiancée. – She's frightfully ugly. Such marriages should be forbidden by law. He didn't take the slightest notice of her.

Spitzer came over and said:

> Watch out, Alma. Take care they don't play you off against her. She – he pointed to Fräulein G. – is probably the one who . . .

I replied:

> I know.

Spitzer left.

They played a serenade by {Josef Suk}.[18] I was particularly taken by the second movement. In the last movement there was a passage:

which was more than I could take.[19] Zemlinsky conducted. At the end of each movement he smiled at me. –

Then they sang lieder by J. Wolff (the unkempt). One was particularly lovely, the last one too, except for the closing bars, which were coarse, mannered and meaningless. Zemlinsky agreed with me – then we left. I'd promised Mama to be home by 9:45.

While I was listening, Fräulein Guttmann fixed me with a stare. But I didn't look at Z. I went the rounds and greeted Frau Radnitzky, Frau Conrat, Dr Horn etc. etc. Although I was aware that Zemlinsky was following me, I didn't turn round. In the foyer he said:

> Can I fetch your coat for you?
>
> Why not, I replied. But step outside with me. There's something I want to tell you.

I leaned him against a bench, planted myself squarely in front of him, and said:

> Let's speak openly: there's someone in there who's very offended when we strike up a conversation. Look, they're all telling me . . .
>
> That's shameful, he hissed.
>
> And why do you never call on us? Because you're not allowed to.

———

Joseph Gänsbacher at the Vienna Conservatoire from 1890 to 1895. In 1901 she emigrated to New York, where she married the painter William Clark-Rice. Her sister Ida married Zemlinsky in 1907.

18 Gap in the manuscript: A.S. had forgotten the composer's name.

19 The phrase does not occur in any movement of Suk's Serenade.

Look, I don't want to hurt anyone's feelings. But the way you're talk-
ing isn't exactly pleasant. And if it was true, what conclusion would
you draw?
I paused – thought it over.
    It's all lies, he shouted, his face reddening.
He promised to come on Monday. I don't believe him. People never tell the
truth.
Gretl and I walked passed Schoenberg and Wolff, and went into the foyer.
Wolff followed us. I congratulated him and said:
    Can you bring me the second song?
    Certainly, where do you live?
    Zemlinsky has my address.
    Fräulein, he's my friend. I can ask him anything – except *that*.
    Very well then: Theresianumgasse 6.
We left. Gretl was overjoyed at having met all the young composers. I was
happy too – but less than her.
At home were Bella Lehrs, wife of the director of the Kupferstichkabinett
in Dresden[20] (a friend of Klinger's – platonic, if you know what I mean)
and Reininghaus. At midnight we all accompanied Frau L. and R. to their
hotels. Bumped into the Kurzweils.

Saturday 21 April
This letter from Khnopff arrived today.
Gird thee with sackcloth and wallow
in ashes.

Monday 23 April
At 11:00, as arranged
– Zemlinsky –
I played him some of my songs, in
which he found much talent but little
ability. He asked me to take the whole
thing more seriously, said it was a
crying shame – that I was full of ideas
but didn't take it seriously enough to
learn properly. Of one turn of phrase he
said:
    That's so good, I could almost have written it myself.

20 Max Lehrs.

He pointed out a few small errors, was kind and witty. One thing though: he wasn't pleased that I'd invited Wolff.

You're very quick with your invitations.

He said I was the worst interpreter of my own music. My playing was too nervous, too fidgety. He asked if he could take three of the songs with him. I'll copy them and send them. –

p.m. at Dr Pollack's.

This evening: 'The Marriage of Figaro' for the first time. I liked it immensely – although 116 years old, it's youthful and modern. There's nothing thrilling, nothing nerve-racking about this kind of music – in contrast to Wagner's – but it's placid, uncommonly neutral and sweet. And hence also the healthier of the two. I must admit that Wagner moves me far more than Mozart. But that's due to the times we live in. Our century, our race, our outlook on life, our blood, our heart – everything is decadent! That's why we prefer operas in which the music whips up every feeling and tears us apart like a whirlwind. We need madness – not dainty pastorales – to refresh the heart and mind. Quite honestly, *today* I learnt to respect Mozart. That I had never previously done so can remain my secret. Respect – yes. I'd always respected him, but never loved him. Now I *love* his music. Afterwards we dined at Bertha Kunz's. With the Sewalds and Magda and old Herr Hirsch.

Gretl, Mama and Dr Pollack were at 'Der verlorene Sohn' at the Carltheater.[21]

Tuesday 24 April

Labor. He liked my two songs.

They're very talented, he said.

For my counterpoint exercises he gave me no marks at all. I'm in despair. On the way home I saw Schmedes's Hun-like figure looming in the distance on the Ring. He went to his front door, looked back, didn't recognize me – and went inside. As I passed by, I looked in. There he stood, waiting to see if it was really me. Recognizing me, he spread out his arms, laughed, rejoiced, came back out and, as a matter of course, saw me home. First I asked him how his wife was, then what was wrong with her. I looked at him sharply, with a sarcastic smile. He was at a loss.

Everything, Alma, everything possible, he joked.

21 The ensemble of the Deutsches Volkstheater was making a guest appearance with *Der verlorene Sohn*, pantomime in three acts by Michel Carré junior, preceded by *Frauen-Emancipation*, a one-act farce by Carl Sonntag.

He'd understood. I said I would never marry, and he replied:

> You know, I believe I'd know how to treat you. All my friends warn
> me: 'Watch your step, she's a dreadful flirt.' I wouldn't allow my wife
> to flirt. Tell me, could you accept me as a husband?

I replied evasively.

He was still jealous of Khnopff. I calmed him down.

> Tell me one thing: are you so sweet to everyone or just to me? And
> then, at the Hellmanns', was that something deeper, or were you just
> playing with me? Do tell me.

I looked into the distance – he'd stopped. I took out my watch, looked at
him ironically and said:

> Oh, it's already 1:30. I must be off.

He called after me:

> Fräulein, wait a moment.

I said:

> Did you know that I don't have a photograph of you?
> Would you like one? I'll give you as many as you like.
> But you must write something nice on it.
> Yes, he said, waving his stick in the air, 'To the young lady who plays
> with everyone.'
> No, I said, that's not true.

We reached the corner. I stopped.

> Well, adieu. – But please: don't make eyes at other men any more. I
> beg you.

I couldn't help laughing. What a droll request! But he's such a dear fellow.
And he has loyal eyes.

Thursday 26 April
This evening: 'Aida'. I like the opera very, very much. Lilli Lehmann in the
title role was wonderful. Some turns of phrases are strongly reminiscent of
'Tannhäuser'.

Friday 27 April
Burckhard to dinner – a dear chap. He told us a few anecdotes about
serving on the administrative tribunal – actually very sad stories but,
the way he told them, amusing. Carl arrived back. I hadn't exactly been
longing for him. He told us much about the poor organisation of the
World Exhibition, the numerous prostitutes, the high cost of living and
the dreadful racket on the streets.

Saturday 28 April
Carl has resigned from the Secession, because Engelhart gave him an official reprimand.[22] Preliminary deliberations on the election. Carl has been nominated for the presidency – unanimously.

Sunday 29 April
Lilli Lehmann, Reininghaus and Burckhard to lunch. Big personalities, those two,[23] worth experiencing. It was great fun. The Asti took its toll.
In the evening: alone.

Monday 30 April
Yesterday morning: at the Secession. Attendance poor. Hancke driven half crazy by recent events.
Today p.m. on the Hohe Warte with Reininghaus. He's in the process of getting divorced.
This evening: Carl was elected president of the Secession. He's just writing to turn it down.

Thursday 3 May
On Tuesday I was at 'Don Giovanni'. It didn't make much impression on me. I remained unmoved by the melancholy drama of both text and music. The beginning of the overture I love.
This evening: Tonkünstlerverein.
    Suite no. 1 by Goldmark[24]
    Lieder – ditto
    Quintet in B♭ major – ditto
His music is too Jewish for my taste. Zemlinsky was noticeably stand-offish. Wolff, who should have called on us today, didn't greet me. Well, I suppose I shall survive without him. I've no idea what's up with Z. –

Sunday 6 May
This evening: 'Die Walküre'. Only the second time this season. I have been frightfully unjust: in its way, the work is unique. Winkelmann and

22 ▶ Letter from Erich J. Wolff, proposing a rendezvous on 26 April.
23 i.e. Lilli Lehmann and Burckhard.
24 Carl Goldmark, an honorary member of the Tonkünstlerverein, celebrated his seventieth birthday on 18 May 1900. Programme: speech by the president (Richard Heuberger); Suite no 1 in D major op 11 (Arnold Rosé, violin, and Ignaz Brüll, piano); songs from 'Der wilde Jäger' op 11 (Agnes Bricht-Pyllemann, soprano); Piano Quintet in B♭ major op 54 (Fitzner Quartet, Carl Prohaska).

Hilgermann very good. Mildenburg really terrific. Reichmann (Wotan) boring as usual. The opera is uniquely beautiful.

Tuesday 8 May
Labor. – We talked at length about our domestic problems. He's like a father to me.
Yesterday p.m. with Erica Conrat in the Prater. She's such a bright young lady.
This evening:
Siegfried
Schmedes unique, terrific; Mime (Breuer) uninspiring; Sedlmair (Brünnh.) poor.
I know every note, every word of this immortal work like my right hand. Schmedes was so handsome again! And sang magically.

Wednesday 9 May
This evening: a wire from Hamburg that Granny was dying. Mama left straight away, although Maria has a feverish cold. Now we're left with all the responsibility.

Thursday 10 May
It just occurs to me: at the Tonkünstlerverein, I asked Dr Horn why he hadn't greeted me, and he got someone to tell me that his attitude is like mine towards Mahler. Since he knows that I know that he likes me, he avoids all contact. – And actually he's right. If you know too much about another person's feelings, the quality of a friendship deteriorates.
This evening: Spitzer, Xandi.
Yesterday evening all the youngsters from the Secession visited 'Venedig in Wien' with the Wärndorfers[25] and Gretl Hellmann. Moser had much to tell Gretl about me. And I'm shocked how he sees through me. But he spoke well of me. – He asked Gretl the opinion of others – of those more competent to judge my music – and was delighted to hear that I have my own standing in the world of music. He said I was such a unique person, he could well imagine it, that there was something irrepressible, invincible about me. He also said:

25 August and Fritz Wärndorfer, heirs to a textile firm. Fritz Wärndorfer was co-founder of the Wiener Werkstätte; he sponsored Josef Hoffmann and Koloman Moser, and also supported Charles Rennie Mackintosh, whose furniture and interior designs were exhibited at the Secession in 1900.

I'll be interested to see who manages to win her favour. She treats all
men with disdain.

How right he is. Once I believed I'd *remedied* the problem. But even that
man wasn't worth it.

I'm fond of Moser. –

Friday 11 May
p.m. Krasny.
This evening:

Götterdämmerung

I concentrated on the orchestration. This Wagner was a smart fellow.
Schmedes wonderful; Mildenburg grandiose.

We have no need to be ashamed of our Opera. The orchestra surpassed
itself. Wagner – I thank you!

Zemlinsky was there too. How small he must have felt.

Saturday 12 May
Lunch at the Conrats' – a certain Dr Kobler, Kraus from 'Die Fackel' and
Zem. Zemlinsky sat next to me, Kraus vis-à-vis. Initially I scarcely spoke to
him. The opportunity didn't arise. I also had much to discuss with
Zemlinsky.

I asked him, in all honesty, why our relationship, which used to be so gay
and unforced, had become so strained. He said he was pleased I'd noticed
it, but when he'd called on us I hadn't been very nice to him. A remark of
mine had so annoyed him that, on his way out he'd said to himself, 'I shall
never set foot in this house again.' After much persuasion, he revealed the
outrage: when I introduced him to Gretl, I said in jest, 'Take your hat off.'
That made him absolutely livid. Even if I consider it petty of him to take
offence at such an innocent remark, he's right in one sense, namely that I
always want to boss my friends about. And he said:

> That's something I just can't bear. I won't let anyone subjugate me –
> least of all a woman.

Bravo, quite right. I like him all the more for that. Then he told me that I
lack all passion, that I do everything by halves – I can only be half a
musician, only take half a pleasure in things – and only marry half-
heartedly, that is: marry a man I don't care for. I shall never approach
things in real depth. –

Alas, *how right* he is, how *very* right. I'm very worried about my half-
heartedness.

He told me he was instantly attracted by my good-natured attitude. I
scarcely knew him, but my conversation was immediately unrestrained,
free of taboos. Later he realized that <u>that</u> was my way of flirting with
people. I said:

> I'm sorry that we seem to have drifted apart, the damage seems to be
> irreparable.
>
> No, we can make it up.

He looked at me and continued:

> Tell me, Fräulein, what's your intention, what exactly do you want?
>
> A nice, innocent relationship, as it used to be.
>
> That's asking an awful lot. You're asking for friendship as between
> brother and sister – that's not always possible.

I frowned.

Frau Conrat ended the meal. We went into the smoking-room. I sat down in
an easy chair, Kraus took a seat opposite me, Zemlinsky a little further
away. Z. said:

> Kraus, you'll have to get up – that chair is reserved for the lady of the
> house.
>
> Oh, excuse me.

And he sprang up.

> Stay where you are, said Frau Conrat. If you get up, Zemlinsky will
> take it, and that really isn't necessary.

At 4:30 Herr Conrat had to go. I took my leave too, as did everyone else.
The discussion revolved mostly around 'Die Fackel'. It struck me as
grotesque, how everyone dragged out their scandalous stories. He listened
attentively – a rag-and-bone man!

We left. In the lobby I was about to take my leave. Both of them offered to
accompany me a little way – Zemlinsky as far as the Ring, Kraus further.

As we reached the Karlsplatz, I realized to my dismay that my right
stocking was falling down. I walked on as far as the tram shelters. There,
stammering helplessly, I stopped. He gloated at my predicament.

> Can't you keep walking while we're talking?
>
> I can't.

After making a series of stupid remarks, such as 'If you weren't so young'
etc., I told him that something was torn. Meanwhile the stocking had
worked its way down into my shoe. I rushed off to the ladies' room. I
re-emerged, blushing for shame. He said:

> Why so petty, Fräulein? It can happen to anyone.

I told him (stupidly) that I was annoyed at the way he kept attacking

Burckhard. Also that he was misinformed about the Secession. We talked about the Klimt affair. I love to talk about Klimt with people who have no idea . . .

We arrived home. I invited him into the garden, where Gretl and Ernst were taking a stroll. Then I showed him the studio, but forgot to tell him that only the redcurrants were in bloom. That would have been amusing. [In the number before last he published a dreadful attack on Carl.][26] He finished his drink[27] and took his leave. He's a handsome man, twenty-six years old, a little handicapped unfortunately, but *so* knowledgeable [?]. His horizon is astonishingly wide.

Ernst Lanner stayed for ages.

In the evening: Pollack and the inevitable Xandi.

Tuesday 15 May

I showed Labor my two latest songs. He liked the one, but found the poem of the other one immoral and badly written. Later I was ashamed at having composed it. My counterpoint exercises were better. We went on to the third species of three-part counterpoint.

Saturday 19 May

Frau Radnitzky has just left. We were talking about marriage, and she said a friend had told her:

You know that Alma Schindler and Olbrich are keen on each other.
I could scarcely hide my feelings. O God, just think what might have been – and has been undone by trivialities. Olbrich – a man of action – a Siegfried. I – a Brünnhilde. Joy and rapture – but quite unattainable. What wouldn't I give to attain it. –

Klimt doesn't enter into it any longer, I've <u>written him off</u>.

Composed very diligently today. A theme and variations.

This letter arrived today.[28] Should I reply?

Tuesday 22 May

Labor. My three-part counterpoint is getting better. At present, I'm obsessed by this idea: I'd like to take lessons with Zemlinsky. If Mama will let me.

26 *Die Fackel*, no 36, end of March 1900, p. 20: '. . . even if someone like Herr Moll pretends to be up to date, that still makes no modernist of him.'
27 Orig.: Weinschorle (wine – usually white – diluted with mineral water).
28 ▶ Letter from Miklós Surány in Budapest.

p.m. to Baroness Bach in Baden. A large, illustrious gathering – including Ehrenstein – but I don't take much notice of womenfolk. Some baroness was introduced to me. Of the men, I made the acquaintance of Count Alberti, a Herr Erhart, Baron Buschmann and others whose names I don't remember. Not much of interest. Little {Moriz} Violin[29] was there too. I feel sorry for him! He plays such a subordinate role.

I learnt nothing this afternoon. The lady of the house sang a few horrible songs by Count Eulenburg[30] – then a few beautiful ones by Schubert etc. Ehrenstein played a paraphrase on 'Götterdämmerung'. The guests smiled charmingly to conceal their boredom, then thanked her profusely for the privilege.

Can't this woman find other ways of relieving herself? It was as if a valve had been opened, emitting a blast of steam which had been accumulating for years. I went there fuming – and came home fuming.

Seligmann travelled with us. When he saw us, he had a nasty turn. On Monday he published an anonymous smear on Carl [in the Sonn- und Montags-Zeitung]. But he soon overcame his shame and had the impudence to talk to us.

August Wärndorfer, whom we met at the station in Baden, invited us to look over his factory. We accepted. It's delightful. All that wonderful, majestic machinery. Human beings feel dwarfed beside it. Thick iron bars are cut and pierced like butter. One thing is clear: the automobile has not yet been perfected. A little more attention to detail – and nothing else will be used the world over. As we were leaving, Seligmann said:

> Today you were like the Kaiser with the industrialists: you held a court circle.

Tuesday 29 May
Labor. He was pleased with my Variations.

---

29 Luise von Ehrenstein was better known as a singer; on this occasion she had been invited to play the piano. The composer–violinist Moriz Violin, a member of the Vienna Tonkünstlerverein, was a close frined of Arnold Schoenberg and Heinrich Schenker.
30 Philipp Graf Fürst zu Eulenburg, an intimate friend of Kaiser Wilhelm II, held diplomatic posts in Paris, London and Vienna. He was active as a poet, musician and architect, and also published a volume of reminiscences, *Aus 50 Jahren* (1923).

Thursday 31 May
This evening: Volkstheater.

John Gabriel Borkmann
Ibsen[31]

The play is magnificent. Was also quite well acted.

Afterwards dinner with Burckhard, Felix, Ernst Fischer, Spitzer, Hoffmann, Stöhr.

Burckhard is delightful. For the first time since I met him, he mentioned his wife.

Klimt was at the performance with one of his models . . .

Friday 1 June
p.m. Olbrich with Peter Behrens.[32]

Not many people can stand the presence of a genius. Carl is not one of them. Olbrich acted a little strangely today. Carl believes he's going off his head. Those eyes, those wonderful eyes. –

Dinner at Spitzer's. Played 'Walküre' and 'Siegfried' four-hands with Zemlinsky. Today I asked him if he'd give me lessons next winter. He promised. – It's *one* of my most fervent wishes!

I didn't speak to Hancke at all. He was livid.

Sunday 3 June
Olbrich for the last time. The farewell was deeply moving. He held my hand longer than necessary. What would I give to win him over! Half my life. And my profit would be the highest yield capital ever realized. I'm immensely fond of him.

He arrived – I was alone in the room.

Does Carl already know? Should I call him?

But why?

He told me he'd send me his play, and that I should devise music to be played between the scenes. It's got to be finished by next spring – but without dividing up the text etc. He wants to open the theatre in Darmstadt with it. Seriously – it's a mad idea. I would never manage it to his satisfaction.[33]

31 One of a series of guest performances by Max Reinhardt's ensemble from the Deutsches Theater, Berlin. The ensemble was simultaneously appearing at the Carltheater.
32 The architect Peter Behrens collaborated with Olbrich on the building of the artists' colony at Darmstadt.
33 Olbrich had evidently written a play, which he intended to stage in the Festival Theatre on the Mathildenhöhe (built in 1901 and pulled down shortly afterwards).

Lunch at Mama Moll's.

p.m. the Leglers – in the evening too.

Before going to bed I had an almighty row with Mama. I shan't go into details – it was just *too* stupid. Let me just say the following: never in my life have I been treated so unjustly. If ever I make something of my life, Mama won't have lifted as much as a little finger towards it. On the contrary – she's put more obstacles in my path than you could imagine. One thought obsesses me: up and away! At home I shall go to pieces.

Monday 4 June

Lunch at the Conrats'. Very agreeable.

p.m. to the Prater. Close of the season. Derby. We didn't want to see the races, so we went down around 6:00 – in Rudolf's cab. All our acquaintances in their finery. Olbrich in one cab, Klimt with three models in another – *none* of those present was more alien to me. Schmedes I missed.

Hustle and bustle, energy, animation, bright colours, luxury – rarely will one find the like of it elsewhere.

I can't stop thinking about Olbrich. 'Mir erkoren – mir verloren.'[34]

Tuesday 5 June

This morning: Labor. When I left, he addressed me as 'my dear friend'. I played 'Meistersinger' to him.

This evening:

<h3 style="text-align:center">Der fliegende Holländer</h3>

Never has an opera pleased me better. Wagner's entire genius is already apparent. Mildenburg was wonderful.

Wednesday 6 June

It's hot, and I feel sluggish and dull. Life is so monotonous. I have *nobody* to love or to return my love. I'm so lonely, one of the loneliest of people.

The other day, at Spitzer's, Hancke came up behind me while I was playing, and asked me to give him my photograph, which he was holding. Half absent-mindedly, half irritated by the interruption, I gave it to him. Zemlinsky, on parting, asked me for one too – adding, with some justification:

---

34 'Destined for me, lost to me' (Wagner, *Tristan und Isolde*, act I).

If you can give one to that little Berlin Jew, you can give me one too. Today this postcard arrived.[35] I don't know what to do. – Would he exercise his discretion? From what I know of him, I have my doubts. If I don't send him one, on the other hand, it would be a downright insult. What should I do?

Friday 8 June
Last lesson with Labor for now. Only now do I realize what they mean to me. I feel as if I'd lost my backbone.
I wish for one thing: that Olbrich might visit us in the summer. I long for him.
My Variations are good. The last song is misconceived.

Saturday 9 June
This evening: Burgtheater
Le Misanthrope and Tartuffe
Molière
Kainz incomparable – magnificent.

Sunday 10 June
At midday: Hancke. I'd expected him to be offended by the events at Spitzer's. But instead, he apologized for his bad behaviour. If you want them to like you, some people need a kick in the backside.
Sent Zemlinsky my photograph.[36]

Wednesday 13 June
This evening: Mayreder and Spitzer. M. still loves me.
p.m. with the Lanners in the Prater. I poured my heart out to them, told them the story of my life (weakness, folly – but suddenly I felt how sincere I have become).
Since the birth of Maria, our family is divided. Carl, Mama, the infant || Gretl and I. – Carl does all he can to prevent us from feeling it, but even the gods are powerless against the laws of nature. He's only interested in his own child. And recently, during an argument, he said:

35 ▶ Postcard from Zemlinsky, with a photogravure of the soprano Selma Kurz in the role of the Princess in *Es war einmal* . . .
36 The photograph was later returned to A.S., and is today preserved in the Mahler-Werfel Collection at the University of Pennsylvania. On the reverse side is her dedication: 'To Herr Alexander von Zemlinsky in heartfelt friendship. X'.

    In *my* house I won't let you do that.
That phrase 'in my house' threw a vivid light on my situation. I'm a stranger. I eat the bread of charity! The sad part of it is that Papa left absolutely
no papers, *everything* went to Mama, and we depend on her generosity. So
we're paupers – *everything* is donated.
Since my chosen profession scarcely permits me to start up on my own, I
don't see the situation ever changing. *All* I want and need is peace and
quiet. But how can I drag out my days in such an unnatural family circle?
... On the other hand, to marry a man I don't love – can only be the last
resort! I haven't a clue when or how. Nor would I wish Papa alive again:
he'd be frightfully unhappy, because as an artist he'd be outdated.

[Corrected 1963. A.M.-W.]

Suite 18

Thursday 14 June
At 10:00 a.m. to Naty Schuster in Dornbach.
Spent the afternoon and the evening at the Conrats'. Annie Leinkauf (pretty as a picture), Karl Kraus, Dr Horn and Herr Fränkel. It wasn't as congenial as usual at the C.s'.
After lunch we were all sitting in a sort of half-circle, and I said to myself: 'Time to go.' An excuse was quickly found. No sooner did Annie Leinkauf hear of it, than she too had some urgent call to pay. So we left together – the others had resolved to play skittles, a game which I don't care for because it bores me stiff.
Outside in the street, we suddenly thought: why do we have to make our calls now? The woods were close by – so we went for a walk. Having climbed a little way, we went into an inn, ordered a bottle of soda water and amused ourselves far better than during the entire lunch party. Later, in the best of moods, we returned to the Conrats'. Somewhat astonished, they asked how it was that we'd arrived together, and we said L. had picked me up from the Schusters'. They appear to have believed us.
At table, I shocked Dr Horn to the core by saying:
> I *can* respect someone with an unscrupulous character if he's otherwise brilliant.
He was aghast, but I said with some conviction that only few artists were honest – indeed, that for a revolutionary spirit it's downright disadvantageous to be honest. –
Use your elbows!
If someone wants to assert their ideas, they need to be cold-blooded and egoistic to the highest degree – outwardly – because, when you think about it, the finest that a person can achieve is to offer up their life-blood, their innermost thoughts, their soul to humanity – for the salvation of humanity, to safeguard the world against brutality, until that becomes an essential quality.
Every birth is beautiful – as is that of a great intellectual achievement – from the conception of the work in the mind of an individual to its

point of maturation and further propagation in the minds of others. Which is the greater artist? He who uses his strength, the full power of his lungs, to impress his ideas upon the greatest minds of his time, and hence demonstrates: 'I have created for you, for *all* of humanity. I am of God – of . . .'

In short, I can't write a monograph on God and Nature – that's wrong too – for God and Nature are but *one*. An artist simply has this mission. He has to scatter his wealth amongst the less abundant, that they too may be enriched.

And then there are other artists, so fearful, shy [and modest] that they conceal their works from the light of day, hoard up their gold, and circulate it only when it no longer gleams so brightly, namely after their death.

Which, then, is the more scrupulous artist: the one with *elbows*, or the quiet, sensitive one? The answer is self-evident.

It rained all day, incidentally, and my white dress cut a sorry figure.

Before dinner, Kraus imitated all the Burgtheater actors – brilliantly. But at dinner there was a major controversy about the Secession. They all went for me, as if I were part of it. Well, I defended them, like a mother her young – their remarks were very wounding. They said that Klimt was mentally deranged, congenitally. His father was off his head, his mother too. It's true, admittedly – but how on earth do they know? Then they pounced on Olbrich. In the end I was so insolent, I was afraid they'd throw me out of the house. Everything they said, I treated as irony. True, the Secession has its problems – but I shall never allow anyone to run them down in my presence.

Saturday 16 June
Composed quite a lot. Two songs. Texts by Richard Dehmel and Rainer Maria Rilke. Half song, half recitation, half chorale – I seem to have come up with an entirely unique art-form.[1]

Two days ago, in the morning, Köpping (from Berlin) was here.[2] The man – professor at the Academy, I believe – has made the most beautiful glasses imaginable – with kaleidoscopic colours and exquisite shapes – and all the

1 The Dehmel setting was probably of 'Wie das Meer ist die Liebe', published in 1924 by Josef Weinberger as 'Lobgesang', the fourth of A.S.'s *Fünf Gesänge*.
2 Karl Köpping, painter and etcher. He read chemistry in Berlin, later studying art in Munich and Paris. During the 1890s he concentrated increasingly on glass painting. He was strongly influenced by the style of Japanese woodcuts.

painters, sculptors etc. consider him as someone of equal rank. He came from Paris, where he'd exhibited a whole case of glasses, and said they were the last he had made – and would ever make.

> The glasses have given me great joy but incomparably greater sorrow. Just consider how dreadfully fragile they are – and how fearfully I have been imitated. I'll keep the last glasses for myself – as a memento – but I shan't make any new ones.

That must have been a difficult decision to take. I find it very moving.

Tuesday 19 June
In the evening: Burckhard, Moser, Hoffmann, Spitzer, the Hennebergs. Zemlinsky cancelled for the umpteenth time. I was sorry, I'd have liked to show him my two latest songs. – His father is ill.
It was great fun. We've planned a cycling trip for the day after tomorrow. Burckhard is to collect me with the coach, and we'll *drive alone* to the Danube (Prater), where we'll meet up with Hoffmann, Spitzer and Henneberg. – I'll believe it when I see it.
Moser was my favourite today, incidentally. – I had a long, stimulating talk with him. In the Schwarzenberg Garden[3] we took a long stroll together. – I like him, and then: he doesn't understand me – and I love that.

Wednesday 20 June
Today my past sins caught up with me. Geiringer came to dinner. Played duets with me. Suddenly he said:

> Yesterday and the day before I heard a lot about you from someone – Schmedes! And he told me a few things I didn't like. That you were angry with him because he hadn't always turned up to the assignations, that he really didn't always have the time etc.

When I see Schmedes again, I shall give him a piece of my mind. And a large piece at that.
Life is full of surprises. And even if I could never trust a tenor to hold his tongue, I had at least credited him with a *degree* of discretion. Just wait till I see him. – Gustav of all people, who has nothing better to do than to tell Christine etc. – The whole business is too stupid, and today, for the first time, I regret it.
Henneberg has called tomorrow off. That puts paid to my lovely cycling trip. O God!

3 Orig.: 'Schwarzer Garten' – the formal garden surrounding the Belvedere.

Thursday 21 June
Dinner in Hietzing at Ernst and Hanna's.
p.m. Carl brought me a bookplate designed by Hoffmann – exquisitely
beautiful! – and a *printed* copy of my three songs – brush-proofs. Moser
will design it. It's very nice of Carl, but to me the whole idea is disagreeable
– a little amateurish – maybe I'll regret it later.

Saturday 23 June
Burckhard, Pollack to dinner – and the inevitable Wilhelm. It was terrific
fun. B. was sweeter than ever. I do like him! Robust in mind, robust in
body. –
At 11:00 we all went down to the cellar to fetch Asti. Living – loving – and
the third: languishing – one must drink each one to the last drop.
Unfortunately I started with the third, then came the second, and the first
has so far eluded me and probably always will.

Sunday 24 June
Morning and noon at the Conrats', afternoon and evening at the
Schusters'. –
I must say, the Schusters were more to my taste. At the Conrats' were Prof.
Grün, the violinist, the inevitable Dr Horn and . . . Spitzer. The latter less
agreeable. The only word for him is 'schmock'. When amongst painters,
he has the eye of an artist; amongst musicians, he's a master in their field
too. The truth is that he's none of that. He has a smattering of this and
that, picked up through social intercourse with genuine artists. I can see
through him, and he feels uneasy when I scrutinize him. I don't care for
him. –
Frau Conrat tried to persuade me not to become a musician – it wasn't
worth it. How does she know? Who gives her the right to deprive me of the
pleasure I take in my work? These Jews are so brazen!
At the Schusters' I was far more at ease. Their youngest insisted on drinking a toast of brotherhood with me – but I wouldn't. He's a handsome
fellow. Tall, well built. Nasty, mean, cynical eyes – I didn't tell him that.
Naty is like a cat – so soft, so sensitive.
Around 6 o'clock we went for a walk on a hill. The air was clear, the view
over the city magical. Somewhere in a field sat a couple, a boy and a
crippled girl. It filled me with joy, because when I see deformity, I often
think: 'You poor, poor things – no love.' I was happy to see my belief
refuted. I wish more for them than for other – healthier, better-looking

people. And how wonderful it is to be loved – or at least to believe you are loved – I know from experience.

What would I give to live that month in Italy over again – despite all the heartbreak!

It's so sad . . . All is lost!

I stayed at Schusters' till midnight. Frau S. made a fabulous punch. I drank five beer-glasses full. Suddenly I felt my mouth watering, always the premonition of a frightful eruption. – I shivered at the thought, swallowed and swallowed – and averted the danger. Was I afraid, so afraid! – But with will-power you can achieve anything.

Alone – actually with three men – I drove home through the night. On the way there, Dick, the chatterbox, called Olbrich a play-actor. I shan't forget that so quickly.

Monday 25 June

This card arrived this morning. Autographed – by Mahler, my idol.[4]

On the reverse side of the first: two {autographs} from Carl's trip to Paris – top right: Carabin, the sculptor – the other two from Hofrat Burckhard.[5]

Klimt, if much later you returned to me, I would say: 'The joys of youth you refused to share with me – keep the sufferings of old age to yourself.'

Friday 29 June

Lunch: Sewald.

p.m. with Mama and Gretl to the Zentralfriedhof – at Papa's grave. Nothing could be more inane than these visits to the cemetery. My heart remains cold, my eye dry – and I keep staring at Mama, who really has no cause to see herself as a faithful wife. As she stood there, rapt in fervent prayer – what on earth was going through her mind? Was she praying? I can't pray! I wouldn't know to *whom*. Yet I love Papa more than all of them. Do I have to go to the cemetery to concentrate my thoughts on him? I can do that at home too – more effectively, more calmly, undisturbed. – I hate all outward show of sentiment.

Since we had the cab, we drove to the Prater and from there to the

4 ▶ Postcard from Paris, dated 22 June 1900, with a view of the Champs Elysées and autograph of Mahler.

5 ▶ Two further postcards from Paris, one with autographs of François Rupert Carabin and several Secessionists, the other with a brief note from Carl Moll; also two postcards from Max Burckhard in Greifenstein and Kremsmünster.

Weissgerberstrasse, to deliver my music to Zemlinsky. I rang – Fräulein Guttmann opened the door. I asked how his father was – she led me into his music-room and told me that he died today – this morning. I was ashamed to leave my cheerful letter and the music. But she put them on the desk and said she wouldn't give them to him until he was calmer.

And there you are too.

She pointed to my photograph, which was standing in the middle of the desk.

I went out – my heart was full . . . I fought back my tears – and observed myself as I did so. I hadn't imagined that I'd be so moved. I, who believed myself free of all excessive show of feeling – felt genuine and honest sympathy. I grieved at the death of the old man, whom I didn't even know.[6] And Fräulein Guttmann commanded my greatest respect. Her eyes were constantly filling with tears, her lips were trembling. The death struggle lasted all night, and she had joined the vigil at his bedside. – She suffers in silence and loves him.

I only hope he will come to love her again. How I *respect* her! She stands far above me, for she is free of social obligations. She was wearing a big apron, seems to be running the household. When I arrived, a girl of the same age quickly left the room – presumably his sister.[7] But she didn't interest me.

Since visiting his house, today, I find him much more sympathetic – his truly artistic, poetic house, his housewife – for I have to acknowledge her as such – but not him.

I'm glad I went.[8]

Sunday 1 July

We left early from the Westbahnhof. Dr Krasny was at the station, got us a compartment and travelled with us. A great pleasure it wasn't. I have my antipathies – can't abide the man!

Once he'd gone, I began to read the 'Divine Comedy' – which, to my surprise, I liked immensely. The book is shaped with such grandeur and beauty, it takes your breath away. Admittedly, some of the opinions are dated, for instance that a noble savage has no place in Paradise, that only

6 Adolf von Zemlinszky (*sic*) died, aged fifty-five, of kidney-stones.
7 Mathilde von Zemlinsky. In 1901 she married Arnold Schoenberg.
8 ▶ Undated letter from Koloman Moser on stationery of the *Vereinigung bildender Künstler Österreichs* (official name of the Secession), concerning the private publication of three of A.S.'s lieder, for which Moser had agreed to design the title page.

a good Christian may be admitted.[9] Such narrow-mindedness seems to have been inherent in the outlook of the time. – As I said, a few such errors and restrictions. But I've rarely read anything so consistently beautiful.

In the evening we reached St Gilgen. Grazerstrasse 78.

Our house is completely hidden by trees, and particularly my room and Gretl's are dreadfully damp. We're also twenty min. away from the lake, and from the veranda we have no view whatsoever. To safeguard us against floods, we're up a steep hill (too steep for cycling). But behind our house flows a stream so torrential, that I fear next time it rains it'll swamp the house. Apart from that, although the house stands high up, it's built so deep into the earth that you have to be prepared for flooding in the cellar at any moment. Altogether: everything you ever wished for from a holiday home. [!!!]

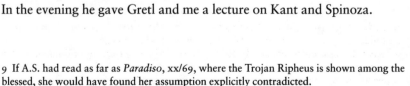

Mama had the unfortunate idea of sending Aunt Xandi here in March to find us somewhere to stay.

Wednesday 11 July

This morning: a huge crate – with Gretl's classics and my 'Tristan' score.

p.m. Gretl and I walked to Hüttenstein for high tea – wine, as a result of which we were more than merry.

On the way home, the Salzburg train passed – who was sitting in it? Burckhard. Now our happiness knew no bounds. We ran as if possessed. Halfway there, he came to meet us – I was expecting that. He's a kind, sharp-witted fellow. –

In the evening he gave Gretl and me a lecture on Kant and Spinoza.

---

9 If A.S. had read as far as *Paradiso*, xx/69, where the Trojan Ripheus is shown among the blessed, she would have found her assumption explicitly contradicted.

Friday 13 July
This morning we started up the Zwölferhorn. Dr {and} Frau Zuckerkandl
came too.
He said:

> Once I knew a lady – she happened to be my wife – and when she was
> annoyed, her nose swelled to twice its normal size. And as she was
> always annoyed, her nose was permanently swollen.

> > The outing was fairly tiring. Burckhard covered the
> > distance three times over, because he kept going up
> > and coming back down. At one stage – he was high
> > up on the mountain – he called down to us. But
> > we didn't know where he was, and kept looking
> > in the wrong direction. Later he said:

> > > If I keep calling to you softly, maybe you'll
> > > recognize my voice better and follow more
> > > quickly.

> I said:

> > You can bet on it, with unmistakable irony.
> > The whole outing was quite delightful.

> > > This evening, Carl complained bitterly that
> > > we were so thoughtless. Burckhard defended

us brilliantly. Carl always wants something in return – always expects
interest from the capital he invests in us. But *no one* will ever succeed in
that. And I don't call it generosity, when something is expected in return. –
The infant's arrival has disrupted our family life. The prevailing atmosphere is icy. Gretl, lucky girl, will be leaving the house in two months. But
me? Must I lead my whole life like this? Impossible.

Sunday 14 July
In the morning: cycled to Lueg.
And then it happened: at midday we had a grand lunch with Burckhard –
the best punch I ever drunk – and got 'smashed' as never before. I shudder
to think of it. Herr and Frau Kutschera[10] were there too.
I drank far too much. After lunch we all lay down in Burckhard's room,
Kutschera on the sofa, Carl on the floor, myself on a lovely, soft armchair.
I dozed off. Suddenly I was awake – my white dress covered in vomit.

---

10 The actor Viktor Kutschera joined the ensemble of the newly founded Deutsches
Volkstheater in 1889. Between 1895 and 1898 he also appeared sporadically at the
Burgtheater.

Quietly I stood up and went to wash it off. Mama saw it and came to help me. Gretl came in from the balcony, where she was joking with Frau Kutschera and Burckhard, saw me and helped me home. But he – Kutschera – saw it {too}. He said:

Alma, sweetie-pie, what's up?

– turned discreetly away, and went back to sleep.

While we were at table, suddenly I had to go, and desperately badly too. I prodded Mama so hard with my foot that she didn't know what to do – finally she stood up and said:

I'd like to go and wash my hands.

Gretl, who for sheer desperation was chewing her nails, and I – we ran outside, overjoyed. Frau Kutschera came too. Gretl set to as fast as she could. I saw her bare bottom, heard a noise, shoved her aside and sat down in her place. She bumped her head on the wall, poor thing, and nearly knocked herself out.

I let Gretl lead me home, concealing the spew on my dress behind my parasol. I got home. I didn't feel ill, was just drunk. Gretl tried to kid Cilli[11] that I'd spilt water over myself, but she said:

I can see you've been an' gorn an' thrown up over y'self. –

It was no use lying. Hastily I got dressed. On the way out, I lifted up my skirt and tried to pull my blouse down. But as I was standing almost on the street, Cilli ran over, pulled it down for me and obscured the view. The miller's apprentices were standing in the gateway over the road. We staggered back. Burckhard said:

Oh look, here come the girls.

They teased me mercilessly.

Kutschera is terrifically witty, his wife very sweet. The others cycled home – B., Gretel and I went rowing on the lake. Mama and Carl walked home.

11 The Molls' serving-maid. Mahler described her (in 1904) as 'ein kleines dickes Weiberl' ('a short, pudgy little woman', cf. *GoR*, p. 225).

We had supper in Fürberg, then rowed home in the most wonderful moonlight. Burckhard is such a dear fellow. I trust him completely. Gesticulating wildly with my parasol, I poured out all my woes to him. Never again shall I drink so much. I feel really ashamed of myself. I give my word of honour that I shall never do it again.

Sunday 15 July
A hangover of modest proportions would be the least of it. This morning Burckhard went for a ride and fell off his bicycle. Cut his knee and his hand. – Poor chap.

All the same, this afternoon he rode with Carl and me to Strobl and Wolfgang. From there we had ourselves ferried back across, and rode through the forest, then later back home along the road. His wounded knee began to bleed more profusely, but he said nothing. In the forest we had to push our bicycles through thick mud. I said I was an epicure, to which he replied:

> Me too, and how. I love gambling,
> cycling, mountain-climbing and –
> young ladies.

As he was saying that, he suddenly sank into a deep patch of mud.

> You see, that's what happens to you with
> young ladies.
> You fall in, hook, line and sinker – I said.
> That's just it – yet I still prefer them. Older
> women are usually such bitches. What
> attracts me to the younger ones is simply
> their sense of decency.

The path through the forest was delightful, later we rode through high corn, and because it was evening, the mountain was swathed in pink mist, the water silvery and vague.

> O world, O nature – your beauty is
> unsurpassable.

Friday 20 July
I had a wonderful dream: Olbrich was mine. Nothing erotic about it, just rational love and mutual understanding. That's all I'd wish for. And all the while I'm not in love with him, no – just an incredible feeling of like-mindedness – of my personality matching his – and of infinite sympathy. Will my wish ever be fulfilled? –

Saturday 21 July
Today there was a long article about Olbrich in 'Dekorative Kunst'. Truly, he's a somebody. And I long for the moment when I can show him that I'm a *somebody* too. I shall dedicate my first major work to him.
Be true to yourself!
At midday the following telegram arrived:
    have bolted to ischl
    dr burckhard
We still don't know – does he mean altogether, or just for today? I miss him sorely – feel almost lost. My work gives me no pleasure, nor does walking etc . . . .

Sunday 22 July
This morning: cycled to Unterach. Met the Kutscheras – it was great fun. Unfortunately the Zuckerkandls turned up just as we were about to take the road to Ischl via Weissenbach. We had to ride back and keep the others company for over an hour while they had their breakfast. Burckhard told them about our last high tea (melon cut in cubes, thrown into a paper bag and eaten with bare hands) – without mentioning any names – and they were all disgusted at the piggery.
Arrived home for lunch pouring with sweat. Burckhard to lunch, swam in the afternoon. At 5:30 rendezvous with him at the boat-house – swam, then rowed out onto the lake, but as a storm was brewing, we landed at the Ochseninsel and disembarked.
I told him how last year Wärndorfer warned Carl about B., and he regretted not having been there to box his ears. Then he began to talk about the Krastel[12] affair:
    I was never open to bribes, so they put rumours of that ilk into circulation. Every actress who got a new role was said to have a relationship

12 Fritz Krastel, an actor at the Burgtheater. Max Burckhard was reputed to have had an affair with his daughter.

with me, every girl who spoke to me I'd got pregnant. I tell you frankly, I never left a woman in any doubt – that is: that I wouldn't marry her. If a woman wanted to do me a special favour – well, I'm not the person to say, 'It's not on.' After all, I'm no saint.

I was at the Krastels' a few times in the summer. And when, after a while, he – her old man – went off to Abbazia and took her with him. When she came back, she'd had a baby. I was so disgusted, I didn't go there any more. –

So we chatted away, all the while observing harmless cloud formations

closing in on us. Eventually we felt it was time to take the boat to Fürberg. We had scarcely cast off, when a wind came up, such as usually precedes a storm, and in a trice the placid lake had become a storm-swept sea. Getting to Fürberg was out of the question, so we tried to land somewhere. The water was spraying right up the rocks. Gretl turned a little pale, Burckhard's eyes were gleaming. They both struck out strongly, while I steered as best I could. B. called out, 'Right – left', in a stentorian voice, as needed, like a weathered coxswain. For a moment, as we were rounding the promontory into Potato Bay, we all felt queasy, the ship was tossed about like a piece of paper, the storm was frightful – the white horses . . .

At last we were out of danger. With a sheer superhuman effort, B. hauled the boat to the shore, and we ran a quarter of an hour in single file to Fürberg. No sooner had we arrived, than a typical mountain storm erupted – with thunder and lightning that made your heart skip a beat – and torrential rain.

We sat down at a table and ordered high tea – in the best of spirits . . .

There was a brief lull, and the lake grew calmer. B. sent out a boatsman to fetch our boat. He'd only just got back, when the wind turned and the storm raged over us all over again.

It was impossible to contact Mama. No boat, no cab . . . We sat back and enjoyed our meal. B. ordered trout, grog etc. – nothing was left out.[13]

At 10:00 the skies cleared. Our boatsman rowed us back. We went aboard, armed with countless plaids and umbrellas. It was pitch-dark, I couldn't see. Gretl got in first, then B., and I last of all. He took my hand. Slowly I clambered aboard. He held on to me until I reached my seat. With a firm

---

13 The drawing is an imitation of a poster designed by Koloman Moser.

grip he held my hand in his – it felt so safe and reassuring. Our hands are made for each other. I could feel it – he too.

I believe in a mutual exchange of feelings.

The water was black, the air was black. Lights flickered along the lakeside. It was blissful.

We got home at 10:30. Mama came to meet us, red-eyed – Carl had lost his temper once again and was nowhere to be seen – that's to say, he vanished the moment we arrived.

Mama was soon appeased.

Monday 23 July
In the morning: B. – At 11:00 a.m. he left. We went along with him, wanted to have a last beer together. On the square: the Loews, the Zuckerkandls. Lots of palaver, but it also saved time, because B. didn't need to call on the Z.s. We wanted to go to the {Hotel zur} Post, hid in a side-street, thought the coast was clear, & re-emerged. We ran into the whole clan[14] all over again. Not a hope. B. fled into the post office and we, like ducklings, followed him inside. – Danger averted.

We enjoyed a last, delightful meal in the Hotel. I suggested we should name the bay the 'Bay of Hope'. B. laughed shamelessly and said he didn't hope it would come true. Carl and Mama came to the station. B. suggested we call the bay 'Ravensbrood Bay'.

It was time to bid him farewell.

There's a legend of seven fat years and seven lean years. –

At first I enjoyed the calm, but once you've tasted blood . . . I miss him already. His candour in artistic matters, his blunt manner with people he doesn't like, his whole, delightful personality.

Gretl – *just* like me – is really sad. The better you know him, the more you get to like him. Such a lovely time, but it's over – well-intentioned, kind-hearted, calm, witty, sensible, stimulating.

p.m. played 'Tristan' – but the hours pass more slowly now.

Tuesday 24 July
B. was so right. 'Bide your time,' he said. 'You don't yet have the right to rebel against your parents' authority. Learn something, achieve something – and all of a sudden you'll find a footing.' – He's absolutely right. I want to study, work hard, that's the *only* way to get anywhere. But I'm just not

14 Orig.: 'Mispocke' (Yiddish).

making any headway – neither with my school-work nor with my
composition.
p.m. at the Loews', went rowing with them. Stayed for dinner too.
Stimulating – pleasant company.

Wednesday 25 July
This evening: the Leglers. They brought a Herr Schöntaler with them who,
I believe, is soon to become a member of the family – Coralie. We played
cards,[15] but in the end I was *simply* too tired, and went to bed.

Thursday 26 July
Mama's name day.
6:00 a.m. cycled to Ischl with Carl, Coralie and Schöntaler. – Coralie fell
twice, Schöntaler and I once each. – At the hotel, I was remounting, pushed
myself forwards and jammed my finger {under the saddle} – ended up
sitting on it.

 The nail split and the flesh laid bare.

Rarely have I been in such pain – but I said nothing, pulled my finger out,
and asked for a glass of water. When the others saw it, they broke into
lamentation. Coralie, who's dreadfully squeamish, was full of praise for
my heroic stance. Afterwards I rode to the chemist's, and got it bandaged.
The chemist was a kindly old gentleman, who asked if he could call on us
in St Gilgen so that I could play to him. – He wouldn't take any money
either.
This postcard[16] was waiting for us when we arrived. Countless letters and
telegrams.
p.m. bathed – after us Bertha L., who has a fantastic figure. Later we went
rowing.
This evening: another stroll. It's unbelievable how I miss Burckhard. I'm
sad because I can't practise. –

Friday 27 July
Carl left this morning. In the end he was very nice to us – thanks to Burckhard. He tore us off a strip, we tore him off a strip . . . and yet he managed

15 Orig.: 'Elephanten'.
16 ▶ Postcard from Burckhard in Igls im Tirol.

to bring us closer together again. I'm much more patient than before. His
words remain implanted in my memory. –

He sent this postcard,[17] which arrived today –
proof that he hasn't forgotten.

p.m. swimming – then these two postcards.[18]
We were all sitting together, and Mama told
us about her youth – how one night she
(the whole Bergen family) had to flee from
the island of Veddel,[19] because after the
war payments weren't coming in, but
Grandpa didn't want to declare
himself bankrupt, and they didn't
even have enough money for the
rent – how their mother, who
was suffering from puerperal
fever after having her twelfth
child, was carried out of her
bed and out of the house by the
children – how, at eleven years
of age, Mama became a ballet
dancer, how she played walk-on
parts for a whole year and became

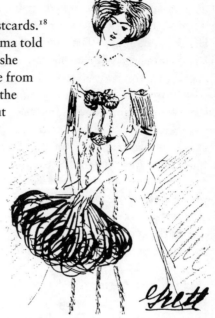

the breadwinner for the whole family – how later she became a nanny,
had to wash nappies and sleep in the cook's room – how she became an
au pair girl, [then a cashier at the baths] and finally a singer. It sounds
almost like a fairy-tale.

And then the first years of her marriage – the debts – and Papa who, when
things were at their worst, would roll over on his stomach and sleep round
the clock. And Carl, who would run from one usurer to the next and pawn
everything he could lay his hands on. What a trouble-free childhood I've
had in comparison with hers. And yet – such an existence steels you, makes
you earnest and hard and ready to face up to anything. The greatest men
grew up in poverty and hardship.

17 ▶ Postcard from Burckhard in Schloss Ambras.
18 ▶ Two postcards from Burckhard in Igls.
19 Orig: 'Fettel' – Veddel, an island between the Norderelbe and Süderelbe rivers in
Hamburg.

Tuesday 31 July
p.m. Else. I had to play. Began with 'La
belle Hélène', 'Orphée {aux Enfers}', 'Die
Fledermaus' – then we talked about
'Figaro'. Then it was time for a chorale by
Handel and, finally, 'Die Meistersinger'.
– Else took her leave. Bertha arrived.
     What, you want to stop already?
     – You must be joking.
I sat down again, and we sang the
closing scene of 'Siegfried' and *all*
of act I of 'Götterdämmerung'.
Mama said, the din wouldn't
have been more ghastly, if
you'd trodden on the tails of
twenty cats.
     In the evening I was
     completely hoarse. –

Wednesday 1 August
We left home at 7:00. Breakfasted with Mama in Hüttenstein. We'd scarcely got back, when we heard a familiar voice from downstairs: Lilli Lehmann and her husband, who's a very nice chap, by the way. She was sweet,
beautiful, sensible – as ever. She's the prettiest woman I ever saw. She
stayed until 11:00, then we went with her to the station. Then it occurred
to her that she could drop in at the local school to show the teacher her
books about cruelty to animals. We went with her. Every famous person
has their weakness. That's hers: she'd rather see twenty people suffer than
one animal.
We waited until the train started moving. Down below we bumped
into Else, who first had to treat us to sugar-candy, then a glass of beer.
Gretl did these drawings of two ladies. I've put them in here, because
they're chic.

Thursday 2 August
Yesterday Lilli promised to take me to see Mahler next winter. I'd go, no
question about it. You have to take your opportunities as they arise.
– Composed today.
p.m. idled around. Breakfasted in Hüttenstein.

Yesterday, when we said that Gretl, Berta & I wanted to learn the Rhine-maidens, Kalisch said:

Shouldn't you learn to swim first?

Saturday 4 August
Could I pull the wool over my eyes? It doesn't work.
I was sitting on the balcony – thinking about the journey to Italy – Genoa – and began to cry, to weep for what I've lost.
I'm so superficial, sometimes I forget my misery. But then they return – my memories – and they're so beautiful, they make me so *indescribably* unhappy, simply because – they're so beautiful.
The kiss in Genoa. I hang on that moment with every nerve fibre . . .
The only person I really ever loved and probably ever will love is Klimt. The very thought of belonging to someone else horrifies me.
Mine – mine – my Klimt.
And even if all the women in the world were to take you. You're mine – for all eternity!
Nietzsche – who says:

Do not commit yourself to any one person – even the most loved. – Everyone is a prison – often also a dead-end.

Didn't you know that they can also be a paradise?
And yet, what would I give to escape – never to have let myself in. I used to say to myself: Klimt isn't far away. Alma, be honest: this past year you haven't lived, but vegetated. Don't be so shameless! Don't accept life without a struggle.

But now, while writing, my little bud of rebellion has withered away. Do I really need love? – The certainty of being able to achieve something in music would make me blissful, more than blissful. So there I stand – half in growth, half in decay. That's the one thing I want – just that . . .

It's raining today. Maybe that explains all these despondent thoughts.
I shall take care to avoid them in future.
I don't want them.

Sunday 5 August
What was the matter with me yesterday? How can one drag all those
skeletons out of the cupboard?
– I don't understand it.
Coralie Legler has announced her engagement to Fritz Schöntaler. I'm so
glad for the poor thing. What else would she have had from life?
I'm composing a cycle of three songs. In the middle one I use two 'Parsifal'
chords. Use? . . . I mean: they came to me of their own accord, and I had no
choice but to write them down. Altogether, writing that song was a curious
experience. From the outset, I knew that I'd do it that way. It just came
over me. Text by Rainer Maria Rilke.
Church fête at St Gilgen – the people amused themselves.
This afternoon, Gretl and I wanted to call on the Leglers and the Loews,
but in both cases we came at an inopportune moment. So we turned
around and went home. Opened the piano and tried through Woglinde and
Wellgunde from 'Götterdämmerung'. It's wonderful, but fiendishly
difficult.

Monday 6 August
Burckhard's letter arrived today.[20] I'm so happy. Unfortunately Mama
doesn't share my enthusiasm. – I want to drop him a hint that, at the time
he wants to come, she'll be in Vienna.
I was working away, when the door opened and Hancke poked his nose in.
We went for a stroll together. He took us into his confidence . . . namely
about the Secession. Opened our eyes to certain things. – He's right: of
thirty-five Secessionists, there are only five or six who actually do anything
for the cause. The exhibitions would have been no different if just those
five or six had contributed to them. All the others are just bystanders,
obstacles. – It won't be long before it comes to that.

Wednesday 8 August
Dr Pollack sent me {Nietzsche's} 'The Birth of Tragedy' and 'Untimely
Meditations'.
In the evening: Bertha. We sang the Rhine-maidens. It's going better.

20 ► Letter from Burckhard in Jagdhaus Hubertus.

Afterwards I inebriated myself with favourite passages from 'Götterdämmerung'.

In those few notes[21] – what unbridled passion. When I see that passage, I could shout for joy. Wagner, you Dionysos, you god of eternal ecstasy. You are so, so great.

I long for the opera, for the coruscating orchestra, for all the Fire of Love and Water of Magic.

Thursday 9 August
p.m. left the house. 7:00 to Lilli Lehmann's. She invited us to supper.
The house in Scharfling is nice – if not particularly well kept. The dining-room is entirely of wood – very attractive. In the bedrooms none of the beds had been made. Over Kalisch's desk hangs a banner with the words 'Patience and Renunciation' embroidered on it. I said it didn't much look like renunciation to me (which in my opinion is a compliment). But he was so offended that he left the room. – He tyrannizes her. And she – such a hot-blooded woman that she'd kill for love or hatred – he winds her around his little finger . . . And she's so beautiful!
Took the last train home. The moon was casting a white halo as large as a rainbow. We went up the hill behind the house and watched the phenom-enon for quite some time.

Friday 10 August
At 9:00 a.m. I drove over to Ischl to visit Frau Redlich, but she was out. I had two hours to wait for Gretl, who was coming on a later train. I went to {Café} Zauner[22], ordered something, read the papers for an hour, also the latest number of 'Die Fackel' which I'd bought – in which he {Karl Kraus} calls King Milan a blackguard to his face.[23]

---

21 'Auf, auf ihm entgegen' – Wagner, *Die Götterdämmerung*, I/iii.
22 Café Zauner, Ischl, Pfarrgasse 7. Like most of the hotels, coffee-houses and restaurants in Vienna that A.S. patronized, the establishment is still flourishing.
23 *Die Fackel*, no 48, end of July 1900, p. 1: 'Currently residing in Vienna is one of the most dangerous blackguards that ever walked the streets of a great city.' Milan Obrenovič became Prince of Serbia in 1868, in succession to his cousin, Prince Michael III. After seven years' rule, he was forced to abdicate in favour of his son Alexander. In 1897 he was appointed

The people in the coffee-house were eyeing me curiously. I stood up, went to the station and spent the second hour waiting there. I felt dreadfully lonely.

Together we went to see Bertha, who was once again the dear friend she used to be. She's undergone an unbelievable transformation during the past year. She wants to study, then take her finals[24] in Vienna, then a Ph.D. in Germany. Good luck to her!

If I didn't have my music and a clear head, I'd do the same. She wants to read Art History. That, I must say, I *don't* understand. I wouldn't care for something so stuffy. I'd far prefer something that belongs to the future: physics – chemistry – medicine. And of the three, the best would be medicine – quotibus non est disputandum.

As I said, Bertha was very sweet to us again. This evening Else Legler called.

When I got home, I found this letter.[25] The matter is awkward. If only Carl had told me from the outset what he intended to do with the songs, a) I would have written them differently and b) shown them to Zemlinsky before they were engraved. Well, it's too late now.

Wednesday 15 August

Just recovered from a nasty bout of tonsillitis.

I feel exhausted, but shan't say anything, otherwise they'll send me back to bed.

Several postcards from B. arrived yesterday. But as there's nothing on them except the names of the places he's staying in – I shan't put them in here. Mama wrote to him today, asking him not to come. I'm sorry about it, but I didn't veto the idea – feel too tired.

In bed I read 'Stilpe' by O.J. Bierbaum.[26] Well-written but highly cynical, the book's message is: 'Lead us not into degeneration' – something one

---

commander-in-chief of the Serbian army, but he remained an unpopular figure, and in 1900, after his son's marriage, he went into exile in Vienna. He died there the following year.

24 Orig.: 'Matura'.

25 ▶ Five-page, black-edged letter from Zemlinsky in Seeboden (Carinthia), dated 9 August 1900: '[. . .] When I received your lieder, I was, as you can imagine, in the most dreadful state. [. . .] Then I took a look at the so-called brush-plates. These three songs are simply bristling with mistakes . . . Also ▶ a long letter from Ernst Moll.

26 Otto Julius Bierbaum was chief editor of the influential journal of the Jugendstil, *Pan*, published in Berlin. His novel *Stilpe* paved the way for the *Ueberbrettl* movement. Highly popular in his day, also as poet and playwright, he is best remembered as editor of an anthology entitled *Deutsche Chansons*.

knows perfectly well, even without reading the book. Nowadays every author seems to write at least one book about some talented songster whose life is ruined by wine and women. And such stories are ever more frequent, more extreme, more erotic. Do these gentlemen really write empirically?

Then I read something greater, something more significant: Nietzsche, 'The Birth of Tragedy'. Some of the details I don't yet quite understand, but all in all it's phenomenal.

Then I started reading the criticism of David Strauss. Full of biting irony, brilliant. I was delighted at the way he lays into the old cultural Philistines.

Friday 17 August
All lit up this evening: tomorrow is the Kaiser's birthday.

Tuesday 21 August
Took the train to Scharfling at 7:00 a.m. and from there we went up the Eisenauer. I talked with Kalisch. We climbed for two hours. It was quite fun. Afterwards I met Lilli L. at the station. We travelled back to St Gilgen together. In the tunnel she gave me two pecks on the cheek. She's as beautiful and cheerful as ever, and today she was positively boisterous.

Meanwhile Reininghaus had arrived. Finding the house deserted, he took the next train up to Schafberg.

Wednesday 22 August
R{eininghaus} came between 4:00 and 5:00. I persuaded him to come cycling with me. He hadn't ridden for seven years. Halfway there, he dismounted and started wheeling his bicycle. He'd given up cycling because of a weak heart, and now he could feel the old ailment coming on. In my eyes, it put him in a poor light. His weakness – it's not his fault, poor chap – served to remind me of the opposite extreme, and all of a sudden I thought of Burckhard – for me a hero.

I left R. behind and cycled on alone to Gschwent. Somewhere on the way back I picked him up again – miserable.

This evening he called on me. The Legler girls dropped in – much ado about nothing.

[Checked in early February 1963. A.M.-W.]

Suite 19

Friday 24 August
This morning: Mama Legler came to tell me that Mama and Gretl would be arriving p.m. Later: Coralie, Bertha and Fischmeister. With the former I played {Beethoven's} fifth. It was terrific, I must say – two hammers got broken. We'd just finished repairing them and were about to start into the 'Choral' Symphony, when the door opened and Reininghaus appeared. After the girls had gone, I had a long, serious talk with R. Like that he's fine – as long as he doesn't start getting familiar.
p.m. the other three returned, and we played the 'Choral' Symphony. Fischmeister cried. Later Mama arrived, and, when I asked Gretl if she'd missed me, she burst into tears.

Saturday 25 August
This morning came the two letters from Z. and B.[1] A cursory glance shows which of the two – sadly – is the more significant. I must say, B.'s letter has absolutely nothing to offer.
At 9:00 to Ischl.

Conversion from Catholicism to Protestantism

The church was empty. Just us and the pastor. He preached a brief sermon, then prayed with his back to us. I found that terribly funny. Gretl, too, was doubled up with laughter.
And now I feel a sense of wistfulness: I detest the Catholic church, but it's not something you just cast off like a dirty garment. Pomp on the one hand, austerity on the other. I was somewhat het up – despite my laughing nonchalance.[2]
Lunch at Bertha Meyer's.
p.m. with Bertha to the quick-photographer – the pictures were no good

1 ▶ Letter from Zemlinsky in Rodaun/Liesing; postcard from Burckhard in the Karersee-Hotel im Tirol.
2 cf. *Mein Leben*, p. 28: '[. . .] My younger sister, who was not particularly self-reliant, was supposed to convert from Catholicism to Protestantism. As she was piteously afraid, I did so too, just for her sake. Thus I became a Protestant without reason and without conviction.

– then to Zauner. I felt dreadful. Headache and aching limbs. – At the station I bumped into Anna Leinkauf. She introduced me to Director Curando. In Strobl he came into our compartment, introduced himself and asked if he could travel with us. I said yes, but was amazed how forward and brazen he was. Gretl was shocked too.

In the evening: alone. Wilhelm and Gretl snapped at each other like rabid dogs – very unpleasant.

Saturday 26 August

Am feeling low – my head – my nerves. I'm so exhausted, I can scarcely move.

p.m. in Hüttenstein. Lilli Lehmann came too. She came over to join us and, on entering the forest, she sang

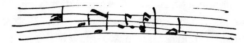

like a nightingale!³ – What a voice, what power, what facility. How happy she must be. 'The greatest happiness known to mankind is personality.'

Tuesday 28 August

Mama and I gave Gretl a good talking-to. She's being nicer to him now.

a.m. Lilli Lehmann's little painter-husband came round to ask me in her name if I would accompany her tomorrow. I was unwilling – before such a public. The matter isn't entirely certain, thank God. An early telegram will decide.

Friday 31 August

My 21st birthday. So old . . . and nothing achieved. –

The night was troubled by bad dreams. With considerable effort I managed to vanquish them.⁴ I dreamt that Klimt had married Gretl . . . No matter how absurd the dream may appear, it still caused me anguish. There he stood, imposingly handsome. My dreams are as clear and well-focused as cinematographic pictures. And in my dreams I see people quite vividly, of whom, when I'm awake, I can no longer evoke an image.

On waking up, I grieved that so beautiful a love-affair had ended so heart-

---

3 Evidently intended as a quotation of the off-stage horn fanfare in *Tannhäuser*, I/ii (the rhythmic notation diverges considerably from Wagner's).
4 ▶ Letter (from Burckhard?), dated 21 August 1900.

lessly. At the Lichtwark party – the rose he threw me and which I put in my buttonhole. That one gesture degraded the experiences of two whole years – of my whole *life* – to the level of a superficial flirt. I wish I'd *never* picked up that rose.

Whenever I look at Gretl and Wilhelm, it always reminds me how happy I once was too – how indescribably happy.

On the 25th, Nietzsche died – in Weimar, where Goethe lies buried. Two powerful minds! For the past eleven years he was insane.

Saturday 1 September

I dreamt of the Tsarina – and of Olbrich. A strange combination, yet not as stupid as it sounds: O. once told me that he knew her.[5]

As for yesterday's dream, I should add that I differentiate between him as a person and as an abstract concept, and that I interpret the latter as pure allegory, as a striving for the highest. – Something to be fought for with grim determination and finally achieved. – What an optimist!

Tuesday 4 September

Gretl has gone. At 11:00, in Ischl, she got married. She cried all night – and took her leave of me time and time again. These last days have been dreadful. I feel terribly sorry for her. I've lost all respect for Mama. I kept repeating to myself: 'Out of my sight, you shameless, conniving hussy' – her eyes gleamed lustfully.

This morning Carl came in and kissed Gretl, then, to conceal his emotion, pushed her aside. I felt he was more moved than she – but she's her mother, while he's merely her stepfather.

|Gretl cried all night. I feel dreadfully sorry for her. Life will never again treat her so well.|

At the station, G. and I waited on the platform and she admitted to me that once, last winter, she was *so* unhappy that she bought a pistol, loaded it and sat the whole morning on the Albrechtsrampe, her mind filled with the most terrible doubts. I simply couldn't believe it. And now she has that loaded weapon in her suitcase. Unbelievable recklessness. I fear for her, my poor, dear Gretl.

The wedding ceremony was quite fun, although the pastor was *not*

5 Alexandra Fyodorovna (Alix, Princess of Hesse-Darmstadt) was a granddaughter of Queen Victoria and daughter of Louis IV, Grand Duke of Hesse-Darmstadt. She married Tsar Nicholas in 1894.

particularly brief. Then we all went for a stroll along the Esplanade, then dined at Hotel Elisabeth. The atmosphere was relaxed, Gretl sweet and happy. We accompanied her as far as the station in St Gilgen, and the couple travelled on to Salzburg. She kept looking at me and lamenting that she wouldn't be seeing me for a long time – my eyes – my mouth.

As we were leaving the church, we bumped into Burckhard – such a dear fellow.

In the evening: I went cycling, thought of him and stretched my arms out. Another cyclist, who was following behind, saw me and smiled.

Mama Moll is here too. She gets on my nerves.

This evening: in my lonely bed I was all but overcome by melancholy. But I picked up a volume of Nietzsche and read my grief away.

Thursday 6 September

What will Gretl do? Be happy to be rid of me – something unheard of. Every morning I now read a section of 'Thus spake Zarathustra'. If others can pray, why shouldn't I? –

And I have need of it.

At 10:00 Mama Moll and Gretl {Hellmann}. It was pretty tedious.

p.m. the door opens – Burckhard. I was so pleased. We had supper at the {Hotel zur} Post, then took a walk on the lakeside.

Saturday 8 September

Yesterday B. suggested an outing to the Almsee, and Mama was *strongly* opposed:

> To play the role of a Marthe Schwertlein[6] is beneath my dignity.

She has no idea how well we two get on together. Thanks to my obdurate silence, we got up at 6:00, took the train at 7:00 and had breakfast in Gmunden at 10:30. He hired a fiacre for Mama, took champagne, partridges, fruit and other things – and we cycled for two hours as far as Grünau. Rather hilly and a little monotonous. There we had lunch and cycled another hour to the Almsee. Beautiful view through forests of tall trees – before us the Grosser Priel.

The Almsee lies also directly at the foot of the Totes Gebirge – so called, I imagine, because no trees grow on them, hence they appear bare, grey,

---

6 Gretchen's neighbour in Goethe's *Faust* I, who takes it upon herself to chaperone Gretchen during her first meeting with Faust (Scene in the Garden).

noble and majestic. Wonderful air too. Totally closed in – calm, peaceful – almost indescribable. We took rooms in a former Benedictine monastery.[7]

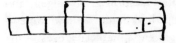 a long corridor without an exit

He allayed our fears and assured us:

    You only need to go through one of the men's rooms.

In the evening, B. somehow managed to persuade the landlady to give us Pater Forstmeister's room, which had been designated to him. Desecration! Before dinner we walked further into the valley and climbed a little way up the mountain – the other two on an outcrop, I on a scree over a waterfall. It was extremely dangerous. Mama stopped halfway up, we continued. The view was a picture – but a picture is kitsch, mere ostentation, while Nature itself is beautiful, expansive.

Our champagne had been chilled, and we swilled it down like students. Then, in the best of spirits, we – Mama and I – went up to bed in Pater Forstmeister's room.

Sunday 9 September

Suddenly I woke up, heard piping voices and saw little creatures merrily hopping about on the floor. As I'm not in the least afraid of rats or mice, I didn't trouble to wake Mama, who's dead scared of them, but calmly went back to sleep.

We left the chapter-house at 7:00 a.m. and cycled on into the Grünau. Initially it was so foggy that you could only see a hundred paces ahead of you. Gradually it grew brighter. The mist was tinged with gold, the sun gradually penetrated. All of a sudden everything was bathed in dazzling light. We dismounted to take a last look at the Totes Gebirge and the Grosser Priel, then rode on into the beautiful forest. Before us, a young stag watched inquisitively, then moved aside, so that we could see it from close range as we rode past. At 11:30 we reached Gmunden.

Once, riding uphill, I dismounted carelessly and took a slight fall. But otherwise, I must say, I rode *very* well. At times we were riding as if through deep sand, later over gravel, narrow pathways etc. Once I had to wheel the bicycle across a temporary bridge (over meadow-land), where in some places just one plank separated you from a considerable plunge.

7 The monastery on the south bank of the Almsee is today still operative as a hotel and restaurant, on lease from the Benedictine abbey at Kremsmünster.

In Gmunden we took our leave of Burckhard. I shall miss him. Mama and I took the boat to Ebensee and from there we travelled home by train. If anyone saw us on our outing, it'll be the talk of the town.

I told B. that Wärndorfer had recently resumed his scandal-mongering, and asked permission to take my revenge. At some social gathering – naturally one to which W. is invited – B. will fabricate a story, namely this particular one, made unintelligible to outsiders by using pseudonyms, but clearly intelligible to him – and told in such a way as to make clear to him what a blithering idiot he is.

The first time we were in Gmunden, we bumped into the pianist and singer Ehrenstein – in the smallest room in the hotel. Fortunately she didn't see B., and Mama didn't mention him.

We travelled home with drunken veterans. We sneaked home, cat-like, with our hand baggage, as we didn't want anyone to see us. – The trip was wonderful, a complete success.

Tuesday 11 September

Am not altogether well – and strangely unproductive. Transposed the A♭-major song a minor third for Mama and made a fair copy of 'Erinnerung', which I wrote last year at the Hellmanns'.

I forgot to mention that Mama Moll and little Gretl plagued us all day yesterday. I got the latter off my back by giving her the libretto of the 'Ring' to read. She devoured it straight off and bothered me no further.

Sunday 16 September

We left the house at 10:00 a.m. and arrived in Vienna at 7:30 p.m. At Ischl I had to hold the baby, which I found highly embarrassing. In the train I stood in the corridor all the way and talked with Dr Holitschek and Paul Jettel, who happened to be travelling with us.

Monday 17 September

All day: clearing up, unpacking, tidying away. I'm dead beat. Krasny told Dr Pollack he'd had the time of his life with me, but had lost interest in me, because I was too egoistic for his taste.

Today, Dr {Pollack} warned me about Burckhard. If they all keep on uttering these dire warnings, one day a harmless friendship will turn into – something less harmless. I gave him my word of honour never – at crucial moments – to forget what he'd told me. That reassured him, poor fellow! He doesn't seem to be aware that there are moments when everything under the sun – including the word 'honour' and all that it stands for – becomes *laughable*.

Hoffmann sent me an ex libris case. Very appealingly fitted out. – Gretl and Wilhelm sent me the complete works of Heine. I'm so delighted.

Tuesday 18 September

p.m. Hancke. He waxed sentimental, and it was no easy matter to prevent him from overstepping the mark. He also made innuendos – which I simply ignored.

Today I went out for the first time {since returning to Vienna}. The atmosphere and the people are intolerable. When our house is ready, in a few days' time, I shall breathe freely again.

Thursday 20 September

News from Darmstadt: Olbrich is getting engaged to an actress, with whom he's been involved for some time.[8] Mama finds that an endearing quality in him. To me it seems somewhat ridiculous – after all his preaching against marriage and for free love. Curiously enough, I *don't* feel sorry. When I heard the news, I felt rather self-conscious, perhaps even blushed. But now I'm quite calm. I recall [happy] hours with him, too, but their memory is dim and not indelible. I'll be glad to know he's happy. Let's hope she lives up to his expectations. One thing I know: he'll go a long way to find anyone better suited to him than me. And anyone who *understands* him better than me. Well – I draw a line beneath the affair. It's not the first time, nor is the line particularly bold or prominent: just a delicate little flourish, the beginning of a large, ornamental letter which has been erased before it was even written down. Better right away than when it's too late. Time is running through my fingers. I feel I should clutch at the hours to prevent them passing too rapidly and without trace.

Today Dr P. sent me 'Aida'. Such luscious sonorities. Nothing but blue and red – red and blue. Beautiful, fiery colours.

Friday 21 September

p.m. Aunt Mie came to fetch me in a rubber-wheeled phaeton.[9] As I found it simply too hideous, we drove to the Graben, had high tea, then hailed the smartest fiacre we could find. And in that we *bruised* through the Prater.

8 The identity of Olbrich's fiancée is unknown. In 1903 he married Clair Morawe (cf. Suite 23, 28 June 1901).
9 Orig.: 'Gummiradler' – a carriage with rubber wheels.

There we saw: Schmedes, Lola Beeth, some of King Milan's[10] retinue etc.

I was so glad to have my dear Mie once again. We talked about everything under the sun – there's almost nothing I wouldn't tell her. She brought me perfume from Berlin and sugar-candy from here. So thoughtful of her.

I've been playing almost nothing except 'Aida' – it's very fine.

Saturday 22 September

I had arranged with Mie that she would give me a chit for her season tickets at the Opera for tomorrow. So far it hasn't arrived, although yesterday evening I telephoned to ask if she'd sent it. But as the box office is only open for season tickets until 1:00 p.m., I brazenly joined the queue, told a few white lies – and got my ticket without a chit. I'm really thrilled, especially since I've only heard 'Meistersinger' twice before.

I'm peeved with Louise: she's deluded me – robbed me of my last illusion. I've often watched dogs copulating – and was always revolted by the pivoting motions of the male. Well, I said to myself, that's just doggy behaviour. But now Louise tells me that humans do it exactly the same way. I'd imagined something calm and dignified ... And that's what Klimt called 'physical union', this jiggling about. It's revolting, disgusting. No, there's nobody I could imagine doing it without feeling revulsion ... Do humans pull the same daft faces as dogs? Ughhhhhhh. When a man introduces himself, I now imagine him rocking up and down on top of me – and can scarcely bring myself to shake his hand.

Olbrich engaged.

Don't stare into the sun or you'll see black rings before your eyes. And anyway – it's bad for them.

Sunday 23 September

I've got a miserable cold. The night before last I left the window open, and it was too cold.

I'm not up to playing 'Siegfried'. The spirit may be willing, but the flesh is weak.

With my filthy cold, I went to Labor. He was awfully pleased to see me and

---

10 Orig.: 'Perser-König Milan' – Milan, King of the Persians.

told me lots about Paris, where he'd been in July. Also something really surprising:

I never heard the 'Maîtres-Chanteurs' as well in Vienna as at the Opéra. By the way, I'm taking charge of his apartment on Tuesday – as cook and bottle-washer.

After lunch I lay down. My knees were trembling and my back ached. And this evening I'm supposed to go to 'Meistersinger' – with a *splitting* headache!

Have just returned from 'Meistersinger'. Hans Sachs is the most touching character ever to have been created. The entrancing music triumphed over my headache.

Monday 24 September

It was wonderful yesterday evening. No single act is my favourite, because they're all equally lovely. There are a few dull spots, however, such as David's monologue in act I. And, to be honest, I get too exhausted to take in the closing scene. None of the 'Ring' dramas or 'Tristan' tire me as much as 'Meistersinger'.

In act II – first Sachs on his own, then he and Eva – it's so unbelievably tender, comparable only with 'The Marriage of Figaro'. In *my* opinion!

Tuesday 25 September

First lesson with Labor. The summer was a bad one for me. He liked the two songs that I wrote in late spring, but all the rest is rubbish, the song-cycle too. In my heart of hearts I already knew it. He was pleased with my 'Lobgesang' and 'Engelgesang'.[11]

I haven't seen or heard a thing from Zemlinsky. I invited him to drop by, but he appears to regret his plan to teach me. – Then let it be. I'm not going to beg him. – I'd considered him a friend – and it peeves me.

At table, Carl said:

Just imagine: Olbrich getting engaged and not saying a word to me about it. It's not nice of him.

I felt the blood rushing to my cheeks, hid my face in my hands – on the side where the light fell – and said nothing. Three minutes later I was able to smile again.

You wicked little actress! Shame on you!

Why shouldn't I laugh, though? Nothing has been taken from me.

11 These are the chorale-like songs to texts by Dehmel and Rilke, of which A.S. writes in Suite 18, 16 June 1900.

Thursday 27 September
In the morning: to Robicsek.
Gretl's first letter arrived this morning. Poor girl. At the very word, I turned hot and cold all over. No, no, no, I shall never marry, that I know. I feel so sorry for her.
A card from Burckhard has just arrived. Cilli brought it in, and I could scarcely speak for joy. She looked at me in astonishment. Why was I was *so* pleased? Involuntarily I kissed the card, and now I long for him. In effect, I've been doing so, subconsciously, since we arrived. My *dear* friend! Come and deliver me from evil, for thine is the power and the glory. – Amen.
This evening: 'Aida' with Aunt Mie. – A beautiful opera!
Afterwards at Meissl & Schadn with Uncle Hugo. He was sweet and kind.

Saturday 29 September
Yesterday evening: Kurzweil, Hancke, Spitzer, Hoffmann, Pollack, Moser. Mama and I on our own. It was awfully nice. Moser is a poppet. Hoffmann is nice too. Hancke and Spitzer got on my nerves. I've become a true anti-Semite. Kurzweil is a quiet fellow with a vacant expression. Moser would like to learn the piano, in order to develop an understanding of music. –
Yesterday I received a letter from Zemlinsky. He's coming on Monday or Tuesday. Is terribly tied up with theatre activities.
a.m. practised. Then Gretl Hellmann – things are not yet as they used to be. She brought me perfume from London, sugar-candy and a pale lilac silk petticoat from Paris. – She's too much bound by convention, loves gossip and all such things.
p.m. to Sewald – he was alone at home – a jovial fellow. Then to Frisch, to fetch the fiftieth number of 'Die Fackel'. I was just picking up the magazine, when Kraus came down the stairs. Joyful reunion. He accompanied me a little way, and I even went a little further and waited while he collected jewellery from Fischmeister's, which was actually not such a good idea. At the Stefansplatz our ways parted. I went down the Kärtnerstrasse onto the Ring. *List* walks towards me. I block his path, he says to himself: 'Good gracious, that's a smart young lady', recognizes me and escorts me home. The walk was great fun. Why can't it always be like this? There's something about Kraus . . .
Aunt Laura called. Later Carl arrived. – He'll probably frown at my Kraus escapade.

Sunday 30 September

This morning: quite a row with Dr Pollack. Liberalism – anti-Semitism, of course. But he's already calmed down again.

Yesterday evening: Richard. He's very morose – poor chap – and only now that his health has improved does he realize just how ill he really is, and how poor his outlook is. I quietly played a few touching passages from 'Meistersinger'. He was visibly moved, sat down right beside me and said in a low voice:

Almerl.

After a while:

> Tell me – does music never make you ill? Sometimes I believe all my suffering comes from music. In Beethoven sonatas or Wagner songs, I often rediscover my misery.

Sadly he stood up – and sadly I improvised an ending. Poor devil! –

Mayreder & Mama Moll to lunch.

This evening: with the latter in the Opera.

Lohengrin

Schmedes incredibly good. Drove me half crazy. The man is quite brilliant. The opera's not bad either. A *wonderful* piece – but Schmedes . . . I saw his little wife, she saw me too, but we didn't greet.

Monday 1 October

Waited vainly for Zemlinsky. –

Had a really lazy day. – Didn't feel in the mood for anything. It was all just too boring – so I did nothing. I love a strong wind or anything you have to work against, because it forces you to stride more powerfully.

Wednesday 3 October

Early to Labor. My first counterpoint lesson. He was sweet to me, so sweet. –

Then rendezvous with Mie outside the Opera.

p.m. with H{ugo} and Mie in the Prater – saw Mahler three times – Schmedes too, but I hope, as he failed to greet me, that he hadn't recognized me.

This evening: première of Hermann Bahr's 'Wienerinnen'. I found it good. The play is specifically directed against those who carp at *everything* – and themselves achieve nothing. He calls them the street-urchins of society. Kraus was sitting in the upper terrace – smiling.[12] He also says: when

12 Obliquely referring to the feast of Yom Kippur, which fell on the same day, Karl Kraus

someone takes the initiative, they provoke the hatred of an entire city. B. came to greet us. Altogether lots of our friends. During the interval, I went up to Aunt Mie's box. Next door were the Wärndorfers. Suddenly Klimt was there and gave me his hand. I simply can't describe my feelings. I couldn't understand myself either, all I know is that my jaw was trembling and that I was so excited, I could hardly stand up. Why was I so shaken at the sight of him?

Mie escorted me back downstairs. Burckhard was there, thank heaven! Not that I felt any love for him – no, just a pleasant, warm feeling – which dispelled the other. –

Afterwards we went to dinner ... with B. at my side. But as it was draughty, I had to move over beside Moser. He's a nice chap too. B. took his leave earlier. [Perhaps he was angry about my changing places.] We all left together, Moser and I far ahead of the others. The dear Wärndorfers were there too, worst luck. He's such a brazen Jew! –

B. is my dearest comrade now.

Friday 5 October
At 8:00 p.m. with Carl to the Secession..
Rendezvous. List, Lenz, König, Mayreder and Hancke accompanied us to the Rathauskeller. I walked on ahead with List.
The restaurant is pleasant and comfortable. Councillor Dr Rudolf Mayreder joined us. The two Mayreders, List and I went into the basement to see the electricity generator and the wine cellar. Dr M. had them call the vintner, who let us taste about thirty different wines. One of them is served only to the Mayor. It was superb. – We went upstairs *very* merry, and I noticed that the more List knocked back, the more roguish he became, indeed he started nudging me with his elbow. I told him where to get off.

Saturday 6 October
Lesson at Labor's. My summer reserves of counterpoint are exhausted. Full of mistakes. Finally he said:
    It's strange: whatever you do, I shall always like you ...
I said:
    I can't imagine ever giving up my lessons with you.

—

wrote: 'Herr Bahr has only the day of fasting to thank that his eminent dramatic impotence was not rewarded by rotten apples and egg-shells' (*Die Fackel*, no 55, beginning of October 1900, p. 24).

He took my right hand, pressed it against his left eye and said:

Don't say such things. I don't even want to think about it.

Arm in arm we went into the lobby, where I put my coat on. Today I brought him Maurice Maeterlinck's 'L'Intérieur'[13] and read it to him. He was absolutely delighted at the curious style and symbolism. I love the calm, drifting, veiled quality of the poem.

In the evening: Docterl. Today is his 45th birthday.

Sunday 7 October

In the morning: at Gretl H.'s. – A frosty atmosphere. On the way there I met Hartwig Fischl and his brother, with wife and child.

Yesterday evening my name was mentioned. Schmedes asked after me – and knew that I was at 'Lohengrin'.

p.m. completed a fugue – sounds well.

In the evening: Pollack and Krasny.

Monday 8 October

a.m. worked.

Lunch: Richard.

p.m. played 'Rheingold'.

This evening: with Mie to 'Rheingold':

Wotan: Frauscher; Mime: Breuer; Fricka: Sedlmair; Freia: Forster; Froh: Winkelmann; Fasolt: Grengg; Fafner: von Reichenberg; Loge: Schrödter (good). All the others mediocre.

I love the opening. The E♭ in the double basses – and the water, the endless waves. A greater musical painter has never lived. |If only I could see Schmedes. For me, when he's not there, the stage is empty.| The second scene-change is also incredibly bold and beautiful.

Mie saw me home – there was bright moonlight. Overcome by a beauty thrown at your feet by the world, wherever you look, I couldn't bear to go indoors.

Tuesday 9 October

This morning: Labor. The fugue is very talented – but lacks proficiency. –

Mie was waiting for me in the Rosengasse. Together we went home. – Höfergasse. Had an opulent meal – then a drive in the Prater.

Mahler – Schmedes.

13 Both 'L'Intérieur' and 'La Mort de Tintagiles' (mentioned by A.S. on 16 October) were published in *Ver Sacrum*, II, vi, 1899, in translations by Friedrich von Oppeln-Bronikowski.

S. looked at me but didn't greet – maybe he hadn't recognized me. In his case, messages don't travel very fast between the eye and the brain. But he's the picture of a man, a hero. So tall and handsome. I love to look at him. This evening:

Walküre
Siegmund: Schmedes; Sieglinde: Kurz; Wotan: Reichmann;
Brünn-hilde: Mildenburg.

Uniquely beautiful. After act I, I felt as if transported. The beauty is indescribable. It was a performance of the first rank.
. . . and the close of act III! . . .

Thursday 11 October
p.m. Mimi Wetzler, Gretl Hellmann. Nothing further to add – but:
This evening:

Siegfried
S.: Schmedes; Brünnhilde: Mildenburg; Mime: Breuer; Wotan:
Reichmann; Erda: Walker. All good except Reichmann. Schmedes –
breathtaking. I've never heard him sing better. What a *man*!

I'd taken Bertha with me – she was dripping with passion – and I no less. *Who* could hear such music and not be moved?

Friday 12 October
In the morning: in town. Once again I didn't meet Schmedes – and actually that's my only reason for leaving the house. How I long to see him – my wonderful Siegfried.
This evening: Mama left {for Stuttgart}. Dr Pollack.

Saturday 13 October
a.m. Frau Radnitzky. Very satisfied.
Began a book: Emile Zola, 'La Faute de l'Abbé Mouret'. Interesting – the style and structure indicate that it was written some time ago.

Sunday 14 October
Composed – read – didn't go out – even that I can no longer bear. I long for a little stimulation – just a little!
This evening:

Götterdämmerung
Schmedes: uniquely good; Mildenburg: magnificent;
Gutheil-Schoder (Gutrune): quite interesting.

Altogether breathtakingly beautiful. Carl came too, and was delighted with Sch.

Monday 15 October
Read all day. A mediocre book. Ernst von Wildenbruch:
Eifernde Liebe[14]
Very mediocre, full of fake sentiment and false passion.
In the evening: at Spitzer's. Hennebergs, Kurzweils, Zemlinsky.
I was well dressed: white shoes, grey dress, pale-lilac petticoat – and looked beautiful, as all agreed – myself included. The feeling is not unpleasant.
Zemlinsky apologized to me for his bad behaviour. He promised to come on Thursday ... I tried to win him back – for I have lost him. He also wanted to revoke the song dedication – and probably will.[15] I shall consent, not beg for favours. – But it hurt. He was as wicked as usual, by the way. Spitzer sang Wotan's Farewell like a pig, but Zemlinsky accompanied wonderfully, and I liked him again. – But he's capricious and unpredictable. He said he had to leave, that he had a rendezvous at 10:00. But I pestered him until he stayed on. I imagine it was Fräulein Guttmann that he left in the lurch this time. – I don't find him ugly. We talked all evening, irritated by the slightest disturbance. Who cares what others think ...

Tuesday 16 October
Labor. I read him 'La mort de Tintagiles', the little marionette play by Maurice Maeterlinck. It's delightful and thought-provoking. He was so unbelievably dear, placed my hand on his eyes, and suddenly I felt: 'Stop – your behaviour is false and underhand. Yesterday you made a contract with an immature young artist – and today you accept these privileges.' He asked me to come round in the evening some time. I promised I would.
On the way home, I felt that I was being unjust and that I shan't be upset if the Zemlinsky business – as I all but expect – does *not* come off. During the summer, our friendship has cooled – more than ever.

14 The playwright and novelist Ernst von Wildenbruch, born in Beirut. His father was an illegitimate son of Prince Louis Ferdinand of Prussia. *Eifernde Liebe* was published in Berlin in 1893.
15 Zemlinsky did ultimately keep his word: his Lieder op 7, published in the autumn of 1901, bear the dedication: 'Frl. Alma Maria Schindler zugeeignet'.

|Gretl H. wrote today to say that Lola Beeth had told her that Schmedes had told her that he was in love with me. What an idiot.| When I see him again, I shall give him a piece of my mind. Such an ass.

Thursday 18 October
Zemlinsky is due today . . .
And he *came*. Half an hour late, admittedly, but he came. I played him 'Lobgesang' and 'Engelgesang'. He was completely dissatisfied. – The atmosphere not captured – and he explained why. He was so incredibly interesting, everything he said was so right. I was – and still am – delighted.
His appearance at our house provoked a chorus of dismay. I find him neither hideous nor grotesque, for his eyes sparkle with intelligence – and such a person is never ugly.
Whatever will Labor say? I have no choice. Labor is only concerned with technique. He doesn't care whether a song captures the atmosphere of a poem. I believe – in my heart of hearts – that he has almost no idea of the modern lied. With his rapid intuition, Zemlinsky grasped the spirit of the poem at once and showed me just *what* I'd done wrong. But to my dismay I realized that I'm incapable of anything better.
I am empty. –
. . . And Zemlinsky is one of the most sympathetic people I know. – He's supposed to return on Monday. I do hope he does.
In the evening: Walter {Bopp}. We were alone together for some time. For a moment his words grew confused and his voice failed him. Had I not manoeuvred smartly, I believe he would have given himself away. He stayed until 9:30, then I threw him out.

Friday 19 October
Early to Labor. Yesterday Z., today Labor – the combination promises well. – My exercises were pretty bad.
On the Ring. Some way ahead of me: Schmedes with his little wife. He strode out boldly like a Siegfried, while she toddled along beside him. I had to laugh out loud – and involuntarily I murmured 'Gutrune'. – He didn't see me, of course.
p.m. at home – composed. Z.'s reproaches spur me on. –
This evening: alone. Studied the score of 'Tristan' – act III. Isolde, how beautiful you are.

Saturday 20 October
Frau Radnitzky. – Composed.
p.m. with Carl {at the Secession}. Moser and Hoffmann. Wall-panels by Macdonald[16] – mannered but fine. Moser was friendly.

Absolutely *delighted* to see you, he said when I arrived.
Then to Laura's. With her to Demel – tedious. Then to the Schusters. Naty and Mikosd. Frau Schuster blurted out that I was engaged. –
This evening: Mie. I asked her to stay for supper. Carl said:

By the way, Schmedes sends you his regards. I saw him.
Siegfried sends me greetings.

Sunday 21 October
Composed. Finished one song.
At 11:30 rendezvous at the Secession. The Hennebergs bought a silver-edged casket from Scotland. Moser and Hoffmann were there too. I do like Moser. I'd like to have him – as a friend. On Wednesday is 'Tristan' – I wanted to invite him to sit in the Hennebergs' box, but as there's a committee meeting and he won't be free, I said nothing. It would have been great fun.
When Zemlinsky comes tomorrow, I'll tell him – but I have little hope. Ah well, I can enjoy 'Tristan' on my own too. – I do look forward to it.
This afternoon: Gretl Hellmann. We warmed a little. That doesn't mean much – we had drifted so far apart. And what embarrasses me: she's become so vulgar, spends all her time thinking about sexual intercourse, which I find revolting, disgusting. I don't think about it often, and even then, I don't talk about it as blatantly as she, who keeps saying: it's supposed to cause pain, you bleed etc. I must say, the idea appeals to me very little – if you think about it . . . And then: music can compensate for everything, everything. – Gretl is, literally, ready for marriage. I shall never entirely warm to her again.

Monday 22 October
Zemlinsky didn't come. I'm absolutely furious with him. – What kind of behaviour is that? I shan't write to him any more.
This morning Mama arrived back from Stuttgart. She said:

How Gretl towers over Wilhelm intellectually.

16 Margaret Macdonald, wife of the Scottish painter and architect Charles Rennie Mackintosh. Together with Herbert Macnair and Macdonald's sister Frances, they formed a group known as 'The Four'.

Poor Gretl! That's the worst, the most difficult. As long as there's some physical attraction, it's all right – but later, when the relationship develops into friendship based on mutual respect, she'll feel it dreadfully.

p.m. Jettel, Else Legler, Dr Sewald.

This evening: played 'Tristan'. Nietzsche, the great visionary, says: 'Tristan' is actually the opus metaphysicum of *all art*. He is right. Nothing can approach its beauty.

Tuesday 23 October

This morning: to Labor. On the way there, from the cab, I spotted . . . Schmedes. – He didn't see me. But it gave me a jolt. And the upsurge of emotion frightened me. I realize now that I feel attracted to him with unbelievable violence. Admittedly without a hint of love. For that I don't *respect* him enough – it's nothing but lust.

    Love without lust – causes pain.

    Lust without love – bodes disdain.

I desire him with body and soul. Oh to talk to him again, to see him, feel his presence. He's right: I'm in love with him. And I believe he also knows – how.

p.m. Aunt Clara's funeral. Although I was personally very fond of her, I didn't want to drive to the graveyard – didn't know why. When I realized that Carl dearly wanted me to go, I agreed to all the rigmarole, dressed in black and did as all the others.

In the train we met Dr Egger, father of the Herr Egger with whom I once played the Schumann A-minor concerto in Grundlsee, and we had a stimulating conversation – about music and the deceased. In the graveyard, her husband, Fritz Knörlein, received us with tears in his eyes. The only next of kin whose emotions were genuine. And Carl wept . . . It was the second time I had seen him weep – once before, on Sylt,[17] and today. He was terribly fond of Clara . . . The pastor's sermon and all the paraphernalia struck me as ridiculous. But when the coffin creaked as it slid into the grave, I was horrified. I stood there dry-eyed. Everyone was pinching themselves to make the tears flow. I *only* felt sorry for her husband, who truly loved her, just as she had loved him. And I ask: wouldn't it have been far more beautiful if he had accompanied the hearse to the graveyard on his own – without that mob of relatives and without the priest? I'm convinced he would silently have

17 i.e. on the occasion of the death of Emil J. Schindler.

delivered a heartrending farewell speech. He on his own – that would be beauty.

After the burial service we went to the coffee-house, then took the five o'clock train back to Vienna.

When we got home, we heard that Burckhard had called and gone away again. I was so sorry. I sat down and played and sang 'Tristan'. Tomorrow I'll see the performance.

Wondrous moment!

My longing grows from hour to hour.

Ernst and Hanna were with us. He confessed to me some of his outrageous deeds. Afterwards Mama told me that new debts have come to light.

At 8:00 Carl returned from the Secession. Brought Moser with him – such a nice chap. He stayed until 10:30. Easy-going and sweet-natured – nice expression on his face. He should have accompanied me to 'Tristan'. But Carl called it off – because of a stupid committee meeting.

Wednesday 24 October
Rendezvous with Mie at the Opera. Dined there.
Spent the afternoon at the Schusters'.
Champagne with lunch and p.m. cider. I fear for my digestive system. – Young Schuster said:

In my opinion, Tristan is the most *revolting* of all Wagner's operas.
I've just got back from 'Tristan'. The most wonderful work ever created. – I'm in ecstasy.

Thursday 25 October
It was uniquely beautiful. – Mildenburg wonderful. Winkelmann good too. In some passages my heart stops beating. Moser did come after all. – Afterwards we dined at Leidinger – Carl, Kurzweil and Moser, who were at the Deutsches Haus, came too. It was pleasant and enjoyable, I got to bed at 2:00. The experience was delightful.

Friday 26 October
Labor. He was touchingly affectionate to me. I learnt little today.
Burckhard to lunch.
This evening: 'Meistersinger' at home on the piano. – Only 'Figaro' can match its sweetness. Act I. The fugal ensemble of the Masters – classically beautiful. Act II. The passage for Eva and Sachs (E♭ major) – sweet.

And then, at the close, Walter's Prize-song. The amazement of the people, who softly hum the uniquely beautiful melody, which builds and builds:

up to Eva's motif 'Keiner wie er zu werben weiss', which tops the jubilation and enthusiasm.

Both in conception and realization, it's unique.

'Tristan' – 'Meistersinger' – the 'Ring'.

And people say: 'Today there are no miracles.' A god has descended . . .

Sunday 28 October

Today this letter.[18] He's such a dear fellow, so strikingly level-headed. I expect much of him.

a.m. at Naty's. Lily was there – came along with me.

At 2:00 Burckhard collected us in the buggy. Together we drove to his little house in Franz-Josephs-Land. A living-room, a washroom, a kitchen, an attic, a balcony and a terrace overlooking the Danube. His boat down by the river. Flowers, white-painted walls – everything bright and airy. Altogether pleasant and delightful. He'd chilled a bowl of punch. First we swilled that down. Then we went for a walk on soft, white Danube sand. Deliciously fragrant ambience. The Danube itself wide, flat, clear, bright, fine – truly beautiful.

We returned home. We were spirited, animated. I didn't regret the visit at all. B. is a fine fellow and very sensible. Once we'd arrived, he stayed a while, then went to see Karlweis.

In the evening: Spitzer, to whom the above-mentioned qualities do not apply.

Take care not to trip over stones that don't lie in your path. You must learn to look the other way.

---

18 ▶ Humorous, pseudo-biblical letter from Zemlinsky, apologizing for his failure to appear to a lesson.

Tuesday 30 October
For once, Labor was satisfied with my exercises.
Mie fetched me, and we went to buy accessories for a hat, which we made p.m.
This evening: Moser, Hoffmann, Hofrat and Frau Zuckerkandl. Although he's very kind, Moser paid little attention to me. What I mean is: I can't succeed in winning him over. – Hofrat Zuckerkandl is one of the most level-headed, amiable people I know. He spoke in a rather Jewish way – but well – about his student days. Delightful anecdotes.
This winter, Moser won't be able to design our things. He'll prepare a few himself. But I shall call the whole thing off.
I would so like to show everyone what *I* can do. A beautiful song, a masterpiece – something finer. Chorus and orchestra – but when will it happen?

Wednesday 31 October
a.m. worked, then finished my needlework for the Secession – and now . . . Once again I'm waiting for Zemlinsky, in vain of course! His behaviour is remarkable. He sent me a cancellation note, saying he'd only just finished at the theatre, had been there since 9:00 a.m. – checked out at 6:00. I forgive him.[19]
In the evening: Aunt Xandi.

Thursday 1 November
Yesterday Mama was at the Deutsches Haus with almost all the artists (Secession), I didn't want to go, indeed I stayed away . . . Don't care to be ignored . . .

All Souls' Day / All Saints' Day
Today a.m. to the Zentralfriedhof. Obedient to the last, I went along too. Lots of people were standing at Papa's grave, but Mama prayed and wept. I looked at them, but couldn't bring myself to simulate emotion, to strike theatrical poses. In my presence, Mama was somewhat embarrassed. Show your false, shallow feelings. – But I really loved Papa – and still love him, shall always be thankful and love him – as long as I live. –
p.m. worked hard.

---

19 Zemlinsky was rehearsing the operetta *Des Kaisers Garde (San Toy)* by Sidney Jones, which was due to open at the Carltheater on 9 November 1900.

In the evening: Richard.

Have finished reading the 'Fridthjof Saga'.[20] Am surprised that no one has set it to music. The story would be good. –

Saturday 3 November
{in the margin:} Moser, Hoffmann, Ashbee, Mackintosh
              Spring Exhibition at the Secession[21]

Later they pointed out his {Klimt's} sisters-in-law to me. They're in all his pictures. One of them – the younger – is unique. Strange eyes. Experienced, sad, floating. He wasn't there. I went the rounds with Minister Wittek. They all praised my embroidery, my hat and my face. The phrase most frequently heard was:

> You're a danger to the Secession, because, once they've seen you, nobody can appreciate the beauty of anything else.

I don't know how seriously to take remarks of that kind. But I believe I really did look good.

p.m. I went back in with Mama. Led Winkelmann around all afternoon.

[corrected Alma Mahler.]

20 *Friðþófs saga ins Frœkna* (The Tale of Fridthjof the Bold), an Icelandic saga, dating from the thirteenth or fourteenth century. A.S. probably read the German translation by J.C. Poestion (Vienna, 1879).
21 Josef Hoffmann and Koloman Moser were responsible for the presentation of the 8th Secessionist Exhibition (3 November–27 December 1900). Two halls were devoted to pictures from the Paris gallery of Julius Meier-Graefe, 'La Maison Moderne'; a further attraction were works of the Scots *art-nouveau* school, including the celebrated tea-room designed by Charles Rennie Mackintosh.

Suite 20

I was born to be lonely –
and loneliness is my destiny,
for I feed off my own thoughts . . .
Once again a planet has flown by – close by.
We went our separate ways, lost in the distance.

Monday 5 November
Dinner at Spitzer's. Zemlinsky cancelled. I was pleased, because it put paid to Sp.'s boastful 'When *I* invite him, he always comes.' It was a pleasant evening, incidentally. Mama, Laura [&] Bernhard, and Aunt Mie played tarot – the rest of us sang. Half act II and all of act III of 'Siegfried'. The cast:

> Wotan: Dr Spitzer
> Erda: Hugo
> Brünnhilde: me
> Siegfried: all three

I also played – and well, I should add. Hugo and I were carried away by the music. We scarcely touched the ground! Spitzer kept annoying us with incoherent expressions of delight. At regular intervals – I believe he was timing himself with his watch – he would exclaim, 'Wonderful', 'Grandiose' – in the middle of a phrase – causing an irritating hiatus.

Tuesday 6 November
Labor. Less satisfied this time. Mie came to fetch me, and he cross-examined her minutely. – She was fairly forthright, admitted that she didn't care for music in spoken drama or for pictorial and verbal elements in absolute music. He found that most interesting. I agree with her about spoken drama – but with absolute music –
No!
At home {with her}, I busied myself with my needlework, and at about 6:00 she took me home.
I sat down at my desk and began a letter to Zemlinsky, bidding him farewell for ever. But then I thought better of it and asked him to come another time. I do *want* to study with him, after all. And pride is well and good – if you don't suffer from it.
While I was writing, there was a knock at the door and Burckhard came in – brought me a book by Darwin and an epic poem. Later we played 'Tristan' for a while and he told a few good stories. We were in the

antechamber, Mama called Aunt Xandi into the dining-room. We were alone. He took both my hands in his and squeezed them hard. I offered no resistance – let it happen – on the contrary, I gave him my hands – just had to . . . But it made me despondent, and that he noticed. – Then Mama returned, and he gave me his hand again – formally. Oh God!

Sunday 11 November
At midday:
> Schubert: Mass in E♭ major
> Soloists: Naval, Hochmeister, Frauscher, Schemmel,
> Dr J. Mayer.

Beautiful and majestic.
Lunch with the Hellmanns.
p.m. I played through almost half of 'Die Meistersinger' – Paul sang. Then to tea with Mimi Wetzler.
This evening:

Die Meistersinger
with Reichmann, Hesch, Gutheil-Schoder (good),
Winkelmann, Hilgermann, Felix.

The whole performance magnificent. I sat alternately with Aunt Mie in her box, and with the Wetzlers.
Then Burckhard joined us for dinner – (Mahler was dining at Hartmann[1] too). Burckhard has no idea how much I like him. He's sweet and *so* bright. He said:

> Let me show you a pitiable sight. Look at those two old gentlemen sitting behind me. They were both friends of mine at high-school, they're no older than I am.

I looked across.

> Their hair used to be *black*, now it's – *white*.

Monday 12 November
I didn't want to write anything, because you easily write too much, and years later, when your outlook has changed completely, you're surprised, angry, no longer understand yourself. But – I must. I have to admit that throughout yesterday's performance I was in a terrible state of physical excitement. I looked – had to keep on looking – down to where he was sitting. He never looked up.

---

1 A restaurant near the Hofoper.

I was hot and cold all over.

Although I know that B. will never marry, I was so pleased when he said:

> I could well imagine having a wife . . .

– spoken with a strange inflection – left hanging in the air. And once, when we were discussing the possibility of my getting married, he said:

> But you'll wait a while, won't you? Time is on your side.

And all the while – those adorable eyes.

I've been thinking of him all day – can't stop myself. My dear one – dearest one.

Night has fallen. I spent the whole afternoon at the piano, in a fever. Just imagine:

> Brahms: Symphony in F major
> Bruckner: 'Romantic' Symphony
> Bruckner: A-major Symphony
> The 'Choral' Symphony – the greatest, most lofty work ever written.
> I love every note of it.

My partner was Coralie, who needed plenty of prodding.

Then on my own: 'Meistersinger'.

The Sewalds came for supper. I feel quite lost – what with 'Meistersinger' and the powerful impression of yesterday evening. – I can no longer think straight. – My music and my pitiable love-life.

Up, up arise! Intimations of eternity! Rise to light, to love, to eternal, sun-drenched love. Burckhard – my Burckhard! –

Tuesday 13 November

I feel more placid today. Perhaps too placid. I would be sorry if the whole thing were to come to nothing.

At 11:30: a loud knock at the door – Zemlinsky. I was playing Bach and, quite honestly, had forgotten all about him. Moreover, I was scarcely expecting him. So I said:

> Now you are mine. Herewith I begin my first lesson.

He: And when's the next?

I: That's up to you.

He: Well then, what shall I teach you?

I: Form.

He: Show me what you've got then.

I played him my latest piano piece.

> It's got qualities, shows talent – but it lacks technique and aptitude.

Then he tested my knowledge of harmony, looked at my latest counterpoint exercises, and we *both* agreed that my capabilites are slight – almost *non-existent*.

And that after *six* years of Labor . . .

What's more, his strict counterpoint is stricter than Labor's. What a wonderful fellow! And stimulating beyond measure.

One thing, though – if you want to be my pupil, you mustn't contemplate publishing anything for some time yet.

Then we chatted about everything under the sun, and he stayed on for two whole hours. My spirits are soaring. –

p.m. called with Mama on Servaes and Hellmann. Frau H. is a blonde cat, probably capable of the meanest behaviour. I only went along because some admirer – her sole admirer, actually – had written, asking me to. –

In the evening: Spitzer, Pollack. They argued about Wolff. I abide by my opinion – and discount him . . .

I thought less of B. today – actually not at all. My mind was preoccupied with countless other things.

Friday 16 November

Labor. My exercises were better.

You're growing more aware. –

p.m. composed – a text by Mörike. Nice little song.

In the evening: played through the prologue to 'Götterdämmerung'. I'm extremely keyed up. My exertions are driving me into the ground – and it's not just willpower. I simply feel compelled.

Later: two tickets from Burckhard for his lecture.[2] Doesn't interest me, actually – I could never get excited about a lecture. If anything, it will be the pleasure of seeing him again – but in public . . .

Sunday promises to be quite a day. Gesellschaft concert, lunch with the Conrats, p.m. Lanners, the lecture in the evening. I'm glad it's scheduled on a Sunday. Any other day would be even less agreeable. –

Gretl is sick – has taken herself off to bed and feels neglected. Marriage is one of those things. –

Sunday 18 November

In the morning: Gretl {Hellmann}. We played through the Mahler symphony.

At noon the Philharmonic concert:

2 ▶ Postcard from Burckhard, with address (IX., Frankgasse 1).

> Beethoven: 'Prometheus' overture
> Schumann: 'Manfred' overture
> G. Mahler: Symphony no 1 in D major[3]

The 'Prometheus' overture, 'Manfred' – no more need be said. – They *exist*, quite simply, and are *beautiful* too. Which you can't say of the Mahler symphony. Certainly, it's done with talent, but with the greatest naivety and refinement, and not in the best sense of the word. An unbelievable jumble of styles – and an ear-splitting, nerve-shattering din. I've never heard anything like it. It was exhilarating all right, but no less irritating. With pulses raging – scarcely able to speak – I arrived at the Conrats'.

The guests: two Italians, Anni Leinkauf, Fräulein Brandeis, Dr Zweig, Fränkel, Meyer and Zemlinsky. It was pleasant and enjoyable. Zemlinsky and Fränkel escorted me a short way. Zemlinsky went off in another direction, Fränkel accompanied me to the Lanners'. On the way, he asked me to tell him when I shall next be at the Secession, because Peter Altenberg is very keen to meet me.

p.m. at the Lanners'. I was rather taken by a certain Dr Muhr.[4] A Wagnerian but evidently *not* of the stupid kind.

This evening: Concordia, Burckhard's lecture on the concept of modernity in art. This much can be said in his favour, compared with other lecturers: he spoke as briefly as possible – wittily and intelligently. I must admit, though, that the bad company he keeps is causing his pure, Aryan blood to semitify. He's even beginning to look Jewish. I just can't help it. My sympathy for him has waned considerably.

Monday 19 November
Yesterday: dinner at the Conrats'.
Zemlinsky, who was vice-president of the Tonkünstlerverein, has resigned, and isn't attending the concerts any more. Conrat is on the committee. Z. was seething inwardly all evening. Finally the discussion turned to the Tonkünstlerverein.[5] That was his chance:

3 The first performance of the work in Vienna, conducted by the composer.
4 The architect Felix Muhr. He evidently lived in an outlying conurbation (possibly Baden bei Wien), and his name is not entered in Viennese address-books until 1914. *GoR* states (p. 540) that he was a member of the Wiener Circle and the Camera Club; nothing further is currently known of his professional or private life.
5 Zemlinsky joined the Tonkünstlerverein in 1893, became a committee member in 1898 and vice-president the following year. In 1901 the committee, under the presidency of Richard Heuberger, voted against promoting a performance of Schoenberg's *Verklärte Nacht*, whereupon Zemlinsky and Schoenberg resigned.

I've coined a new name for the Verein:
(Incidentally, they recently gave several memorial concerts – whenever
someone dies, whether the deceased was an untalented ass or not, the event
is commemorated.)

Concordia Morticians' Union.
Conrat retorted:

> The title is not inappropriate. After all, Concordia means harmony –
> and since you've left, that just about hits the nail on the head.

And so it went on, blow by blow. It was highly amusing.
– And now –
I'm writing all this down while waiting for him to arrive, the beast. –
At 3:00 he sent a card, making his profoundest excuses. So I worked. Later
Narciss and Anna Prasch came round.
This evening: at the Lanners'. Dr Muhr was there. I must admit I was
rather taken aback. We played trios – Else the violin, he the cello and I the
piano. A trio by Haydn and another by Beethoven. The funny thing was
that every opinion I expressed seemed entirely to agree with his.

> I've never met a girl who speaks so much sense as you.

He repeatedly expressed his amazement at my concisely formulated,
logical opinions.
– The man can't have much of an idea of true logic, otherwise he would
never have seen as much in me. Apart from that, I quite like him, except
that he's not full-blooded – pallid and colourless in body and soul. He puts
saccharin in his coffee . . . Despite all that, he knows and understands his
Wagner, something I always admire. –

Tuesday 20 November
Yesterday evening, Pollack, Muhr and I *walked* home. It was agreeable.
Labor. I played him four songs – 'Unvermeidlich', 'Wandreres Nachtlied',
'Abend', 'Er ist' – an invention, and a piano piece which he dubbed
'Novelette'. One of the songs he liked very much, namely the first. The
Novelette is good too. The other songs not too bad either. –
p.m. Portrait sitting. Carl is painting a family picture. Boring – boring.
Later Erica – a good-natured, sensible girl – and Burckhard. Well, I must
say, I've never met anyone more good-natured, more sensible or sweeter
than him. As he was leaving – we happened to be alone, like last time – I
went outside with him, and, at the very spot where we had experienced
that brief moment of bliss – stood Aunt Xandi. He looked at me, I at him –
we smiled. He *always* knows what I'm thinking, and vice versa.

Thursday 22 November

This morning: Zemlinsky. At 10:00 I'd gone out, because it was cleaning day,[6] an institution that I loathe from the bottom of my heart. I fetched Naty, and we strolled on the Ring for a while. – I got back six minutes late, and I still can't forgive myself.

He was kind and friendly – and we began our first lesson. He took the Beethoven piano sonatas as a model – logical, clear, distinct.

To Richard, who came round p.m., I was able to repeat everything almost word for word. Even he understood it. I'm to give up song-writing for the time being, and for the next lesson I've got to write short movements based on the exposition sections of various sonatas movements. – I shall do it with joy. – Zemlinsky is a wonderful fellow.

p.m. Gretl. I'm invited to the Hellmanns' on Sunday, but as I find them tedious, I shan't go. –

Dinner at the Geiringers'. I didn't drink anything – a virtue in which, as with many others, I follow Burckhard's example – and hence remained affable and clear-headed to the end. Gustav and I played four-handed – and, I should add, very well – from two-handed vocal scores: 'Siegfried', 'Meistersinger', 'Walküre'.

To bed at 2:00 a.m.

Friday 23 November

Had a miserable night. Dreadful cramp in the kidneys – at least that's my explanation for the pain. It was just too awful. And – half in my sleep – the Prize-song {from 'Die Meistersinger'} kept ringing in my ears . . . I could have wept.

a.m. at Spitzer's. Had my photograph taken.

A card from Erica, asking me to be certain of arriving by 5:00. She expects a huge crush – I wonder. –

I found this drawing of Klimt's and am putting it in here. It's robbery, I know, for it belongs to the Secession. But doesn't the whole man belong to me?[7]

So I walked over to the Conrats', went upstairs – and Erica begged my forgiveness, saying she'd only written to make sure that I would come, and that she'd like to go to Demel with me. I was somewhat ostentatiously

6 Orig.: 'Gründlich' – thorough cleaning, spring-cleaning.

7 Gustav Klimt: *To Rudolf Alt on his 80th birthday* (brush proof, reproduced on p. 348). The final version was published in *Ver sacrum*, V, 1900, p. 318, with a motto: 'Be true to yourself, and the times will be true to you.'

dressed – long collar, plumed hat – and at first I didn't want to, but then I did. And it was great fun.

In the latest number of 'Die Fackel', Carl has been dreadfully panned. Kraus refers to him as a well-known dealer who sells art to stockbrokers and coal-merchants.[8] For Papa, on the other hand, he has nothing but praise. – Nice of him . . .

In the evening: Pollack. Until now Carl always read 'Die Fackel'. But now that he and the Secession are under attack, he won't read it any longer. B. gave up reading it after the first issue, in which a friend of his was monstrously slandered. –

8 *Die Fackel*, no 59, mid-November 1900, p. 19: 'Just as every aristocrat used to keep his Jew-in-residence, so today every stockbroker has a Secessionist about the house. Herr Moll is known to be art-agent to the share-pusher Zierer and the coal-usurer Berl, while Herr Klimt initiates Frau Lederer into the art of Secessionist painting. This rapport between modern art and idle-rich Jewry, this rise in the art of design, capable of transforming ghettos into mansions, occasions the fondest of hopes. [. . .] Those who had the opportunity to admire the burgeonings of the celebrated *goût juif* at the recent Secessionist Exhibition will not dismiss such dreams as merely idle.'

Monday 26 November

I'm sitting here, waiting for Zemlinsky.

p.m. Stern-Rechfehlen. As soon as he came into the room I dragged him to the piano – he had to play duets with me. Unfortunately he disappointed me with his incompetence. – We tried through the last movement of the 'Choral' Symphony.

This evening: to Burckhard's. Oysters, lobster, suckling-pig, artichokes, duck, chocolate with whipped cream, ice-cream, cheese, fruit-basket, black coffee, liqueurs, pineapple punch. It was a terrific blow-out. Everything A1. We four were on our own. It was cosy. After a long period of abstinence, I tippled, heavily – but not *too* heavily.

He has three large rooms and two smaller ones. A magnificently elegant house. The apartment is wonderfully large, airy, cool. The walls of the library are crammed from floor to ceiling. – It looks terrific. – In that room, I should imagine, you could take any silly goat for a scholar. Such a pile of books always impresses me beyond belief. – And with that fellow sitting there ... The atmosphere is of his making, and the atmosphere makes him. So complete, so rounded a person as he is a rarity. Confident, clear-headed, composed. Whenever he turns round, sits down or makes some other movement, no matter how slight, he always knows *exactly* why.

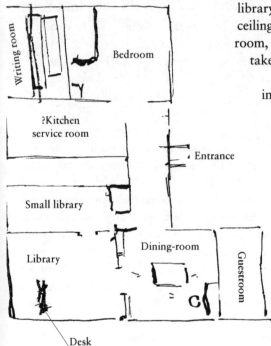

Wednesday 28 November

In the afternoon: Mie at home.

This evening: Mozart concerto. Marie Baumeyer (piano) – accurate but ineffectual – typical woman's playing. Then two pieces by Fuchs – tedious academicism. A Phantasiestück by someone called Klose, entitled

'Elfenreigen'. Finally Beethoven's second Symphony.[9] Didn't care for it.
Then with Hennebergs and Spitzer to Hartmann. Listless.

Saturday 1 December
Letter from Zemlinsky – apologizing. Whenever I read his 'Please don't be
angry', I capitulate.
It's raining, the weather is dull and grey, so dreary and monotonous – I'm
already fed up with it.
p.m. in quick succession: Dr Spitzer, Krasny, Pollack, Burckhard, Richard.
Mama was busy all the time packing. – Krasny was intolerably impertinent
to me. At all costs he wanted to hail a cab and drive with me to the concert.
You can imagine how I reacted to that. Even Carl was annoyed at his
obduracy. In the end I gave Richard a ticket, hailed a cab and took him
with me, at the same time making it clear that I'd been invited by the
Conrats – and hence would have to sit with them for part of the concert.
Conrat and young Wolff were waiting for me at the entrance, gave me
another ticket and offered to escort me inside. Naturally I went with them
and left Richard to his own devices. – After the third song, the usher
sauntered up and gave me the two tickets and the cloakroom receipt. So
why did I give this fellow tickets: to sit next to me, or to hear Gärtner?[10] I
can find no clear answer.
Lieder by Schoenberg, Wolff, Zemlinsky, Strauss, Posa etc. – old folk-
songs. Zemlinsky is the most gifted of them. Schoenberg – an aberration.
Two songs – or lieder, rather[11] – unbelievably showy but without the slightest concession to an ear accustomed to melody. Flabbergasting, mind-
boggling. Not a crescendo reaches its peak smoothly. By no means
uninteresting – but beautiful . . . ?
Afterwards: dinner at the Conrats'. A gentleman with an Italian-sounding
name brought me home in a carriage. –

9 Marie Baumayer played the Concerto in E♭ major K 482 (cadenzas by Josef Labor); the
work by Robert Fuchs was his Andante grazioso und Capriccio op 63 for string orchestra;
conductor: Ferdinand Löwe. Friedrich Klose's symphonic poem *Elfenreigen* was composed in
1892. Klose was a pupil of Bruckner; he taught in Geneva, Basle and Munich.
10 Eduard Gärtner, voice teacher, composer and book illustrator, noted for his performances
of contemporary music.
11 In the original, the contrasting words are 'Lieder' and 'Gesänge' (A.S. employs the latter
to imply a more substantial composition). Programme: Schoenberg, Zwei Gesänge op 1
(world première); Zemlinsky, Gesänge op 8 no 3 and 4; Oscar Posa, 'Frühling'; Heinrich
Schenker, 'Wiegenlied'; Erich J. Wolff, 'Schön Liebchen'; German, Russian, old-English and
old-French folk-songs. Gärtner was accompanied by Zemlinsky.

Sunday 2 December
Mama has left {for Stuttgart}.
To lunch: Burckhard, Richard, Pollack.
Carl, Burckhard and I then drive to Hotel Rabl on the Fleischmarkt, where
B. was to give a dramatic reading of his 'Bürgermeisterwahl'.[12] At the
reception desk we were met by Jewish committee members, who eagerly
led us to a long, smoke-filled room packed with working-class Jews. – He
read well. The play is fine and effective. It was so funny: the fellow who
opened the proceedings, a lad of no more than twenty years, spoke of the
workers' incredible thirst for knowledge, of the spectre of reactionism, of
the influence of the clergy etc., all with a strong Jewish accent, in typically
Yiddish slang. Finally he apostrophized Burckhard as a fine man who had
come to open their eyes. – B. made his entrance to thunderous applause.
Why on earth did he give that reading? For educational purposes? Surely
not because he cares about this degenerate race. Was it just vanity? What
do I know? Enough – I just wouldn't consider it worthwhile to squander
my vocal chords, my good temper like that, for no return. He was so
exhausted that he had to go home . . .
Carl and I walked over to the Secession – he to the office, I to the galleries.
There I bumped into Peter Breithut, with whom I went the rounds. A
bloodless nincompoop.
In the evening: Fischel, Richard, Xandi. Richard was immensely animated,
Fischel immensely boring. He told me once again that the noblest calling
for a woman was to tend the sick.

Tuesday 4 December
Am in a frightfully bad state, very tired. Am working hard for Zemlinsky,
want to make progress.
a.m. to Labor. Letter from Gretl H.: Schmedes in the hands of the receivers
– his wife and Dagmar in Abbazia, the divorce now definitely going
through . . .
This evening: at the Kurzweils'. I went with dreadful misgivings.
Henneberg, Spitzer, Hancke, List, Hoffmann, Moser and Kurzweil's sister
were there. I didn't enjoy it. Carl was rude to me. Was adamant that I
should play. I wouldn't. He fumed. I cannot and will not. – Nothing of
interest to report, I regret having gone.

12 *Die Bürgermeisterwahl*, first performed in 1898, was Burckhard's most successful
comedy.

Wednesday 5 December
a.m. Gound. I played him some of my music, and he liked it. He even asked me to give him some of my songs for his wife.[13]
Lunch with the Hennebergs. I'm not speaking to Carl – and he's not speaking to me either, by the way . . . And the Hennebergs? I find her all too transparent . . . nothing about her ever changes, nothing at all.
Then to Else Legler. Lilli Conrat was there. I introduced her to some of the fruits of my labour, and we had a very pleasant conversation. At the age of six she had lessons all day, at seventeen she took her finals. She's simply learnt the art of learning. – She's engaged – in love, but not physically – the third sex!
This evening I wrote another exercise for Z. and one for Labor.
p.m. Krasny – while I was out. You just can't shake the fellow off. –

Thursday 6 December
Reininghaus to lunch.
This evening: to the Opera with the Hennebergs.
       'Der Bundschuh' by Joseph Reiter
       'Cavalleria rusticana' by Mascagni[14]
I'd never heard 'Cavalleria' before, which, considering its popularity, is quite something. The piece isn't bad, although it already shows signs of wear, but it has a certain lasting value. Above all it's racy, full of temperament, which is more than can be said of the 'Bundschuh'. The music is highly competent, but completely lacks individuality. For sure, as far as being ultra-modern is concerned, he doesn't miss a trick. He keeps the singers in the same register throughout, gives them nothing for it, not the slightest chance to shine. On the whole it's not uninteresting. Sometimes it even makes an exciting effect, but what Reiter lacks is the grace of God![15]
Unfortunately I couldn't hear 'Cavalleria' to the end – Reininghaus, Jettel and Dr Pollack were waiting for dinner at home.
p.m. Gretl H. Once again, she told me all sorts of gossip about me. I

13 The soprano Elisabeth Lauterburg. The *Deutsches Musiker-Lexikon* (Dresden, 1921), gives her year of birth as 1885 (!).
14 The evening ended with *Harlequin als Elektriker*, pantomime in two tableaux, music by Josef Hellmesberger junior.
15 The opera ran for five performances. The Austrian composer Josef Reiter, born in Braunau, worked in Vienna as a teacher and conductor. From 1908 to 1911 he was director of the Mozarteum in Salzburg and in 1917–18 conductor at the Burgtheater. A further opera, *Der Totentanz* (1904), was rejected by Mahler and remained unperformed until 1938.

find it so disgusting. I simply don't *want* to hear all the prattle about Burckhard and me. People who live in glass houses ... Most of those beastly debutantes don't even *know* me. –

Friday 7 December

Actually it's wrong of Gretl to keep telling me what others think of me – it does make me angry. And then – I just don't know – are Hoffmann, Moser etc. justified in accusing me of megalomania? Am I really so hollow? Or am I so gifted that they can't apprehend it?

A song by Richard Strauss, 'Traum durch die Dämmerung', has been running through my head all day. It's so unbelievably beautiful, intimate and sincere. If only I had written it.

This evening: 'Meistersinger'. Winkelmann, Gutheil-Schoder, Hilgermann, Hesch, Felix etc. Wondrously beautiful. – Reininghaus had reserved a box, and I invited Moser and Zemlinsky. We met, quite by chance, on the way in. Carl came with me.

The opera is simply unique! And with Zemlinsky – it was a feast! Altogether – Zemlinsky! A great fellow. The Zierers were sitting next door. To them it was all Chinese. Afterwards we dined at Hartmann. Zemlinsky went home. He was tired! I didn't feel tired in the least. Kolo M. couldn't resist assailing me with a few coarse remarks. Quite why he felt I deserved them, I don't know. I only know this much: we shall never be real friends.

Saturday 8 December

Lunch at the Conrats'. It was great fun. Zemlinsky, Wolff, Spitzer, and others I didn't take note of. Also Fräulein Kusmitsch – the only lady present apart from myself. Zemlinsky sat next to me. Later I spoke at some length with Wolff – last year's misunderstanding was cleared up. My letter never arrived, and he was offended. We really took the mickey out of Spitzer. Zemlinsky was incredibly rude to him. All the others too ... I've come to like Wolff.

Last time I was at the Conrats', they told me they'd written to him anonymously to tell him that he should wash himself. Today he kept asking:

Fräulein – cross your heart and tell me: were you behind that letter?

He showed me the signature, 'A society friend'. I read it very calmly, didn't betray the secret, played my role to perfection, as the Conrats, who were following the proceedings with bated breath and great amusement, later assured me. At the time I felt sorry for him, and silently I cursed the whole Conrat clan.

Zemlinsky and Wolff absolutely insisted on dragging me off to to a musical tea-party in some unknown house, at which lieder by Wolff, Schoenberg, Zem. etc. were to be sung. Of course I couldn't go. These fellows are so free with their opinions. They compared my face with that of a well-known actress, and Zemlinsky said:

> I'd be happy if I could express in music the fine nuance which makes Fräulein Alma the more beautiful of the two.

In the evening: at home. Played 'Meistersinger' – 'Meistersinger' – 'Meistersinger'.

Monday 10 December

During the course of the day I did about ten counterpoint exercises. –

In the evening: dinner at the Loews'. At table I sat next to – Burckhard. I can scarcely describe what I felt when I went in, and the first person I saw – B. We'd never previously met in company. He felt funny about it too.

Before dinner, I sat with Herr and Frau Hesch, Hofrat Zuckerkandl and his wife, Prof and Frau Oserder, Hartel (the Minister of Education), Marschall (architect in charge of the cathedral) and Frau Schödl. Oh yes – and {Rosa} Papier. She arrived late. Everyone was already at table – all of a sudden she grimaced, muttered something and rushed out. Embarrassed silence. If you've got stomach troubles, you should stay at home. – After a while she came back and tried to make apologies, which only made the whole thing worse. It was so embarrassing, one couldn't help laughing.

My dear, dear B. was as discreet as ever, said not a word, just smiled . . . *How* I like him. He said he'd give anything to travel with me. I would dearly have replied: 'I'd give anything to live with you.' I'm so unbelievably fond of him. So handsome, so noble, so masculine, so free!

In the night I dreamt that we had kissed – and I awoke overcome with bliss. O daylight! Horrid, cold, grey daylight! What a dreadful awakening.

Tuesday 11 December

Labor. I'd worked well. He was satisfied. As I was going, he kissed the air – as farewell gesture.

p.m. Zemlinsky. After the lesson he played 'Tristan' – so wonderfully beautiful . . . a dear fellow altogether.

In the evening B. sent me a basket of fruit. I thanked him:

My dear anonymous donor,

Many, many thanks for your sweet greeting. I can scarcely tell you the joy with which I think of you. If only you had been here today. After my lesson, Zemlinsky played 'Tristan' so magnificently! We both sang as well. – It was unique. – My knees were trembling. I also mentioned your reservations about Tristan's death. He refuted everything, would much like to discuss it with you. – My dear Hofrat, do you know how beautiful 'Tristan' is?[16]

I picked up the letter and smiled at myself.

How I would love to talk to you, paper is so stupid. – I must close. – I send you a thousand greetings.

Al{ma}

Thursday 13 December

This morning: Mama returned from Stuttgart. And a reply arrived to yesterday's letter. What a dear, sweet man. Does he know how much I like him?

p.m., while I'm hard at work: Reininghaus. I was very put out. –

Later Pollack. The defamatory tactics of the anti-Semitic faction are making him ill. God knows, I'm glad I wasn't born a Jew.

In the evening: alone – working. Let me progress. I must, I shall. My sole desire: to achieve something in art – in my art, something beautiful, substantial, sacrosanct. That's my only wish . . .

It's curious. When B.'s letter arrived today,[17] I blushed from head to foot. I was alone, I knew it. As I read it, I grew hugely excited, I kissed it. I dream of giving my body to him, just once, even if it's only a kiss . . . As far as dear Burckhard is concerned, my thoughts go no further, and I know also that all the thoughts in the world can change nothing.[18]

A kiss is the noblest, purest gift of Nature for saying 'I am yours' Everything that follows serves a specific purpose, an ulterior motive, can never be as selfless, as pure as a kiss. It's the most beautiful thing I've

---

16 In *AtB*, A.S. implies that this experience led directly to an erotic encounter: 'This was the beginning of our love. To me it was a time of absolute music. He played *Tristan* for me, I leaned on the piano, my knees buckled, we sank into each other's arms.' (p. 18.) From *The Diaries* it transpires that several months were to pass before A.S.'s relationship with Zemlinsky became more intimate.

17 ▶ Letter from Burckhard, dated 12 November 1900.

18 cf. *AtB*, p. 16, where A.M.-W. writes of Burckhard: 'I was seventeen and very innocent . . . On my side, our relationship lacked any erotic tinge.'

experienced. All the rest I know only instinctively, and instinctively I dread it. And yet – if B. were here . . .
What am I saying? . . . !

Friday 14 December
a.m. Frau Radnitzky. Else Legler with her fiancé.
I'm simply shattered . . . I was getting dressed – about 7:00. The doorbell rang, it was Burckhard. We didn't know what to say – he brushed my cheek with his hand, I resisted. He didn't desist, came closer and closer, and finally he kissed me – and this was the worst of it – touched my mouth with his tongue. – That put paid to any illusion of passion. How I had been longing for that moment – and how horrid it actually was. I shall never forget the disillusionment . . .

   Klimt's kiss and
   Burckhard's kiss
– the former was Heaven – today it was Hell – an abyss opened before my very eyes . . .
B. and Bertha accompanied me to the Tonkünstlerverein. – The programme was:
   Gound concert:
   much ado about nothing –
   a few lieder performed by a scandalously bad soprano.
Then with Spitzer to Bertha Kunz, where we were joined by Sewald, Mama and Hancke. Saw Muhr. Drank champagne. I got sozzled – on purpose.
I can't stop shaking all over – I really love that man – but his insidious behaviour disgusts me. –
What a day!!

Saturday 15 December
Unveiling of the Goethe Memorial. –
First: lesson with Labor. It was pretty grim.
I'm still suffering from the shock of yesterday. We – together with Felix Fischer, Karlweis, Sewald – went to Bertha Kunz and swilled champagne. I'm still tipsy from it. – Apart from that, I also spoke to the wife of Director Taussig, Helene Neumann, Junke, List, Hancke, Eger, Rainers etc. My much-despised beloved wasn't there. Oh, if only he hadn't done it with his tongue. I'd been longing for the moment – and now . . . the very second he came in, I knew what was up. We were sitting together and didn't know what to say. And then, when he started making passes, I kept repeating:

No – that leads to nothing, don't, it's not right. –

But listen, child, if you only do what's right . . .

Then he took my left hand and smothered it with kisses.

Tell me,[19] how come you have such a <u>sweet</u> little visage? . . .

Later, as I was resisting more violently:

> . . . Don't you like me any more? Tell me . . . Then it's over, that I know . . .

> Our friendship is wrecked, I know it.

> Come now, what makes you say a thing like that? Come now – he said, slightly more earnestly.

I went outside. I wouldn't have betrayed Klimt's kisses for anything in the world. After a while I went back in again, and that's when it happened . . . The man is so self-assured . . . I hate him . . .

Monday 17 December

I'd really like to know whether I like Burckhard or not. My feelings for him aren't tender – it's just that he excites me physically. For a moment we were standing alone. He said:

> Why are you holding your head so high? You used to be different. Are you reminding me of a moment of weakness that will *never* be repeated? Very well – I shall remember it.

(as if he wanted to punish me – and in reaction to the lustful look in my eyes)

> That would be very unkind. –

I must say that I'm disgusted at his easy-going attitude to the whole affair. At the outset, when he arrived, he looked me over and asked:

> Why are you so sad?

But you *can't* be cheerful if you take it all seriously. Afterwards I laughed. But that laughter still horrifies me. I long to be alone with him again and to tell him: 'I'm not and shall *never* be your plaything.' Once – we were drinking a toast with Asti – he looked at me – so very meaningfully, promisingly, questioningly. Sweet – so sweet. But *so* frivolous. –

How did Klimt manage to account for his frivolous attitude towards me? And how is it that he understands women far better than this bogus Don Juan? By the way, all the gossip that's circulating about him – I believe it, every word. He's trying it on with me in just the same way . . . But I don't

19 Despite the intimacy of the moment, Burckhard retains the impersonal form of address ('Sie').

know whether to call a halt or let things run their course. I'd prefer the latter – but the former is more attractive.

– Vederemo –[20]

a.m. in town with Bertha Legler.

p.m. Auchentaller, to whom I played endlessly from 'Siegfried' and 'Götterdämmerung'.

Zemlinsky, naturally, failed to show up again . . . the miserable hound!

Tuesday 18 December

Labor. We argued again.

Lunch: Richard.

This evening: 'Walküre' –

  Winkelmann, Hilgermann, Hesch, Reichmann, Kurz, Mildenburg. The performance? Orchestra often scrappy. Reichmann inaccurate as usual. In the intervals I spoke with Hollitscher, Muhr, Paul Hellmann etc. – To write about the work – again – would be ridiculous. Only this: this time I found some sections too long-winded. Half of act II, for instance, where you're constantly being told things you already know from 'Rheingold'. It's a concession of Wagner's to the public, so that they can understand the story even if they only see the one opera. They could cut those passages with a good conscience. –

Afterwards: dinner at Hartmann with Mie and Hugo. –

Friday 21 December

Ghastly night. Colic and pain in the bladder, also chest pains and heartburn. Thou shalt not – booze!

And yesterday at the Opera – the Wärndorfers with . . . Klimt . . . What would I have given for him to see me with *Burckhard* – whom, formerly, he simply couldn't abide.

Saturday 22 December

At the last performance of 'Siegfried' Schmedes was hoarse and Reichmann kept coming in wrong. Some consolation, at least.

One thing though: Burckhard was there. He'd said:

  In that case I shan't go . . .

But he did go.[21]

p.m. Spitzer, Reininghaus, Richard, the two Conrat girls, Pollack. Gretl is

20 'Vederemo' (Ladino): we shall see – a favourite expression of Zemlinsky's.
21 ▶ Letter from Zemlinsky.

ill and very nervous. We're concerned that she's in the first stage of 'hope'.[22] – Poor thing. Is that living? –

The Hennebergs, Spitzer, Carl and I drove to Café Museum. Bernatzik and List joined us for supper, the Kurzweils came too. And Bernatzik spoke with Carl about Burckhard. He said that B. doesn't make full use of his talent, that his talent and his character have been ruined by his director-ship. – If he hadn't accepted it, he could have risen to a leading position, but those dogs of journalists have ruined him. At the same time he's intensely ambitious. – His readings at the Concordia and the Workers' Club are the logical outcome of his unfulfilled vanity. He's lost hold on himself . . .

I was only half listening – was saddened – *because it's true* . . .

I should make it my job to help the man back on his feet, to cure him of his unbridled frivolity. Only now do I realize *how warm* my feelings towards him really are.

I'm grateful to Bernatzik . . .

Sunday 23 December
Pollack to lunch.

This evening: 'Götterdämmerung'. I wasn't carried away . . . Winkelmann sang Siegfried. The performance was dull and lacked vigour. Unenthusi-astic on the whole. Mildenburg excellent. – Alfred Zierer came up to the third circle. That's a greater achievement than Siegfried penetrating the fire. Muhr had a seat in a box in the first circle. He's an attentive listener, which I like. – Next to me sat two pretty girls, who greeted me cordially as 'Fräulein Alma', even though I didn't remember ever having seen them before. –

Monday 24 December

Christmas

{My presents:}

Burckhard	1	Grillparzer
	2	Shakespeare
	3	Uhland
	4	Schopenhauer / 30 volumes
Mayreder	5	Gottfried Keller
Mie	6	domestic encylopædia
	7	Knut Hamsun

22 Euphemistic expression for pregnancy (cf. Klimt's eponymous paintings of 1903 and 1907–8).

Hellmann	8	cardigan
Mama Moll	9	collar
Mama	10	blouse
Fischel	11	clasp
Spitzer	12	Gretl's picture
	13	Goetz: 'Der Widerspenstigen Zähmung'
Hancke	14	stationery
Ernst	15	picture of Wagner
Horwitz	16	handbag
Gretl H.	17	handbag
Flora	18	handbag
Pollack	19	two volumes of
	20	Nietzsche
Xandi	21	perfume
Mama	22	visiting cards
	23	gloves
Lanners	24	chatelaine

Quite enough, actually. Burckhard's present gives me the greatest pleasure, because the thought behind it is so kind and touching. Thirty volumes just from him. My whole room is full of books, which are my favourite anyway.

The coat from Frau Hellmann is somewhat ostentatious but chic. And poor Gretl got almost nothing at all. All *she* has is her husband. And that's not much.

Thursday 27 December
Lydia Hardy has got herself engaged. To think that such *ugly* girls can find themselves husbands – as long as they have money – revolting!
p.m. talked to Louise about kissing. I told her I didn't understand how she could bear to kiss her husband, who has protruding teeth.

After all, when you kiss you feel the teeth.

But Almschi, how do you know that? You're talking of erotic kisses. Married couples, once they've cooled off, don't do that any more. And then there's another sort – she said – but that's only possible if you're *very* fond of each other.

With the tongue? I asked.[23]

Well, well, Almschi, you are quick on the uptake . . . If you know that.

23 ▶ Letter from Zemlinsky, thanking A.S. for the photogravure of Wagner (cf. Suite 21, 31 January 1901), that she had given him for Christmas.

You're right: if two people are very fond of each other, they kiss with
their tongues.
In his case I consider it mere frivolity. – But it's strange: since our conversation, I long to kiss him again. My dear, singular, errant friend!
This evening: lesson with Zemlinsky – it was like a thermal bath. Invigorat-
ing, quickening, soothing. And his refreshingly sharp tongue. A wonderful
fellow. I want to keep on working hard. –

Suite 21

I have acted very foolishly –
with a rashness that will torment me
for the rest of my life. –
And a star has arisen,
dazzling and distantly radiant.

Saturday 29 December
p.m. Muhr. First we played the 'Choral' Symphony, but neither of us really entered into the spirit of it. Then I played him three of my songs. After 'Einsamer Gang' he smiled and said:
God created you on a Sunday.
Tea was served. I got up – he barred my way and pressed an envelope into my hand. I opened it absently – and inside . . . a letter from my beloved Wagner. – I was really delighted. It's so very generous and kind of him. I shall have it framed. After high tea, we played 'Siegfried' – with *more* spirit, as, to my shame, I have to admit.
Before lunch I'd been at Labor's. On the way home I exchanged the silver chatelaine for a big gold pin with two diamonds, and a locket, into which I put Papa's picture.

Thursday 31 December
New Year's Eve. – Composed.
Yesterday Mie gave me a lovely handbag. –
Have a cold and a stiff neck.
In the evening: the Sewalds, Prof Wolff, Pollack, Xandi. I was pretty well sozz . . . First Heidsieck, then punch. That was asking too much of my temperance. I was also too befuddled to write anything sensible. And today I can't think of anything to say.
The year hasn't been too bad. But I still think it would be better never to have been born.

Friday 4 January 1901
|This evening: operetta. Première at the Carltheater.| Eduard Gärtner's 'Die verwünschene Prinzessin'. Attractive overture – the closing scene ruined by a vulgar ditty. Good on the whole. Zemlinsky conducted. Has orchestrated it beautifully for Ed too. |He took a curtain-call . . . |

Monday 7 January

This morning: Zemlinsky. Punctually. My variations: not bad, one of them splendid. He is delightful, kind – and uncivil. I asked him to play the prelude to 'Es war einmal', but he wouldn't. – I made so bold as to tell him I hadn't gone to 'Tristan' because he wasn't there. He said:

> You know, Fräulein, you are becoming tiresome. – You may be able to keep all your other young men under your thumb, but with me – that won't work . . .

And he's right. *What* do I want of him? Yes, I like him – beyond words . . . But when he arrived – his incredible ugliness, his smell. And yet – when he's there, I get strangely excited.

It's remarkable how impudent, how rude the fellow can be.

Monday 14 January

p.m. at the Secession. This time the exhibition is monumental.[1] – The Segantinis look superb, Klinger and Rodin no less so. It's a true master-exhibition.

This evening: at home alone. Mama, Carl and I got a little tipsy on Saturday's punch. – As a result I fell on the stairs and sprained my foot.

Wednesday 23 January

This evening: Strauss concert.

> Till Eulenspiegel
> Several lieder, of which 'Wiegenlied', 'Befreit' and 'Traum durch die Dämmerung' should be singled out
> Ein Heldenleben[2]

Programme-music in the worst sense of the word. In both works you have to wade through endless pages of prose, just to gain some vague idea of the composer's intentions.[3] In the papers 'Ein Heldenleben' was advertised as the opening item. But they changed the order, and Hugo and I, who didn't

1 The exhibition (13 January–28 February 1901), designed in Byzantine style by Alfred Roller, included fifty-six paintings by Segantini; also on display were busts by Rodin and Max Klinger.
2 Programme: *Till Eulenspiegels lustige Streiche;* three orchestral songs (world première): 'Meinem Kinde', 'Muttertändelei', 'Wiegenlied'; *Ein Heldenleben;* four songs with piano accompaniment: 'Befreit', 'Ein Obdach', 'Traum durch die Dämmerung', 'Heimliche Aufforderung'; prelude to act II of *Guntram* ('Ein Siegesfest'). Pauline Strauss-de Ahna (soprano) was accompanied by the Kaim Orchestra (Munich), conducted by the composer.
3 The programme-book included the following note: 'A booklet with full explanatory texts to *Ein Heldenleben* and *Till Eulenspiegels lustige Streiche* can be purchased from the ushers for 30 Kreuzers (both analyses). Song texts: 10 Kreuzers.'

know about it, listened to the whole of 'Till' under the impression that it was 'Heldenleben'. – Dear God, I realized afterwards that they might just as well have swapped the titles! We laughed heartily at our [and Strauss's] mistake.

Richard Strauss is a brilliant pig – I can find no other word for it. The whole thing is larded with illogical, unnecessary and hideous discord. The volume at which these dissonances are given out is [unnecessarily] ear-shattering. According to the principles of natural selection, future generations will be born with double-strength eardrums. That's the gist of it: on no account use a chord that anybody else has ever used before. – If these people only realized *what* harm they do themselves. They're all too ashamed to spell out a melody – for fear of appearing banal. They shamble, ramble and scramble about unceasingly – but never succeed in walking upright, in surmounting every obstacle, in pursuing their goal! –

Thank God: on Sunday is the
'Choral' Symphony

Thursday 24 January
This evening: Tonkünstlerverein.
> Prohaska: String quartet[4]
> Hugo Wolf: Harfner lieder
>> sung by Ed. Erhard
> G. Fauré: Sonata for violin and piano
>> perf.: H. Scalero, Prohaska
> R. Strauss: Three songs
>> sung by Ed. Erhard

It was about as stimulating as a vicarage garden-party – quite lacking in verve, impetus and objective. Richard Strauss looked in for half an hour. Sat quite close to me. Then we all went to Café Parsifal. But I was tired . . . I spoke with Wolff, Horn, Stern, Spitzer etc. Strauss's face is composed – cold – Germanic. But his eyes – are dark craters.

---

4 The composer-pianist Karl Prohaska was a disciple of Brahms. From 1901 to 1905 he taught in Warsaw, from 1908 at the Vienna Conservatoire. On this occasion his String Quartet op 4 was performed by the Fitzner Quartet.

Sunday 27 January
A.M. Bertha. Then to the

'Choral' Symphony[5]

I'd taken my score with me, and followed the performance with it. I believe nothing has ever excited me more than this monumental composition. The first movement, the second – God knows – the whole work. All of a piece, one *beautiful whole*.

> Ahnest Du den Schöpfer – Welt?
> Über Sternen muss er wohnen.

First the loud question, then the soft answer. Before such beauty one prostrates oneself. I scarcely dared raise my eyes. Such lofty passion – sublime sensuality.

I spoke to Bernatzik – his eyes were glazed . . . On the other side of the hall I spotted Klimt.[6] – We met in the cloakroom. He looked at me gravely – I shook his hand. |I bumped into Wengraf, who fetched my coat. I put it on – he took his leave. I went towards the exit – Klimt followed me with his eyes. – Outside stood Ernst, waiting for someone or other. I stood with him and waited for the Zierers, with whom I walked home.| – After a while, Klimt came out, saw Ernst and greeted him. I averted my eyes. What I had always suspected now became blindingly clear. Even if my sensuality awakens and occasionally overcomes me – attracts me to a man – he's the only one I shall ever *love*. When I see him, I tremble from head to foot. Down in the cloakroom, I stood for a moment and stared at him. I would kiss every atom of him – there's nobody else of whom I could say that. But now we have grown apart, so *dreadfully* far apart. My greatest desire would be to win him for myself again – for ever. [Somehow!]

The strange thing is that last night, in bed, my thoughts turned to Burckhard, and I worked myself up into a regular frenzy of desire, fooling myself that this love was dead . . . And today follows the refutation.

Whenever I believe myself cured, my old ailment breaks out with renewed severity. – Why do I go on living? Only for fear of death. For I have nothing more to live for. No happiness beckoning to me through distant clouds and spurring me onward, only music. And I can do no better than to quote Gretchen:

> Daß, wo er nur mag zu uns treten,

---

5 Soloists: Elise Elizza, Karoline Kusmitsch, Franz Pacal and Moirtz Frauscher, with the Vienna Singakademie, the Schubertbund and the Vienna Philharmonic, conducted by Mahler.
6 Shortly after this concert, Klimt started work on his *Beethoven-frieze*.

Mein ich sogar, ich liebte dich nicht mehr![7]

Today, I couldn't drum an opening into my heart, it was so bursting with love for this unforgettable man. – But then, they were only the opening bars . . .

|This evening: at Frau Radnitzky's. It was uneventful.|

Tuesday 29 January

Labor – satisfied. After I'd played my counterpoint exercises, he suddenly said:

> Tell me, aren't you composing any more? – It's a long time since you
> last brought me a song. Why's that?

How fortunate that he's blind: he couldn't see that I was blushing profusely . . . What if he hears that I'm spending every free moment working for the quizzical praise of another teacher . . . ?

|In the evening: dinner with O. Sachs in Hotel Sacher. I talked most of the time with Zemlinsky and Gärtner. Later all the others played tarot, and I joined them, together with Dr Holländer, Engel & Alfred. Weisse, from the Volkstheater, doubled up with me. It was very amusing. At 2:00 a.m. everyone went home. – Those of us who'd put our coats on took them off again and stayed until 3:00. Gärtner and Zemlinsky played duets – Gärtner's operetta, later Strauss. It was delightful. Zemlinsky tore me off a strip in front of the assembled company. Said I was superficial and untalented. Was altogether brusque. At one stage I was talking to Berl, and Zemlinsky went off to play cards with Lanner. I said:

> Why are you deserting us?

Whereupon he replied in a booming voice:

> If you insist on spending your time with people who don't interest me.

Berl gave him an astonished look and said:

> How now, sir? Do we have the pleasure of having been introduced?

Wednesday 30 January

To lunch: Prof Herterich (Munich), Hölzel (Munich/Dachau), Prof Schrödter (Graz).[8] Herterich is adorable – intelligent and engaging. A true

---

7 Goethe, *Faust I*, 3496–7 (scene in Martha's garden). Gretchen: '[It overcomes me so much too,] / That when he [i.e. Mephistopheles] only comes our way,/ I even think I've no more love for you.'

8 Ludwig Herterich, a member of the Munich Secession, made his reputation with the interior decor for the Festsaal of the Rathaus in Bremen. Adolf Hölzel, from Olomouc in Moravia, exhibited at the Munich Secession from 1893 onwards; until 1919 he was professor

artist. We spoke at some length about the widespread decadence in the arts. Herterich blamed it on Jewish infiltration amongst both artists and patrons. Feeling has given way to <u>intellect</u>. – He's absolutely right . . . There's no simplicity – just mathematical accuracy.

This evening: Konzertverein.

> Mozart: Symphony in E♭ major
> Hermann Goetz: Violin concerto[9]
> Wöss: Symphonic poem 'Sakuntala'
> Beethoven: Fifth Symphony

For the first time in my life I hissed, namely after hearing 'Sakuntala'. It was shameless. Shabby plagiarism. I hissed like a snake. – The Beethoven began badly, but ended quite well.

|Hugo came to collect us. Together we went to Hartmann. Henneberg and Mie, who also attended the concert, had a frightful row. Hugo was unbelievably beastly to Mie.| Altogether, the sun is shining none too brightly over their marriage. I did my best to avert the shadows . . . He said:

> Alma, did you ever hear of a husband who hadn't betrayed his wife in eight years?

Mie was very angry, and so was I. How very tactful! She said, quite rightly:

> Come to think of it, you haven't much to boast about . . .

Thursday 31 January
|p.m. at Zemlinsky's.| The room radiates unbelievable poetry. – Schoenberg opened the door with his gob full – I believe poor Zem. is besieged by spongers. One wall is full of laurel wreaths etc., including a bust and a picture of Brahms. The photogravure of Wagner that I sent him for Christmas hangs over the desk, above it the sprig of mistletoe that I fixed to the wrapper. *My* photo still stands on his desk. Even if I mean nothing to him – personally – at least he can take pleasure in looking at my picture.

He gave me my first lesson. Before and after, we chatted disparagingly about mutual acquaintances. Particularly those present at the last dinner-party. Afterwards he accompanied me to the cab-stand.

I'm endlessly fond of him. His lessons are the high-point of the week.

---

at the Academy in Stuttgart. Hans Schrödter, painter, graphic artist and book illustrator, was a pupil of Hans Thoma.

9 Hermann Goetz's single-movement Violin Concerto in G major was composed in 1868. From 1899, Joseph Venantius von Wöss worked for the music-engraving firm of Waldheim-Eberle; from 1908 he was employed as copy editor by Universal Edition. He composed primarily sacred music.

|This evening: tarot party at the Sewalds'. As soon as dinner was over, I grabbed Dr P. by the arm, and he walked me home. I worked until 11:30. At dinner an argument arose between Carl and Blum, and the sparks flew. |Spitzer, that prize idiot, kept on interrupting with comments such as:

Carl is in magnificent form today. – Exactly that! – Quite so . . . etc.
Sewald and I scarcely dared look at each other for fear of laughing.

Friday 1 February
p.m. Muhr. |The fellow's growing very tiresome. He's arrogant and limited – two characteristics that usually go hand in hand. A ghastly alliance.| Spent the rest of the day working.
In Zem.'s room also stands his bust. I told him the likeness was very flattering, which <u>really</u> annoyed him. He showed me the score of 'Es war einmal'. How I envy him:

This is *my* work, *my* talent, my heart and my love . . .
If only I could say that too.

Monday 4 February
p.m. Zemlinsky. – He gave me a thorough dressing-down: I may be very productive, but I don't use my brain properly. Will I ever learn to? I try ever so hard.
I sounded him out discreetly about his early years.

Coming from so poor a background, I asked, how did you succeed in becoming a musician? A profession which brings in so very little.
So he told me: he learnt the piano by chance. The son of one of his father's friends, who lodged with them, was allowed to take piano lessons. And this friend let little Alex learn along with him. Naturally he soon surpassed the other. – He was given a teacher of his own, whose fee was 3 fl per month and high tea. Then came a dreadful period: wherever he was invited, he had to play 'The Monastery Bells', 'The Maiden's Prayer' etc. Mozart sonatas, which he knew by heart, were forbidden. –
Once the whole family was in a restaurant in the Prater, and the proprietor's daughter played a piece, 'Maria', which moved all the guests to tears. His mother promptly borrowed the music, and he had to learn it. He so hated the piano that they had to carry him to it – he would burst into tears.
Later, at high-school, the teachers took note of him and advised his parents to send the boy to the Conservatoire. – They were persuaded they would save themselves the tuition fees. That helped. But they were mistaken. They

had to go on paying for two years, for nothing. – Later, admittedly, he won scholarships, prizes etc., but until then he had to give lessons [morning, noon and night] for 60 fl . . .

Yes – I've seen very hard times – and that isn't the worst.

I told him:

I feel that one can never again be *entirely* happy, a certain bitterness remains for the rest of one's life [naive].

He said:

You grow hardened, lose your finer touch.

I replied:

You mature . . . The only thing that gives me joy is composing. I never had a childhood – no youth. I was always amazed at the youthfulness of other girls of my age – how old and mature I appear by comparison.

I feel that my hands are too rough to lay on his. Soft, everything that touches him should be soft. Every one of us should do everything in their power to help a man like him. Not for pity's sake, but out of deepest respect. – Nothing would deter me from making him happy.

Tuesday 5 February
Labor.
p.m. composed.
Mama underwent minor surgery: removal of a polyp in the uterus. Maria has fever. The atmosphere is sad and gloomy.

Sunday 10 February
Had the flu. Not badly, but bad enough.

Friday: Tonkünstlerverein.
Saturday: Siegfried
Sunday (today): Gesellschaft concert
Monday: Burgtheater

All called off, because there was no question of going out. I'm so exhausted – have a headache too.

I consoled myself by giving my ticket for 'Siegfried' to Zemlinsky – who wrote to me – and by sending today's concert ticket to Labor. I believe the distribution is just. My God, if I were rich!

Had a dreadful night. Not a wink of sleep until 7:00 a.m. – just creepy dream-visions. Initially, I must admit, it was rather fun.

I was playing Z. one of my piano pieces. It began softly and came to a wonderful climax, shot into the air like a rocket. But suddenly the music stopped – I saw only the arc of the sheaf and the dripping balls of fire. What an after-glow . . . And then hordes of dogs crawled in through the closed door, snuffling along the floor, searching. I was terrified that they would all jump at me, but they were looking for something else. Then a creature at my bedside. I stretched out my hand – and it went straight through. But the creature laid its hand on my heart and gradually froze. The whole house was alive – a frightful night.

Wednesday 13 February
|a.m. Frau Horwitz and Laura. Carl left yesterday evening – for Stuttgart etc.|
p.m. Zemlinsky. But he came so late that we did without a lesson and chatted the time away. He's such a nice, sensible fellow. He's looking for a libretto – is bursting with ideas. How I envy him! What fecundity! What fortune! There's so much to him – unlike me. He raged at the whole world today. There's nobody I enjoy talking to more than him.
|In the evening: Felix Fischer.|

Saturday 16 February
|Frau Radnitzky. I had been dreading the lesson. She's asked me to partici-pate in her next concert, namely to play a Fantasiestück by Rietsch[10] with her on two pianos. I wrote, curtly, that I didn't care for the thing at all.| Labor and Zemlinsky were unanimous in their disapproval. I myself dis-liked it at first glance. Lots of tremolo (not at all pianistic), many borrow-ings, little original material – and whatever was original . . . No, there were no two ways about it. She also made no further attempt to persuade me. But only five minutes later she asked me to participate in her pupils' con-cert in the Ehrbarsaal. I wouldn't dream of it – just imagine: bowing and scraping before the public . . .

Sunday 17 February
Called on Zemlinsky in the morning. First time out of the house since my illness. To begin with, two of his pupils were there. The first, Hoffmann,[11]

---

10 Heinrich Rietsch succeeded Guido Adler in 1900 as professor at the German University in Prague. In 1909 he founded the Prague Institute of Musicology.
11 Rudolf Stefan Hoffmann read medicine, then studied both piano and composition with Zemlinsky. For some years he was chorus-master of the Philharmonic Chorus and the Vienna Singakademie. He published important monographs on Schreker (1921) and Korngold (1922).

played a sonata he had just written. – Well ... I've heard better. The second, an ex-pupil of his, is now studying with Fuchs at the Conservatoire, so as to acquire an official diploma.[12] – That's what I call an artistic standpoint. Nevertheless, the young man goes to Zem. as final arbiter and plays him his pieces. I would never do that. – Zemlinsky also handled him pretty roughly. That made me happy. In the end they were both standing around and didn't know how to take their bow. Zemlinsky said:

Well, gentlemen: adieu – good day.

And with that he simply threw them out. I'd brought a piece that I'd stolen from Schumann. He recognized it as such from the first bar. After the lesson he brought Schoenberg in, who wanted to say good morning. We spoke a few words, I somewhat foolish and tongue-tied in the face of such sharp repartee ... Zemlinsky himself went out to hail a cab for me, which I found dreadfully embarrassing – he had a dreadful cold. I feel so at home with him. –

|p.m. Spitzer.

This evening I composed like one possessed. – |

Wednesday 20 February

Worked. In the afternoon visitors, worst luck: Ilona Abel with her dragon-like lady-friend.

This evening: Orchesterverein. First a novelty:

Overture to the opera 'Maria Tudor' by Josef Foerster.

It didn't sound bad. Surprisingly fine – for a young man – I said to myself. And when it was over, a white-haired old man came on stage to take his bow.[13] – How sad! Nobody has ever heard the opera, and doubtless he himself won't live to see it performed. Such a work takes everything out of you – love, involvement, endless care – terrific amounts of mental and physical energy.

Dvořák's Cello Concerto

R. Hausmann (Berlin). The piece is fine but tedious.

{Beethoven's} seventh Symphony.

Fine too – but not tedious. The second and third movements magnificent, the fourth somewhat trivial.

12 Probably Karl Weigl.
13 At the time of the performance, Foerster was forty-two years old. While teaching the piano in Hamburg, he made the acquaintance of Mahler, who later invited his wife, Berta Lauterová, to join the ensemble of the Vienna Hofoper. Between 1893 and 1936, Foerster composed six operas, all of which were first performed at the National Theatre in Prague. *Maria Tudor* was never completed.

'Calm Sea and Prosperous Voyage' – Mendelssohn.
Also beautiful, noble.
|Afterwards Mie saw me home.|

Friday 22 February
11:00 a.m.: rendezvous with Mie at the Secession. The Segantini, which was only hung at the last minute, is the finest of all:

Love at the Fountain of Life

A valley of Alpine roses – in the background snow-covered mountains, in the near distance two lovers walking towards the observer. Lightly dressed, transfigured, almost fused together. In the foreground, to the left, sits a white angel. His huge wings, which span half the picture, hang over a fountain. It's uniquely beautiful! The truth of Nature – but also poetry – truth and fantasy wonderfully combined – the 'Tristan' of painting, but purified [ice-cold].
Then we popped into the court-room to see Bahr v. Kraus.[14] Since several literary figures were involved, it was an uncommonly interesting case. Kraus spoke excellently – but too long. He quoted some old article of Bahr's. The jury was asleep, the judge was asleep, the two assessors (or whatever their title is) were asleep, the public was asleep. Although he spiced his argument with witticisms, he didn't mention much of relevance to the case – one soon lost interest.
I had lunch at Mie's. At 4:00 we went back to the trial.
They called Schnitzler (the writer), Dr Wengraf, Fraenkel (spy for 'Die Fackel'), Josef Holzer etc. into the witness box. Kraus read out a list of critics whose plays are currently in the repertory. That made quite an impact. It's true: every Viennese critic is also a playwright, and all their works get performed – for the simple reason that they're critics. Young authors with far greater talent suffer neglect.
This evening: Tonkünstlerverein.[15]

14 Ever since *Die Fackel* came into existence, Hermann Bahr had been a regular target for attack by Karl Kraus, who complained of the 'incompatibility of his being a critic and simultaneously a playwright, whose works are performed by theatre directors who have obligations to him' (*Die Fackel* no 69, end of February 1901, p. 3). The lawsuit was occasioned primarily by Kraus's allegation that Bahr had received the land for his villa in Ober-St-Veit as a gift from Emerich Bukovics, director of the Deutsches Schauspielhaus. The case was dismissed, but Kraus was ordered to pay the costs.
15 Carnival concert: Ševčik: *Böhmische Weise und Tänze;* piano pieces by Scarlatti and Smetana; Schubert: German Dances, arranged by Eusebius Mandyczewski for women's voices, violin and cello. Zemlinsky's Walzergesänge op 5, originally scheduled, were not performed 'due to the composer's unavailability'. The evening ended with dancing.

Zem. wasn't there. Gound conducted Schubert (dances arranged for female chorus). Wolff saw me, took both my hands in his and thanked me for my letter. He was altogether very, very kind. He's a good-looking fellow. – If only he weren't so unwashed.

I spoke with lots of people. Ignaz Brüll[16] etc. Then Mama and I went to Hartmann. Muhr joined us. We met up with Carl and the Hennebergs. At 11:30 we went over to Hotel Imperial. Kraus came in, saw me, but didn't greet . . . Carl was sitting with me.

Saturday 23 February

a.m. Zemlinsky. He's just wonderful. – One thing I deeply regret. I showed him my diary, namely the entry in which I write deprecatingly of him – where I accuse him of plagiarizing Wagner, ridicule his appearance[17] . . . Some devil must have possessed me. I regret it now. Only a few days ago I wrote that to touch him your hands should be soft, that I feared my hands were too rough. And today I seized him with a glove of iron. I'm really sorry.

p.m. returned with Mie to the court-house. Today it was the turn of Bahr's attorney [Dr Harpner], then of Kraus's [Dr Kienböck]. Bahr's was by far the cleverer – also the more agreeable. He cast the most lurid light on Kraus's activities. His muck-raking, his phoney campaign against corruption etc. – In a word, he was at his throat. Then it was the turn of Dr. Kienböck. We didn't stay to the end. He was just as long-winded as Kraus. In the Herrengasse we bumped into Burckhard, who was on his way to see us. Mie accompanied us as far as the Opera, then we went home on our own.

In the evening: König, Pollack, Xandi – and B. I played 'Siegfried' and 'Meistersinger'. – B. was on edge, I too . . . We weren't alone . . . thank heaven.

I can scarcely take my eyes off the man!

Sunday 24 February

Philharmonic concert:

>   Weber: Overture to 'Turandot'
>   Dvořák: Serenade for wind instruments

16 Ignaz Brüll, a close friend of Brahms, was director of the Horák Piano School in Vienna. His reputation rested primarily on the opera *Das goldene Kreuz*, first performed in Berlin in 1875.
17 Suite 16, 11 February 1900.

Bruckner: Symphony no. 5 in B♭ major[18]

I'd brought Zemlinsky with me . . . and learnt to *listen* – to differentiate. He's such a dear fellow, and I shall never forgive myself for offending him yesterday . . . for I really did offend him. My behaviour is so strange!

Today – we were sitting close together – when he turned to me, it caused me physical pain – sheer sensual over-anxiety. My greatest wish, that he should really take fire for me, will remain unfulfilled, because he knows me too well – my faults, my limitations, my stupidity. What he thinks of me, I can read in his eyes. It's not exactly flattering. Everything he says about me – my dreadful superficiality, my deficient education, my upbringing – poor in certain respects and thoroughly one-sided – everything. How I envy him! He is everything I would like to be!

|p.m. worked.

In the evening: Dr Heinzen, Richard, Xandi – the former rather tedious. But I played 'Meistersinger' and amused myself.| To begin with, Richard and I were alone for a while, and he said he had something to tell me. Recently he was in company, and they told him the saga of Burckhard and Krastel, namely that Krastel's daughter was expecting a child from him – disgusting gossip, which others say is untrue.

> Whereupon a certain Dr Meyer, whom I don't know, volunteered: 'And now he's got his claws into Alma Moll.' I just wanted to tell you, so as to put you on your guard. Don't let yourself be seen with him.

Well I must say, that gave me something to think about. Ultimately they'll be saying I'm pregnant, and wherever I spend the summer – wherever I go, out of Vienna – will be spoken of as my hideaway, the place where I secretly give birth. Unfortunately these brazen gossip-mongers are never *entirely* wrong. – I know only too well that Burckhard's intentions towards me are not exactly unsullied. But I know just as well that I shall never succumb to his advances. I swear it. No more than a kiss! – But kisses can be so sweet . . .

Wednesday 27 February
To lunch:

Max Klinger

with Hofrat Wiener, Herr and Frau Marx, Bernatzik, Gound and his wife. It wasn't as lively as usual – too many women! Dull, silent women at that. Oh Börne:

---

18 Conductor: Mahler. All three works were receiving their first performance in Vienna.

A silent woman is an empty casket with seven bolts.
I spoke to almost nobody except Wiener.[19] A pleasant, intelligent man.
After dinner Frau Gound sang. Very pretty – a little dull. As I said: a silent
woman . . .
At 6:00 dinner at Spitzer's: Hennebergs, his nieces, Zemerl.[20]
After all the fuss and bother of getting changed etc., I was very agitated. I
probably said some wild things – in a word, they all thought I was drunk.
Zemlinsky kept repeating, softly:

Nasty . . .

and spoke only little and brusquely with me. Mie, Hugo, Zem. and I drove
together to the Opera:

Meistersinger

Zem. hoped to get a ticket, but they were sold out. We had our season
tickets. The performance was good. Slezak, a guest, first-rate. A typical
tenor in appearance, but [nevertheless] sympathetic. The voice big and
well-schooled. In the last act he could be heard clearly above the chorus
and orchestra (Prize-song), one of the most exacting tests imaginable for a
singer.
Well, Herr Schmedes . . . ?
Forster dull and insignificant – both in voice and appearance. Otherwise
everything as usual. By now I know every note and every word of it. This
opera sits at the right hand of the god Tristan . . .
Unfortunately I noticed that my favourite passages – despite their beauty –
left me *unmoved*, i.e. I didn't *lose* myself [but remained objective], which is
a dangerous sign, as far as my state of mind and my artistic receptivity are
concerned. I observed my neighbours, observed myself, studied my every
movement and the impression it made on others. – It's frightful when you
can see through yourself.
|Afterwards at Hotel Imperial.|

Thursday 28 February
Lesson with Zem. I'm dreadfully stupid. He proved it again today.
But he's sweet! Frightfully sweet! And our conversation flows like honey
. . . We talk about *everything*!

I'm so happy, he said, that I feel calmer now. The solitude I was going
through was dreadful . . .

19 Hofrat Karl von Wiener, departmental councillor at the Ministry of Education, also sat on
the committee of the Gesellschaft der Musikfreunde in Wien.
20 i.e. Zemlinsky (familiar diminutive).

I'd like to really know him – just for a day – find out who he really is . . .

|p.m. Gretl H. She told me categorically that Zem. was engaged to Fräulein Guttmann. – | I would find that most regrettable. He shouldn't get married, otherwise he'll suffer the same fate as Gound – he'll run to seed.

Saturday 2 March

p.m. Muhr. Played duets. In the evening with Zem. to hear:

Dvořák Requiem.

Beautiful sonorities, refined structures. He saw me home. He said:

I envy you one thing: your German name. 'Zemlinsky' is in itself unobjectionable, but a musician must have a German name . . .

We came to the front door. We both regretted already having arrived.

I'll accompany you back, I said.

My God – how well brought up you are. No. But seriously: I really enjoy making conversation with you. – During our lessons, in company . . . Actually I only tease you so, because I love to see how you wriggle your way out.

I'm not averse to you either, I said . . .

I lowered my voice to a whisper and said, flatly:

Good night.

He laughed . . . I crossed the courtyard in a dream . . . I believe my relationship to him is closer than fitting between a pupil and her teacher . . . There's nobody with whom I would rather be. And, I must say, I really do find him good-looking. His eyes are velvety. He can be so sweet. When he speaks to me, I feel a strange joy.

I could enumerate several other such points. Whether they amount to what is commonly known as 'love', I don't know – don't want to know. Clarity is not always the brightest light . . . dreams can shine even brighter . . .

Sunday 3 March

I can't help thinking about yesterday evening – of our conversation in the dark silence of the doorway . . . Even now I remember every word. My God, if he only knew *how much* I liked him . . . I've been longing for him all day. – And tomorrow he'll fail to show up again . . .

Monday 4 March

He was here – but came so late that I couldn't have my lesson, as I had an invitation for dinner at Taussigs' at 7:00. I came out onto the stairway to greet him with reproaches. He wasn't expecting that. Was indescribably brusque. I just laughed it all off . . . but inwardly I was very galled. He said:

> Either you compose or you socialize – one or the other. If I were you, I'd stick to what you do best – socialize.

What a fix. Our friendly, cheerful tone was gone. As if the varnish had been scratched away. We either exchanged long, baleful looks or – averted our gaze.

I went to Taussigs' determined to amuse myself. And I did. I was young again. |Carl Taussig led me to my place at table. I danced mostly with Alfred Rappaport, a gorgeous, brawny young rascal.| I was the prettiest. They arranged contests for the victor ludorum – Alma Schindler. I danced like one possessed. The Taussigs are decidedly upper-class Jews – distinguished and easy-going. I must say, I felt very much at ease.

But what would Zem. have said about this form of amusement? I often found myself thinking of him – and at 2:45 this morning I wrote him a perfectly sober letter.

|The Rappaports took me home in their cab. Alfred's eyes glowed in the dark like hot coals.|

Wednesday 6 March
Outside it's fine spring weather.
I'm young. Feel young too – wonderfully young.
p.m. called on the Zierers. Then lesson with Zem. He arrived in a state of considerable excitement. On his way over he'd been reading a mime-drama by Hofmannsthal,[21] which he found uncommonly interesting, as I did too when he told me about it. Unbelievably imaginative and poetic. He was sweet today – really sweet. I'd brought quite a good piece of work along – an Adagio.

I feel uplifted. Our words, our glances, our movements – everything harmonizes. He told me that my Adagio reflected one aspect of my personality: my unpredictability – my unexpected changes of mood . . . I live in him . . .

Later Burckhard arrived. He was somewhat depressed – taciturn. Nobody can be cheerful when their mother has just died. –

In the evening: to Zuckerkandls. Was introduced to Schönaich, the music critic. Had a long conversation about Wagner – modern art – the public

---

21 *Der Triumph der Zeit*, ballet in three acts. Zemlinsky worked on the project from April to December 1901, but only completed the short-score. In 1904 he revised act II as an independent piece, entitled *Ein Tanzpoem*.

and its ineffable stupidity. I told him my story about Frau Hellmann getting carried away by Grünfeld's interpretation of a Beethoven sonata 'because you didn't feel it was by Beethoven'. He had a few good anecdotes too. Then a pupil of Rosa Papier was asked to sing. We didn't listen. I detest convulsive music-making. And in *those* surroundings, music was indeed convulsive, superfluous. She sang a few potboilers by <u>Lassen</u>.[22] Then an aria, at which we turned up our noses. Schönaich said:

That must be from an operetta. –

To me it sounded more operatic. So we asked what it was, and were told, to our acute embarrassment, that it was from 'La Juive'. – I had the excuse that I'd never heard it. But Schönaich – the music critic – told me he'd seen it twenty times.

I made the mistake of agreeing to dance with Fritz Wärndorfer, which irked me all through dinner. – Kolo Moser and Hoffmann were sitting at my table. Moser is quite a dear fellow. A little shallow, perhaps, but he's working hard to better himself and will soon get to the heart of the matter.

Friday 8 March

This evening: Tonkünstlerverein, incl. Zemlinsky lieder. He accompanied. Fräulein Guttmann was there with the whole family. I don't know her, but they kept looking at me through their opera glass – what a cheek.

Zemlinsky stayed in the green-room, didn't greet me. He saw to it that the song 'Irmelin Rose', which is mine, was performed twice.[23] Spitzer said:

Zem. was here, saw you & went away.

That hurt! And now, while I'm writing all this down, I couldn't care less. My attitude is: you Jewish sneak, keep your hooked-nosed Jew-girl. She's just right for you. – I feel a strange indifference. And a certain amount of hatred. And now I can see that a little of that hatred used to be love – yesterday, that is, and this afternoon still. So little love? And so much indifference. Or do I really mean it? One thing is certain – when I next speak to him, I shall radically cut back the warmth in my voice.

Otherwise it was pretty tedious. I dined at the Conrats' – nice people.

22 Eduard Lassen, a Belgian composer of Dutch origin, whose opera *Le roi Edgard* was performed in Weimar under Liszt. He composed numerous songs, which enjoyed considerable popularity at the end of the nineteenth century.
23 Op. 7 no. 4, to a poem by Jens Peter Jacobsen, from the volume of lieder which Zemlinsky dedicated to A.S..

Saturday 9 March
Nobody can imagine how plagued I am by minor setbacks. – I'm pretty, not unintelligent, talented, most people like me, and when I'm in company, men usually sit at my feet. But when I feel the urge to approach one directly – let alone stretch out my craving hand to his heart – all human emotion goes up in smoke.
Zem. simply can't be entirely indifferent towards me. It's *just* not possible. His behaviour yesterday: so dishonourable – so cowardly. For me the most dreadful quality in a man.
This afternoon: played duets with Muhr – 'Tristan', act I. It drove me almost crazy. Nothing is more beautiful. Afterwards: the Radnitzky concert. Classy but tedious. Zemlinsky wasn't there.

Sunday 10 March
This morning: Ernst Zierer and his father called. I went to the Kuhs to cancel Tuesday.
Then to the Philharmonic:
> Dvořák: Overture 'In nature's realm'
> Beethoven: Piano concerto in G major
> „   : Symphony no. 8 in F major[24]

Zemlinsky was there. I greeted him more coolly. He felt it at once.
> What's wrong? Tell me, so that I can defend myself. – Are you angry with me?

I replied:
> Oh no, not angry!
> Offended, then – hurt?

He thought it over, even though he knew exactly what was up. Finally he guessed:
> Should I have waved to Fräulein Schindler from the concert platform?

I gave him no reply. I shall remember the tone of voice with which I spoke to him: cool, reserved yet amicable. If only I knew how to tell him. In such a way that he remains my friend, yet is prompted by my indifference to realize that it's a one-sided friendship and that I've had to restrain my feelings. It's also not my intention to compete in any way with any of his friends. And then I'd like to call him a 'sneak' to his face . . . That would be all! . . .

24 Since Mahler was indisposed, the concert was taken over at short notice by Joseph Hellmesberger junior. The soloist was the Hungarian pianist Ilona Eibenschütz, a pupil of Clara Schumann.

Monday 11 March
And Zemlinsky was here. –
I didn't tell him any of those things. But he told me a thing or two! He asked me if I'd been invited to the Tonkünstlerverein, and who had invited me. And then the bomb dropped . . .
Last Wednesday he asked me if I wanted to go, and I said I'd be too tired, the previous day was long . . . But I did go. And {now} he told me he'd written to the secretary asking him to invite me, but in Wolff's name, not his own.

> You see, I hadn't invited you, and your presence was an embarrassment to me.

I was shaken rigid, had no answer.
As he was leaving, I took his hand and asked him to forget the whole affair. One thing hurt me deeply. I asked him how things had turned out with Hofmannsthal, and he said it was none of my business, his artistic affairs were no concern of mine. He would continue to take an interest in my artistic endeavours but asked me not to reciprocate, at any rate, he didn't expect it of me. From his tone of voice, I could tell that he was mortally offended. I'd give anything to make amends for my thoughtlessness. But it's no good apologizing, that alone can never right the wrong . . .
In the evening: Hennebergs, Spitzer, Hanna, Ernst. Maria very ill.
I'm shattered!

Tuesday 12 March
Labor. Mie.
This evening: 'Tristan' – with Zemlinsky. I told him I felt like a fallen angel.

> I want to open your eyes above all to the minimal interest you've taken in my art. I've noticed all along that my request – that you should in future take no interest in my art – means no more than if I were to ask you to address me in your letters as 'Dear Herr von Zemlinsky' instead of 'My dear Herr von Zemlinsky'. That's all. I've been asking myself all along, how it is that 'Tristan' moves you so. There must be some very special affinity . . . because nothing else interests you in the least. Fräulein, this may be the last time I see you for the time being – if, for instance, I spend the coming year out of Vienna.[25]

I must say, I had never before experienced such a 'Tristan'. Act III began – so terribly sad and lonely. I could scarcely suppress my tears.

25 Zemlinsky was musical director of the Carltheater. For the following season he hoped to be offered a new appointment in Breslau.

So I've really lost him for good. He's rejected my friendship. If he only knew what he's taking from me. On the way home and upon arrival, I felt utterly crushed. –

During act II I scarcely spoke to him. Occasionally he looked my way, from time to time he made an ingratiating remark – as if to comfort me.

No: I don't ask him for *forgiveness*. The next time I see him, I shall change my attitude towards him entirely. Calm – cool.

And now I shall read the latest edition of 'Die Fackel'. Let my heart turn to stone. It already has, incidentally. I no longer feel the pain. Quite right too. *Swallow the bitter pill!* One can swallow *anything*, even if it's indigestible.

Zemlinsky – all hail to you! All hail to you and your art.

My sympathies are with you, even if you can hardly feel them. –

Wednesday 13 March

Yesterday I read 'Die Fackel'. I thought that a touch of cynicism might help. Scarcely had I put it aside, when my thoughts turned black. I had seen blue sky – not much, but a patch – and now all is black. The last weeks were so lovely . . . living for someone else. And now . . . completely alone again. I can't cry – I'm too sad. What have I done? With incredible stupidity, thoughtlessness, momentary lack of interest – I shall never overcome the loss to the end of my days.

No sacrifice would be too great! But none is even expected of me.

He is beautiful and so immeasurably great that my eyes cannot apprehend his full stature. I'm at my wits' end. I can't compose, my eyes are full of tears. God, God, what have I lost? Everything. Whatever I touch ends in failure.

I would gladly go to him, beg him on my knees to return what is lost. Without him I can live no longer. Today my thoughts return to a certain day, two years ago – the one with the cross – except that this time it's *my* fault. Mine entirely. Why did I do it? Not a word did I have for his wonderful songs – not one word.

What would I give to go through the past week a second time.

Thursday 14 March

Yesterday evening: concert.

> Beethoven: 8th Symphony
> Beethoven: Overture 'Leonore' no. 3

Bruckner: 7th Symphony

The Bruckner: very beautiful! Particularly the Adagio and the Scherzo. But with Aunt Mie – the pleasure was moderate. She all but dozed off. How different with Zem., himself a musician to the core.

Then dinner at Hartmann. Quite agreeable. I told them the whole story. They – like me – found my behaviour incomprehensible. Yes, there's no explanation for it. Today I composed a little. But nothing worked out. My thoughts were too full, my eyes too moist.

Just got home. Was on the Ring. Bumped into Schmedes . . . for the first time in ages. In five minutes he'd run down Slezak, his wife and the public – the triangle of his possible conversation. [All the same] I enjoyed talking to him. |The man always gets me so excited.| Despite his stupidity and superficiality. But his physical presence is overwhelming, and that means a lot. Sometimes it can replace an overwhelming intellect. I'd like to see him again.

Have composed quite a bit. Would like to write *just one* song that embodies and relives all my grief. But no musical key can unlock my heart. I compose with the ear – not with the soul.

All day, I've been considering what I shall do now that Zem. is gone. I shall come to grief, no doubt about it. I hope for a miracle. I'm still so young! Something must surely come along to help me. –

Friday 15 March

10th Secessionist Exhibition[26]

Klimt's 'Hygieia' – wonderful, mad. In the right-hand corner a pregnant woman naked – a curious ideal of beauty. Carl comes over well, not stunningly. Klimt and Olbrich are the two cornerstones. The rest are rocks of greater or lesser value. Some are just pebbles – nomen odiosa sunt. All the tribes of Israel were assembled, as ever, like on a feast-day at the synagogue.

p.m. Auchentaller – down in the dumps. – Justifiably so . . .

Spoke to Krasny. Spoke to Burckhard – but *so* remote.

This morning I had a long stroll in the garden with Gound. It was beautiful and sunny. Composed two songs. Downright bad. – Have just played through my earlier pieces. – Where did I find all that feeling at that time? Yes – that time – Klimt . . . I set my hopes on the spring!

26 The exhibition (15 March–12 May 1901) was one of the most significant in the history of the Secession, with over 38,000 visitors. The picture to which A.S. refers as *Hygieia* was *Medicine*, Klimt's second controversial painting for the main hall of Vienna University.

Zem., although I sent him tickets, wasn't at the Secession. He must be very angry.

In the evening: Prasch, Pollack. I went upstairs.

Saturday 16 March

Letter from Zemlinsky, written in an unbelievably icy tone. I carried the letter about with me all day like a wound. If only we could make things up! Dinner at the Hellmanns'. Sat next to Moriz Rosenthal (the pianist) – a cynical fellow, with typically Jewish disrespect. It wasn't much fun. I shocked him with the following observation: the orchestral player is paramount. For me, the piano is actually just a surrogate. Altogether the most profane of instruments. – Our piano-acrobat buried his head in the menu . . . The evening was pure piggery. Gallons of champagne. Free-range opera singers, without a care in the world, squawking out little ditties at 100 fl a piece. Schrödter and Foerster. Ilona Eibenschütz played Scarlatti – in such surroundings, pearls before swine . . . Everywhere plunging necklines, rolls of Jewish fat. Uuuugh.

After dinner, I spoke mostly with Dr Mathias, a superbly educated, kind-hearted man who, like me, found it all faintly ridiculous. At the end, Kramer[27] from the Volkstheater made a few speeches that were supposed to be funny – and the engagement party was over.

My dress was immaculate – as always, when the occasion is dull.

I have nothing to add.

Monday 18 March

Yesterday, I almost forgot: Carl said I always fell for people who were missing some extremity or other – as yesterday with Dr Mathias. So I whispered to B.:

> And what are you missing?
> Well, if you have any particular suspicions, I shall be happy to prove you wrong – but you'll have to be quick . . .

He's a designing rascal – and I'm a disgusting flirt!

p.m. Zemlinsky. I lured him into the garden and brought up the hateful topic once again. He said it really was of no consequence.

> I'd noticed that about you from the start.

And now I remember it too. The first time was with his opera. I didn't say a word about it. – I told him it's so hard to talk to an artist about his work,

27 The actor Leopold Kramer. In 1918 he was appointed director of the Deutsches Landestheater, Prague, where Zemlinsky was musical director.

but that made little impression. His heart is embedded in a block of ice, which even my most ardent glances simply can't melt. My loss is infinite. Perhaps even greater than I can at present imagine. He was very pleased with my two songs. And they were written with such grief! Together we went to the opera.

Première: Lobetanz

Text by O.J. Bierbaum

Music by Thuille[28]

Wonderful libretto, lively, Germanic. The music – a mish-mash of 'Meistersinger', 'Tristan' etc. Excellent performance. Particularly Gutheil was superb. Pretty, graceful and intelligent. –

Afterwards we dined at Hartmann. Half the Secession was there.

This morning I received a letter from Olbrich. The poor fellow is quite off his head. I showed Zemlinsky the letter too. I'd scarcely given Olbrich a thought. And now, all of a sudden . . . ! Shame – I used to think differently of him.

[corrected A.M.-W.]

28 In 1896, with his opera *Theuerdank*, Ludwig Thuille won the Luitpold Prize in Munich (shared with Zemlinsky's *Sarema*). The fairy-tale opera *Lobetanz*, first performed in 1897 at Karlsruhe, enjoyed considerable success in Germany and Austria. In 1909 it was also staged at the Metropolitan Opera, New York.

Suite 22

Saturday 23 March
Labor.

I've been hearing terrible things. Mama told old Frau Legler behind closed doors: the reason for Gretl's illness was that she hadn't yet been given sexual fulfilment. He always goes so far but no further, to avoid children. Poor Gretl. Isn't it beastly of him, and so insulting. Sexually unfulfilled, even now.

This evening: Muhr. We talked about everything under the sun. – He confessed various sins of his youth. Finally he asked me to marry him. I was thunderstruck, taken completely by surprise. I *simply* cannot see myself getting married. He's an agreeable, well-educated fellow, but I feel *absolutely* nothing for him. I like him, yet I simply can't return his love. He doesn't touch me. He's right, we would certainly be happy together, but I just can't imagine it. It would be marrying out of friendship [for common-sense reasons] – in the best sense of the word, admittedly, for I haven't the slightest interest in his money. But what about my profession? He wants to leave everything to me, the greatest freedom; he wouldn't be jealous. Yes, for sure – but . . . what about the great love of my life? |Alma, that already lies behind you. You can't expect it a second time.| I would wither away, become an old maid, remain unfulfilled. And yet . . . marriage . . . I shudder at the prospect. To give my body to a man I don't love. But then: the prospect of never giving my body to anyone! Never maturing, never being fulfilled. Half measures . . . always half measures – it's too dreadful.

At the same time – I [quite] like him. With my two darlings close at hand:
|Burckhard – Zemlinsky
free-thinking – big-hearted
and between them – a Muhr!|

Sunday 24 March
Yesterday evening I composed like one possessed – 'Ekstase' by Bierbaum. It just welled up from within me. One positive outcome, at least. Mama left {for Hamburg}. I only told her of Muhr's proposal as she was leaving. –

This morning I discussed it with Carl. He didn't dissuade me. On Saturday, I want to tell Muhr that I don't know him well enough, that he should wait six months. By then . . . perhaps I shall have nothing . . . It's too sad: people whom I love scarcely take notice of me, and people whom I don't love [who mean nothing to me] love me . . .

Midday: with Zemlinsky to the Philharmonic:

    Haydn: G-major Symphony[1]

    Tchaikovsky: Symphonie Pathétique

    Overture: 'Leonore' no. 1

We skipped the latter. – I invited him over for lunch [since everyone was out] and fetched a bottle of Asti from the cellar, which we drank to the last drop. We found much to discuss. Without mentioning names, I told him of Muhr's proposal – he advised me to accept. I understood only too well. Then he spoke of the closing line of the letter, which I had correctly interpreted. At the concert, I'd told him that Mama was away – that ruined everything for me. It was my excuse for not going to see 'Es war einmal'.[2] At table, out of the blue, he suddenly asked:

    When did your mother leave?

I told him the truth:

    Yesterday.

    Aha – I was only asking . . .

Afterwards I explained everything, begged him to believe that I really was interested [in his music]. We parted on good terms. I feel such sympathy for him – such close sympathy! He's wonderful – glorious . . .

At 3:00 Frau Gallia collected me from the Prater. High tea at home with her. Then I went home to get dressed.

This evening: 'Die rote Robe' (Brieux) at the Burgtheater. Splendid, serious play. Well-written and well-observed. Witt, Sonnenthal, Hartmann, Devrient: all good.

Later Dr Pollack came round. We discussed the Muhr affair at length . . . He advised me to accept.

Monday 25 March

This morning: Secession.

At midday: Hancke. Proposal of marriage – the second this week! Like in a penny-dreadful. Straight out, with considerable show of self-confidence, he

---

1 Haydn, Symphony no. 88 in G major. As Mahler was still ill, Franz Schalk took over the concert.

2 The performance of *Es war einmal* . . . mentioned here took place on 22 March 1901.

asked if I'd marry him, adding that I didn't need to decide immediately. But I did decide immediately – in a hard, implacable voice, I said no. He insisted on asking why, wanted to know the reason.

So I said:

Why did you come here?

Because I love you and want to marry you.

Just why? – Tell me.

Well – er – because . . .

You see, you have no answer. Because there is none. I have no intention of getting married. But if I did, I'd have to be certain: 'Yes, he's the one for me.' With you that isn't the case – forgive me for hurting your feelings. You know perfectly well that I never encouraged you. My attitude towards you has always been one of friendship . . .

And so on, for some time. He tried to take my hand – I recoiled. Initially he'd spoken with Carl, who advised against calling on me. He was furious at being rejected, left the house very much on his dignity. Menfolk are unbelievably dumb – plain stupid!

5:00: chamber music. How tedious! Nothing but fatuous scraping – the very essence of petty bourgeois music-making: nothing hazardous, nothing spine-tingling. They played

Labor's Piano Quartet

sundry lieder

Kreutzer Sonata – Beeth.

Everything was so still – calm – neither verve nor warmth! How irksome! In the evening: Pollack.

Thursday 28 March

This morning: on the Ring.

p.m. Hofrat Catharin, who found everything 'secessionist'.

Then Zem. He was delighted with my work. Said it was a pity I wasn't born a boy, that it was detrimental to my talent.

As a girl, if you want to make your mark, you'll experience countless setbacks.

And I *want* to make my mark. For me, Muhr is far away. I won't even consider the possibility of getting married. I just want to study | – to climb ever higher!| To be a somebody!

Oh, to sense the heights. To be a mountain – not just another mole-hill. To be great, swollen up, |pregnant,| to beget. Oh, to [be able to] let myself go. |Just once|.

Zem. is my rock and my foundation. If he really settles in Germany, I shall go to pieces!

This evening: Siegfried.

> Schmedes (excellent), Sedlmair (poor), Demuth (good), Breuer (very good).

This part of the Ring always drives me to a frenzy. The whole of act I, the first half of act II. And act III, which is uniquely beautiful. So much bright green! And so much bright red! Wagner is right when he says: you shouldn't listen to music just with your ears, but soak it in with all your senses. Your whole body is stimulated – every nerve, every muscle. It always makes me want to jump out of my seat and run around, make expansive movements. I can scarcely sit still. My unstilled passion drives me to a frenzy . . . Oh to *live*! – Just once!

Monday 1 April

It's beautiful outside. It makes me feel young. I would like to love . . . to live . . .

Two days ago I bought a book, and yesterday I finished it:

La Terre – Zola

Never have I read anything more ghastly. It's so gross and oppressive – and yet I found myself reading malodorous passages several times over, until my whole being revolted . . . I could scarcely control my inner excitement. What should I have done? The book has made one thing clear to me: man is born only to procreate. – That's the goal of all our striving.

Wednesday 3 April

Gound.

Worked. Read – 'Gugeline' by O. J. Bierbaum. Not as good as 'Lobetanz'.

Zemlinsky called. We went into town together. I went to the concert. There's such a heart-felt give-and-take between us . . . nothing I wouldn't discuss with him. I'm unbelievably fond of him.

Bach's B-minor Mass. Some passages grandiose, others a crushing bore. I kept thinking of Zem., his dear words, his whole, dear being. He distrusts me, considers my behaviour coquettish. What if he's right? No, a thousand times . . . no!

Thursday 4 April

Mama arrived on the early train. This morning I was in town. In Berté's showcase I saw Zemlinsky's 'Sarema', and bought it for 6.50 fl. Some passages are delightful, but I haven't quite finished playing it through.[3] Worked hard. I think of Zem. with joy.

Wednesday 10 April

A beautiful day: blossom and scent all around. My heart beats faster. Springtime. –

a.m. Percy Miles [the little composer]. Then Zemlinsky. We had our regular lesson. Afterwards we sat together. I told him I'd written him a letter but not sent it off. He begged to see the letter. I brought it. He read it.

He told me I was playing with him, that he thanked God for his common sense. Suddenly our gaze met and didn't waver. I asked him to come on Saturday. He asked if that was important to me. I said yes. [He said: 'So it's true.'] He kissed my hands, bent his head over them. I laid my head on his. We kissed each other on the cheek, held each other for an eternity. I took his head in my hands, and we kissed each other on the mouth, so hard that our teeth ached . . .

{In the margin:} He told me he had struggled all winter against his love for me.

Oh, how happy you can make me! Don't be so sweet to me . . . I beg you. We couldn't bear to part.

Now I shall write, compose – everything for you! It's such a joy that you have talent, that you're an artist too! We shall always have that in common. If tomorrow you have regrets, then write and tell me. I shall never trouble you again.

I got dressed, and together we took a cab to the Weihburggasse. We held each other tight.

Oh, you're so sweet – so sweet.

And next year he'll be leaving Vienna . . .

Spent the evening at Horwitz's. Sense of vacancy. Flicked through Carl's scores with him. Then he played some of them to me – his own compositions. More technique than feeling. My pieces are better.[4]

---

3 Zemlinsky composed *Sarema* in 1894–95. The opera won a prize awarded by Luitpold, Prince Regent of Bavaria and was first performed in Munich on 10 October 1897. The vocal score was published in 1899 by Berté, Leipzig.

4 ▷ Letter from Zemlinsky: 'I can understand your silence – because I'd been anticipating it.'

Thursday 11 April
My thoughts are constantly with him – in everything I do, I see him before me – feel him. He's so dear to me. I long for him . . . I see everything in a new light. The trees are greener, the sky bluer.
p.m. Krasny. He made a fool of himself. Kissed my hands over and over, I felt sorry for him. How different it was on Wednesday. Today was nothing but a bore. He's still jealous of Burckhard. If only he knew!

Saturday 13 April
Have a bad cold. Was agitated all day. My longing for him and his letter made me ill. At dinner: Dr and Frau Servaes, Herr and Frau Epstein, the Gärtners, Felix and Senta Fischer, Mie and Hugo, Moser, Hoffmann, Pollack, Muhr, Spitzer – Zemlinsky.
At table I was fairly placid. I had to listen to Muhr's inane twaddle. I asked Z. if he'd brought the letter. He said he had . . . After dinner we went into the studio. Frau Servaes was about to burst into song.[5] I asked Z. to come up to my room to fetch music. Actually I just wanted him alone for two minutes. All he could say was:
     I'm not your plaything . . . You shan't have the letter.
I begged and begged. Carl poked his surprised face round the door. Shortly afterwards Mama came up and said the guests were asking after me. Whereupon Z. ups and aways like lightning down the stairs, with me in hot pursuit. That's the one thing I hate about him: his fear of public opinion [of being ridiculed]. *Fear*! I don't know – if someone asked me: 'Are you in love with Z.?', I wouldn't be embarrassed. I'd say yes, at all costs. Incidentally, I've already said so once – to Mie and Muhr, some weeks ago. At the time I simply said:
     I love – Z.
Because I said it outright, nobody believed me. That's how stupid people are! They understand innuendos more readily than the honest truth . . .
Afterwards we danced. – From then on, I don't remember anything. I was so bitterly disappointed! To fight back the tears, I laughed out loud. |A proper Kundry!|
As the guests were leaving, I again asked for the letter. – He gave me his hand, like all the others. Just that. Not a smile, no secret glance of familiarity. Looked back through the window and slipped away like an eel. Almost as if he were afraid that *I* would compromise <u>him</u> . . .

5 Martha Servaes (soprano) was a concert-singer of some repute.

I went to bed. Until 7.00 in the morning I lay awake, brooding . . . crying! Couldn't sleep. A night not to be forgotten.

My next lesson is on Wednesday. Another three days! I asked him to come tomorrow. And tomorrow is – Sunday. He cancelled my regular time on Monday: a more important commitment! Quite right too! Why am I so dumb? I could take ten others in his place. And what of me? – His feelings for me aren't *deep* or *genuine*, otherwise he certainly wouldn't be behaving like this. –

Monday 15 April

My letter is still in the tray. I can't send it off – for pride! Or is it defiance? Probably, but he's no better. Why didn't he bring his letter with him? – Everything would have remained as it was. But like this – I can't even write to him. If I make such a display of my love, he'll lose all respect for me. On the other hand, he's so sceptical, he may consider the whole affair on my part to be a mere crush.

On the dance-floor, he asked me why I lacked the fire I'd shown with Muhr. The answer was very simple: you can only do that if you're dancing anti-clockwise. I said nothing. The question shocked me! Surely he has some idea of how much I love him, how, when I look into his eyes, I'm lost to the world. I feel very poorly, by the way. And there's no consolation!

Worked all afternoon. Wrote to him. But only a few words. Asked him to come tomorrow. Let's hope he doesn't have a rehearsal. I can't wait to see him again. I thirst for him. |I thirst for his life-fluid.|

Thursday 18 April

With him, I feel that I am always the giver, the bestower – and since I love him so fervently, I take advantage of my position. With outstretched arms, I would like to shower him with golden blossom – until we reach the wall, that white wall which marks the point of no return. I would consume myself with sheer giving . . . With Klimt, I was always on the receiving end. Why, I don't know. Has it to do with outward appearances and the associated joy of victory? – He took me in his arms and kissed me.

I kissed Z. – yesterday too. I took his hands. I embraced him. He kept saying:

You have no idea what this means to me.

He doesn't trust in his masculine appeal [rightly so]. – I don't find him ugly. I love his appearance. He's so small . . . when we walk together, he reaches up to my shoulder. [But then] all famous men were small – almost all. I believe he loves me truly, more truly than I love him, for I haven't yet lost my head. [Never!] [Only] in spirit.

I carry his letter in my pocket, read it, kiss it, put it away again, and go about my daily duties. Not as calmly as usual, but calm all the same. Incidentally, my sexual organs are strangely disturbed . . .

On Saturday evening I played three bars from 'Sarema' and asked him if he recognized it. He said no. Yesterday he brought the matter up again, and asked me how I came to know it. So I showed him the vocal score. He played a few passages from it and was very pleased.

p.m. Krasny.

I liked him better today. I played him two lieder. He liked them. He kissed my hands. I showed him my books. He asked me, if one year from now he had a million to his name, whether I would take him. I said no. It would most certainly be too awkward. He stayed a long time. –

This evening: worked.

Friday 19 April

Worked well. Between Wednesday and today I've written a whole rondo. Look forward warmly to my dearest one. Warmly – but no longer as *intensely*. It seems to me that this affair won't endure much longer. I'd regret it. It gives me much stimulation – I'm working well – and I'd be doing him a serious injustice. – It <u>must not be</u>. –

p.m. he was here . . . He came in, hand in hand with Maria. We sat down at the piano. I took his hand, we kissed, but I was already much calmer than the first time. I don't believe myself capable of penetrating to the depths of a true, intense passion. The ecstasy has worn off <u>so</u> quickly. I do still long for him desperately – but it's no longer as *wild* as in the first week. Anyway, it's his own fault – his constant questioning has cooled my fire. He maintains that everything about me is hollow, not sincere or genuine. And he's not entirely <u>wrong</u>. He's so *astute* that he senses it. Asks repeatedly:

Tell me, do you really mean that?

And every time I reply:

Would I say so otherwise?

But at such words I grow cooler . . . We kissed and embraced again, but since his attitude is mostly passive – motivated by reverence and modesty – my love is waning. A woman should be the taker . . . has no right always to be the giver. I long for him to hug me tightly and *shout out loud*, 'Alma, my Alma', as Klimt once did. But he addresses me as 'esteemed Fräulein' and is noticeably offended if I forget to call him by his first name. – When I asked him why he still calls me 'Fräulein', he looked at me affectionately and said:

I don't <u>dare</u>.

I detest people who don't |dare| . . .

Sunday 21 April
I'm ashamed to admit it, but in spirit I keep sinning against Z. I thought for a long time about Muhr's theories on marriage. The freedom of his concept appeals to me. I could well imagine . . .

I'm disgusted at myself. My *poor beloved*! –

Have just returned from Bertha Legler's wedding. How sweet a couple they make, with their undying love. Touching – enviable. And I pictured to myself: if I were to stand at the altar with Z. – how ridiculous it would look . . . he so ugly, so small – me so beautiful, so tall. I can summon up no feelings of love for him, no matter how hard I try. I *want* to love him, but I believe, as far as I'm concerned, it's already over. Should I go on deceiving him or – tell him the truth? For me it would be better if I were to marry . . . ['someone or other']

Since love departed from my heart, my music has died within me. I feel uninspired, am completely sterile. What a <u>wretched feeling</u>.

It's evening. The whole afternoon I struggled for some kind of inspiration. This is Z.'s revenge. I've just reread his letter . . . It's *so* sweet. I do believe that I'm still fond of him . . .

Vederemo.

Tomorrow will decide.

Monday 22 April
My heart is quite calm. I long for him no more – am saddened. That explains the white wall. Often I press myself against it, that it might fall. But my strength deserts me. It's not the wall that's too rigid, it's my passion that's too weak. I'd like to know if he still loves me as much as before.

Yesterday Mama was at the Zierers'. Several people asked her:

Is it true that your daughter is in love with Zemlinsky, and that she doesn't go out in the evenings because he won't allow her?

Mama replied, with a laugh:

There's no need to get excited: she's taking her lessons very seriously, that's all.

She also had to explain at least fifty times that I had a *sore throat* – she was asked so often. Many people said

Your daughter is the prettiest girl I know. – Don't let her get so bottled
up in herself. It's a sin against her flowering youth.

You hooked-nose race of numskulls, do you really think that my good
looks are there for your benefit? I flower for my art – and for my friends. A
week ago I would have said – for my beloved. Today that would be a lie!
He knows everything . . .

Lunch with Spitzer. He sang Z.'s lieder – very well. Then we went home
together. Z. told me that my letter was insincere. I had to agree. He told me
that my intention was to flirt but <u>never</u> to marry, and that was the saddest
part of it.

I must admit that I never seriously considered marriage.

He told me that he loved me, but that I was far too superficial to return his
love sincerely. How right he is. He can see into the depths of my soul. Just
imagine: I marry him – share his poverty-stricken [ugly] life, and then . . .
his love endures for six months, and there I stand . . . Yet today I could still
feel: there's nobody in the world I ever loved more than him.

We took a roundabout route. Frau Hardy and Lydia drove past and drew
up in front of our house. I barricaded myself behind my umbrella. I felt
unspeakably sad. And yet I have this feeling that *nothing* really moves me.
|I am, truly, only half a person.| I'm deeply saddened – no, I'm incapable of
being *deeply* sad. Tepid – just tepid! I feel sorry for anyone who sincerely
loves me. |I'm disgusted at my behaviour. – He said:

> You're just made for men like Herr Zierer. Once you've married some-
> one like him, remember me, and that I have nothing in common with
> people of his ilk.|

Tuesday 23 April

I feel so empty – so dreadfully empty. Nothing moves me. Neither joy
nor sorrow! I wrote to him, saying that I felt exactly as I had on the first
evening. – But it's not true – <u>I lied</u>. I wouldn't want him to be sad on
my behalf. Only beauty and warmth. And how I'd love to make him
happy.

Labor – <u>dissatisfied</u>.

p.m. at home. I'm so terribly sad. All day I've been thinking of how best to
do away with myself. Slash my wrists? Tonight – and by the morning I'd be
dead. How lovely that would be. I have nothing left in the world. Nothing
more to expect. And should I live aimlessly, vegetate? Heaven, give me
strength! I long for the deed. I shall never make anything out of my life. I
was born only half a person! –

I have only half a soul – he has only half a body. One of us should have been born <u>complete</u>.

I composed and wept while doing so.

In the evening: to Wetzlers. Gretl Hellmann was there. She gives me joy. I regret nothing. To bed at 12:00. Quietly read a little Darwin – quite calmly, as if nothing had happened. I don't understand myself!

Wednesday 24 April

After dinner: alone in the garden for a long time. Thought of Z. – with *great* affection.

The morning was spent packing – very calmly. I'd expected that the house would mean something to me. But I feel utterly unmoved. A little regretful, true, but quite unemotional. When I think that Z. is lost to me, my heart ceases to beat!

This afternoon he came – as dear as ever! We kissed. Together we sang 'Tristan'. We were holding hands. Once he squeezed me round the waist. – I love him. –

Thursday 25 April

I've been considering whether to marry Z. With him, I believe, I would regain my mental equilibrium. I feel so *at one* with him that I *simply* can't imagine ever leaving him. Hence, when he's not with me, I feel my music trickling away. Should I write and tell him? Muhr's money is all well and good – but what an oaf!

Yesterday Z. told me he would send me the ballet – I should be the first to hear it. How |unbelievably| happy that makes me! – His love elates me. If only I'd met him earlier! I would have become an entirely different person.

While clearing up, I found this concert programme. Shall keep it here.[6]

This evening: Verdi memorial concert.

> Requiem
> Soloists: Uffreduzzi, Walker, Marconi, Navarrini.
> Conductor: P. Mascagni.[7]

Some passages were dreadfully insecure. The tenor wobbled. The

---

6 cf. facsimile on p. 246.

7 Part of a two-day festival commemorating Verdi's death on 27 January 1901. The soloists were Giuseppina Uffreduzzi (Teatro alla Scala), Edyth Walker (substituting at short notice for Virginia Guerrini, Teatro alla Scala), Francesco Marconi (Teatro Argentino, Rome) and Francesco Navarrini (Teatro alla Scala). The Singverein, the Vienna Männergesangverein and the orchestra of the Hofoper were conducted by Mascagni.

soprano's voice was too small. But the work is so sublime, it can take even that.[8]

|Afterwards: dinner with Moser, Pollack and Spitzer, who attended the concert with us.| Went on ahead with Pollack – couldn't talk, my thoughts were only of Zem. Do I love *that man*! Honestly, truthfully? – The whole day I've been thinking about marrying him. It's only that ... poverty stifles. Would it not be bound to stifle my love?

Saturday 27 April
Gound called on me.
While still in bed, I read Z.'s letter. It was like reading the Bible. Gound's face betrays the burden of having a family to feed. Zem. must never suffer that fate! I have no wish to be a millstone around his neck – he must be *free*!
p.m. Muhr. He expounded his views on marriage. I said:
    I need the *greatest* freedom – in thought and deed.
He agreed! – We were only talking in general terms. Mama asked him to stay for dinner. She demands everything. – He hasn't the first idea about the visual arts, doesn't fit into the family circle at all. One day I'll let him think that I'll take him, the next that I shan't.
When I'd gone to bed, I read my old diaries for a while. How harmless and innocent I was then – at the time of my burgeoning love-affair with Klimt. I always thought him so nice – merry, kind. I didn't have *the slightest idea* with whom I was involved, how eminent he really was. That's why ...
'You, little Alma, my wife?' He was right. –
And Olbrich ... I don't know what that was all about. Was it also – love? If so, then quite different. Perhaps *he* was the greatest loss of all. In fact I'm certain of it. If only I'd taken him by storm! And Zem.? Yesterday he sent me this postcard,[9] which gave my affection a severe jolt. A coffee-house in the Leopoldstadt ... Is he one of those little half-Jews who never succeed in

---

8 cf. Mascagni's own account of the event: 'The contralto was Virginia Guerini [*sic*]; the soprano was a phenomenon for the power and sweetness of her voice and for the expression of feelings. She was very young, a Sicilian contessina by the name of Giuseppina Uffredursi [*sic*] who had finished her studies at Santa Cecilia at the time. [...] The enormous Viennese public was incapable of resisting the enthusiasm which seized it while hearing that music and those four voices which they will never hear again in the world. The most frenetic applause exploded at every phrase. It was the greatest triumph of Italian art abroad' (David Stivender, op. cit., 160).
9 ▶ Postcard from Café Haus Maendel (II., Praterstrasse 33): '12 o'clock midnight, at the start of a booze-up', with a few bars of music.

freeing themselves from their roots? Just to think that he goes off with a fellow like Wolff – that unwashed Jew – to booze the night away ... He told me that life had lost its meaning for him, that he *wanted* a life of dissipation. Fine – but then at least in such a way that you have something to show for it ...

The melody comes from 'Sarema' – the text runs:

> And with his arms he pressed me firmly to him ... [But not the way they wanted.][10]

On that fateful evening I played it (he didn't know that I possessed a copy), thus establishing a point of contact that nobody else could understand. The postcard uses the same ploy ...

He should never have sent that card! ...

Wednesday 1 May

Moved out. – Mie fetched me in the morning. I bade farewell to the house where I'd spent my finest – and saddest hours. Actually it wasn't as hard as I'd expected.

At Mie's, I found Z.'s letter waiting for me. – Composed.

In the afternoon: went for a walk, high tea in town.

In the evening: composed.

Thursday 2 May

Once again, Z. didn't show up. Anticipation and frustration are making me ill – physically ill!

He came – a little later. He's so dear – so dear ...

I hauled him into the smoking-room – an ideal place for lovers. We fell into each others' arms. |Kissed the living daylights out of each other ... I sank down, he on top of me.| With an *insane* jolt I pushed him away. He asked:

> Why?

He knew exactly why. And he said:

> It's the first time that a girl hasn't staled on me. Even when I'm with you, I long for you ...

I longed for him too – if only he knew how much. He'd brought a letter with him. I've just answered it.

Mie invited him to stay for dinner. He's so witty, so intelligent. Brought the Hofmannsthal scenario with him. Read it to me. It's terrifically poetic.[11]

10 From *Sarema*, act I/ii. The significance of A.M.-W.'s remark is unclear.
11 At this point a page of manuscript is probably missing.

Saturday 4 May

Never have I had less idea how I should behave. – I keep asking myself how such a passionate affair as this last could die so swiftly, how it is that it can't even survive a few scornful remarks. Yesterday B. said:

For heaven's sake *don't marry* Z. Don't corrupt *good* race . . .

Somewhere that rang a bell. He's right – my body is ten times too beautiful for his. That his soul is a hundred times too beautiful for mine – that didn't occur to me. And now, too, my letter is calculated, not heartfelt. I asked Uncle Hugo:

How would you react if I were to marry Z.?

That would be pure Krafft-Ebing.[12] A cold-bath cure.

|He could only imagine that I was joking.|[13]

Friday 17 May

p.m. in the Prater. Sent Z. – I mean Alex – my song. –

Supper in the Prater. Have rarely felt sadder than now. Once before, when we were leaving for Italy . . . I can't stop thinking about my beloved Alex. Does he miss me too? I cling to him with my whole being. I hope and pray that it will stay that way. – I want to live for him. That's my only wish. How sweet he was yesterday – *uniquely* sweet. We were sitting interlocked, my knees between his. He pressed me hard – hard – kissed my thighs. *There's* a man you can't forget, once you've possessed him . . .

Saturday 18 May

7:00 a.m. departure – at the station Ernst, Mama Moll, Spitzer, Hugo and Krasny. The latter had reserved a compartment for us, and accompanied us as far as Hallein. He kissed my hands over and over. – All day my thoughts were of Alex.

Changed trains at 3:00 in Ischl. The following exchange took place:

Mama: I know you were *very* annoyed with me about 'Tristan'. I had no choice. It's come to my notice that Z. is in love with you. I wanted to prevent you from being *alone* together . . . That will lead nowhere. You are not the person to make sacrifices – nor is he. On a diet of

12 The German neuropsychiatrist Richard von Krafft-Ebing, a pioneer of sexual psychopathology and author of *Psychopathia Sexualis* (1886).

13 At this point several pages are missing, presumably removed by A.M.-W.. During the intervening days, A.S. established with Zemlinsky the personal (du) form of address; from now on she refers to him as 'Alex'. From Zemlinsky's letters, it transpires that he and A.S. attended a performance of *Tristan und Isolde* (on 15 May 1901), during the course of which there were moments of considerable intimacy.

bread and water even the strongest love perishes. I have nothing against him – but he should at least have a *few* groats to his name.
I remained silent and said to myself: all in good time.
In the evening: St Gilgen. The villa is delightful – right by the lake. –

Sunday 19 May

It's lovely here. Snow on the mountain-tops, blossom in the valley. This morning I went to the post office to find out about the poste restante. I chose the number 1003. I long for a letter from him . . . My dearest beloved.
Then I went to Ratz and took a look at B.'s boat – terrific!
Then home – to write. My whole existence was centred around him and his being – and now I'm already beginning to feel the emptiness. – Lord knows what the summer will bring.

Tuesday 21 May

It's wondrously beautiful here. I feel that I don't <u>deserve</u> so much beauty. –
Scent over the water. The purity of nature. No strangers, no intruders. –
p.m. piano delivered. Worked a bit. Then into the woods with Mama to look for lily of the valley. It was uniquely beautiful. Fields of blue forget-me-not . . .

Wednesday 22 May

p.m. to Ischl. Fetched Mie. She said she'd spoken to Klimt about me (he's painting her portrait).[14] He spoke often of me, asked if I was still contemplating marriage. Said I would have a hard time of it . . . etc. etc. The conversation – highly interesting . . .
Mie travelled with Mitzi Fischer, who said:
> Is it really true that Alma's going to marry that hideous little musician? That would be dreadful! –

What people! – What business is it of theirs? People who live in glass houses . . .

[Read and abbreviated A.M.-W.]

14 Klimt's *Portrait of Marie Henneberg* (Plate 15), today at the Staatliche Galerie Moritzburg in Halle.

Suite 23

Thursday 23 May
A bad start![1]
This morning I composed with a will. Then to the post office, to see whether a letter had arrived. I took it, bursting with joy. It made me unspeakably sad. I answered at once.
p.m. walked to Fürberg – with Mie. I didn't speak a word the whole way. Just couldn't. All my pleasure is gone – my zeal partly too. I started on a book by Hofmannsthal, by the way – but with little enthusiasm.

Saturday 25 May
Burckhard. Sailing with him all day – wind and waves fairly rough. Didn't think of Alex *for one second*. If he doesn't want me *the way I am*, with all my faults, he can do without . . .

Thursday 30 May
Received a card from my vis-à-vis in the Höfergasse. His name is Dr Kainer. I could put it in here, by the way – with a letter from Muhr, which isn't so stupid – and none from Alex.[2]
Spent the afternoon at Aunt Mie's. Naturally, the conversation turned to marriage. She said she wished a famous artist for me, but also someone with heart and soul.

Aunt Mie, you'll have to look yourself. I can't find anyone of the kind. We talked of Alex.

Oh dear, you can't marry *him*. He's a Bohemian, you wouldn't feel the rift until you were married. He's still a nobody, and that won't change for some time yet, because he's so stubborn. As his wife, that's what you'd constantly have to put up with.

1 ▷ Letter from Zemlinsky, discussing the question of his alleged ugliness: 'Your letter has brought something out in me that I have long been suppressing and often wanted to get off my chest. My dearest, often – as often as you can – you stress how pathetically small I am and how little I possess, how much about me is unworthy of you!'
2 ▶ Letter from Muhr.

You're wrong, I said, nobody is easier to manage than he.

No, no, Alma. He's not for you.

And so I went home.

Almost nobody I know means so well for me as Mie, and even she is trying to dissuade me, not with common arguments such as:

He's too poor. He's too ugly.

but:

Your outlooks and opinions differ from his.

You move in completely different circles.

He's a Bohemian – the gap can *never* be bridged.

All the fighting has turned him sour . . .

It's all running through my head – but also:

He loves me – I love him.

He will educate me, raise me to his level – and I will educate him – raise him to my level.

That woman has a remarkable talent for hitting the nail on the head . . .

Tuesday 4 June[3]

One thing pleased me: I kissed O. and didn't feel a thing. When I dream of Alex's kisses, it's a different matter altogether. I write to him often, think of him often.

Don't find much time for writing my diary . . .

How I long for him. Sometimes I lay my head between my arms on the table and think about us for hours at a time . . . I must say, I can't imagine giving myself to anyone but him.

– Not even Klimt!!

Friday 7 June

Worked, reread his last letter, thought of him, longed for him . . . And one day is much like the next. There are bright days, on which I receive his dear letters, dark ones, on which his letters are not so dear, and the indifferent ones, nameless – grey days, on which I hear nothing from him.

Monday 10 June

Sent Alex my half an act – I fear the worst.[4] Does Monday set the tone for the week? –

---

3 One page missing from the manuscript (3 June and part of 4 June). Where the text resumes, A.S. is evidently recounting a dream.

4 A.S.'s setting of an operatic scene. In his accompanying letter, Zemlinsky describes the text

p.m. climbed the face of the Falkenstein.

In the evening: Pollack. He will stay as long as he can stand it. He told me that Hancke *really* loves me & is fearfully unhappy. For all I care . . . ! I'm not happy either! –

Tuesday 11 June

Received a letter from Muhr with a *wonderful* autograph letter of Wagner's. My first reaction was to return the gift and call the whole thing off. Mie agreed. I wrote to him – showed Mama the letter. I really can sense *how* kind he is. Talked it over with Pollack, & suddenly he had divined my secret. He was appalled. –

For heaven's sake – not Z.?

Isn't it strange how *all* my friends are trying to *dis*suade me. – Just let them. Carl asked:

You mean Z.?

Yes, I replied, I would far rather marry him than Muhr.

All through lunch – talk, talk, talk! My aesthetic feelings – the *first* kiss would make me sick. He's so poor, has nothing to his name! And Lord knows what else.[5]

Thursday 13 June

At 6:00 p.m. Gretl arrived. I was entirely calm. Gradually I warmed to her. She sensed it . . . had brought Zola's 'Le débâcle' with her. Advised me against getting married. Her facial expression has changed, and physically she's changed too. – She's been very ill!

Friday 14 June

This morning: my manuscript from Alex. – My work is a complete failure.[6] Today I keep telling myself: why must I be blessed with this little bit of talent? Why can't I be *nothing* but the woman in his life. [?] – *His* wife [?] – and only that! [?] But like this I feel called to higher things that I shall *never* attain. [?]

Pollack, Gretl and I today discussed both affairs – Muhr and Zemlinsky.

---

as 'a long dialogue, with nothing particularly dramatic, also nothing lyric about it'. Judging by his description, this was probably the scene between Dianora and the Nurse in Hofmannsthal's *Die Frau im Fenster* (published in 1898).

5 ▶ Letter from Muhr.

6 Zemlinsky's accompanying letter includes what amounts to a beginner's guide to operatic form and structure.

Both dissuaded me . . . & when I think that my heart could ever hesitate!
And on the other hand . . . I haven't posted the letter yet . . .

Saturday 15 June
Pollack & Gretl are plaguing my conscience, & they aren't entirely wrong.
Alex needs a devoted *woman about the house*. Can I be that for him? I have
the choice: to be Alex's wife – just that – with financial restrictions and
a neurotic husband who disdains my music. Or to be Muhr's wife – a life
of luxury, respected, honoured, loved, spoiled. But – Alex I love, and,
I believe, steadfastly. Muhr doesn't mean a fig to me. What should I do? I
have *nobody* who sees things objectively. They all laugh about Alex being
small and ugly . . . and that's enough for me. Pollack, for instance, who
said:
> The first time you kiss Z., you'll be terribly disappointed. –
I just laughed. His first kiss – how beautiful it was!

Sunday 16 June
Today: this postcard.[7] Yes, Olbrich I'd take on the spot. There's a fellow for
you. Incidentally, I don't look well. The affair is troubling me *greatly* . . .
Pollack has left. He advised me to marry Muhr on trial . . . Methinks that
wouldn't be so foolish – and then divorce him and return to Alex with
plenty of money.

Monday 17 June
Mie has just left. She said:
> Alma, you don't look well – your eyes are red-rimmed.
> That comes from all the clandestine letter-writing.
> The time will come when you remember my words.
> I do remember them, I replied.
> Yes, but – be careful with letters. They're evidence that can be used
> against you.
My heart missed a beat. I'd *never* thought of *that*. My candid declarations
of love, dragged into public display . . . Alex would *never* do that. He's a
high-minded artist! – But then . . . The danger is there. And I'm so dam-
nably frank . . .
Today I wrote to Muhr – neither accepting nor rejecting him . . . I shall end
by falling between two stools and landing in a heap – that will be my fate. If
only I could fuse those two men into . . . one single one.

7 ▷ Postcard from Olbrich in Darmstadt.

Gretl felt sorry for both of us. She told me that Alex was far too weak for me, that he would be unable to give me satisfaction. She made a comparison with a water-glass & a finger. I feel warmly about Alex – the ill-feeling of the last days has dispersed. Once again, I want to be his! Lord of heaven, help me out of this labyrinth . . .

Friday 21 June
I'm not allowed to compose or play. Every sound irritates Gretl – so here I sit, with tears in my eyes. Muhr writes: my negative reply has perturbed him. I should remember that nobody is rushing me, that we have time on our side, that I should think things over carefully . . .
Never before have I been so rudely thrust off my calm, secure path. I find Muhr perfectly sympathetic [no longer], but Alex I *love*! I don't love him as fervently as last spring – but still warmly. I keep asking myself: with Alex, will something become of me, or shall I be engulfed in petty domestic troubles? Then again: for me Alex is immensely stimulating, Muhr not *in the least*. What use is money, comfort etc., which only makes you lethargic and dull-witted, when there's not a hint of stimulation? *Never* before have I had to grapple with such an intractable problem . . .
I can & will not go on living at home! I too want to *live*!
I wasn't allowed into my room all day. Gretl couldn't stand the sound of the piano. I was like a dog without a master. Went cycling, rowing – in the end I howled all evening. To crown it all, Mama told Gretl that she wouldn't let Alex come to our house any more. *Just* let her! – Then I'll go to him! – That will be the moment where defiance sets in, the thin end of the wedge! Instead of sitting here contemplating, brooding & despairing, the matter would be settled once and for all. Then I would say: Alex – or nothing! But I was deeply affected all the same. My eyes filled with tears – and I cried all evening.
When Carl (who has a cold) had gone to bed, the three of us talked things over more critically. I told Mama she should leave *me* to choose, judge and act. In plain language: not to meddle in my affairs. She replied that she would never give her consent. Good – bene! Then it's up to *me*. It *all* just serves to draw me closer to Alex! My dear – poor friend!

Friday 28 June–Thursday 4 July
Darmstadt – and Olbrich!
Monday. 7:00 a.m. departure – Carl and I. 12:00 arrival in Munich. Herterich at the station. Lunch with him. His wife: pretty but insipid.

International exhibition: whistle-stop tour. A few good pictures: Hodler, Bergh etc. This time, Stuck is fine. Hölzel and his wife came over from Dachau to meet us.

4:00 departure – 12:30 a.m. arrival in Frankfurt. {Hotel} Frankfurter Hof.

Tuesday. Up early. Goethe's house – unmoved. Posh house, aristocratic. Sightseeing tour of Nizza. The city elegant, prosperous. The banks of the Main terrifically picturesque, colourful. Carl called on Frau Spier, a friend of Papa's. She came with us, just for our sake.

10:00: to Darmstadt. Olbrich at the station. Dressed in white – dandy. *Not* to my liking. His achievements are remarkable. His own house, the Ernst-Ludwig-Haus, several others – Glückert, Habich.[8] Behrens too, who has built his own – fine. It's just like a music-drama: the interior and exterior of the house merge together. Not one running parallel to the other, but like a loving married couple.

Servaes is here too.

Dinner with Olbrich.

p.m. Spier.

In the evening: Herr and Frau Morawe.[9] She is Olbrich's sweetheart. He arrived with her. In the afternoon I had quietly locked myself up in one of his rooms. Was just *too* tired. He went to pack his bags. We were all at table when the two of them arrived. She is pretty but unrefined, tarty. Her husband sat there & safeguarded *his* interests – ugh!

The next day we travelled on. Already late. On arrival, this letter from Alex, which Gretl had fetched for me. A large volume of poetry: Bierbaum's 'Irrgarten der Liebe' – the poems – numbered copy on hand-made paper, parchment binding with gold lettering – *wonderful.*

Frau Spier – very sensible, intelligent – with her son, who immediately became familiar and started making advances. She told me that, when Carl called in the morning, she kept looking into the cab to see if I was a real Schindler. Papa had told her lots of things about me. He always used to say: in me he had a son and a daughter at once. He also had high hopes for my music. –

She was very sweet. At dinner she sat next to me, & we had a lively

8 In 1900–01 two houses on the Mathildenhöhe were built to Olbrich's designs for the furniture manufacturer Julius Glückert, and a further house for the sculptor Ludwig Habich, himself a member of the Darmstadt artists' colony.
9 The architect Ferdinand Morawe, an associate of Olbrich in the Darmstadt artists' colony, and his wife, Clair. They divorced in 1903.

discussion about modern literature. She's a personal friend of Bierbaum, Dehmel etc., calls Dehmel the 'burnt-out devil'. He's said to be a lecherous old beast, changes his women as often as his shirts . . . But he's scarcely capable any more – is all but past it. When Bierbaum comes to Vienna, she'll see to it that he calls on us . . . He had a blonde wife, pretty & devoted 'till death us do part'; he was also friendly with a young musician [Fried]. He invited him to his castle in Tyrol, left him in the care of his wife & went off on a short trip. On his return, he found neither wife nor friend . . .

What a pity that Frau Spier is so conspicuously Jewish . . . it hits you in the eye.

p.m. I was so exhausted by all the travelling & sightseeing that I asked Olbrich to open a room in *his* house, & sat down for a short rest. To crown it all, while still in St Gilgen I'd been bitten by a horsefly, and my leg was sore and inflamed. It was no joke!

I bumped into Servaes, and we sat together in Olbrich's anteroom & discussed our impressions in a pleasant, objective manner. The view over the entire colony was really beautiful.

I sent postcards to Alex & Burckhard. Then we met up with the others & strolled – limped – from one house to the next . . . until dinner time. I must say: the way Olbrich made his entrance with Frau Morawe, as if it were a matter of course, momentarily took my breath away. He noticed it. But I talked cheerfully & gaily with Servaes & Frau Spier, and scarcely looked his way. Olbrich thought me irritable. My neighbours contradicted him vigorously . . . Not I! –

He asked me to play, and I said:

My word of honour: this evening I shan't play a note.

He smiled . . . This morning, by the way, I'd played a few bars on a piano he's had made to his specifications. But in front of his sweetheart – no!

Incidentally, he paid for her meal, gave her morsels off his fork, behaved as if he was her husband. Now and then she nodded cheerfully across to her spouse.

They both accompanied O. to the station. He gave her a voluptuous look. He was very excited, forgot to carry his bags into the compartment, forgot his tickets, forgot everything around him. Then he blamed it all on his artistic temperament . . .

I *know* him! –

The journey was appalling. I was supposed to share a sleeping-car with two women and two children. Was forced to, despite bitter complaints. Slept only two hours, couldn't get to sleep: O.'s ideas droned on like Wagnerian leitmotifs. Otherwise I felt calm and unmoved about everything I'd seen & heard. I also *didn't* think about Alex. –

I got up at 5:00, sat down in the corridor and worked on a little song.

We reached Munich at 7:00 and had breakfast together. Carl called on the Loews in their hotel, while O. and I waited for some time in the reading room. We talked about all sorts of things. But not as we used to do. Much stands between us. He spoke of his former colleagues with a supercilious smile. – He was offended by my letter of refusal last winter. Particularly when I wrote that I would, if he wished, recommend songs by younger composers. That annoyed the arrogant fellow.

In Munich, with him and the Loews, we visited the Crystal Palace – this time with more leisure. Then with Carl to

Franz Stuck

I'm really *glad* that I went. He made a lasting impression on me. The house[10] – his living quarters – partly genuine antique, partly in his own imitation antique style. – He received us in the studio. He's tall, with fiery black eyes and an air of powerful benevolence. He showed us his current work: a portrait of himself and his wife or, shall we say, of the Master and Frau Stuck! – Then he led us to his living quarters. His little white dog accompanied us. The living-room – or rather the reception room – has golden mosaics, bright red curtains & pictures set into the walls. The effect is wonderfully elegant, colourful – & rich. I told him:

One has the impression that only a Stuck can live here.

He found this was as it should be. – The library – wonderful tapestries etc., carved Japanese wooden chests – comfortable yet magnificent, aristocratic. The dining-room & a smaller living-room – all in the same style. Colour, colour everywhere – but refined nevertheless. Large, iridescent green butterflies in vitrines. Gold – lots of gold – black & white mosaics. – Splendour. And in the midst of it all, this fellow with a bull-neck & the keen eye of a Siegfried.

What virility!

He spoke with awe of Klimt. He would dearly have liked to purchase his 'Judith'. He led us into the garden, which is laid out in arcades. Busts mounted on pedestals, everywhere vines & blue clematis. In the room with the grand piano, Stuck more or less

10 The Villa Stuck, on the Prinzregentenstrasse, serves today as a museum specializing in exhibitions of *Art nouveau*. Much of Stuck's original decor is still preserved.

invited me to play. He said it had a good tone, & rattled the lid. I refused. Now I regret it. To be able to play for such a man is an honour.
In his studio he has

> PHIDIAS
> TITIAN &
> MICHELANGELO

and a fourth, whose name I've forgotten.
At 12:30 lunch with O. at Loews'. Champagne – lots of champagne. Then we took our leave of O. He held my hand for a long, long time & looked into my eyes. He also volunteered that he would come {to Vienna} in the autumn, which I *simply* don't believe. And then he was gone . . .
– Go! –
Carl & I went to the station and, as soon as the train moved off, we fell asleep. Our relationship is curiously asexual. I was tired, & he said I should rest my head on his shoulder. I did so, & it felt something like an old woman's – complete equanimity.
At the station in Salzburg: <u>Spitzer</u> & <u>Gound</u>. Back home: Willy & Martha {Nepalleck}, but they left this afternoon.
As I said – on arrival I found the wonderful book & the letter. I was very pleased.
When I speak of the trip, then only of STUCK. O., by comparison, is insignificant. He rejects Stuck, finds him coarse & brutal. But he – O. – is <u>too</u> elegant, <u>too French</u>. If I were to make a comparison, then – Chopin . . . And Stuck . . . ?

Wednesday 10 July
Worked – with inspiration.
p.m. in the menagerie. Poor, strolling players with a few beautiful animals. A tame panther, a tame boa constrictor, all kinds of apes, sand foxes, armadillos etc. Carl bought meat & gave them money. They were unbelievably grateful. Poor devils.
Then with Mie by boat to Ravensbrood Bay. On the way home we discussed Alex again. She *simply* can't believe that I love him, spoke denigratingly of him. But I do love him! – My marriage plans shocked her to the core. She can't hurt my love. There are many obstacles to the marriage. I'd like to convince him of it bit by bit, so that *he* can tell me. – I can and will not lose him!

Sunday 14 July
Lunch with Burckhard. Trout – punch bowl – pineapple etc. Acute brain-fever – fuddled, but in moderation. Just to annoy B., I drank a toast of brotherhood with Kutschera.
In the evening: rowing. Great fun.
B. is a person of whom you have to be *very* wary. I like him ever so much – but calmly. But Alex too: I feel sorry for him.
And now, a few hours later, my heart is filled with love for him. What kind of girl am I? – My thoughts are with him constantly, and so intensively that I can't even work. Right now, I feel that living with him would for me be the very essence of happiness. Yet at this very moment he may perhaps be reading my nasty letter. – I've written to him again, & I'd like to write time after time, talk to him, tell him *everything* that's on my mind. Today I feel once more what he means to me: it's more than just <u>physical</u> <u>love</u>. I love the tiniest hair on his body just as much as his greatest thought. – I love *everything* about him, infinitely. I long for him to clasp my hand, to kiss me, to be near me, I long for his whole being.
My dear, *poor* Alex, a simple country girl deserves you more than I do.
Yesterday, at table, they were all poking fun at him again. His diminutive stature, his chin, everything. And yet he's *a hundred* times taller than *all* of them. I'd marry him just to show these people what he is, how dear and handsome he really is.

Tuesday 16 July
This morning: 'Lobetanz' from Dr Pollack. I was overjoyed. Played it through right away. The music is so tender and warm.
At midday: Burckhard, who came with sugar-candy. Later he tried to stroke my face.
Calmly but firmly, I moved his hand away.
No, my Alex – I remain true to you!
Then I played him the most attractive passages from 'Lobetanz'. Mama had to sing along too.
All day I didn't think for a moment of Alex. As far as I'm concerned, it's over. I can feel *nothing* more for him, nothing at all. We would *certainly* have been happy together. How is he going to answer my letter? He'll be furious! –
Went for a stroll in the evening, and met Minister Rezek with wife and daughters. Spoke to him.

Friday 19 July

At 7:00 a.m. with two boats (Hennebergs, B. and us) to Wolfgang. From there on foot to the Schwarzensee for a rendezvous with the Kutscheras. Picnic de luxe. Then siesta. Kutschera wanted à tout prix to claim his kiss of brotherhood. While the others were sleeping and B. was climbing a nearby mountain, we wrestled silently on the ground. Then down the narrow gorge to Unterach. The outing was great fun – spirited, merry. In the evening: dead tired.

Monday 22 July

B. had ordered caviar, sardines, goose-liver, aspic etc. He prepared debardeurs, which we had for lunch, washed down with Asti. Mama brought a wonderful pineapple. A gourmet meal – outrageous. He knows what he's about!

High tea at Rudolf's. I went sailing with B. But first to the doctor, who diagnosed apical pneumonia. The weather grew stormy, & I demanded that we return to shore. B. called me a cowardly hussy. That hurt. I paid him back today, and now he's angry. What do I care. –

Today, while sozzled, I caught myself running my eyes lustfully over his loins. Oh so lustfully . . .

Tuesday 23 July

Mama & Carl in Salzburg. I stayed home.

Around midday: Burckhard. We were sitting in the little room, examining a bicycle which the local repair-shop (an agent of Styria Cycles) had offered me for 60 fl in part-exchange for my present bike. So there we sat – when suddenly he takes my left hand, kisses it, strokes it, puts his hand in my lap, strokes my knee, kisses it, strokes my face, strokes my legs – from under my skirt down to the knees, then back up again. It felt wonderfully tender & pleasurable. Resisting only gently, I just let it happen. But suddenly I felt:

    Enough. –

Gently but firmly I took his hands away & placed them in his lap. All the same, I would have given anything for him to kiss me – & more . . . I was consumed with desire.

Later I was eating on the balcony, he was watching. I wouldn't let him touch my face.

Alex – what if you knew! He must *never* get to hear of this. But it was *so* lovely. The man really knows how to create an atmosphere – I felt so snug and weak-kneed.

And now I feel: even *then*, when I was lying on the sofa with Alex |and I could feel his male member hardening – even then I wasn't as excited.| Alex is right . . . me too! To burn with desire and yet feel so unsullied – that only happens *once* in a lifetime.

It's so strange. B. – as a person – leaves me *completely* cold, but my desire – my cursed, churned-up desire – seethes and boils over.

And Alex? My soul reaches out for him, just as my body. I love him truly. Full of desire, yet chaste. Yes, a thousand times yes. You, my angel. And this abominable seducer, who's only interested in my sweet face & my ample curves, did I *for one moment* give him my body?

– Shame on me –

I'm disgusted with myself. And he takes no blame at all . . . It was *I* that let it happen. I, who belong to Alex. My poor dear. Don't follow my example. I shudder at the very thought.

The funny thing is that Alex also stroked my knees, kissed my thighs – & I found nothing dishonourable in it. On the contrary, it aroused me. |I gave him my tongue – let him feel me all over.| For me it was a matter of course. But now, today, I'm shattered. A curse on B. and his eyes (at the time |his eyes were shining like a wild animal's|) & his exploring hands. A curse on me and my sensual temperament, *on the whole affair*. Forgive me, Alex – I rented out your house to a lodger. *Your house.* I long for *your* kisses, [Alex], for *your* embrace.

Wilhelm just looked by – complained that Mama & Carl weren't giving him enough money. I placated him as best I could. Blamed it on his rebellious behaviour.

Then came Mie & Hugo. She was a little cool, and I told her as much. She replied:

>   I've lost my faith in you. You must restore it . . .

She deprecates the *best* of me. She would deprive me of my love for Alex, *my all*, would alienate me from my most beautiful, most wondrous, purest thoughts and desires. I laughed out loud & said:

>   Flirt? Me a flirt?

[But that's not what she meant!]

How disgusting!

This evening, in pouring rain, Burckhard came to my window, soaked to the skin. I spoke to him, but was too exhausted to feel any resentment. Once he'd gone, I returned to the piano, but with little enthusiasm.

Wednesday 24 July

Gretl, Wilhelm & I went for a walk – B. followed. Later he saw me home. We were alone . . . he started making advances. I staved him off firmly and sat down on the window-sill. Told him that his eyes were calculating, evil-minded & gross. That he found unforgivable.

> I'd rather not read the expression in *your* eyes. They might reveal something far worse {he said}.

He wanted to go. I held him back.

> No, I said, you must justify yourself!

He said I had changed. He's not entirely wrong. A kiss – nothing against that – but as for running his hands all over my body!! And I – offered no resistance! I added that it was neither flirtatiousness on my part nor calculation, merely a passing whim.

> You mean – at the time, you wouldn't have *cared* who it was?

I don't love him and never shall. But I find his physical presence enthralling. I made eyes at him, let him hold my hand longer than necessary. In short, the implicit message was: come closer. And now that he's come closer, I'm saying: go to the devil. I'm really very sorry – I can only repeat that over and over.

Why am I so boundlessly licentious?

I *long* for *rape*! – Whoever it might be.

Saturday 28 July

I wrote to Alex to say that I might be coming to see him in Ischl. I'm so happy, I can hardly think straight. To see him again – my protector! I long for his pure embrace – only then shall I feel human again. My longing is unbounded. I believe he's the only man I can ever love, that I ever loved. My love for Kl. was a thin gruel compared to the thick broth of my present feelings. If it weren't for all the others – all those smart, pernicious, conventional people – I would already be his wife. But like this, it's conceivable that they'll keep on bombarding me with common-sense reasons until I lose myself – which would mean losing Alex as well.

p.m. My feelings for him are stronger than ever. I have never loved him more – *never*. I would love him even more – freer, less inhibitedly – if that ominous word 'marriage' were not beckoning from afar. For the idea of marrying him, of bearing his children – little, degenerate Jew-kids . . . On the other hand, I would be perpetuating his name. I love the word 'Zemlinsky'.

This morning Burckhard dropped in and asked me to let him read from the novel he's writing. He wanted an opinion – and my encouragement. The idea is to tell the life-story of a man who attends the cathedral school at Kremsmünster, loses his reputation through the perfidy of his colleagues, goes out into the world, experiences betrayal and infamy, returns to the monastery and takes holy orders – well aware that the clergy is no better or worse than the laity, but that a life dedicated to good can best help him overcome his anguish.

The idea is not new. There's {Bierbaum's} 'Stilpe' – a novel about a boy's development to manhood – and Zola's 'Rome', the story of a priest who so detests his fellow priests that he leaves the church. Well – that's part I.

I encouraged him to finish the story. Although it's full of detail, it has a good flow and is finely observed. It took him almost all morning. We were sitting in the boat, and he was reading swiftly & with a flat voice. I'd like him to do something creative again. It would raise him up. Last winter I discovered how wonderful it can be to *really* learn something. How much more wonderful is true *creativity*.

That's what I long for.

Towards evening I noticed to my surprise that I couldn't take my eyes off the bulge in B.'s trousers. My sensuality knows no bounds. I simply *must* get married. It would be much nicer without the institution of marriage. A wedding coram publico is something frightful. A thing of wonder, reduced to the banal – how hideous, how base. –

Monday 29 July
Yesterday p.m. with Gretl, B. and Wilhelm in the woods. – My hands are so swollen by insect-bites, I can scarcely write.

I shall miss B. He wants to leave tomorrow.

My God, I only hope I'll be able to meet up with Alex in Ischl. It would be wonderful. Last night I dreamt of him. I'd returned to Vienna unannounced and sought him out – with his colleagues and lady-friends – in a small inn. He came slowly towards me, kissed me casually on the mouth, as if it were a matter of course. Then he rushed off, sent me flowers – with a ribbon on which were written the words: 'Alma Maria Alexandra Schindler'. Then Mama and Carl joined us. I explained that it was a joke of 'Herr von Zemlinsky's'. They believed me, laughed.

If only I could look into the future. Oh, what nonsense! I *myself* shall shape my destiny. Only *myself*.

I'd love to know *which* of my two souls will triumph. My loving soul – or my calculating soul.

Saturday 3 August

Worked, composed with a will – a chorus for mixed voices, poem by
Gustav Falke. I don't want to lose the manuscript, so I'll pop it in here.

p.m. Muhr. I'm beginning to warm to him.

In the evening we rowed out onto the lake. We remained a long time in the
boat-house. He asked me how his chances stood.

    Fifty-fifty, I replied.

    Is the answer likely to be no?

I told him:

    At present more likely yes.

He was overjoyed, kissed my hand with warmth and passion. And it gave
me pleasure – *real pleasure.*

If I weren't in the throes of my affair with Zemlinsky, I'd take him on the
spot.

Thursday 8 August

At 6:45 to the station. Nearly missed the train. Studied the score intently.
Arrived {in Salzburg} at 8:45.

Strolled around in town. It's actually rather tedious – I thought to myself –
being so *completely* alone. Went to Café Tomaselli & ordered a Mary
Cobbler. Suddenly I was spotted by Max Lichtenstern, who came over with
Prof. Simandl. But soon they had to leave – for rehearsal.

I was on my own again. Went for a walk. Suddenly I noticed Hofrat
Wiener. I put my hands over his eyes – he was *very* pleased to see me. Asked
me when I was leaving. I answered, 'Two o'clock,' but he said that wasn't
on, and that I should travel with him at 4:00. In the end he invited me to
lunch. After some hesitation, I accepted. Then we went happily to the
concert.[11] Everyone treated us like a young couple. –

Programme:

    'Tannhäuser' overture

    Beethoven: 'Emperor' concerto

        Emil Sauer

    Haydn: Recitative & 'Winter' aria from 'The Seasons'

        Herr Klöpfer

    Mozart: Sextus' aria 'Parto, ma tu ben mio' from 'La Clemenza di Tito'

        Edyth Walker

    Beethoven: 8th Symphony

11 Salzburg Music Festival; concert with the Vienna Philharmonic Orchestra.

Conductor: Josef Hellmesberger
Orchestra: Vienna Philharmonic.

The difference between him & Mahler is incredible. Mahler commands –
Hellmesberger entreats. The players just love it. They were beaming with
pleasure. I was so starved of orchestral music that I pounced on every note
like a wild beast. The public was almost entirely Viennese – the Reimers,
Dumka etc., Epstein. Before the concert, we two wandered up and down
the university quadrangle. I saw Stecher and other musicians. Then we
walked to the hotel together, discussing how we should announce ourselves. We agreed: a friend of his wife – whom I don't even know. Bösendorfer[12] & Sauer were initially somewhat surprised at his unexpected appearance. But soon it transpired that Bösendorfer was a friend of Papa's, & that
Sauer knows Carl. I congratulated the latter on acquiring a picture by
Besnard – and so the conversation turned from the Secession to Carl. The
situation was explained. Sauer is a genuine artist, highly knowledgeable &
with a fine understanding of the visual arts. He spoke well: witty, urbane –
and without allures. His fingers are as nimble as an ape's. He can do
anything with them. When he eats chicken, he spits the skin into his hand,
then runs his fingers nimbly round his mouth to remove the fibres between
his teeth – with incredible speed. He's going to give master-classes.[13] I'm
so pleased to have met him.

Friday 9 August
Anniversary of Papa's death. Maria's birthday.
As I write these words, I feel overcome by a deep resentment of the poor
little child, even if it's not her fault that she's alive. Sad – sad. The memory
of my dear, dear Papa doesn't grieve me in the least. Since we speak of Papa
as if he were still alive, I don't feel his loss so directly. I often think of him
as if he were still amongst us. And then – even when I remind myself that I
shall never see him again, I still feel no intense pain. *Nothing* moves me.
This evening: at Mie & Hugo's.

Sunday 11 August
Hancke to lunch. Afterwards inexplicably tired – from cycling etc.
Since yesterday, my rendezvous with Alex is no longer certain. I haven't
heard any definite news from him, and today Mama suddenly decided to

12 Ludwig von Bösendorfer, proprietor of the eponymous firm of piano manufacturers, and
an influential personality in Viennese musical life.
13 Sauer led a master-class at the Vienna Conservatoire from 1901 to 1907.

drive to Ischl tomorrow. If she does, I'll have to wire Alex a last-minute cancellation. –

The strangest thing is: after so long an absence, my heart should be beating faster for him than it actually is. I feel absolutely *nothing*. If I see him – fine. If something comes between us – fine too. *A curious calm.*

Unfortunately I had to let Mie into the secret, to prevent her going along tomorrow. She said:

    You're a card!

I've no idea what tomorrow will bring. If I lose him, then I know that I shudder above all at the thought of losing a wonderful teacher. The lessons with him were a joy. It would never be possible to make amends . . . I'm such a fool!

Monday 12 August

I found this {card} this morning[14] & was actually relieved at the outcome . . . ! It took a heavy load off my mind. – I have *absolutely* no regrets. Also cards from Burckhard & Hermann Bahr.

[Corrected A.M.-W.]

---

14 ▷ Postcard from Zemlinsky in Ischl, addressed to '1003': having vainly waited for news from A.S., he cancels the planned rendezvous.

Suite 24

[!!!Mahler!!!]

Wednesday 21 August
A cycling trip was planned, but I felt unwell, & we called it off.
Wieners & Hennebergs to lunch. Riotous time. Everyone teased me
terribly about the pain in my breasts.
p.m. rowed out to Ravensbrood Bay, climbed the rocks and came
home again. Wiener & I went to the piano: Tristan act I. |Really great.|
I was photographed countless times. – The day was lovely, pleasant,
delightful.
They're so unaffected. Hugo too. But Mie . . . I've never seen her smile –
really smile. People smile less frequently than they really weep, & it's much
nicer. How poor – not to be able to laugh! Burckhard can't laugh either. I
discovered that his kisses are dishonest too . . . Maybe that's just as rare &
just as beautiful. |My Alex – how beautifully you laugh and kiss!|

Saturday 24 August
His letter. As I was reading it, my eyes filled with tears. I feel certain that
he's bored with me, at the same time I sense how *very* much I love him. He
is my second self. At the very moment when the chasm opened between us
– that's when I knew it. I've written to him – earnestly, calmly. At the end I
wrote:
       All my love is yours, my life! –
I believe this is the greatest truth I ever felt. – And yet he's thinking of
giving up my lesson-time to one of his friends. If so, I shall abandon my
studies. Let myself go – *get married*! But not |him, my one and only
beloved| – <u>no</u> – some Semitic moneybag. –
How could he possibly forget me? Just an ugly little fellow – and me, an
eminent young lady, a belle! He's a somebody – I'm a nobody. He has his
circle of admirers – I have none. He is unique – I am one of many.
There you have it.[1]
And Hancke, that idiot, couldn't suppress his unambiguous remarks – if I

1 Half a page removed from the manuscript.

so disliked the Hohe Warte, there were always ways and means of living in town. I replied:

> I've had more than one such offer: they all disgust me. I choose the lesser evil: the Hohe Warte . . .

Tuesday 27 August

Alex's dear, sweet letter. It gave me such joy. I *can't* say how much. My love for him is unbounded, my every thought is of him – my one and only beloved! –

Saturday 31 August

[My birthday] |Early this morning: to the post office. Received the letter & a delightful Ueberbrettl song – I enclose it here.[2] It gave me *so much* pleasure.|

At home: Mie, *Hugo, Burckhard*. Mie gave me a blouse, Hugo a subscription to 'Die Insel' for 1901–2. B. twelve cans – *of lobster, caviar etc. etc.* Later the vicar came with dried *cognac pastilles – cognac pralines wrapped in silver foil*. This evening they all came to dinner. Had a great time. Mie proposed a toast:

> Thank you, Anna [my mother] – for having given us Alma, the goddess.

I was in particularly high spirits. Had plenty of Asti too. Twenty-two years . . . wasted.

Sunday 1 September

At 4:30 a.m. with B. to Ischl, met up with Wieners. Cycled to Offensee – caviar – beer – beer – caviar – pineapple. A few more such trips & I'll return to Vienna a fatted calf. Cloudburst, got wet. Return was all right – Offensee quite charming.

Monday 2 September

Birthday present from B. – Middle High German classics in the original versions. Twelve volumes. I'm so pleased.

a.m. to Loew on the off-chance. Worked a little. Went for a stroll with B., and he told us all sorts of splendid things about his career as a theatre director. He said:

> I joined the Ministry by playing cards[3] – to the Burgtheater playing

---

2 Probably Zemlinsky's setting of 'Eine gantz neu Schelmweys' (Dehmel), mentioned in a letter to A.S. a few weeks earlier. The manuscript is lost.
3 Orig.: 'Preference'.

skittles. So you see, everything I've ever achieved came about through self-indulgence – drinking – gambling etc.

One thing he didn't mention was his great talent. For, *although* he tippled etc., he was still a brilliant worker. Everywhere they created special posts for him. The pity is that his great potential now lies fallow. We told him as much too – and added that the time would come when they would call him back. He answered, with blazing eyes:

Certainly not. Everyone knows me now, knows that I'm a rabid Social Democrat, that my attitude towards everything connected with government and the clergy is destructive ... That's the last thing they'd do ...

The man has more to him than meets the eye. –

Thursday 5 September
p.m. with B. Heidsieck etc. Much talk about my future plans. – He advised me simply to study & thus establish my independence, not to contemplate marrying for love but without money, nor for money but without love, as a) is impractical and b) disgusting. How right he is. –
I prefer not to think about the future at all. – Basta! –

Tuesday 10 September
B. has left. *I feel nothing* for him – my thoughts are always |of Alex| & why he hasn't written for ten days. Is he angry or – [is there some truth which he suspects?]
I don't know what to think. Haven't a clue what's up with him.
p.m. went walking with Mie.

Sunday 14 September
Yesterday Reininghaus made me a very strange proposition. He asked me to visit him next winter in his apartment – on my own – for a super-fine champagne dinner. I said no. – He said he found me blasé. If it were Alex – yes, but Reininghaus! To compromise myself & gain nothing from it – not on your life.
Alex hasn't written for fourteen days now. I simply can't understand why. Doesn't he feel the longing to write to me? – I consider him moody & fickle. But I still don't understand it. I'm beginning to wonder whether my character is mature enough for him, as it once was and as I now fondly hope.
Last night I dreamt of him. He was angry – but wouldn't tell me why. His

parents (his father was still alive) were really sweet to me. I'd called on them with Carl. They were living in Gmunden. A flood was expected. In the afternoon, Alex went off & left me with his parents. When we left, he didn't even come to the station.

What does that mean? – If only I had some notion of how I should shape my future!

p.m. at Vilma Robicsek's. Had a nice long talk on many topics. She's a hero.

Sunday 15 September
This evening Gretl popped over to Vilma's.

For me, our conversation yesterday afternoon was a great event. She has *high hopes* for me, for my future. She found that in one year I'd matured considerably. –

Suffering ripens –
Joy ripens.

She said I had a harder burden to bear than others – that it's an encumbrance to be saddled with the heritage of so famous a father. – I wasn't entirely honest: I, of all people, spoke of lust dismissively. Yet I'm a lustful person, indeed very much so.

p.m. in Wolfgang with Mie etc.

This evening: an earnest discussion with Mama. About Alex too. She said categorically that she would *never* let me visit him at home again. – Yet I'd been so looking forward to it. She told me to be sensible, that one can't marry a man like him. Yet I'd been in the most boisterous mood all day, because he'd sent me another letter! Isn't it crazy not to love someone just because they're ugly, a man in whose arms I've tasted the *very highest* of pleasures? For whom I chafe, tremble & yearn!?

Absolutely crazy!

I just want to be a woman – pure woman. Live and die in his arms . . . and now we're talking about reducing him to a mere friend. –

I love him. Mama feels it, knows it. She knows *everything*. Maybe – if he wants me – I shall marry him after all. Money is well and good – but nothing compared with love! I love him so *utterly and completely*. I *cannot* contemplate us being just good friends again. He is my lover, and so it must remain.

Mama won't let me enter his house any more – and that means the world to me. How *beautiful* it was. –

Monday 16 September
Composed – rondo completed.

Tuesday 17 September
a.m. letter from Alex. Tender & passionate again, at last. I feel that he is a piece of my life. My thoughts are with him always. –
p.m. at Rotballer's, who called on us in the morning – in Fürberg – with Restranek. We played a delightful game of dice.⁴ I amused myself – something *different* for once . . .
This evening, although unwell, {cycled} almost as far as Fürberg. With Mama, as Mie wasn't around. She blamed it on missing a train.

Thursday 19 September
Mama has written to Alex. She said:
> Let me tell you this: only as long as you behave correctly & sensibly. As
> soon as you two start whispering, exchanging glances etc., it's all over.
How is that going to work? It will be like talking to a stranger – and I love him so. We'll have to be very wary. Except when we're *completely* alone, then not. –
I long for him so – I can scarcely say how much. |All my senses cry out for him.| And I let B. kiss me?! To be quite honest: I don't blame myself *in the least*! Even if I had let Muhr kiss me! [Ugh!] – That's how I am. Nobody has any kind of *right* to me. Not even my Alex. I can betray him whenever I want to – my poor dear! But he doesn't really believe in me. As far as *that* is concerned – *he knows me only too well*!
I'd like to know if it would be *very* foolish to marry him . . . At least I'd know for two days what happiness really is. [?A.M.-W.] To be his, methinks, would be bliss. [?A.M.-W.] Whenever I read anything erotic, I always think of Alex. I love him so. If only I can manage to bluff my way through the winter – <u>then</u> I'd have time to think it all over. Maybe by then everything will have changed. –
Chi lo sa! –

Tuesday 24 September
I've just been watching two flies copulating. They were so still & so imperturbable. Now & then a shiver ran through their wings. I blew at them – they flew off lethargically, the one with the other, & resumed their activity a little further away. How I envied them. The breath of the world

4 Orig.: 'Kreuzerlschupfen'.

caressed me. How could anyone find that offensive? The flow of the one into the other – I find it beautiful, *wondrously* beautiful. How I long for it. Alex, my Alex, let me be your font. Fill me with your holy fluid.

It will *never* come to that. And there is *nobody* on this earth that I love more than he. –

Leaving here will be *terribly* hard. I feel death closing in on me.

Wednesday 25 September
The first night on the Hohe Warte.[5]

I cried in the train – couldn't stop myself. The house is really nice – it would be even nicer if it were closer to the city centre.

Alex's letter made me very sad. Even I don't know why. It's written so <u>heartlessly</u> – <u>unlovingly</u>.

Thursday 26 September
Just about *finished* my room. – It's white and pale green. The central attraction is a big bookshelf, which I shall never in my life be able to fill. At present I feel *nothing* at all, neither joy nor sorrow.

For the time being I *shan't* be writing to Alex. –

Tuesday 1 October
My dear Alex – my thoughts are constantly with you. If only I could see you. I've been in Vienna almost a week – & still haven't seen him. And we *never* even meet by chance! I long for him unceasingly. I've thought of everything . . . I'm not even allowed to go alone to concerts any more . . . & that was my greatest joy.

Thursday 3 October
Yesterday evening: Pollack, Krasny. This morning: Burckhard. Letter from Zemlinsky.

Zemlinsky can't come today, has a dress rehearsal.[6] I'd asked him to come out to the Robicseks'. It would have given me untold pleasure.

---

5 The Molls had moved into their new, semi-detached villa (XIX., Steinfeldgasse 8, cf. Plate 14). Their new neighbours were Koloman Moser, Victor Spitzer and the Hennebergs.
6 On 4 October 1901 Zemlinsky conducted the première of Alfred Zamara's operetta *Die Debütantin* at the Carltheater.

p.m. I'm not so sure if I would have been so pleased. One thing is certain: his cancellation didn't *really* put me out *at all*. I went to Robicsek to get a tooth capped. I'll probably have to wear the temporary bridge for a fortnight. I feel as if there's a hole in my mouth.

This afternoon: Moser came up again. Carl was as pleased as punch about the exhibition in the Gartenbau – wanted to visit it with Moser. But when the latter <u>didn't want to accompany him</u>, Carl stayed home too. That's typical of his wretched relationship to Moser.

Friday 4 October
Couldn't get Alex's picture out of my head all morning. I love him with all my soul. I long for him endlessly. His face, his eyes, his mouth, his hands – everything. |How I'd love to kiss him – suffocate on his kisses!|

Saturday 5 October
Spent the morning with Bertha Kunz. We drove out with Sewald for breakfast – I made a few embarrassing remarks – |and was rewarded with a well-deserved round of derisive laughter.|

Now I'm standing here waiting for *my* Alex. And he won't be able to come . . .

My Alex did come – Alex my sweet. I opened the gate, led him up to the room. Our kisses were less wild but more tender than in the spring. We stared into each other's eyes, held hands. He found me changed, couldn't say why. He could only stay a little while, had missed a train and had to conduct in the evening. He <u>didn't</u> give me a lesson . . . At parting, we kissed so hard that I had the feeling I was melting! My body became unbelievably pliant & clung to his. |My longing for him – for his embrace – knows no bounds.| I love him more than I can say. And his eyes – those dear, sweet eyes. –

Sunday 6 October
Spent the whole day in Franz-Josephs-Land with Burckhard. The cab was waiting for me. He gave me a wonderful bunch of roses. Then down to the house. For a moment we were alone. He kissed me |wildly & with his tongue.| I let it happen . . . It seemed to me like desecrating a temple . . .

Heidsieck etc. had the desired effect – we became merry. Very merry.

He spent the evening at home with us. He asked if he could come again during the week. I said, 'Well . . .', in a downright impudent tone of voice. I don't know – all of a sudden I found him so dreadfully <u>tedious</u>. –

I went up to my room. My first thought: Alex. It's no ordinary carnal desire – I *really* love him. I long for him … I would give him everything – *everything*!

Monday 7 October
How long must I subsist from the last kisses |my Alex?| It's not like with Burckhard. He gives – I take, but give nothing in return: with Alex we fuse together. And then that slow separation of our lips, that unbelievable gentleness and abandon – mutually. I love him. My whole being breathes for him. I wish to be his for eternity. To be his wife, his beloved. Ever, ever with him, close to him.
I wonder if he feels the same? Does he still love me, or have I disappointed him? While I was away, he must have moved my picture. I ran my hand through his hair, he his through mine. He stroked me – on the cheek. God – how I long for him. |You my sweetheart!|
I can't work at all. I keep lowering my head and dreaming, speaking with him, |my dear master, my master!| Yes – *he* shall command me – for ever and ever. Let me be his vassal. Let him take possession of me. He is my lord and master.
When he kissed me, although he twisted my spine & pressed his body against mine, I had the sensation of something holy. A powerful, searing rite – like something God-given. Is it not so: is this not the preparatory ceremony for the holiest act, during which one feels the measure of eternity? *A drop of eternity.*
I would gladly be pregnant for him, gladly bear his children. His blood and mine, commingled: my beauty with his intellect. I would gladly serve him in his professional life, |live for him and his kith and kin, breathe {for him}, attend to his every happiness, wait on him with a gentle hand.| God give me the strength and the will-power to do so. If not, I would be committing a crime against myself. He is dearer to me than everything, everything in the world.
This evening I played 'Tannhäuser'. My technique has gone to pieces. I shall try to freshen it up. Today it sounded quite amateurish. Otherwise my thoughts are of nothing but Alex – very curious, how he *lives* in me. Morbid, really!

Tuesday 8 October
I confessed to Labor. I would never have expected that it would affect him so. His faced twisted into a grimace. He said:

Then I see no need for you to study with me any longer. –
I replied:

I'd sooner give up Z. than you –
I repeated over and over:

Only if you don't object . . .
We shook hands several times. When I was leaving, he knelt down and kissed them. I feel awfully sorry for having offended him . . . yet I'm glad the secret is out.
My Alex – *you* I could never give up.
At midday I called on Mie.
This afternoon: through town to the Karlsplatz. There was a hat I couldn't take my eyes off . . . will buy it tomorrow.
Later we entertained the Andrés, Mie & Hugo.
This evening: read through act III of the ballet (in the September edition of 'Die Insel').[7] It's unbelievably colourful and imaginative. – If he can set *that* to music, then I take my hat off!

Wednesday 9 October
In town all day – bought the hat etc. Lunch at Mie's, then waited for Alex – in vain. I'd asked him not to delay the first lesson until Friday – I'm so terribly uneasy, and the day is ruined, written off. I waited for him, and he didn't arrive. How often shall I have to write that in future?

Friday 11 October
Alex is due – I'm waiting – that says it all. Enough now. One hour of intolerable waiting. My tenderness knows no bounds – | in his hands I melt like wax. – | I love him *inexpressibly* . . .
We kissed *so* hard. I played him my summer harvest. He found that some of it was *very* fine. In some passages he even *envied* me. I want to get back to work in earnest.
He had his arm around my waist. When he got to a good bit, he stroked my back & said:

Well done.
Then he sat at the table – |embraced me, placed his whole body between my legs and pressed them hard. Our tongues sought each other.| How I love *every* part of him. Everything. He said:

7 Hofmannsthal's text for 'Der Triumph der Zeit' was published in *Die Insel*, September 1901, pp. 323–363. Although Zemlinsky had been working on the music since April 1901, he ultimately failed to reach an agreement with Hofmannsthal about the dramatic structure of act III.

It can't go on like this. What is to become of us? You are even sweeter
than last year – much more tender.
Let me be the carpet beneath his feet – carry him on my hands – be a bed
for him to lie on – soft as could be. Yes – Alex. –

Monday 14 October
Finished my chorus. Today my Alex lives in me once more – wonderfully
warm and tender. My music & my Alex – *my all*. Wanted to write a song –
the text was good, the atmosphere mediocre.
Dr Mayreder with his young wife.
This evening: 'Kreisleriana', half of 'Götterdämmerung'.

Tuesday 15 October
Labor. He's lost for ever. Has abandoned me.
    I *can't* do it, he said. Either Z. or I. But both – no.
I was sobbing quietly. He must have noticed ... Otherwise he was
uncommonly sweet – soothing my wounds. At the time it hurt me deeply.
I've been studying with him for six years – haven't learnt all *that* much, but
always found him a warm-hearted, sympathetic friend. – And a true artist
as well. A dear, kind fellow.
Mie came to collect me. She didn't observe my pain. I forced back the
tears.
An episode of my life has ended – my old teacher & friend has stepped
aside – into the shadows.
A day I shall take note of.

Thursday 17 October
Am unwell – and bad-tempered. I long for Alex again, much more so than
during the last few days.
|Burckhard called in the evening – he doesn't excite me.|
Today I read Plato's 'Symposium' – outrageous, but fine.

Friday 18 October
Yesterday evening: Hofrat Burckhard – Hofrat Burckhard called – in his
accustomed manner. Hofrat Burckhard – is slowly getting on my nerves.
But that really doesn't matter. How stupid, how audacious.
Today is my 'day of waiting'. Oh Alex – |sweet Alex.|
Muhr wrote to say he was coming, & I had to call it off. But I don't regret
it. Yesterday I read Plato's 'Symposium' – often I had to laugh *out loud*.

The way he writes of pederasty as something self-evident, even virtuous. It's just too funny. Aristophanes tells of a miraculous invention. Socrates plays a faun-like role. I liked it more than I can say.

Oh, how lovely it was today. We worked – kissed – worked again – kissed again – and so on. Once we simply couldn't separate. He pressed my right hand between his legs, & I, who love *every* part of him, had a greater sensation of bliss than ever before. I am *firmly* resolved to marry him . . . I feel unbelievably drawn to him. Come to me, Klimt, and take this dreadful weight from me. Make me free. |Once again, our teeth and tongues fought a hard battle. I love him.| He played me the first act of his ballet – sweat was pouring off his brow. – I couldn't bear to take my hands out of his. He coiled himself around me like a spring – pressed me *madly* close. I wish for one thing only – |wedlock, union.| I want to feel him within me – to open my womb to him . . .

I would *never* have imagined that I could love anyone so. |Alex, my golden one – |

Sunday 27 October

I don't know how things will turn out. I lie in bed open-eyed, thinking and longing. I shouldn't be writing all this down so frankly – it will make us both meaningless. And *that may not be*! If he were here right now, I wouldn't be able to resist him. |My whole body burns for him – my soul thirsts for him.| For his sacred fingers! – What does a man understand? He goes to some whore & relieves himself of his pent-up energy. But I – what can I do to calm the wave swelling deep inside me?

My one and only. |I love his hands, his teeth, his tongue,| his dear, soft-brown eyes – what don't I love about him? Everything, everything.

Once – we were sitting together – I laid my head on his chest, put my arms round his neck & stayed in that position for some time. He kissed my breast, my eyes, my forehead and finally my mouth, which I purposely kept shut, so that he'd have to force it open. |Oh, how I love him, love him. My master.|

I think, once I am his, he will kiss the ground I walk on. But no – *I* want to do just that! I would never have believed that I could ever so humiliate myself as to |kiss a man's hand!| – But I do so, do so with pleasure. I have the feeling of having climbed down from a high pedestal. But the further I descend, the taller grows my horizon. And when my descent has ended – at his feet – I shall find myself on a pedestal *infinitely* higher than the one from which I descended. –

I shan't post the letter. Even with your *own* husband, you should always leave things a little nebulous. I'm glad that I brought myself to do it. Now I'm calmer, much calmer, shall try *not* to think of him, will do everything to silence my poor, aching soul.

Thursday 31 October
I haven't written anything for several days now. Now I must. My feelings for Alex are overwhelming. His image stands clear and shining before me. During the past days, my thoughts were but *rarely* of him.
p.m. drove over to Mie.
Tuesday evening: concert, the first for a long time. I soaked in sound through every pore. Never before had I taken such pleasure in music.
      Schumann: 2nd Symphony & Coriolan –
      were the two peaks.
Then dinner with Hugo. If only Mie were a *little* more musical! It bores her stiff, poor thing.
On Wednesday, after spending the night at Mie's (yellow silk bedding & a cambric night-gown), with her in town.
To lunch: Gretl & Spitzer. Was quite pleasant.
Today Gretl went home. I'm afraid to say, I couldn't care less!
Then Mama and Carl drove out to Papa's grave [ugh!]. Are these people really such simpletons, or are they frivolous? I made my excuses, because visiting graveyards & the like is for me merely theatrical – *insincere*. And then I don't care to go. I [surely] think of Papa more often than Mama or Carl [ever did]. So I stayed at home – working!
I asked Gound to give me counterpoint lessons . . . and he sent the following reply:
      Let's talk it over.
      Gound greets Schindler.
I rather suspect that he won't take me . . . Then I'll go to Schoenberg . . . But I'd prefer Gound. For my taste, Schoenberg is too Jewish.
I think of Alex very, very fondly. I feel his lips perpetually pressed against mine, his hands . . . his eyes, I can see those dear, brown eyes – |my Alex.|
Worked in the evening, after freeing myself from my self-hypnosis (Alex – at my side). My work gives me pleasure. It's a longer poem by Goethe – alternately for the master, his apprentices, a chorus, a trio. I don't know if it's any good; and whether Alex will like it – !? Parts of it are deliberately naive . . .

Friday 1 November
At Spitzer's with Alex & Gound. I arranged for Gound because of the counterpoint lessons. Alex spoke to him too. In the presence of others we can't find the right tone. We are quarrelsome and spiteful to each other. Then Spitzer sang & Gound accompanied. Alex was sitting near me – I asked him to come closer. He said I was treating him like a discarded lover. I replied:

Don't talk such nonsense.
He came to me, face to face – I stroked his hair & he kissed my hand. – I'm so fond of him.
At that moment he seemed so handsome – previously, at table, he struck me as being unspeakably ugly.

Saturday 2 November
Today too – all my thoughts are centred on this one person, this ugly, sweet little man. I knew it yesterday at Spitzer's – he came in, I took his hands, even *that* was a pleasant thought. *Nothing* about him is disagreeable, unappetizing, I love everything about him. He played my song 'In meines Vaters Garten'[8] more beautifully than I ever could.
I'm sitting here waiting, & Alex hasn't shown up. It's the first time that he's kept me waiting like this. Maybe he's angry – he certainly hasn't forgotten.
And then he arrived. Slowly he gave me his hand, didn't kiss me, didn't look at me, corrected my work, found mistakes, got annoyed. And I – at first I asked for caresses, then I was silent. Only much later – I don't need to write it down. His letter tells all! – I couldn't bear it, threw myself at him and begged him for affection. We wrestled in silence. He tried to resist – fought with me and with himself. At last I found his lips – & he responded to my kisses like one possessed.
Later – he clasped my hips, I slid between his legs, he pressed me with them, and we kissed to the accompaniment of soft exclamations. He forced me onto his lap, our lips would not be parted. I sucked on his mouth. Suddenly I felt him |salivate – again and again – & I drank eagerly from his mouth – blessed impregnation! – | And then again – he forced me roughly into a chair, leaned over me, kissed my eyes & forehead – & then on the mouth. Afterwards I felt completely shattered – I could scarcely come to my senses.

8 Published in 1910 as no. 2 of the *Fünf Lieder*.

How far will it go!? I drank from a man's mouth, kissed him all over his hands, his head. I love him! –

He kept repeating softly:

I'm going crazy, Alma.

We both quivered with boundless longing. I long to bear him a child. I want to be a wife to him, as never a woman has ever been before. To marry for money – what does that mean? You only live *once* – and you have to enjoy life while you can. And I can get more out of life in simple, modest style with my beloved husband than in luxury with some smug, boring Jew-boy [man].

This evening: Burckhard, the Hennebergs, Spitzer, Moser, Hoffmann. Alex didn't stay, although everyone did their best to persuade him.

Thursday 7 November

Card from Alex! I was overjoyed when I saw the handwriting. |My dear sweet!| God, how I long for him! –

Muhr called in the afternoon.

This evening: at the Zuckerkandls'.

Met Mahler.[9]

Present were: Frau Clémenceau, Burckhard, Spitzer, Mahler and his sister & – Klimt. With the latter I barely spoke two words – was perfectly calm. Nor with Mahler at first – but then: a highly interesting controversy arose concerning Alex's ballet – about artistic cross-fertilization in a time of cultural decay. He denied the justification of ballet as an artform in its own right etc. Klimt, Carl, he and I led the discussion. Then it turned to Alex personally. He described him as restricted – in a certain sense he's right too. He described the ballet [Hofmannsthal] as unperformable.

[By the way, I don't understand it.]

I'm *dreadfully* sorry to hear it.

[My reply:

I can explain the scenario to you, but first you should expound 'Die Braut von Korea'[10] to me – one of the most stupid ballets ever to have been staged.]

He said he found it very good of me that I spoke of Alex with such respect,

9 Zemlinsky was conducting a concert at the Musikverein with Jan Kubelik (violin) and Rudolf Friml (piano) as soloists, and was hence unable to attend.
10 Ballet by Josef Hassreiter, ballet-director of the Hofoper, with music by Josef Bayer. Due to the obscurity of its scenario, the work was poorly received.

and it was also a good sign for Alex that, when you know him better, you get to like him.

He asked me to bring him one of my pieces – even wanted to know exactly *when* I would call on him. I promised to come as soon as I had something worthwhile. That didn't satisfy him – he asked me at least to announce myself. –

I must say, I liked him *immensely* – although he's dreadfully restless. He stormed about the room like a savage. The fellow is made *entirely* of oxygen. When you go near him, you get burnt.

Tomorrow I shall tell Alex *some* of this . . .

Friday 8 November
This morning: to Zuckerkandls' – she, Frau Clémenceau & I to the Opera. Mahler gave us a warm welcome and led us through all the corridors into the auditorium, carrying my coat. As he took his leave, he said:

   Fräulein, don't forget: 'A man's word is as good as his bond.'
It was the dress rehearsal of 'The Tales of Hoffmann'. The second act fantastically atmospheric, the effect of the third unbelievably dramatic. Gutheil masterly. Mahler came twice to the railing & spoke to us – really kind. Astonishing what he can hear and see at once – when a doubling is out of tune, or the lighting wrong, when a singer makes an awkward movement – unbelievable.

Afterwards he led us out again.[11]

[Zemlinsky]
   No, no, you can't do that either.
(Me) I can & will not.
Then we played duets, but I was inwardly so restless that I could scarcely read the music. I reminded him of the passage in my letter in which I longed to be the mother of his children. He kissed me on the forehead, & said he would never have expected that of me.

I walked home from the station with Hoffmann & a painter named Kainhart.

11 One page missing from the manuscript.

This evening: Burgtheater première
Der Apostel
by Hermann Bahr

The play is downright <u>bad</u>.

Then supper at the Riedhof with Mie, Hugo, Burckhard, Moser, Kainhart.

Kainz was excellent, all the others mediocre. Yesterday B. accompanied Mahler on his way home. B. ventured the opinion:

> Fräulein Schindler is a sensible, <u>interesting</u> young lady, don't you think?

M. replied:

> I didn't care for her at first. I thought she was just a doll. But then I realized that she's also very perceptive. Maybe my first impression was because one doesn't normally expect such a good-looking girl to take anything seriously.

Today he brought me my songs.

Saturday 9 November

A new idea occurred to me: art is the outcome of love. While love, for a man, is a tool for creativity, for a woman it's the principal motive. I was never less productive than when I was in love. I sit at the piano, waiting and waiting – & nothing comes. I can concentrate on nothing else.

I took a careful look at my songs, which Alex brought round. They're very morbid, but also very beautiful. They give me untold pleasure.

I just sit & dream. Thinking of him – you, my beloved. If only I knew:

a) if he does *not* give himself entirely, whether my nerves would suffer, and b) if he *were* to give himself entirely, whether there would be any unpleasant consequences. Both alternatives are equally dangerous, yet I madly desire his embrace. I shall never forget the touch of his hand on my most intimate parts. Such fire, such a sense of joy flowed through me. Yes, one can be *entirely* happy, there is such a thing as *perfect* joy. In the arms of my beloved I have known it. One little nuance more, & I would have become a *god*. –

Once again: everything about him is holy to me. I would like to kneel before him & kiss his loins – kiss *everything, everything*.

Amen!

Sunday 10 November
Midday: Gesellschaft concert

Saul
Oratorio by Handel

Terrifically beautiful and stimulating. Magnificent choruses, a few tedious passages too – but, all things considered, very fine. I'd invited Gound [the musician] to accompany me.

p.m. Richard, the »Grethe« Loews, later Gretl Hellmann. –
This evening: the inevitable Fischel.
My thoughts were less of Alex, thank God, and I was calmer. Otherwise I shall drive myself to distraction.

Monday 11 November
Called on the Hennebergs.
This evening: première of 'The Tales of Hoffmann' – delightful, graceful. I'd like to hear it a third time. Afterwards Muhr, whom we couldn't shake off. He joined us for dinner.
Felt dreadful all day. Stomach pains. –
Acts II and III – fabulous.

Wednesday 12 November
Shopping in town with Mie.
p.m. at home. Worked, but with no inclination or desire – entirely without inclination [& desire!]. I can't even think of writing to Alex. I feel *absolutely* nothing for him.[12]

Tuesday 19 November
Yesterday evening:

Orpheus – Gluck[13]

I was thoroughly bored, but there was the Director's box, & I stared up into it, and Mahler stared down ... At first he didn't recognize me, but then he did. I just kept on staring. After 'Orpheus' we went into the foyer ... Suddenly M[ahler] was there. He asked:

Is that your mother?

I introduce her – the Hennebergs withdraw. He invites us up to his

---

12 Entries for 13–18 November removed from the manuscript. It was probably at this time that A.S. received the anonymous poem 'Das kam so über Nacht!' which, as later transpired, was written by Mahler (the complete text is reproduced in *GoR*, p. 54).
13 The evening was rounded off with Delibes's ballet *Coppélia*.

office – we follow. He offers us tea ... We talk about everything under the sun – he is fascinating, kind. Mama invites him to call – he accepts. Let's hope he really does come. We shook hands with vigour. From the gist of what he said, it appears that it was he who wrote the poem. – I shan't do anything of the kind. We stared at each other, stared and stared ...

Alexander von Zemlinsky – who is he?

Dinner at Hartmann. With B. Was he jealous!

This evening: Konzertverein with Loews.

> Mendelssohn: 'Melusine'
> Beethoven: Violin concerto
> > Prof. Rich. Sahla
> Tchaikovsky: 4th Symphony in F minor

Just wonderful – & the orchestra! –

Afterwards: dinner with the Geiringers. Mie took a fall – almost provoked a nervous collapse. Oh my dear, so highly strung ...

Wednesday 20 November

It's just too dreadful, I should be ashamed of myself ... but *Mahler's* picture is graven in my heart. I will pluck out this poisonous weed – make room for the other again – my poor Alex. – If only the poem had come from him. If only!

I could hate myself!

Friday 22 November

I'm expecting Alex to call. Conceivably he won't be coming – I haven't written to him again ... My longing is for ⊖.

Alex was here. He spoke no loving word, |didn't kiss me|. As explanation he gave me the letter – |we kissed each other once, just once. My longing for him again knows no bounds.|

This evening: Burckhard – pretty tedious. And Alex is in dissolute company this evening. Alas, poor Alex. –

Thursday 28 November

Mahler was here – I can think only of him, only of him. He had to make a telephone call.[14] We walked to Döbling together. He told me how much

14 Mahler had to tell his sister that he would not be coming home for dinner. As there was no telephone at the Molls', he walked with A.S. to Döbling, where he realized that he had forgotten his telephone number (cf. *MaL*, p. 19).

he liked me. I didn't tell him how much I liked him. We talked of many things – not everything . . .

A barrier divides us – Alex . . . He doesn't know it, but senses it nonetheless! – I'm not <u>certain</u>, but I <u>believe</u> I love him [Mahler]! I want to be honest. Recently I no longer felt anything for Alex.

Friday 29 November

8:00 a.m. The walk was lovely yesterday – through <u>snow and wind</u>. Initially we didn't know what to say. Then he told me how much he had been thinking about me, & how worried he was, because his life was preordained. Only his art – and now his thoughts are of other things.

Later this too: to maintain *complete* freedom of action. His sister has always helped him. He wouldn't object in the least to handing in his resignation right away. But if he was committed to somebody else, the situation would be quite different.

> Well, I said, what if that somebody also possessed a modicum of artistic sensibility?

We want to get to know each other, that's our mutual wish. My thoughts are only of him – memories of the other are already fading.

. . . The day before yesterday, Muhr said:

> Well then, when are we going to marry?

In the evening I went up to my room. I don't know why, but I was ashamed. Now I regret every kiss, every caress, every amorous glance. – The hour of <u>remorse</u> has come!

I would have wished to meet him pure, <u>completely</u> pure! But that can no longer be. Now I feel – the stains will *never* fade.

B. doesn't bother me as much . . . He didn't get his money's worth this evening – brought me flowers & a book by Ibsen. But Alex, whom I would rob of years of his life, to whom in my last letter I still swore:

> You are the *only* man to whom I would belong!

And now: I am glad I never yielded to his entreaties – and anyway, I never should have done so. – My lips are |profaned!|

At midday Mahler sent me all his songs, which disappointed me because they struck me as insincere. I shall tell him so as well. –

Alex called, a little peeved about M[ie],[15] but otherwise as sweet as ever. I had the feeling: *that's* where I belong. –

15 A.M.-W.'s expansion of 'M.' to 'Mie' seems nonsensical; 'Muhr' or even 'Mahler' were more likely objects for Zemlinsky's annoyance.

Saturday 30 November
A battle is raging within me. Alex against Mahler. My trust for Mahler is
boundless.
Yesterday, Alex and I discussed his songs – he sarcastic and mocking, I
unimpressed. Truly, they don't relate to his personality. This studied
naivety and simplicity, and he the most complex of characters. I'd like to
tell him so – but fear he might be insulted.
Look forward to Monday.

Sunday 1 December
Sang through the Mahler songs all morning. I'm beginning to like some of
them. It's pretty dour stuff.
Midday: Philharmonic concert
    Mozart: Sym. in E♭ maj.
    Sauer: Concerto (pfte. Sauer)[16]
    Brahms: Academic Festival Overture
The Sauer was pleasing – simple and melodious – wouldn't have expected
it of him,
Then lunch at Mie's.
p.m. Mahler songs. Nice afternoon! Alone, undisturbed, left to my own
devices. –

Monday 2 December
This afternoon: Mahler.
He told me that he loved me – we kissed each other. He played me his
pieces – my lips are sealed . . . His caresses are tender & agreeable. If only I
knew! He or – the other.
I must gradually get Alex off my mind. I'm terribly sorry. If it weren't for
all that, I would have got engaged today. But I couldn't respond to his
caresses. Someone was standing between us . . . I told him so – without
mentioning names. I *had* to tell him . . . If only he had come three years
earlier! An unsullied mouth!

Tuesday 3 December
I'm on the horns of a *terrible* dilemma. I keep repeating the words 'my
beloved' and follow them with 'Alex'. *Can* I really love Mahler as he
deserves and as I am really able? Shall I ever understand his art, & he

16 Emil Sauer's Piano Concerto in E minor was receiving its world première.

mine!? With Alex the sympathy is mutual. He loves every *note* of me. Mahler just said:

This is really serious. This I didn't expect!

How shall I break it to Alex? – I'm on first-name terms with Mahler now. He told me how much he loved me, and I could give him no reply.

Do I really love him? – I have no idea. Sometimes I actually think not. So *much* irritates me:

his smell,

the way he sings,

the way he speaks [can't roll his rrrr's].

And longing? How *madly* I longed for Alex – when we first met . . . every minute, every second – & now: well, I long for him, but no longer with the *same* fire. Maybe I cannot love anyone *like that* a third time. He's a stranger to me. Our tastes differ.

He said to me:

Alma, think it over – carefully – if ever I disappoint you, you must tell me.

At present I can live it down, though it's not easy – but in four months? Maybe it will no longer be possible.

And I don't know what to think, how to think – whether I love him or not – whether I love the director of the Opera, the wonderful conductor – or the man . . . Whether, when I subtract the one, anything is left of the other. And his art leaves me cold, so *dreadfully* cold. In plain words: I don't believe in him as a composer. And I'm expected to bind my life to this man . . . I felt nearer to him from a distance than from near by.

I shudder.

But if today I say 'no' – a long-cherished dream will turn to dust!

We kissed – |drunk greedily from each other.| Although his hands are expressive, I don't love them as much as Alex's. You can get used to a lot of things – given time . . . but patience is not Mahler's strong point. –

What should I do?

And what if Alex were to become famous? – In my letter I wrote that I hadn't the *slightest idea* what was going through my mind.

This morning I played music from act I.[17] I feel so much sympathy for it.

One question *plagues* me: whether Mahler will inspire me to compose – whether he will support my artistic striving – whether he will love me like Alex. Because *he* loves me utterly.

---

17 i.e. from the short-score of *Der Triumph der Zeit*.

Wednesday 4 December
At Spitzer's. Had my photograph taken.
Then to Gallia – Gound. Later Erica.
This evening: at the Opera.

The Tales of Hoffmann

My Gustav conducted. At every curtain he looked round – so sweet. If only
he were here *now*. –
If only I had already spoken to <u>Alex</u>. My thoughts are always with the
other. Muhr was sitting in our row – my God!
If he doesn't call before his departure, I shall go to him. –

Thursday 5 December
My thoughts are ever more frequently of him. His dear, *sweet* smile. – *This*
is the man I kissed. Or rather – he kissed me. Now I believe that I really
love him. Alex weighs on me like lead. I long for him really badly now,
have to think constantly of him, of his dear, sweet eyes. – If only I'd already
broken it to him. It will be *dreadful*.
Let's hope I see Mahler before his departure.
p.m. Gound, Mandlick.
In the evening: this letter.[18] – I could weep! I believe I've lost him – and in
spirit he was already mine – what a fate! I feel quite wretched. I must see
him before he leaves, *must* see him. –
He doesn't want me! He's written me off. That last sentence – that *terrible*
last sentence! – Now I can feel how dear he is to me – suddenly I feel so
empty. Tomorrow I *must* go to him. My longing is *boundless*.
Eva and Hans Sachs – a feeble excuse. It can't be true. –

Friday 6 December
He loves me no more – I'm unhappy. Today I shall go to him and won't find
him in. I'd like to weep on his breast. Eva and Hans Sachs – I wasn't
prepared for that.

Saturday 7 December
Gustav was here. –
We kissed each other over and over again. In his embrace I feel so warm. If
only he still loved me as much – but I consider him fickle, dreadfully fickle.
He tried to convert me, in many senses.

18 ▷ Undated letter from Mahler (cf. *GoR* pp. 71–72.) The closing sentence reads: 'Think of
our dear friends: Eva – and Hans Sachs!'

I shan't be seeing him for nineteen days. On Monday he's going to Berlin. I don't know what else to write, but my feelings are <u>for him</u> & <u>against Alex</u>. *Never* before have I watched the clock as avidly as today. I couldn't work for sheer longing.

At the thought of next Tuesday I *tremble*. |My poor Alex.| I'm convinced he knows *everything* . . . feels *everything* . . . Constantly I see Gustav's eyes before me, so kind and sweet – & *always* questioning. His lovely hands somewhat disfigured by nail-biting. He'll write to me from B[erlin]. Never in my life have I met anyone as alien as he. How alien [and yet so close!] I cannot say. Maybe that's one of the things that attracts me to him. But he should let me be as I am. Already I'm aware of changes in myself, due to him. He's taking much away from me and giving me much in return. If this goes on, he'll make a new person of me. A better person? I don't know. I don't know *at all*. –

More than ever, a huge question-mark hangs over my future. Everything is up to him. Today he confessed everything to me, all his sins – I even confessed some of mine.

He guessed Alex's name & was *appalled* – *couldn't* understand it.

Enough now – for both of us – and *no* concern for the mysteries of 'tomorrow'. Today <u>is real</u> at least, and is *beautiful*, yes – beautiful.

[He is the *purest* person I ever met – because my love-affairs were few and, thank God, just mechanical experiences.]

Suite 25

[!!!Mahler!!!]

{*Saturday 7 December*}
We were playing piano duets and he said:

> There's a crotchet missing here. But I'll grant it you – I'll grant you half the bar. Yes – I'll grant you the whole bar – everything.[1]

Sunday 8 December
I feel that my world is in chaos. Everything is collapsing and growing anew. A new outlook on life – new belief. If only I can live up to his love. He is capable of giving infinitely. I am quite unable to work. I don't know why. Alex had already given me *everything* – and I had absorbed so much from him. But now I have to discard so much in order to take in new things, better things.

At midday he sent me 'Das klagende Lied'. The text is excellent, the melody a little impoverished, but the structure firm and effective. I can imagine some passages sounding quite passable.

p.m. at the Opera: 'Die Zauberflöte'. Heavenly performance. Only now do I realize the true greatness and beauty of this work.

Then I looked over to Gustav and had to smile as if transfigured. At the end of each act he gave me such a touching smile – particularly at the end – as if casting out a line to me.

Then we drove past him [on the street]. He was walking with his sister and [Natalie Bauer-]Lechner, and didn't see me. My dearest Gustav – think, just think of me!

Monday 9 December
I simply can't work – walk around the room, go over to his picture, reread his last letter – I love him!

At midday he sent me a big box of pralines and this dear, sweet letter. I believe I shall become a better person, he purifies me. My <u>desire</u> for him is unbroken.

1 Untranslatable pun on 'Viertel' (quarter-note or crotchet), 'Halbe' (half-note or minim) and 'Ganze' (whole-note or semibreve).

This afternoon: Muhr. We made a lot of music together. Finally he again asked how things stood with me. I had no choice but to tell him the truth, no matter how *hard* it was. He stood before me, pale and trembling:

Fräulein, if you turn me down, I shall kill myself.

I felt so sorry for him. I do like him very much – as a friend – and am convinced that I wouldn't be doing badly if I accepted him. But some things lie beyond our power.

My love and longing is boundless – Gustav, my dearest, my love . . . I have but one wish, one dream: to be yours alone . . .

Muhr said today that a doctor had told him that Gustav was suffering from an incurable disease and that he was weakening perceptibly. – Dear God, I shall nurse him like a child. I will not be the cause of his downfall. I shall restrain my longing and my passion – I want to cure him – let him recuperate through my strength and youthfulness.

My beloved Master . . .

Tuesday 10 December
I didn't get a wink of sleep all night – tossed and turned in my bed – thinking of my uncertain prospects, of Gustav's ill health, of his sister, whom I've already taken into my heart – and of him, of him – you, my beloved.

Today Alex is due – that will be difficult for me.

And yet another morning has passed. To no effect, fruitlessly. I am simply incapable – my dear, sweet Gustav.

Gretl sent me reviews from the Stuttgart daily papers – of Gustav's third symphony.[2] *Dreadfully* rude. It robbed me of some – not all – but some of my faith in him. Why is he not here now, at this difficult time?

|What will Muhr do?

Another poor devil – Zemlinsky – when he arrives, he'll approach me with *pride* and bluntness. *I know him well.*|

I'm still waiting for Alex [Zem.], with fear in my heart. He's due at any moment. If he doesn't come, I shall write to him – but it would be better to talk.

And my Gustav? In Berlin, amongst strangers. When shall I receive his first letter? What hasn't all been going through my mind this past fortnight! |I've grown so old!|

---

2 *Recte* 4th Symphony (cf. *GoR*, p. 81).

This evening: 'Tristan' – in every note, in every bar, my thoughts were with him.

Spent the night at Mie's.

Wednesday 11 December
a.m. in town.

p.m. at the Zuckerkandls'. Gustav asked me to go, as his sister would be there. Although she has a slightly deflected look [in plain English, a squint], she feels deep sympathy for me – I recognize him in her. We got on quite well together. I only hope I can feel something for her. I really don't understand why Gretl doesn't cultivate greater affection for Wilhelm's sisters. I found them *immediately* sympathetic. Well, I only hope she likes me. I *fervently* hope so.

On Saturday I shall be visiting her. – What are we going to talk about? How are we going to face up to each other under these uncertain circumstances?

Thursday 12 December
I feel *really* sorry for him. Who knows, perhaps it might be – well, really! But his love is so *touching*. His immense ardour frightens me – my Saviour!

This evening: 'Meistersinger'. Although the piece is so wonderful, I must admit that I was dead tired. It took five hours. The second day that I haven't been feeling well – etc. On the other hand | in the same row sat the young Dr Adler,[3] whom I find tremendously attractive. I flirted with him outrageously.[4] Finally we exchanged smiles. And suddenly I realized, to my horror, that Muhr was sitting next to him and had probably been observing the entire manoeuvre. I felt ashamed of myself, absolutely ashamed. All the same, I noticed that M. was looking the other way, so I quickly turned my head in his direction, and we exchanged a voluptuous glance – for a long, wonderful moment – regardless of onlookers. Such a glance can be stunningly sensual – and he's the very picture of a man, his eyes are black pools and ... in short, a face that appeals to me. There's good stock for you.| Mahler can't compete with that. But otherwise I remain independent and, at heart, faithful to Gustav. My bold glances didn't come from deep inside. I've written to Alex – he'll be furious, will *never* forgive me. I wrote:

3 The gynaecologist Dr Louis Adler, who graduated in general medicine at Vienna University in 1900 (cf. *GoR*, p. 82). At the time of this chance encounter he was twenty-five years old.
4 Subsequently altered to: 'I flirted a little', then crossed out.

Alex,

You haven't called because you know everything. You know all that has happened. You can read even my most secret thoughts. For me, the last weeks have been torture.

You know how *very* much I loved you. You fulfilled me *completely*. Just as suddenly as this love came, it has vanished – been cast aside. And befallen me with renewed power!

On my knees I beg your forgiveness for the evil hours I have given you. Some things are beyond our powers. Maybe you have an explanation for that. You – you know me better than I know myself.

I shall *never* forget the joyous hours you have given me – don't *you* forget them either. One thing, though: don't desert me! If you are the man I think you are, you will come here on Monday, give me your hand – and our first kiss of friendship.

Be a dear fellow, Alex. If you so wish, our friendship could be really meaningful. We could stick together always, as old comrades.

Above all, answer me at once and without reserve – Mama will not read the letter.

Once again: forgive me – I no longer know myself.

Your Alma.

Friday 13 December

Still no word from him today, not even a breath sealed within an envelope. I long for him . . . am terribly anxious. Is he thinking of me just as hard? Gustav, if you could have seen me this afternoon . . . amidst eight debutantes! I felt myself *far* superior, made a few really good quips – some of which shocked the demure, well-brought-up young ladies to the core – and amused myself by observing them. <u>What</u> these girls all find interesting! Unbelievable!

The fateful letter to Alex has been posted. And what will be the upshot? He'll write me a wickedly sarcastic letter in return and *never* show his face again . . . My loss is immeasurable. Such a wonderful teacher! I've seriously miscalculated this time . . . Whatever happens, I must accept it . . . all my own fault! But it was so lovely . . .

And Gustav – such a prodigal – has had affairs with them all – Mildenburg, Michalek, Kurz etc. – with all of them. [Later I discovered it was all lies!]

Saturday 14 December

Today's letter is cooler. – I knew it before I'd even read it, because it's all my fault. I answered at once. Now I'm waiting for Alex's reply – which I dread . . .

p.m. at Justine's. She was uncommonly kind and courteous to me. I went into his room – stood in front of his desk, greeted his bed, his books, his surroundings. The apartment is decorated in pseudo-modern style, but *tastefully* and unostentatiously.

While I was there, a letter arrived for her, which also included something for me, namely the programme of his 2nd Symphony in C minor.[5]

Sunday 15 December

Philharmonic Concert[6]

> Massenet: Overture to 'Phèdre'
> Heuberger: Variations on a theme of Schubert
> Beethoven: 7th Symphony

Then dinner at Hotel Imperial with Mie and Hugo.

p.m. Gretl Hellmann, later Burckhard. He advised me against Gustav, saying that when two strong personalities come together, they usually fight until one of them is forced into submission. And that would probably be me – which he would regret.[7]

Must *I* be subdued? I can and will not. And yet I feel that I stand at a far *lower* level – and it would do me no harm to be drawn up to his.

Monday 16 December

|*Today* the letter included below. He's such a fine fellow. My longing is indescribable.| And my poor Alex – he's fuming, ignores me, hates me – with some justification. I could weep that I have caused him such sorrow – the poor, poor fellow. My love for him is [was] boundless.

p.m. – being inexplicably tired, I'd only just got out of bed – suddenly I could feel something special in the air. I went to the door and – in came Alex. I was speechless. He came into the room, paler than usual and very quiet – I went to him, drew his head against my breast, and kissed his hair. I felt so strange. Then we sat down and talked seriously, only of matters

---

5 Mahler wrote several, slightly divergent versions of the programme. The complete text, as copied by A.S. into her diary, is reproduced in *GoR*, pp. 87–89.

6 Conductor: Josef Hellmesberger jnr. The works by Massenet and Heuberger were receiving their first performances in Vienna.

7 One page removed from the manuscript.

concerning us both – side by side – we two, |whose bodies had coiled in love's wildest embrace.| He a little sarcastic, as ever, but otherwise kind, touchingly kind. My eyes kept filling with tears. But my will stood firm . . . Today I buried a beautiful love [feeling]. Gustav, you'll have to do much to replace it for me.

Although I told him that I no longer loved him – and that it was actually he who should be shamefaced – it was *I* who felt it more deeply. He seemed so noble, so pure, stood so *high* above me! Had he uttered just *one* angry or accusing word, I would never have begun to feel that way. Alex, I *respect* you – my respect for you is endless.

This evening: Richard, Mayreder and Moser. The afternoon had so upset me that I could scarcely speak to them. But then Gustav's letter arrived and helped me over the worst. –

|My poor Alex| – I could see the suffering on his face. You noble man!

Tonight Gustav's 4th Symphony is to be performed in Berlin. Those curs will cause a rumpus once again. Never mind.

The trials and tribulations of the past week have made me physically ill.

Tuesday 17 December

Early this morning to Mie – and happy to go, as it would concentrate my thoughts on something else.

Rendezvous with Mayreder. A shopping spree. Then home, where I found this letter. He's such a dear man. How I look forward to his return. How kindly and nicely he writes . . .

And Alex – if only I knew what he's feeling – |my poor devil.|

Strange though: yesterday I was calm and remained so, looked at him, and suddenly felt, with a shudder, just how ugly he is, how <u>strongly</u> he smells etc. [Midsummer-night's dream!] All things I'd never noticed before. That *is* strange. [?!] Is there really some extrinsic force that controls us? Sometimes I believe so. These last weeks will remain *rooted* in my memory.

Wednesday 18 December

I must say, the letter has me foxed.[8] I take the greatest pains to make friends with Justine, and she observes me with an eagle eye – every word, movement and sensation – and promptly passes on her <u>fears</u> to Gustav . . . That annoys me because, if she perseveres in observing me so closely, it could become |dangerous| [unpleasant]. What, for instance, if she should

---

8 A.S. appears to have destroyed the letter to which she refers, in which Mahler made critical remarks about her relationship to his sister Justine (*vide GoR*, p. 101).

come to realize [believe] that I'm heartless and unloving – things that I only confide, discreetly, to my diary – that I'm incapable of warmth, that everything about me is sheer calculation, cold-blooded calculation? [All untrue!] No – he's a sick man, his position is insecure, he's a Jew, no longer young, and as a composer . . . [deeply in *debt*]. So where's the calculation on my part? Is it all just folly, then? No, for there is <u>something</u> which draws me to him – without a doubt!

But if Justi intrigues against me, and his interest wanes, I shall – |*not* die| [love him and stand by him].

I can hardly say how Gustav's letter has me foxed . . . and how this loss of warmth distresses me. I must be fond of him! My Gustav! – I long for him *disgracefully*.

This evening: 'Walküre'. I scarcely listened, have *absolutely* no head for music right now. During act II, I stayed at the back of the box and took a break, chatted with Pollack. Anyway, the performance was mediocre.

But I'm inexplicably restless. I feel that Justi is poisoning his love.

Thursday 19 December

|Yesterday again I flirted madly with Louis Adler. The fellow is so damned good-looking. And Muhr was watching . . . If only Muhr were as handsome as he – there's a captivating fellow. He knew it too, kept looking over his shoulder. Unfortunately I was sitting rather far away. The music gave me no pleasure. My ears were shut, my eyes incapable of seeing. – |

p.m. Frau Lanner with Else. Then a lesson with Gound.

This evening: Pollack. We talked a lot about Gustav. I managed to talk my rage away. I had to make a clean breast of all that was seething within me. If it ever comes to my marrying him, I must do everything *now* to stake *my* rightful claim . . . particularly in *artistic* questions. He thinks *nothing* of my art – and much of his own. And *I* think *nothing* of *his* art and much of my own. – That's how it is! Now he talks unceasingly of safeguarding *his* art. I *can't* do that. With Zemlinsky it would have been possible, because I have sympathy for his art – he's such a brilliant fellow. But Gustav is so poor – so *dreadfully* poor. If he knew *just* how poor he was – he would cover his face in shame . . . And *I* am supposed to lie, lie for the rest of my life? And he – that's all right – but Justi, that woman! I feel she's spying on me everywhere . . . And I *must* have my freedom!

Complete freedom!⁹

9 The editors of *GoR* (pp. 125–126) date the passage beginning 'This evening: Pollack' to 16 January 1902. By comparing tears in the paper, however, it becomes clear that it belongs with the rest of the entry for 19 December 1901.

Friday 20 December
Early this morning: to town, shopping with Else L. in an open fiacre.
a.m. at home – *this letter*.[10] My heart missed a beat . . . give up my music –
abandon what has until now been my life? My *first* reaction was – to pass
him up. I had to weep – for then I understood that I loved him. Half-crazed
with grief, I got into my finery and drove to 'Siegfried' – in tears! I told
Pollack, and he was incensed – he would *never* have thought it possible. I
feel as if a cold hand has torn the heart from my breast.
Mama & I talked it over until late at night. She had read the letter . . . !
I was dumbfounded. I find his behaviour so ill-considered, so inept. It
might have come all of its own . . . quite gently . . . But like this it will leave
an indelible scar . . .

Saturday 21 December
I *forced* myself to sleep the night through. This morning I reread his letter –
and suddenly I felt such warmth. What if I were to *renounce* [my music]
out of love for him? Just forget all about it! I must admit that scarcely any
music now interests me except his.
Yes – he's right. I must live *entirely* for him, to make him happy. And now I
have a strange feeling that my love for him is deep & genuine. For how
long? I don't know, but already *that* means much. I long for him
boundlessly.
This morning, Mama called on Klimt. That doesn't bother me at all.
Before lunch I went shopping in Döbling – just to get out of the house. My
heart trembles in anticipation. On the way I met his servant. I read his
letter on the street. How right he is about everything.
     I love him!
He arrived – as kind and loving as ever. Our kisses were hot. I am wax
in his hands . . . I want to give him everything. My soul is his. *If only*
everything was clear! –
Tomorrow I shall call on Justi.

Sunday 22 December
How *lovely* it was yesterday!
My longing for him is indescribable. Everything about him is lovable &

10 ▶ Letter from Mahler, in which he indicated that he expected his future wife to abandon
her ambitions as a composer (published in *GoR*, pp. 104–110).

familiar, his breath so sweet . . . I have the <u>feeling</u>: I could <u>live</u> . . . <u>exist</u> for him alone. If we marry, it will be in the spring, just as I thought.

I long to bear his child. If he has the strength. He hopes so.

Nothing, absolutely nothing – but to obey him.

p.m. at Justi's. Initially we were somewhat inhibited. But then Gustav arrived, and as a *trio* we were quite happy. Whenever Justi went out, he kissed me. They brought me home in the cab – we held hands.

My thoughts are continually of him. No work gives me pleasure. My beloved Gustav – my thoughts are *only* of him.

I got home: Mayreder was there, had waited all afternoon – for me.

p.m. Fischel.

This morning Carl came up to talk to me . . . kindly & seriously. – He explained all the possible eventualities. I know *everything*. He's sick, my poor dear, weighs under 10 stone – *far* too little. I shall care for him like a child. My love for him is infinitely touching. – What a shame that he can't pronounce an r. Strangely enough, he'd prefer my name to be Maria, because he loves the strong r in the middle. Strange and . . . !

Today Justi spoke of Arnold (Rosé),[11] who also gave her |a lovely ring . . . |

I'm *so* afraid that his health will let me down – I can scarcely say. I can just see him lying in a pool of blood. –

He's right. On the one hand he could be satisfied, he said, because he believed {the affair with} Gustav wouldn't last much longer . . . But in my case he thinks quite differently.

I have no heart [? too much] & feel so warmly for him. And I have the feeling that he elevates me, while Burckhard's company brings out my frivolity. When Gustav is listening, I feel ashamed of my loose tongue – and can scarcely express all my thoughts. Are you happier when you live frivolously, unscrupulously, or when you acquire a beautiful, sublime outlook on life? . . . Freer in the former case, happier. {In the latter case} better – purer. Does that not hinder one's path to *freedom*? Yes, yes, a hundred times yes, I tell you – stand firm!

He's right – we make a good match – like fire and water – outwardly and inwardly. For sure! But <u>must</u> one of us be subordinate? Isn't it possible –

11 Justine Mahler and Arnold Rosé were engaged to be married.

with the help of love – to merge two fundamentally opposing points of view into – *one?*[12]

Monday 23 December
I'm waiting – waiting – for Gustav & Justi! How I resent having to wait. It's torture – an eternity. He does me wrong.
Well, they came, and this evening I got engaged – officially, in the presence of Carl and Mama. From now on *only he* shall have *a place in my heart* – *only* he. Never more shall I cast my roving eye on a good-looking young man. I shall give him everything – *my* husband[!]. Our bond is already so close that it can scarcely grow closer. If my relationship with A.Z. was wild and carnal, then with Mahler I feel imbued with the holiest feelings. Once I told Z. I wanted to be mother of his children. I was not speaking sincerely. I then believed I could never feel anything so profoundly beautiful – today I said nothing: *but I felt it.* When we sit there, cuddled together, I feel him as *my* body. Nothing remotely *foreign* – so unbelievably dear ... I can scarcely wait to see him again tomorrow.

Tuesday 24 December
I can't entirely let my joy overcome me. For fear of the gods, who cannot bear to contemplate pure joy.
I await him *eagerly* – today.
Gustav doesn't want it to be known, for fear of the newspapers – of crazy gossips.
I can neither think nor act clearly. Everything begins and ends with Gustav. My longing is infinite. I would give everything for him – my music – *everything* – so powerful is my longing! *That*'s how I want to be his – I am *already* his – I belong to him and Justi, who I love, because she's of the same blood.
Justi told Mama that Gustav kept saying:
> Isn't it a crime that I – the autumn – should bind myself to the spring? She will forgo her summer.

No, my Gustav, no!

---

12 This paragraph and the preceding one were written (probably on the same day) on a separate sheet of paper, whose exact position in the chronological sequence is uncertain. 'He' presumably refers to Carl Moll.

Christmas Eve. And this year I couldn't care less.

Gustav was with me up here. We felt our blood pounding – followed our instincts, and were happy. As to the presents, I shall write about them tomorrow – the day after – they mean nothing to me. Only one will I mention – a {diamond}-edged pin, from *my* Gustav.

In the evening: Burckhard and Moser. Burckhard suspects it all – Moser is like a child. B. is edgy & imprudent. He teased me about my waning enthusiasm for Nietzsche. In Gustav's presence. What do I care. Only to him will I give myself.

Wednesday 25 December
Wieners, Burckhard, Moser etc.

p.m. at Gustav's. He was already waiting. I sat on his knee the whole time. I love him more than I can say. We melt into one another.

He had to conduct – 'Tannhäuser'. I stayed with Justi. I'm fond of her.

Thursday 26 December
Gustav called.

This afternoon: Mama Moll. Gustav met me at the station and we drove home in a rubber-wheeled phaeton.

Friday 27 December
This evening the bomb dropped. In big, bold letters it stood in the papers:

Director Mahler engaged
etc. etc. etc.

He was very put out. For fear of the personnel at the Opera.

Saturday 28 December
Frau Hellmann sent me a wonderful ostrich-feather fan. Gretl, who called yesterday, is half crazed. Letters, telegrams, flowers – & the papers. Everywhere my beauty, my youth – & my musical talent are stressed. According to the 'Fremdenblatt', *I am brilliant*. Lord – and whatever else! p.m. Ilse and Erica.

In the evening with Gustav. Drank a toast of brotherhood with A[rnold] Rosé – but otherwise mostly alone with G. in his room. We stood a long time in the dark corridor and were happy. *That* is my only wish, to make him happy. He deserves it!

Sunday 29 December
a.m. Wärndorfers & Loews etc.
This evening: at the Opera. For the first time in the Director's box – Mama,
Justi and I.
Then to Hartmann. Gustav & I walked alone for a while. We resolved to
get married in mid-February. – Let's hope it works out.
My appearance in the box was a veritable début. Every opera-glass was
focused on me – every single one. I felt offended & withdrew. Mildenburg
came down to meet me – *awfully* sweet.
And he was sitting down there – so far, so far away from me!

Wednesday 30 December
p.m. rendezvous with G. We failed to meet, & he got so angry that I had
difficulty in calming him down.
Today we all but joined in wedlock. He let me feel his masculinity – his
vigour – & it was a pure, holy sensation, such as I would *never* have
expected. He must be suffering *dreadfully*. I can gauge his frustration by
mine. Nobody knows how I long for him. And yet – I cannot imagine
giving myself to him before the appointed time. A sense of injustice &
shame would degrade the whole, holy mystery. My lover – in God.
When I'm on my own, I feel the emptiness – the missing other half.
We could scarcely bring ourselves to part. Why these *dreadful* conventions? Why can't I simply move in with him? *Without* a church wedding.
We're consumed with longing, are dissipating our strongest desires. He
bared his breast, and I put my hand on his heart. I feel: his body is *mine* –
he and *I* are *one*. I love every part of him in turn – nobody exists other than
he. No other thought!
I'm wearing my hair loose now – he loves it that way – and our bodies cried
out for union. Oh – to bear his child!
My body
His soul
When shall I be his! Another ninety nights!

New Year's Eve
At midday I was with him.
p.m. at Zierers'.
In the evening he, Justi and Arnold [Rosé] called on us. Very, very nice!
More than that – Oh God. Once I was upon the point of giving myself to
him. Then I thought: how awful if he had to leave straight after – and I

remained alone with my torment. No, no. His beloved hand explored my body, and mine his. We clasped each other tightly. No – I want to give myself freely, without constraint, with no fear of disturbance. I love him. I have only one wish: may the New Year not shatter my dream. I love him – & so I close. My life is his, he shares my joys, I his sorrows.

Amen!

New Year's Day 1902

What I have to write today is terribly sad. I called on Gustav – in the afternoon we were alone in his room. He gave me his body – & I let him touch me with his hand. Stiff and upright stood his vigour. He carried me to the sofa, laid me gently down and swung himself over me. Then – just as I felt him penetrate, he lost all strength. He laid his head on my breast, shattered – and almost wept for shame. Distraught as I was, I comforted him.

We drove home, dismayed and dejected. He grew a little more cheerful. Then I broke down, had to weep, weep on his breast. What if he were to lose – that! My poor, poor husband!

I can scarcely say how irritating it all was. First his intimate caresses, so close – and then no satisfaction. Words cannot express what I today have undeservedly suffered. And then to observe his torment – his unbelievable torment!

My beloved!

Wednesday 3 January

|Bliss and rapture.|

Thursday 4 January

Rapture without end.

Friday 5 January

This evening: at Gustav's. His friends ... all conspicuously Jewish.[13] I could find no bond ... amused myself by stunning them with unprecedented impertinence, said I didn't care for Gustav's music etc. On the way home we laughed and laughed. It had been so tedious.

---

13 The guests (according to *MaL*, pp. 25–26, and *GoR*, p. 124) were Siegfried and Clementine Lipiner, Anna Mildenburg, Albert and Nina Spiegler, Justine Mahler, Arnold Rosé, Koloman Moser, Anna and Carl Moll.

Saturday 6 January
A wonderful afternoon.
Yesterday he sent me his 4th Symphony – today we played it through together. It really moved me – pleased me very, very much.[14]
And my poor Gustav is under doctors' orders. An inflamed swelling – ice-bags, hot baths etc. etc. All because I resisted him so long – he has to suffer!

Thursday 16 January
For a long while I've been truly happy, and therefore haven't written anything down. But in the last few days everything has changed. He wants me different, completely different. And that's what I want as well. As long as I'm with him, I can manage – but when I'm on my own, my other, vain self rises to the surface and wants to be let free. I let myself go. My eyes shine with frivolity – my mouth utters lies, streams of lies. And he senses it, knows it. Only now do I understand. I *must* rise to meet him. [For I live only in him.]
Yesterday afternoon . . . he begged me to talk – and I couldn't find *one* word of warmth. *Not one.*
I wept. That was the end . . .
To be like him – my *only* wish.
I have two souls: I know it. –
Only one – which is my true soul? If I lie, will I not make us both unhappy? – And am I a liar? When he looks at me so happily, what a profound feeling of ecstasy. Is that a lie too? No, no. I must cast out my other soul. The one which has so far ruled must be banished. I must strive to become a real person, let everything happen to me of its own accord.

---

14 On 12 January, at a concert with the Vienna Philharmonic Orchestra, Mahler conducted the Viennese première of his 4th Symphony.

About the manuscript

The original manuscript (Suites 4–25), consisting of twenty-two exercise books (white paper with faint red page ruling, bound in blue soft covers) supplied by the stationers J. Mayr & A. Fessler (I., Kärntnerstrasse 37), is preserved in the Mahler-Werfel Collection, Special Collections, at the van Pelt-Dietrich Library Center, University of Pennsylvania. The whereabouts of Suites 1–3 and of all later diaries are not known.

A.S. wrote with diversely coloured inks, pencil and crayon, while her line-drawings are executed, almost without exception, in black ink; A.M.-W.'s amendments are written with ball-point pen. Most dates and all sub-headings – announcements of exhibitions, theatre and opera perform-ances etc. – are written in an ornamental hand, influenced by *Jugendstil* graphic design. Comparison of inks and handwriting reveals that A.S. reread and altered the text on more than one occasion. Some of her cor-rections were evidently intended to clarify passages particularly difficult to decipher, others enlarge or comment upon the original text. The numerous commentaries, deletions, signatures etc. dating from the period 1962–63 indicate that A.M.-W. actively considered publishing her own edition of *The Diaries*. Several passages are struck out (with varying degrees of emphasis), but only a few words of the original are obliterated entirely.

Supplementary material

Numerous mementos (letters, concert programmes, playbills, newspaper articles, postcards, visiting cards, photographs etc.) are inserted into the manuscript. A.S. fastened them securely to the page by making four clean, diagonal cuts in the paper, and inserting the corners of each object through them, much in the manner of a photograph album.

Exceptionally, the brush-proof of a lithograph by Klimt (p. 348) is gummed onto the page. A.M.-W. later removed most of Zemlinsky's letters and all of Mahler's, marking their original positions with abbreviations (e.g. 'Zem. 17'); her typewritten transcripts of this material are preserved separately in the Mahler-Werfel Collection.

Punctuation

A.S.'s original punctuation varies according to her mood, with copious use of dashes and dots (in place of a full stop, sentences usually end with a comma followed by a dash). While endeavouring to maintain the flavour of the original, the editors have unified the punctuation and adjusted it to clarify sentence structure.

In the later Suites, A.S. often begins each sentence on a new line. In the interests of space, these isolated periods have been combined into paragraphs, which are grouped according to time of day, event or subject. Quotations and passages of direct speech are indented throughout.

Titling

The quotation from Kant, 'Always act as if the maxims of your will-power could be accepted as the principles of a collective legislation' (*Critik der practischen Vernunft*, Riga, 1788), is written in bold letters on the outer covers of Suites 4–12. Although several later Suites bear other headings or subtitles, it seemed appropriate to place these words, as an all-embracing motto, at the beginning of the book.

Artwork

Although the size of A.S.'s handwriting prevents an exact reproduction of her original graphic layout, the reproductions of her line-drawings are positioned within the text in a manner similar to that of the original manuscript. Larger drawings that appear to be unfinished, and smaller ones that amount to little more than doodles, have been omitted.

Facsimile: from the entry for Sunday 15 July 1900 (Suite 18).

Facsimile: from the entry for Sunday 22 July 1900 (Suite 18).

Index of Alma Schindler's Compositions

General Index